The Dreaming

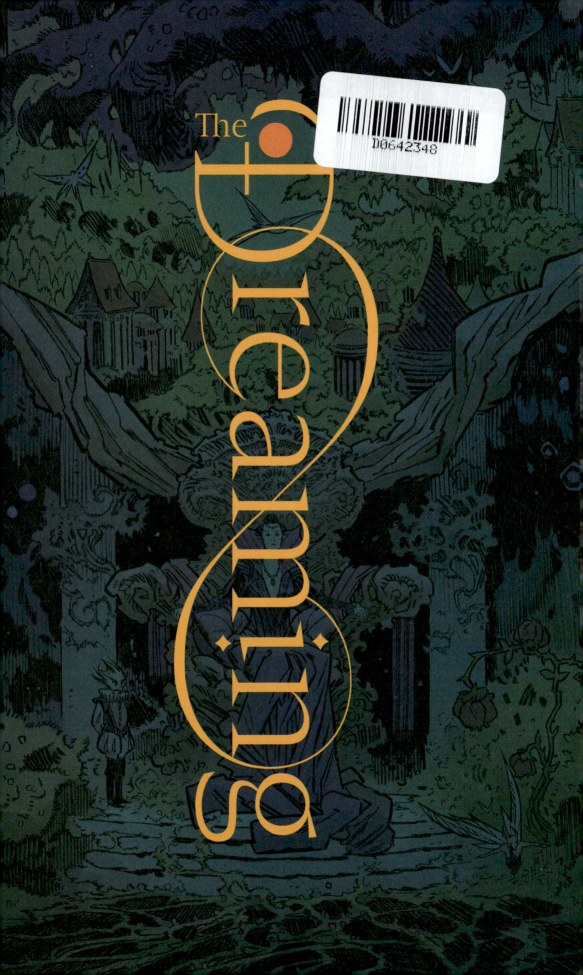

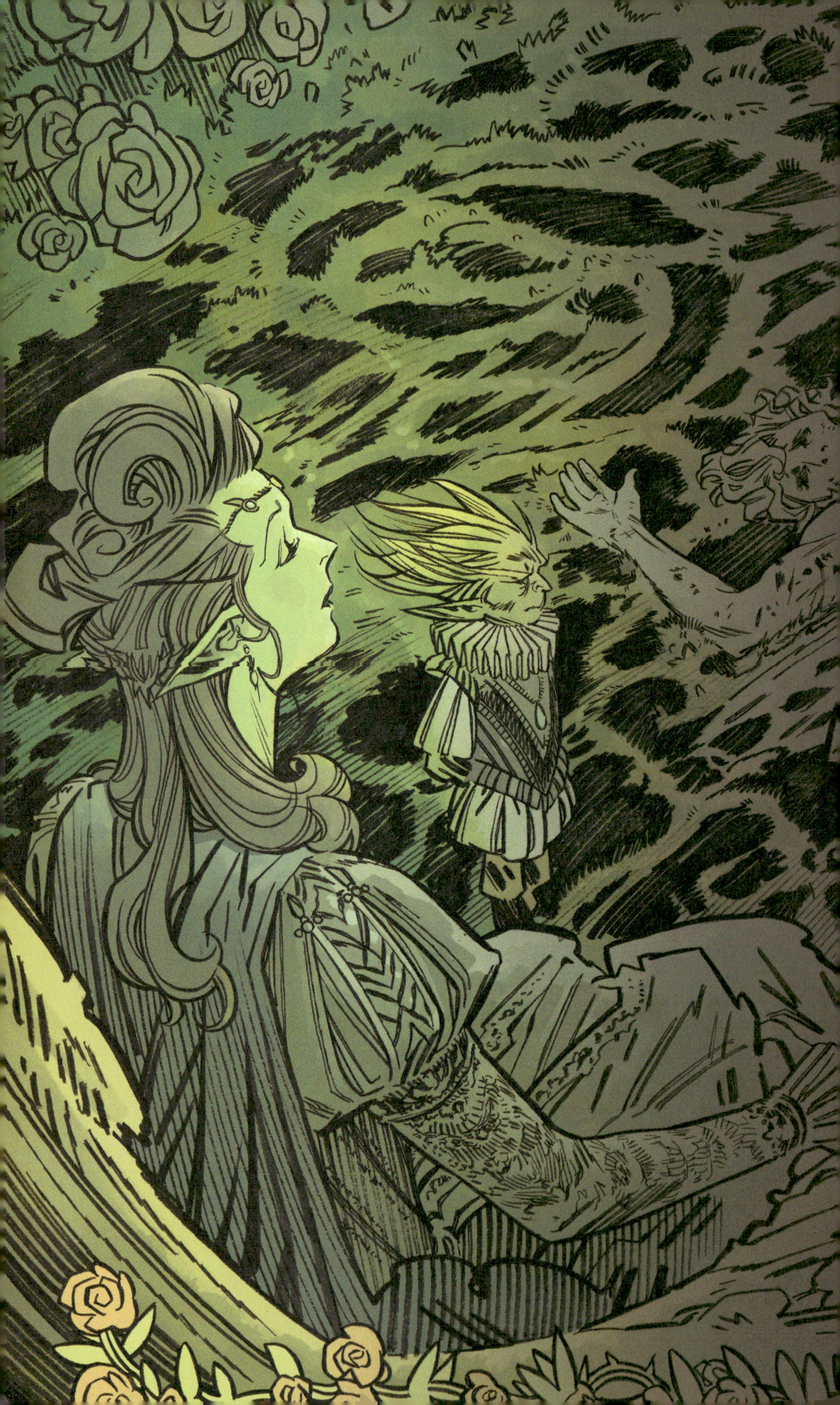

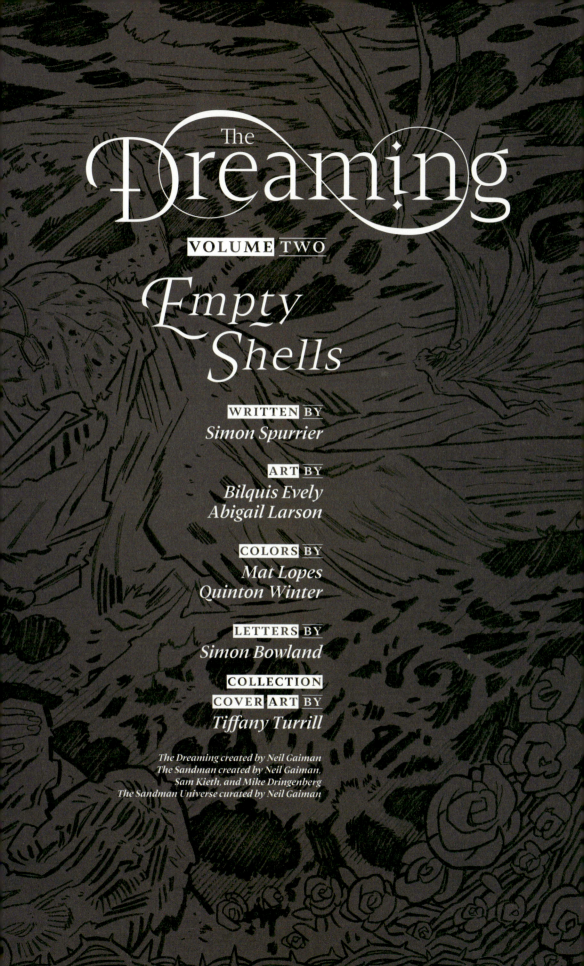

The Dreaming

VOLUME TWO
Empty Shells

WRITTEN BY
Simon Spurrier

ART BY
Bilquis Evely
Abigail Larson

COLORS BY
Mat Lopes
Quinton Winter

LETTERS BY
Simon Bowland

COLLECTION
COVER ART BY
Tiffany Turrill

The Dreaming created by Neil Gaiman
The Sandman created by Neil Gaiman,
Sam Kieth, and Mike Dringenberg
The Sandman Universe curated by Neil Gaiman

MOLLY MAHAN
CHRIS CONROY   Editors – Original Series
AMEDEO TURTURRO   Associate Editor – Original Series
MAGGIE HOWELL   Assistant Editor – Original Series
JEB WOODARD   Group Editor – Collected Editions
SCOTT NYBAKKEN   Editor – Collected Edition
STEVE COOK   Design Director – Books
and Publication Design
TOM VALENTE   Publication Production

BOB HARRAS   Senior VP – Editor-in-Chief, DC Comics
MARK DOYLE   Executive Editor, Vertigo & Black Label

DAN DiDIO   Publisher
JIM LEE   Publisher & Chief Creative Officer
BOBBIE CHASE   VP – New Publishing Initiatives & Talent Development
DON FALLETTI   VP – Manufacturing Operations & Workflow Management
LAWRENCE GANEM   VP – Talent Services
ALISON GILL   Senior VP – Manufacturing & Operations
HANK KANALZ   Senior VP – Publishing Strategy & Support Services
DAN MIRON   VP – Publishing Operations
NICK J. NAPOLITANO   VP – Manufacturing Administration & Design
NANCY SPEARS   VP – Sales
MICHELE R. WELLS   VP & Executive Editor, Young Reader

THE DREAMING VOL. 2: EMPTY SHELLS

DC Comics, 2900 West Alameda Ave., Burbank, CA 91505
Printed by LSC Communications, Owensville, MO, USA. 12/6/19. First Printing.
ISBN: 978-1-4012-9563-9

Library of Congress Cataloging-in-Publication Data is available.

PEFC Certified

This product is from
sustainably managed
forests and controlled
sources

PEFC/29-31-337   www.pefc.org

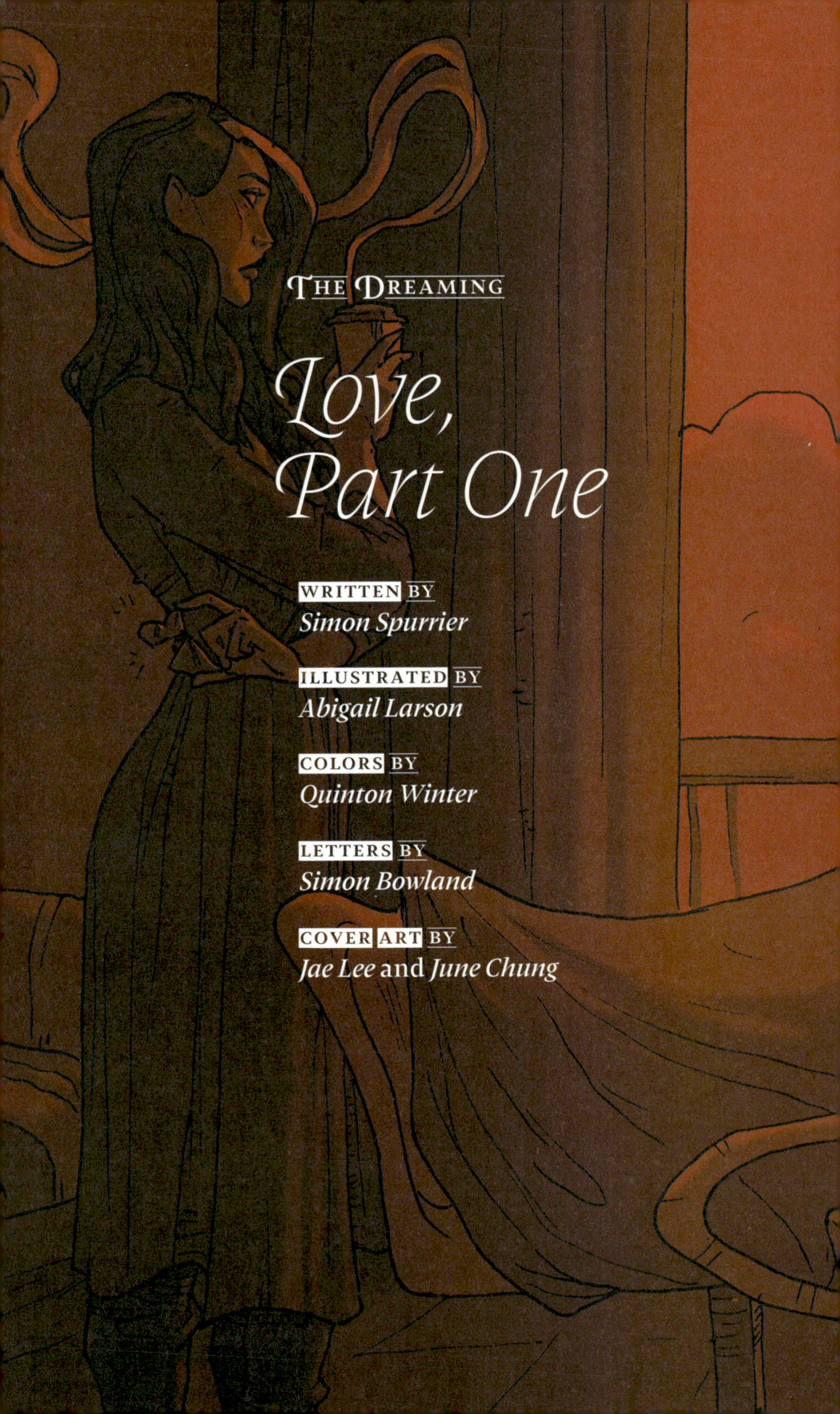

THE DREAMING

Love, Part One

WRITTEN BY
Simon Spurrier

ILLUSTRATED BY
Abigail Larson

COLORS BY
Quinton Winter

LETTERS BY
Simon Bowland

COVER ART BY
Jae Lee and *June Chung*

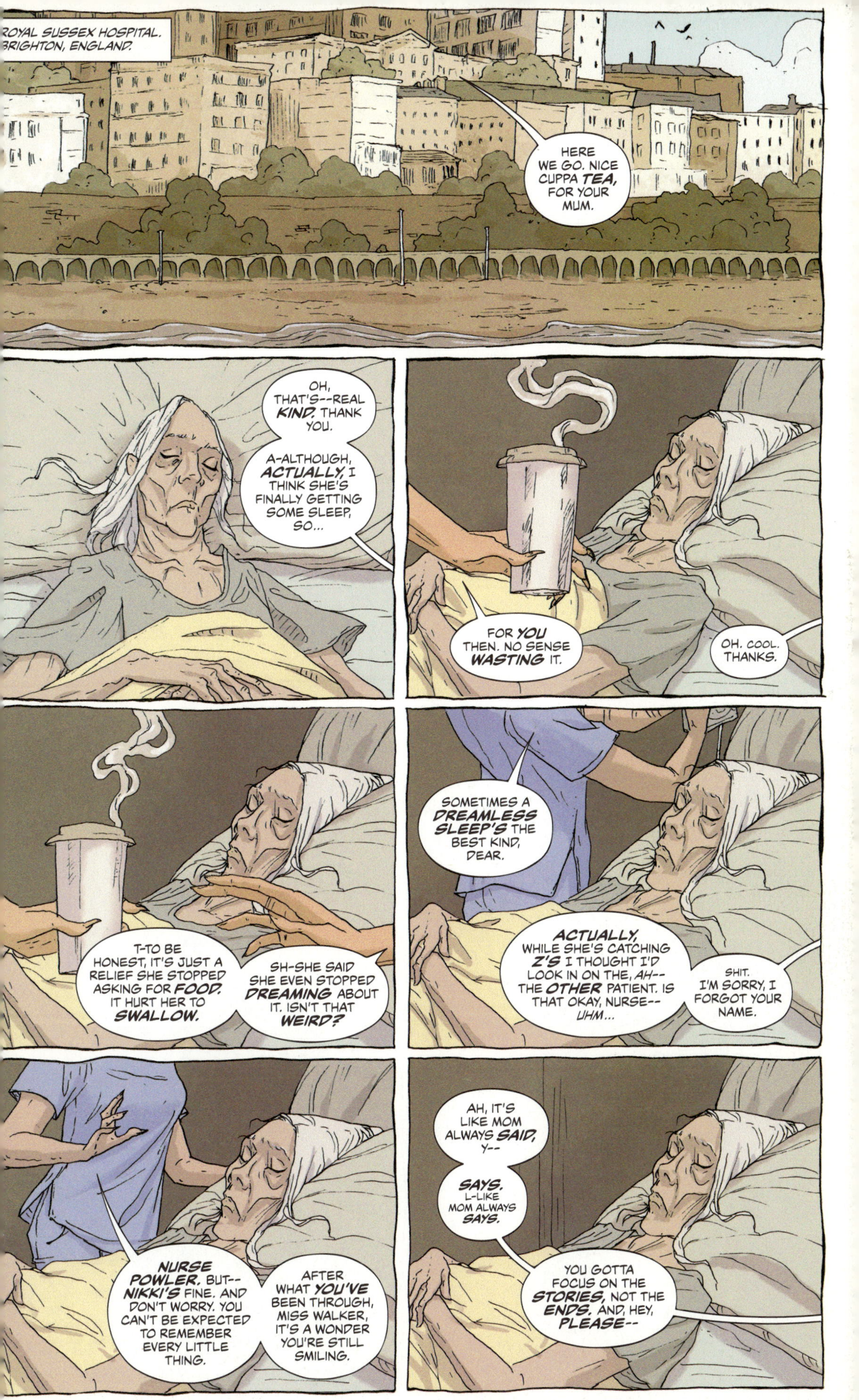
ROYAL SUSSEX HOSPITAL. BRIGHTON, ENGLAND.
HERE WE GO. NICE CUPPA TEA, FOR YOUR MUM.
OH, THAT'S--REAL KIND. THANK YOU.
A-ALTHOUGH, ACTUALLY, I THINK SHE'S FINALLY GETTING SOME SLEEP, SO...
FOR YOU THEN. NO SENSE WASTING IT.
OH. COOL. THANKS.
T-TO BE HONEST, IT'S JUST A RELIEF SHE STOPPED ASKING FOR FOOD. IT HURT HER TO SWALLOW.
SH-SHE SAID SHE EVEN STOPPED DREAMING ABOUT IT. ISN'T THAT WEIRD?
SOMETIMES A DREAMLESS SLEEP'S THE BEST KIND, DEAR.
ACTUALLY, WHILE SHE'S CATCHING Z'S I THOUGHT I'D LOOK IN ON THE, AH-- THE OTHER PATIENT. IS THAT OKAY, NURSE-- UHM...
SHIT. I'M SORRY, I FORGOT YOUR NAME.
NURSE POWLER. BUT-- NIKKI'S FINE. AND DON'T WORRY. YOU CAN'T BE EXPECTED TO REMEMBER EVERY LITTLE THING.
AFTER WHAT YOU'VE BEEN THROUGH, MISS WALKER, IT'S A WONDER YOU'RE STILL SMILING.
AH, IT'S LIKE MOM ALWAYS SAID, Y--
SAYS. L-LIKE MOM ALWAYS SAYS.
YOU GOTTA FOCUS ON THE STORIES, NOT THE ENDS. AND, HEY, PLEASE--

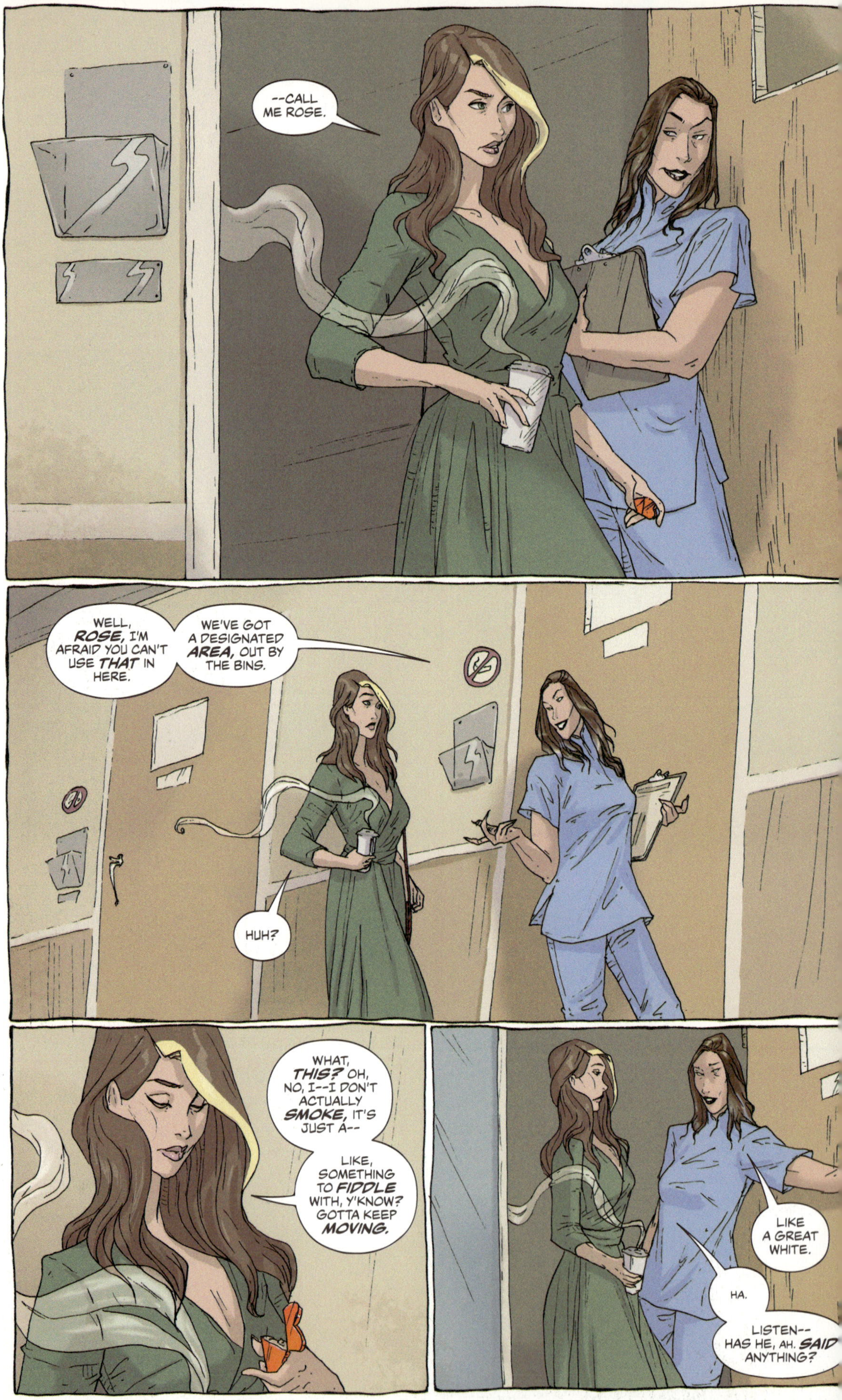
--CALL ME ROSE.
WELL, ROSE, I'M AFRAID YOU CAN'T USE THAT IN HERE.
WE'VE GOT A DESIGNATED AREA, OUT BY THE BINS.
HUH?
WHAT, THIS? OH, NO, I--I DON'T ACTUALLY SMOKE, IT'S JUST A--
LIKE, SOMETHING TO FIDDLE WITH, Y'KNOW? GOTTA KEEP MOVING.
LIKE A GREAT WHITE.
HA.
LISTEN-- HAS HE, AH. SAID ANYTHING?

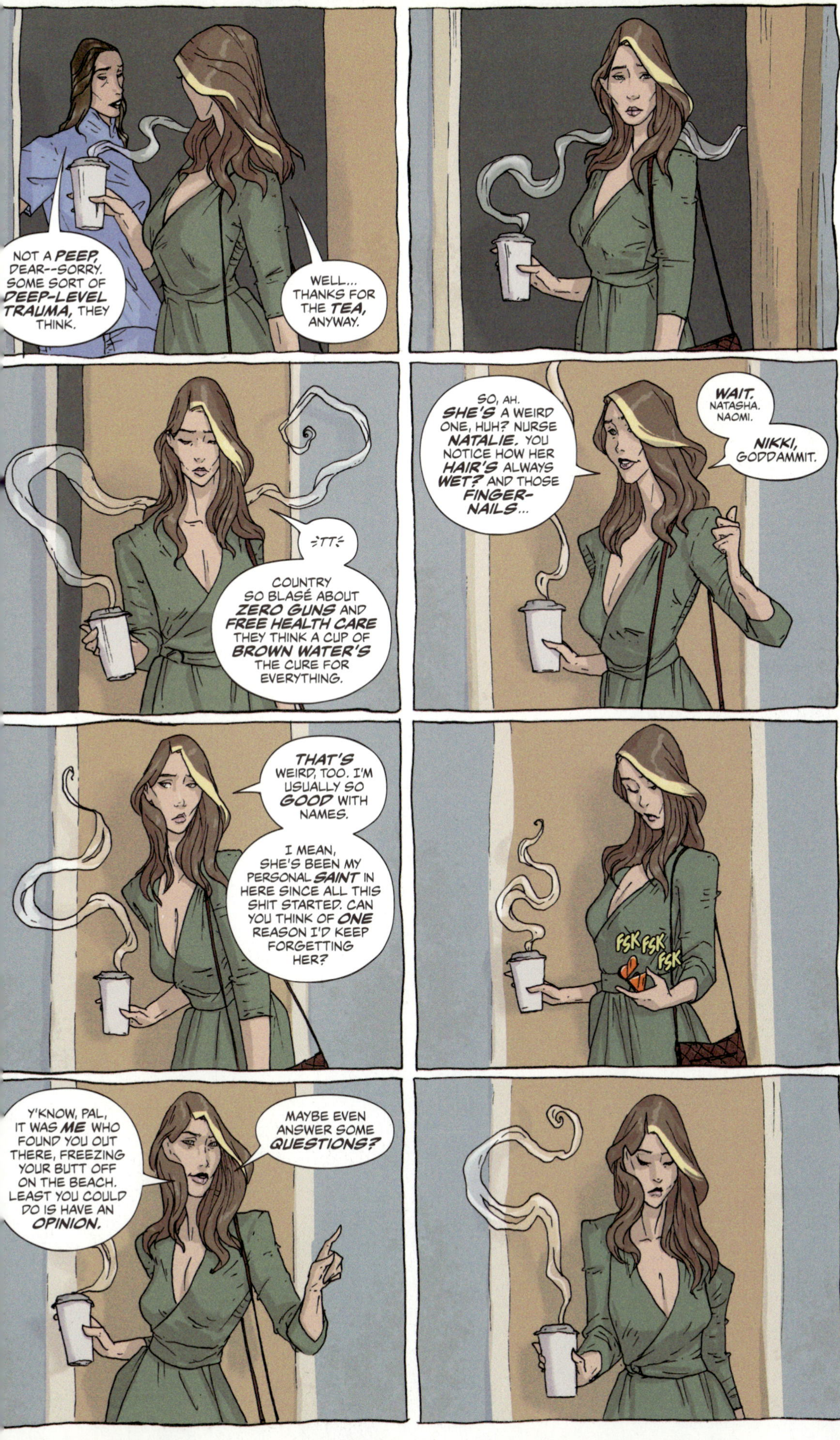
NOT A PEEP, DEAR--SORRY. SOME SORT OF DEEP-LEVEL TRAUMA, THEY THINK.
WELL... THANKS FOR THE TEA, ANYWAY.
TT
COUNTRY SO BLASÉ ABOUT ZERO GUNS AND FREE HEALTH CARE THEY THINK A CUP OF BROWN WATER'S THE CURE FOR EVERYTHING.
SO, AH. SHE'S A WEIRD ONE, HUH? NURSE NATALIE. YOU NOTICE HOW HER HAIR'S ALWAYS WET? AND THOSE FINGER-NAILS...
WAIT. NATASHA. NAOMI.
NIKKI, GODDAMMIT.
THAT'S WEIRD, TOO. I'M USUALLY SO GOOD WITH NAMES.
I MEAN, SHE'S BEEN MY PERSONAL SAINT IN HERE SINCE ALL THIS SHIT STARTED. CAN YOU THINK OF ONE REASON I'D KEEP FORGETTING HER?
FSK FSK FSK
Y'KNOW, PAL, IT WAS ME WHO FOUND YOU OUT THERE, FREEZING YOUR BUTT OFF ON THE BEACH. LEAST YOU COULD DO IS HAVE AN OPINION.
MAYBE EVEN ANSWER SOME QUESTIONS?

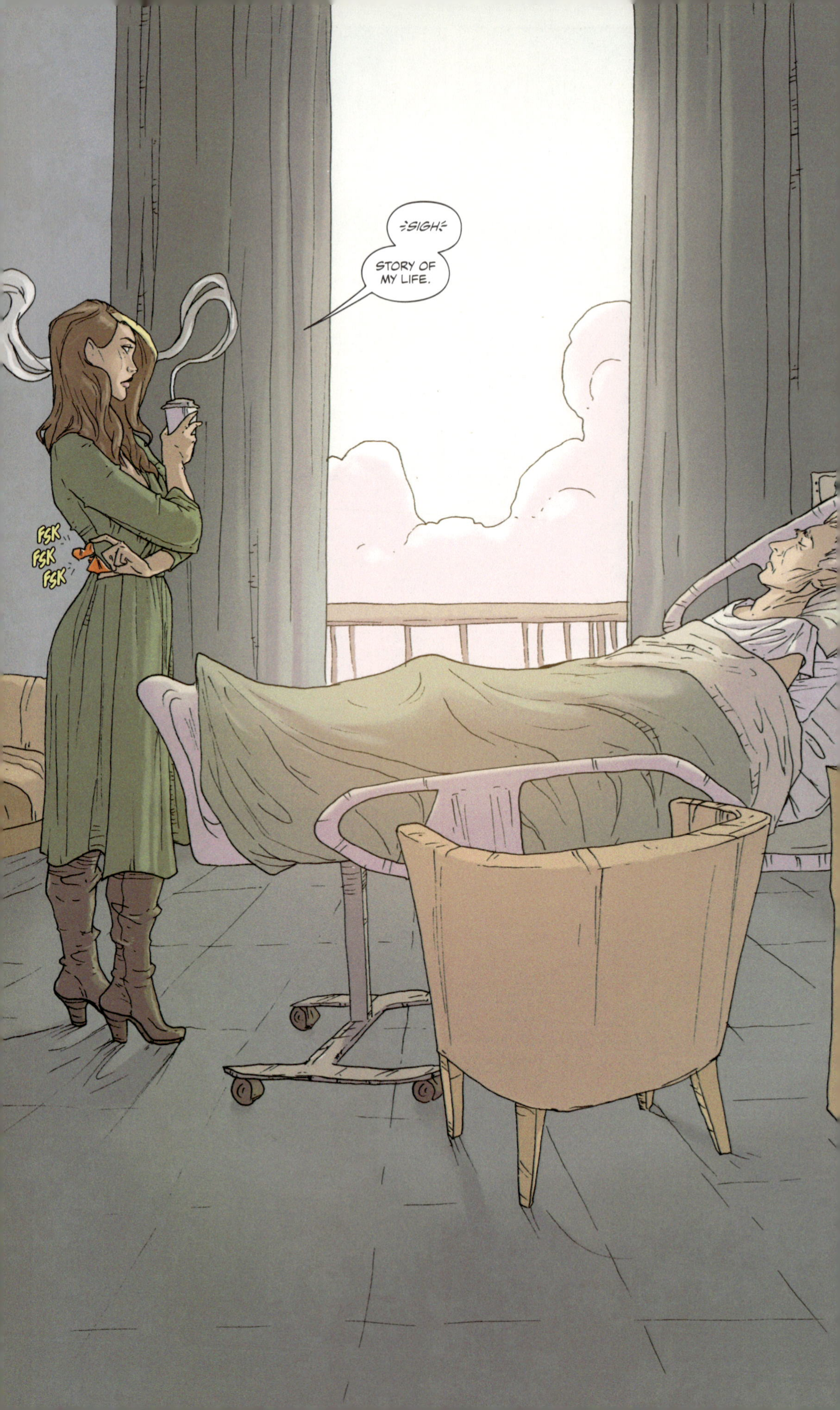

FSK
FSK
FSK
-SIGH-
STORY OF MY LIFE.

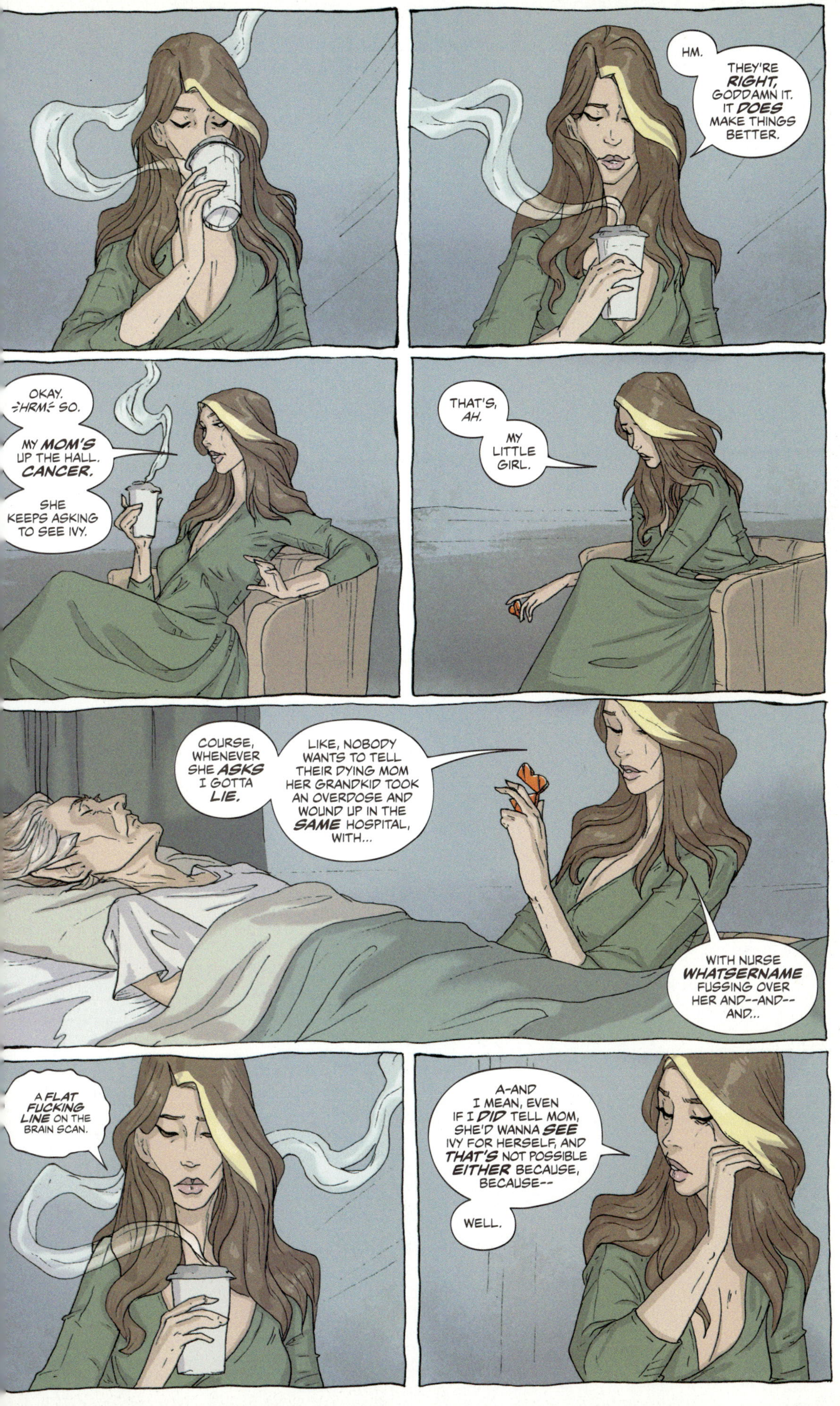
HM.
THEY'RE RIGHT, GODDAMN IT. IT DOES MAKE THINGS BETTER.
OKAY. ≠HRM≠ SO.
MY MOM'S UP THE HALL. CANCER.
SHE KEEPS ASKING TO SEE IVY.
THAT'S, AH.
MY LITTLE GIRL.
COURSE, WHENEVER SHE ASKS I GOTTA LIE.
LIKE, NOBODY WANTS TO TELL THEIR DYING MOM HER GRANDKID TOOK AN OVERDOSE AND WOUND UP IN THE SAME HOSPITAL, WITH...
WITH NURSE WHATSERNAME FUSSING OVER HER AND--AND-- AND...
A FLAT FUCKING LINE ON THE BRAIN SCAN.
A-AND I MEAN, EVEN IF I DID TELL MOM, SHE'D WANNA SEE IVY FOR HERSELF, AND THAT'S NOT POSSIBLE EITHER BECAUSE, BECAUSE--
WELL.

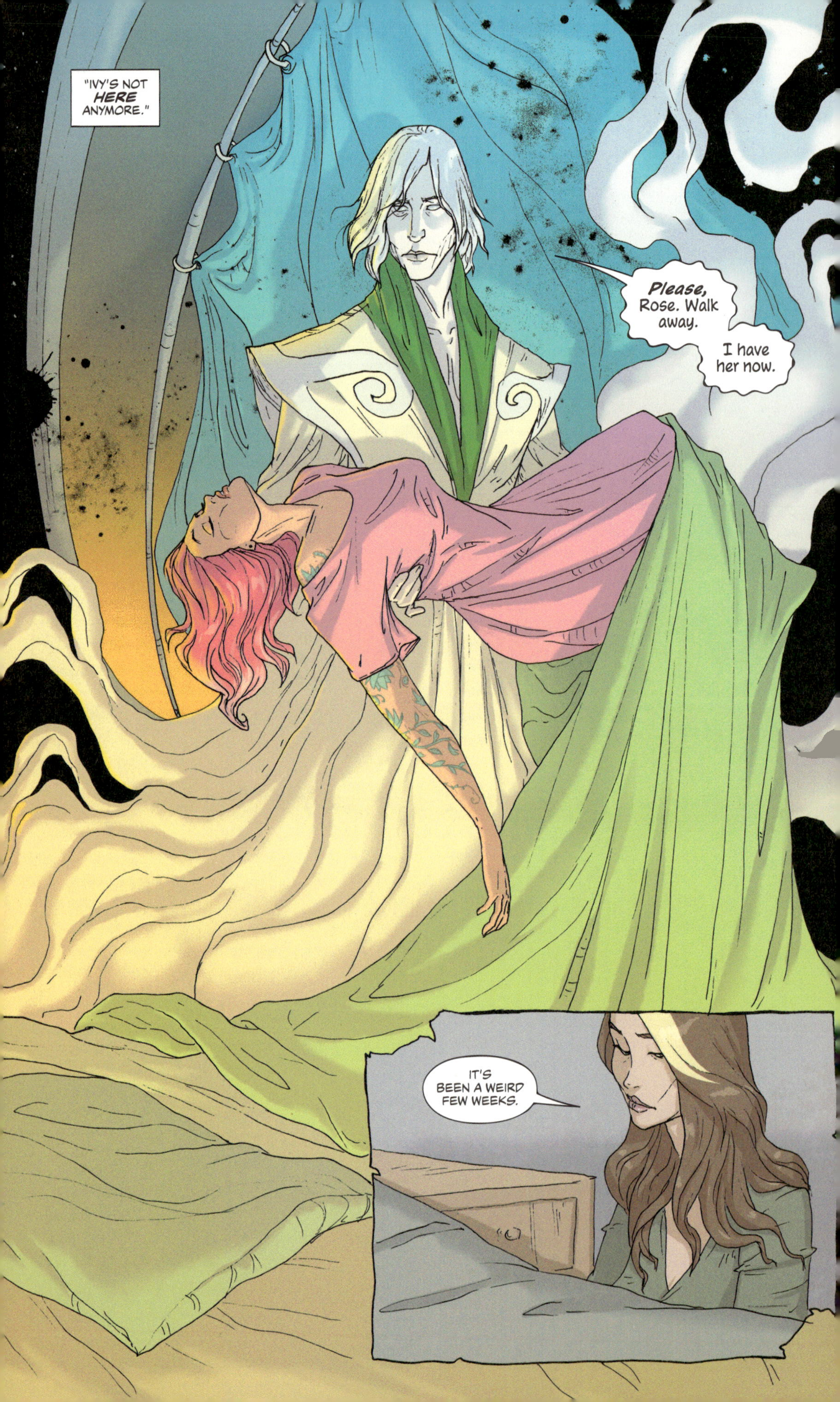
"IVY'S NOT HERE ANYMORE."
Please, Rose. Walk away.
I have her now.
IT'S BEEN A WEIRD FEW WEEKS.

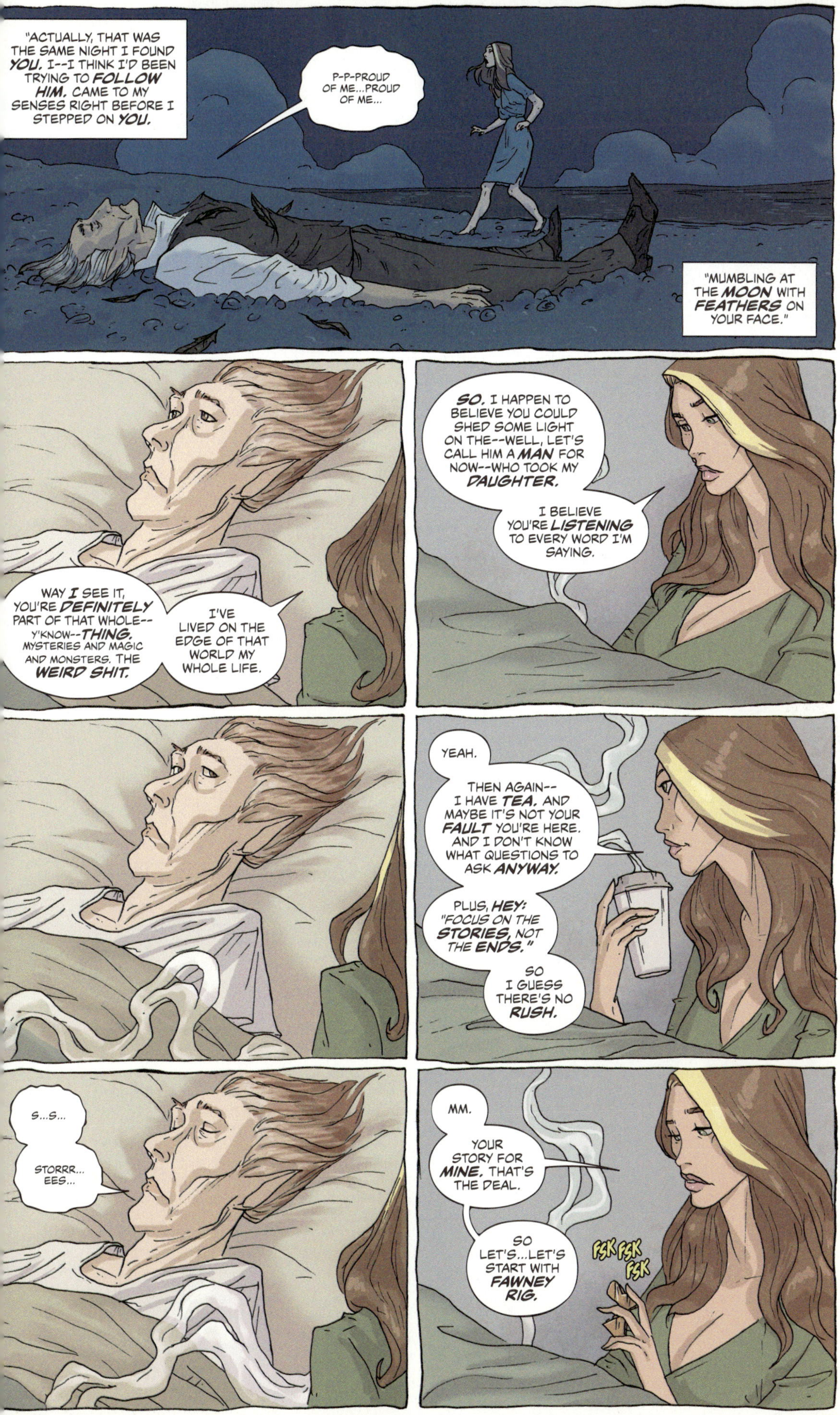
"ACTUALLY, THAT WAS THE SAME NIGHT I FOUND YOU. I--I THINK I'D BEEN TRYING TO FOLLOW HIM. CAME TO MY SENSES RIGHT BEFORE I STEPPED ON YOU.
P-P-PROUD OF ME...PROUD OF ME...
"MUMBLING AT THE MOON WITH FEATHERS ON YOUR FACE."
WAY I SEE IT, YOU'RE DEFINITELY PART OF THAT WHOLE-- Y'KNOW--THING. MYSTERIES AND MAGIC AND MONSTERS. THE WEIRD SHIT.
I'VE LIVED ON THE EDGE OF THAT WORLD MY WHOLE LIFE.
SO. I HAPPEN TO BELIEVE YOU COULD SHED SOME LIGHT ON THE--WELL, LET'S CALL HIM A MAN FOR NOW--WHO TOOK MY DAUGHTER.
I BELIEVE YOU'RE LISTENING TO EVERY WORD I'M SAYING.
YEAH.
THEN AGAIN-- I HAVE TEA. AND MAYBE IT'S NOT YOUR FAULT YOU'RE HERE. AND I DON'T KNOW WHAT QUESTIONS TO ASK ANYWAY.
PLUS, HEY: "FOCUS ON THE STORIES, NOT THE ENDS."
SO I GUESS THERE'S NO RUSH.
S...S...
STORRR... EES...
MM.
YOUR STORY FOR MINE. THAT'S THE DEAL.
SO LET'S...LET'S START WITH FAWNEY RIG.
FSK FSK FSK

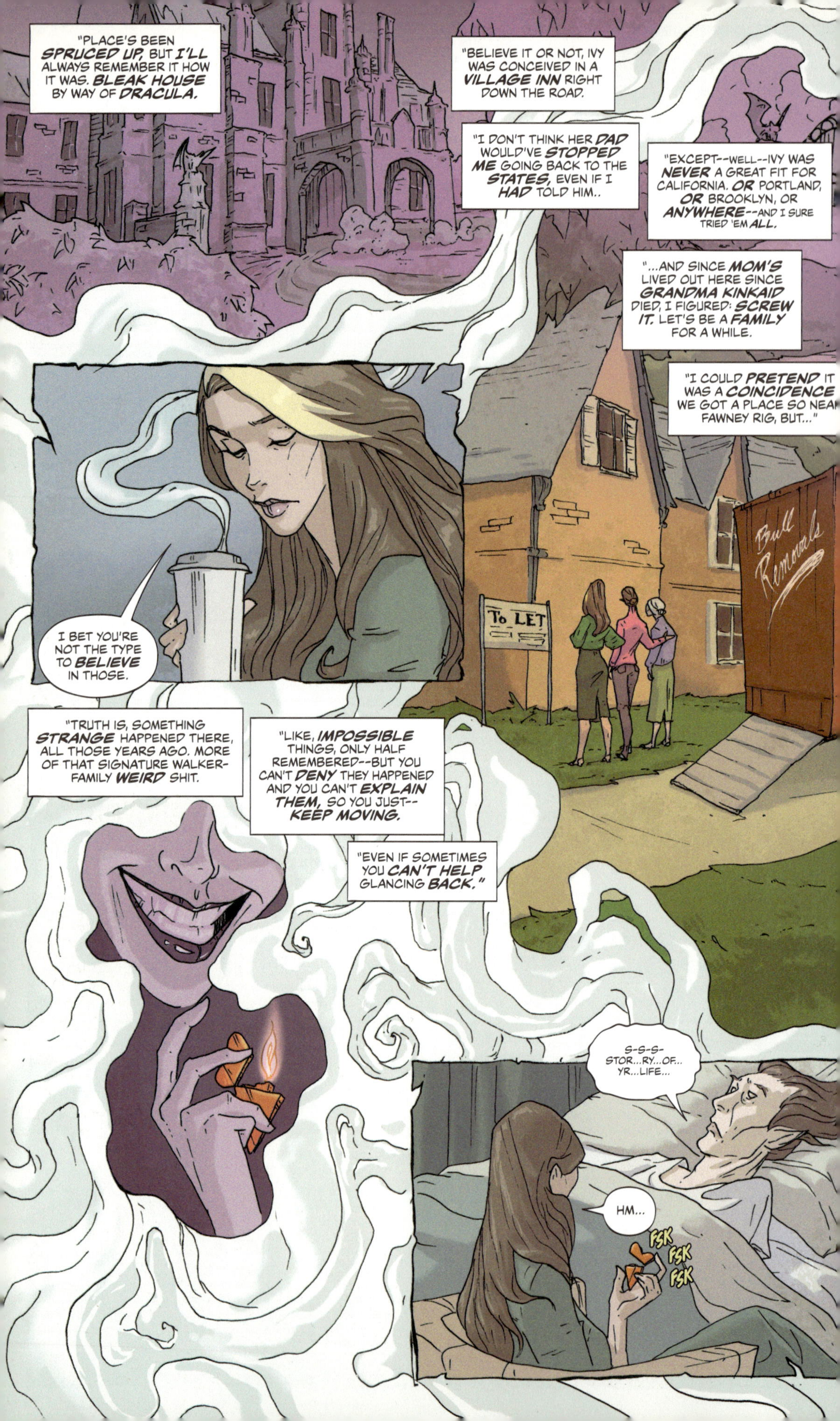
"PLACE'S BEEN SPRUCED UP, BUT I'LL ALWAYS REMEMBER IT HOW IT WAS. BLEAK HOUSE BY WAY OF DRACULA.
"BELIEVE IT OR NOT, IVY WAS CONCEIVED IN A VILLAGE INN RIGHT DOWN THE ROAD.
"I DON'T THINK HER DAD WOULD'VE STOPPED ME GOING BACK TO THE STATES, EVEN IF I HAD TOLD HIM..
"EXCEPT--WELL--IVY WAS NEVER A GREAT FIT FOR CALIFORNIA. OR PORTLAND, OR BROOKLYN, OR ANYWHERE--AND I SURE TRIED 'EM ALL.
"...AND SINCE MOM'S LIVED OUT HERE SINCE GRANDMA KINKAID DIED, I FIGURED: SCREW IT. LET'S BE A FAMILY FOR A WHILE.
"I COULD PRETEND IT WAS A COINCIDENCE WE GOT A PLACE SO NEA FAWNEY RIG, BUT..."
TO LET
Bull Removals
I BET YOU'RE NOT THE TYPE TO BELIEVE IN THOSE.
"TRUTH IS, SOMETHING STRANGE HAPPENED THERE, ALL THOSE YEARS AGO. MORE OF THAT SIGNATURE WALKER-FAMILY WEIRD SHIT.
"LIKE, IMPOSSIBLE THINGS, ONLY HALF REMEMBERED--BUT YOU CAN'T DENY THEY HAPPENED AND YOU CAN'T EXPLAIN THEM, SO YOU JUST--KEEP MOVING.
"EVEN IF SOMETIMES YOU CAN'T HELP GLANCING BACK."
S-S-S-STOR...RY...OF... YR...LIFE...
HM...
FSK
FSK
FSK

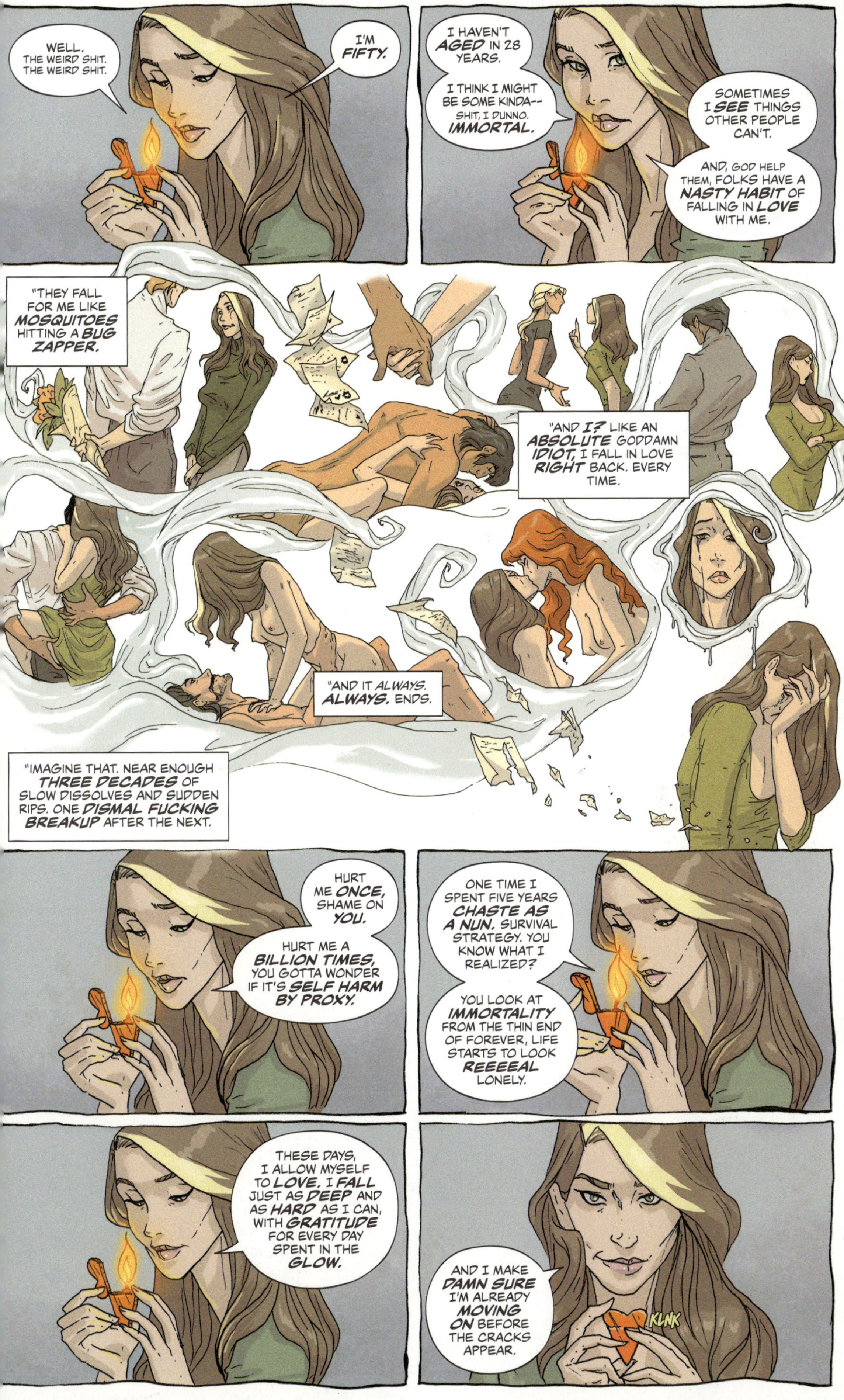
WELL. THE WEIRD SHIT. THE WEIRD SHIT.
I'M FIFTY.
I HAVEN'T AGED IN 28 YEARS.
I THINK I MIGHT BE SOME KINDA-- SHIT, I DUNNO. IMMORTAL.
SOMETIMES I SEE THINGS OTHER PEOPLE CAN'T.
AND, GOD HELP THEM, FOLKS HAVE A NASTY HABIT OF FALLING IN LOVE WITH ME.
"THEY FALL FOR ME LIKE MOSQUITOES HITTING A BUG ZAPPER.
"AND I? LIKE AN ABSOLUTE GODDAMN IDIOT, I FALL IN LOVE RIGHT BACK. EVERY TIME.
"AND IT ALWAYS. ALWAYS. ENDS.
"IMAGINE THAT. NEAR ENOUGH THREE DECADES OF SLOW DISSOLVES AND SUDDEN RIPS. ONE DISMAL FUCKING BREAKUP AFTER THE NEXT.
HURT ME ONCE, SHAME ON YOU.
HURT ME A BILLION TIMES, YOU GOTTA WONDER IF IT'S SELF HARM BY PROXY.
ONE TIME I SPENT FIVE YEARS CHASTE AS A NUN. SURVIVAL STRATEGY. YOU KNOW WHAT I REALIZED?
YOU LOOK AT IMMORTALITY FROM THE THIN END OF FOREVER, LIFE STARTS TO LOOK REEEEAL LONELY.
THESE DAYS, I ALLOW MYSELF TO LOVE. I FALL JUST AS DEEP AND AS HARD AS I CAN, WITH GRATITUDE FOR EVERY DAY SPENT IN THE GLOW.
AND I MAKE DAMN SURE I'M ALREADY MOVING ON BEFORE THE CRACKS APPEAR.
KLNK

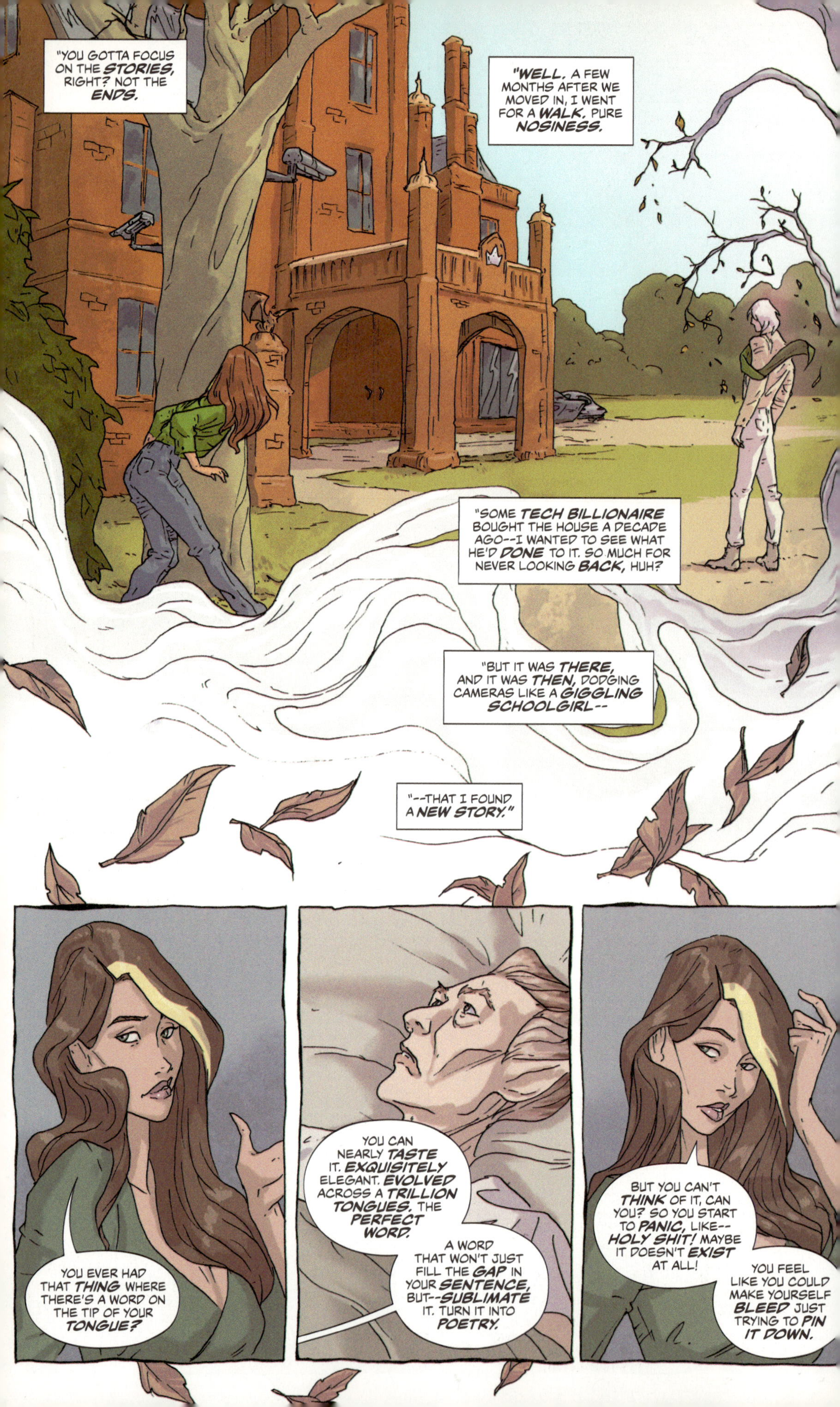
"YOU GOTTA FOCUS ON THE STORIES, RIGHT? NOT THE ENDS.
"WELL, A FEW MONTHS AFTER WE MOVED IN, I WENT FOR A WALK. PURE NOSINESS.
"SOME TECH BILLIONAIRE BOUGHT THE HOUSE A DECADE AGO--I WANTED TO SEE WHAT HE'D DONE TO IT. SO MUCH FOR NEVER LOOKING BACK, HUH?
"BUT IT WAS THERE, AND IT WAS THEN, DODGING CAMERAS LIKE A GIGGLING SCHOOLGIRL--
"--THAT I FOUND A NEW STORY."
YOU EVER HAD THAT THING WHERE THERE'S A WORD ON THE TIP OF YOUR TONGUE?
YOU CAN NEARLY TASTE IT. EXQUISITELY ELEGANT. EVOLVED ACROSS A TRILLION TONGUES. THE PERFECT WORD.
A WORD THAT WON'T JUST FILL THE GAP IN YOUR SENTENCE, BUT--SUBLIMATE IT. TURN IT INTO POETRY.
BUT YOU CAN'T THINK OF IT, CAN YOU? SO YOU START TO PANIC, LIKE-- HOLY SHIT! MAYBE IT DOESN'T EXIST AT ALL!
YOU FEEL LIKE YOU COULD MAKE YOURSELF BLEED JUST TRYING TO PIN IT DOWN.

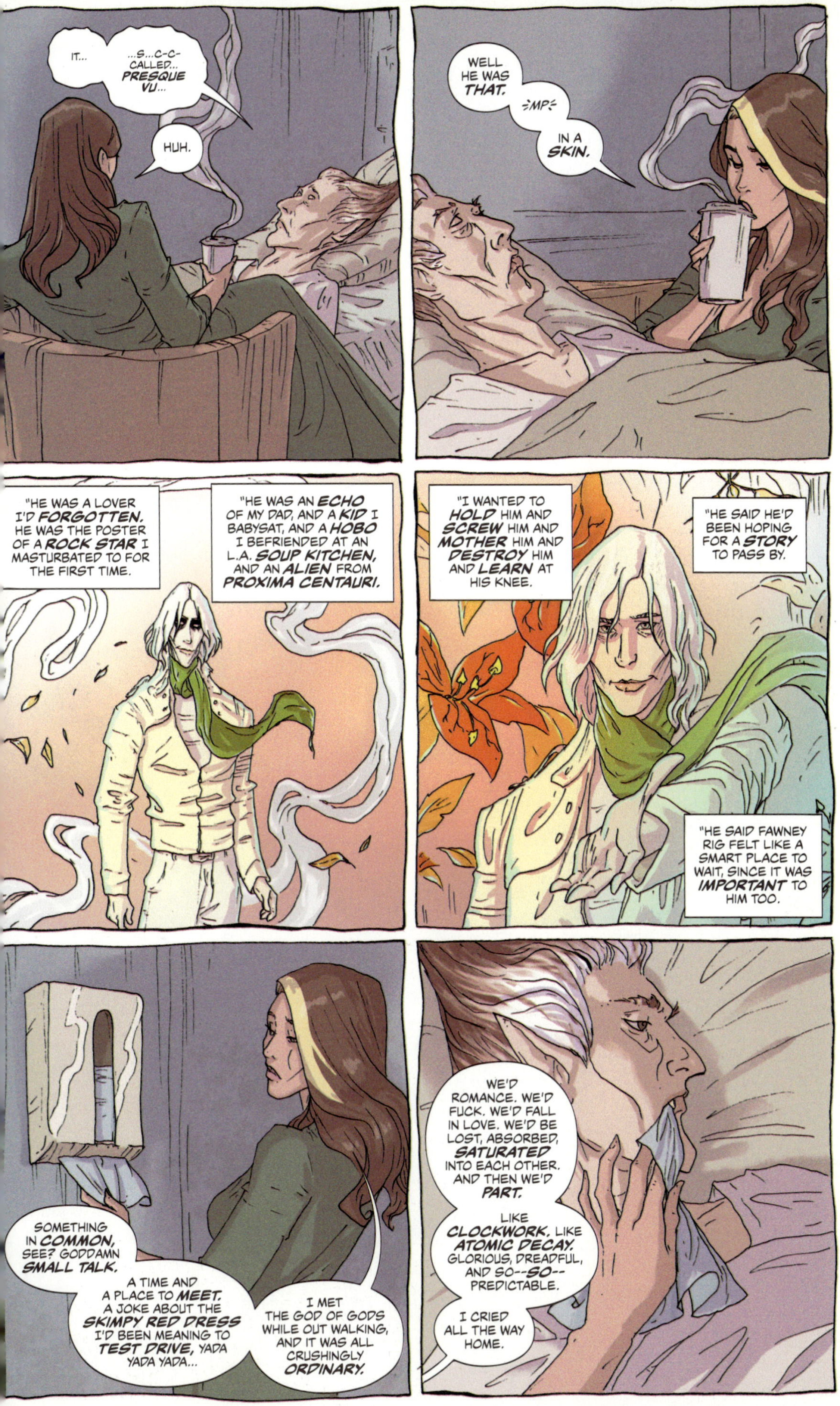
IT...
...S...C-C-CALLED... PRESQUE VU...
HUH.
WELL HE WAS THAT.
MP
IN A SKIN.
"HE WAS A LOVER I'D FORGOTTEN. HE WAS THE POSTER OF A ROCK STAR I MASTURBATED TO FOR THE FIRST TIME.
"HE WAS AN ECHO OF MY DAD, AND A KID I BABYSAT, AND A HOBO I BEFRIENDED AT AN L.A. SOUP KITCHEN, AND AN ALIEN FROM PROXIMA CENTAURI.
"I WANTED TO HOLD HIM AND SCREW HIM AND MOTHER HIM AND DESTROY HIM AND LEARN AT HIS KNEE.
"HE SAID HE'D BEEN HOPING FOR A STORY TO PASS BY.
"HE SAID FAWNEY RIG FELT LIKE A SMART PLACE TO WAIT, SINCE IT WAS IMPORTANT TO HIM TOO.
SOMETHING IN COMMON, SEE? GODDAMN SMALL TALK.
A TIME AND A PLACE TO MEET. A JOKE ABOUT THE SKIMPY RED DRESS I'D BEEN MEANING TO TEST DRIVE, YADA YADA YADA...
I MET THE GOD OF GODS WHILE OUT WALKING, AND IT WAS ALL CRUSHINGLY ORDINARY.
WE'D ROMANCE. WE'D FUCK. WE'D FALL IN LOVE. WE'D BE LOST, ABSORBED, SATURATED INTO EACH OTHER. AND THEN WE'D PART.
LIKE CLOCKWORK. LIKE ATOMIC DECAY. GLORIOUS, DREADFUL, AND SO--SO--PREDICTABLE.
I CRIED ALL THE WAY HOME.

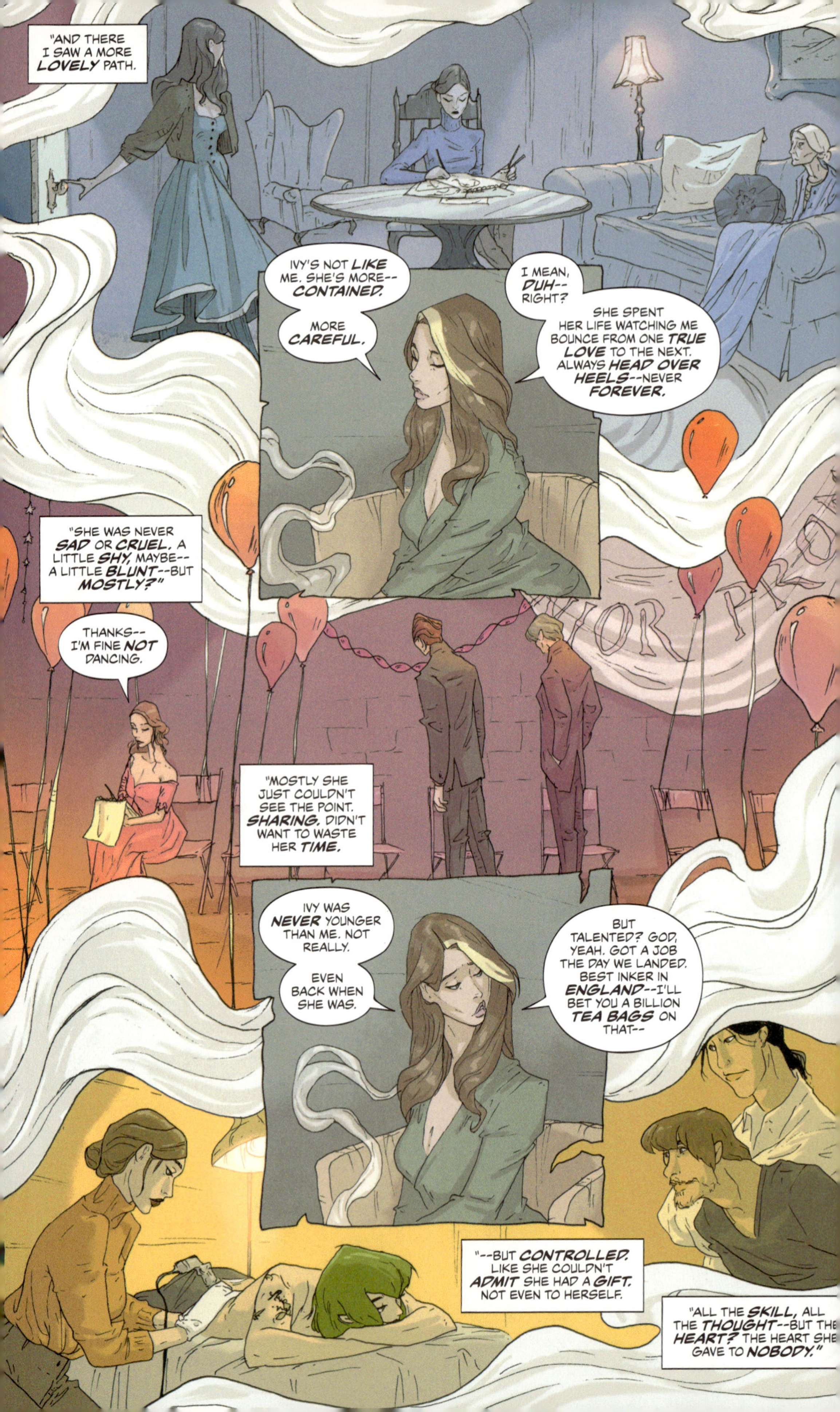
"AND THERE I SAW A MORE LOVELY PATH.
IVY'S NOT LIKE ME. SHE'S MORE--CONTAINED.
MORE CAREFUL.
I MEAN, DUH--RIGHT?
SHE SPENT HER LIFE WATCHING ME BOUNCE FROM ONE TRUE LOVE TO THE NEXT. ALWAYS HEAD OVER HEELS--NEVER FOREVER.
"SHE WAS NEVER SAD OR CRUEL. A LITTLE SHY, MAYBE--A LITTLE BLUNT--BUT MOSTLY?"
THANKS--I'M FINE NOT DANCING.
"MOSTLY SHE JUST COULDN'T SEE THE POINT. SHARING. DIDN'T WANT TO WASTE HER TIME.
IVY WAS NEVER YOUNGER THAN ME. NOT REALLY.
EVEN BACK WHEN SHE WAS.
BUT TALENTED? GOD, YEAH. GOT A JOB THE DAY WE LANDED. BEST INKER IN ENGLAND--I'LL BET YOU A BILLION TEA BAGS ON THAT--
"--BUT CONTROLLED. LIKE SHE COULDN'T ADMIT SHE HAD A GIFT. NOT EVEN TO HERSELF.
"ALL THE SKILL, ALL THE THOUGHT--BUT THE HEART? THE HEART SHE GAVE TO NOBODY."

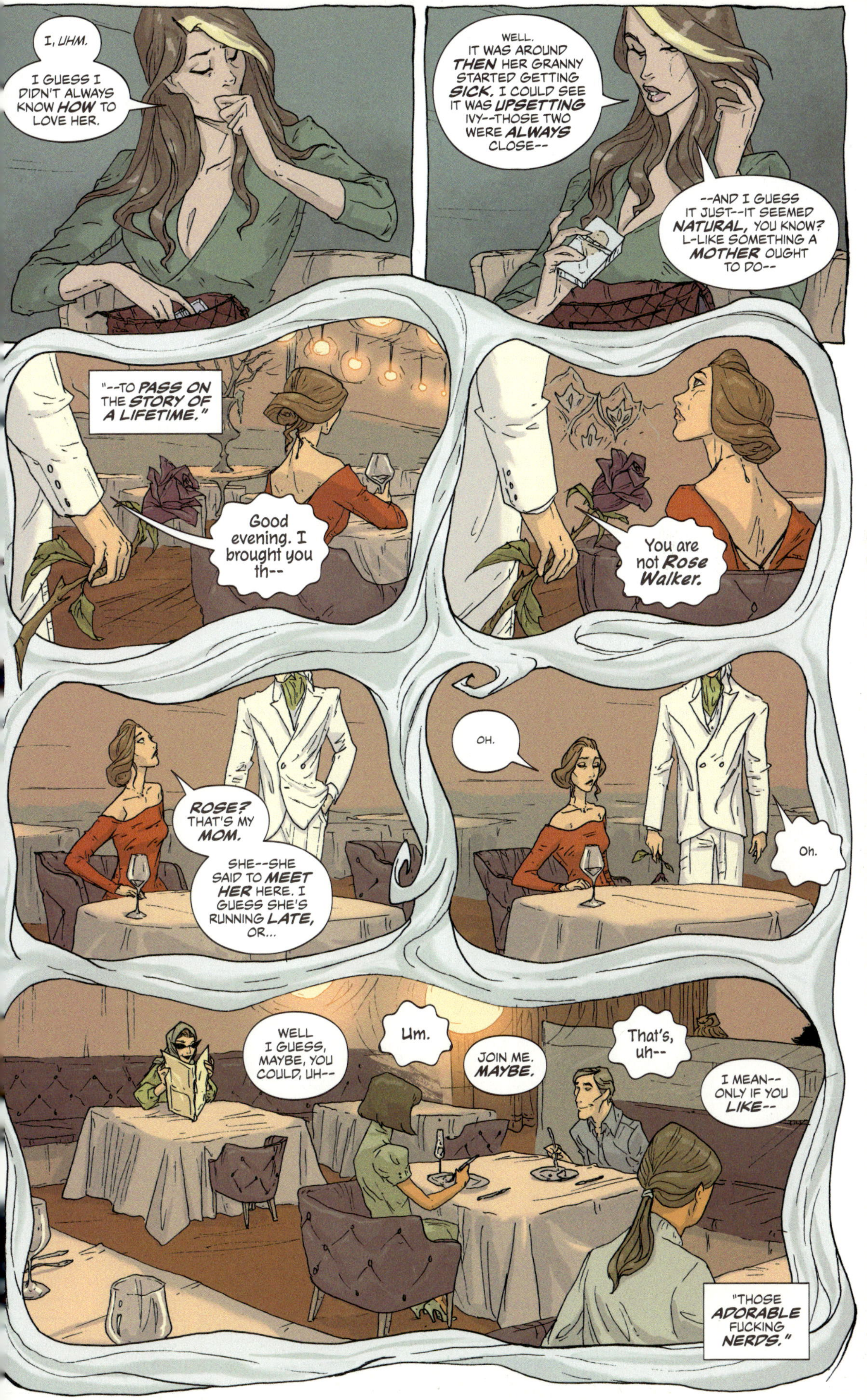
I, UHM.
I GUESS I DIDN'T ALWAYS KNOW HOW TO LOVE HER.
WELL. IT WAS AROUND THEN HER GRANNY STARTED GETTING SICK. I COULD SEE IT WAS UPSETTING IVY--THOSE TWO WERE ALWAYS CLOSE--
--AND I GUESS IT JUST--IT SEEMED NATURAL, YOU KNOW? L-LIKE SOMETHING A MOTHER OUGHT TO DO--
"--TO PASS ON THE STORY OF A LIFETIME."
Good evening. I brought you th--
You are not Rose Walker.
ROSE? THAT'S MY MOM.
SHE--SHE SAID TO MEET HER HERE. I GUESS SHE'S RUNNING LATE, OR...
OH.
Oh.
WELL I GUESS, MAYBE, YOU COULD, UH--
Um.
JOIN ME. MAYBE.
That's, uh--
I MEAN-- ONLY IF YOU LIKE--
"THOSE ADORABLE FUCKING NERDS."

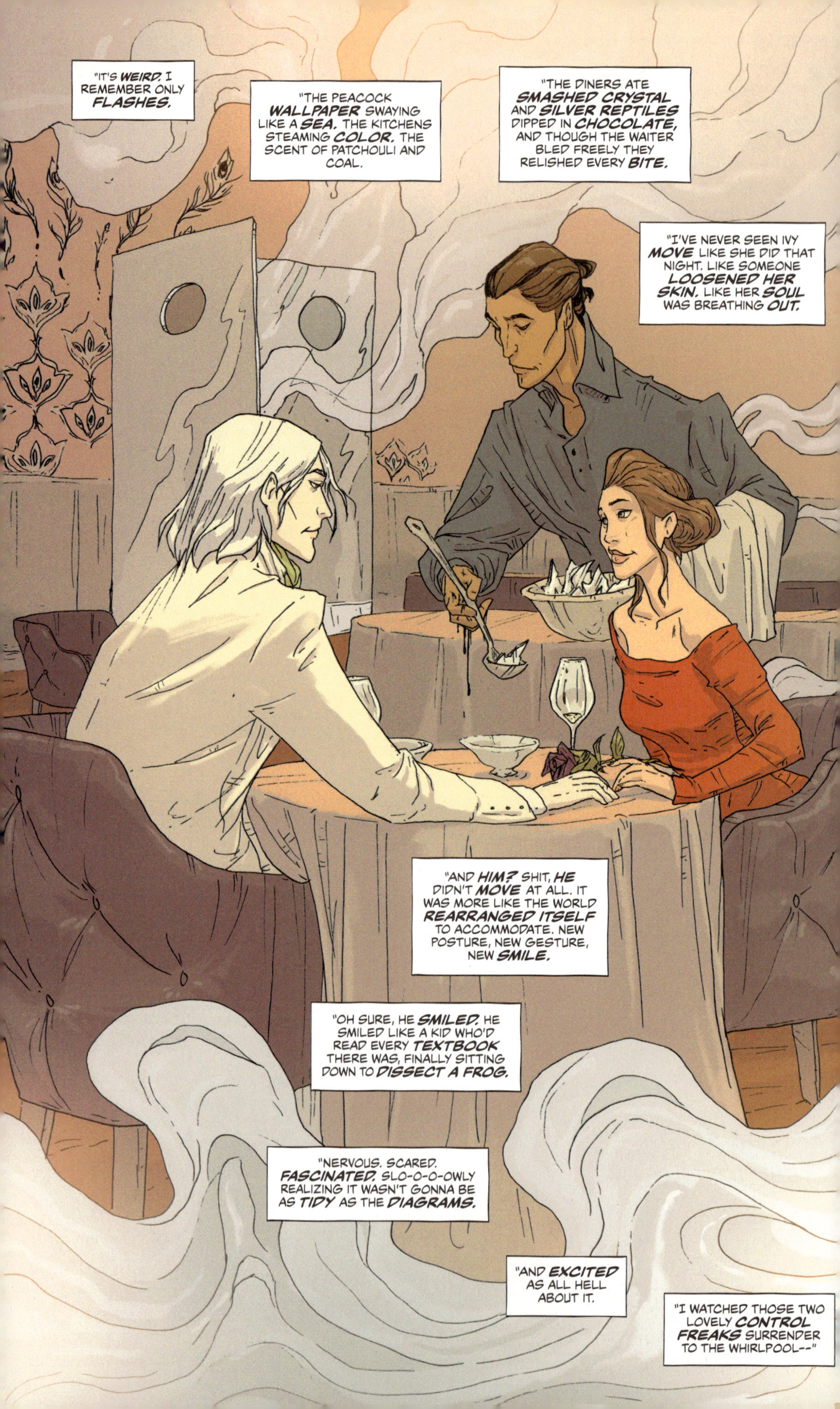
"IT'S WEIRD. I REMEMBER ONLY FLASHES.
"THE PEACOCK WALLPAPER SWAYING LIKE A SEA. THE KITCHENS STEAMING COLOR. THE SCENT OF PATCHOULI AND COAL.
"THE DINERS ATE SMASHED CRYSTAL AND SILVER REPTILES DIPPED IN CHOCOLATE, AND THOUGH THE WAITER BLED FREELY THEY RELISHED EVERY BITE.
"I'VE NEVER SEEN IVY MOVE LIKE SHE DID THAT NIGHT. LIKE SOMEONE LOOSENED HER SKIN. LIKE HER SOUL WAS BREATHING OUT.
"AND HIM? SHIT, HE DIDN'T MOVE AT ALL. IT WAS MORE LIKE THE WORLD REARRANGED ITSELF TO ACCOMMODATE. NEW POSTURE, NEW GESTURE, NEW SMILE.
"OH SURE, HE SMILED. HE SMILED LIKE A KID WHO'D READ EVERY TEXTBOOK THERE WAS, FINALLY SITTING DOWN TO DISSECT A FROG.
"NERVOUS. SCARED. FASCINATED. SLO-O-O-OWLY REALIZING IT WASN'T GONNA BE AS TIDY AS THE DIAGRAMS.
"AND EXCITED AS ALL HELL ABOUT IT.
"I WATCHED THOSE TWO LOVELY CONTROL FREAKS SURRENDER TO THE WHIRLPOOL--"

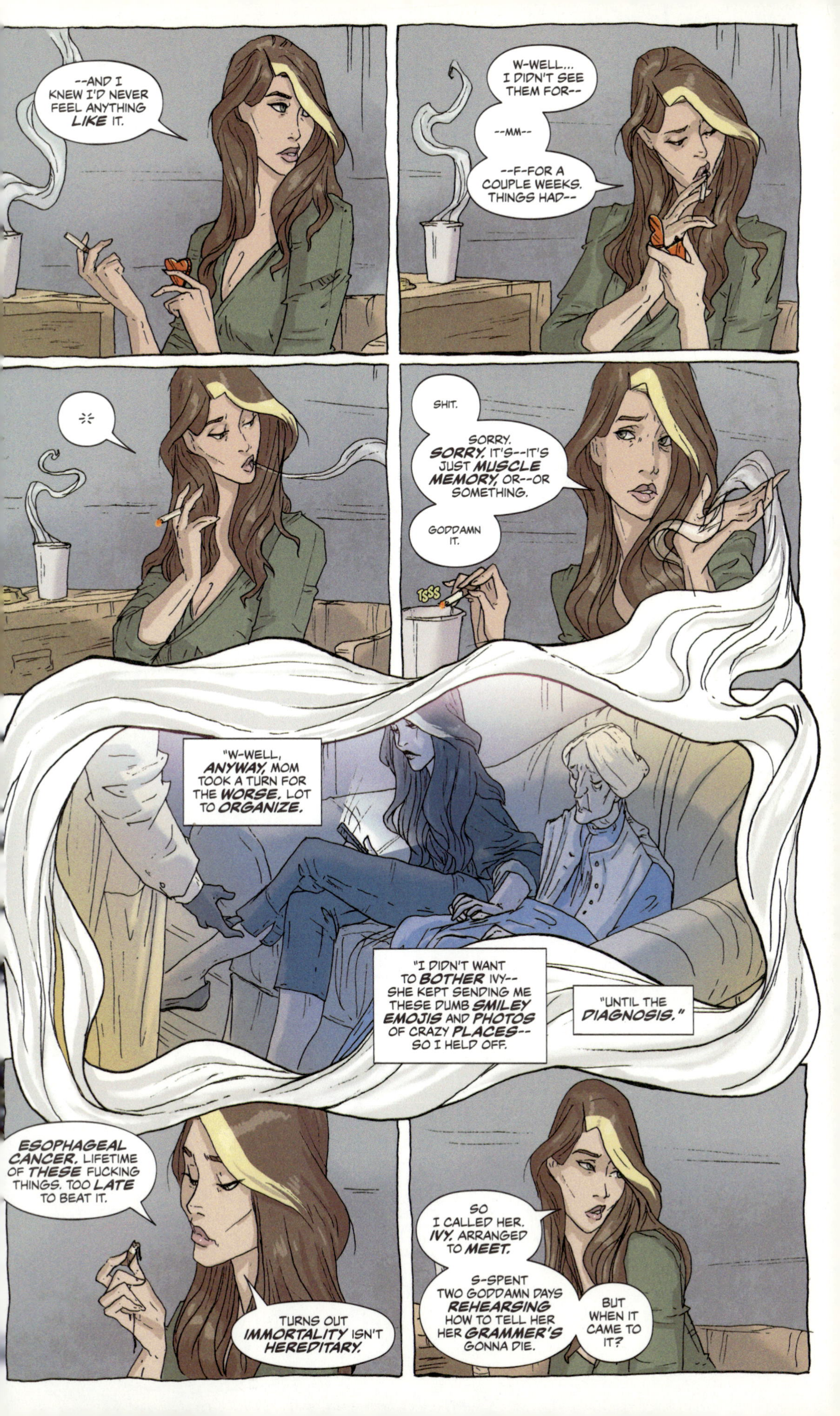
--AND I KNEW I'D NEVER FEEL ANYTHING LIKE IT.
W-WELL... I DIDN'T SEE THEM FOR--
--MM--
--F-FOR A COUPLE WEEKS. THINGS HAD--
SHIT.
SORRY. SORRY. IT'S--IT'S JUST MUSCLE MEMORY, OR--OR SOMETHING.
GODDAMN IT.
TSSS
"W-WELL, ANYWAY, MOM TOOK A TURN FOR THE WORSE. LOT TO ORGANIZE.
"I DIDN'T WANT TO BOTHER IVY--SHE KEPT SENDING ME THESE DUMB SMILEY EMOJIS AND PHOTOS OF CRAZY PLACES--SO I HELD OFF.
"UNTIL THE DIAGNOSIS."
ESOPHAGEAL CANCER. LIFETIME OF THESE FUCKING THINGS. TOO LATE TO BEAT IT.
TURNS OUT IMMORTALITY ISN'T HEREDITARY.
SO I CALLED HER. IVY. ARRANGED TO MEET.
S-SPENT TWO GODDAMN DAYS REHEARSING HOW TO TELL HER HER GRAMMER'S GONNA DIE.
BUT WHEN IT CAME TO IT?

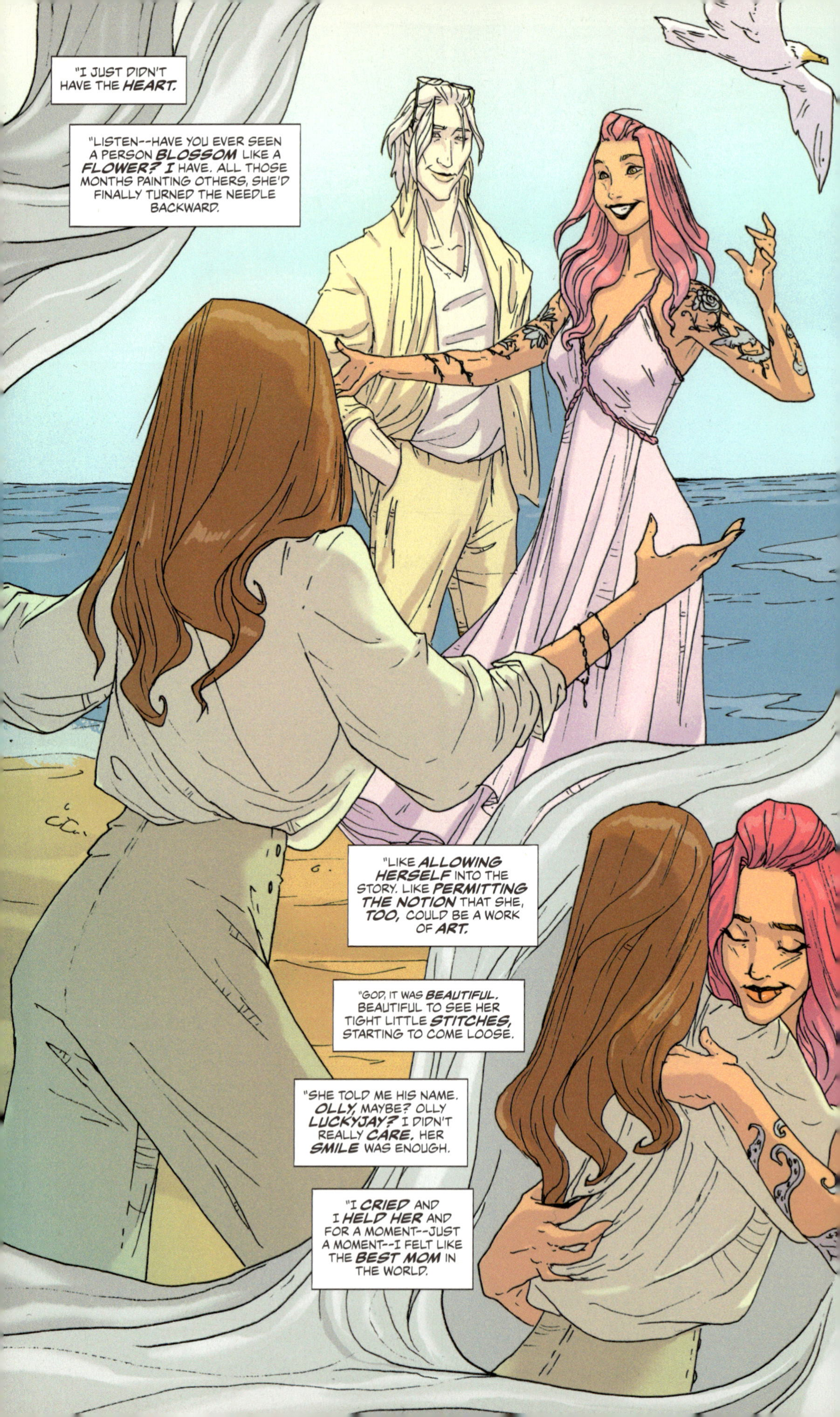
"I JUST DIDN'T HAVE THE HEART.
"LISTEN--HAVE YOU EVER SEEN A PERSON BLOSSOM LIKE A FLOWER? I HAVE. ALL THOSE MONTHS PAINTING OTHERS, SHE'D FINALLY TURNED THE NEEDLE BACKWARD.
"LIKE ALLOWING HERSELF INTO THE STORY. LIKE PERMITTING THE NOTION THAT SHE, TOO, COULD BE A WORK OF ART.
"GOD, IT WAS BEAUTIFUL. BEAUTIFUL TO SEE HER TIGHT LITTLE STITCHES, STARTING TO COME LOOSE.
"SHE TOLD ME HIS NAME. OLLY, MAYBE? OLLY LUCKYJAY? I DIDN'T REALLY CARE. HER SMILE WAS ENOUGH.
"I CRIED AND I HELD HER AND FOR A MOMENT--JUST A MOMENT--I FELT LIKE THE BEST MOM IN THE WORLD.

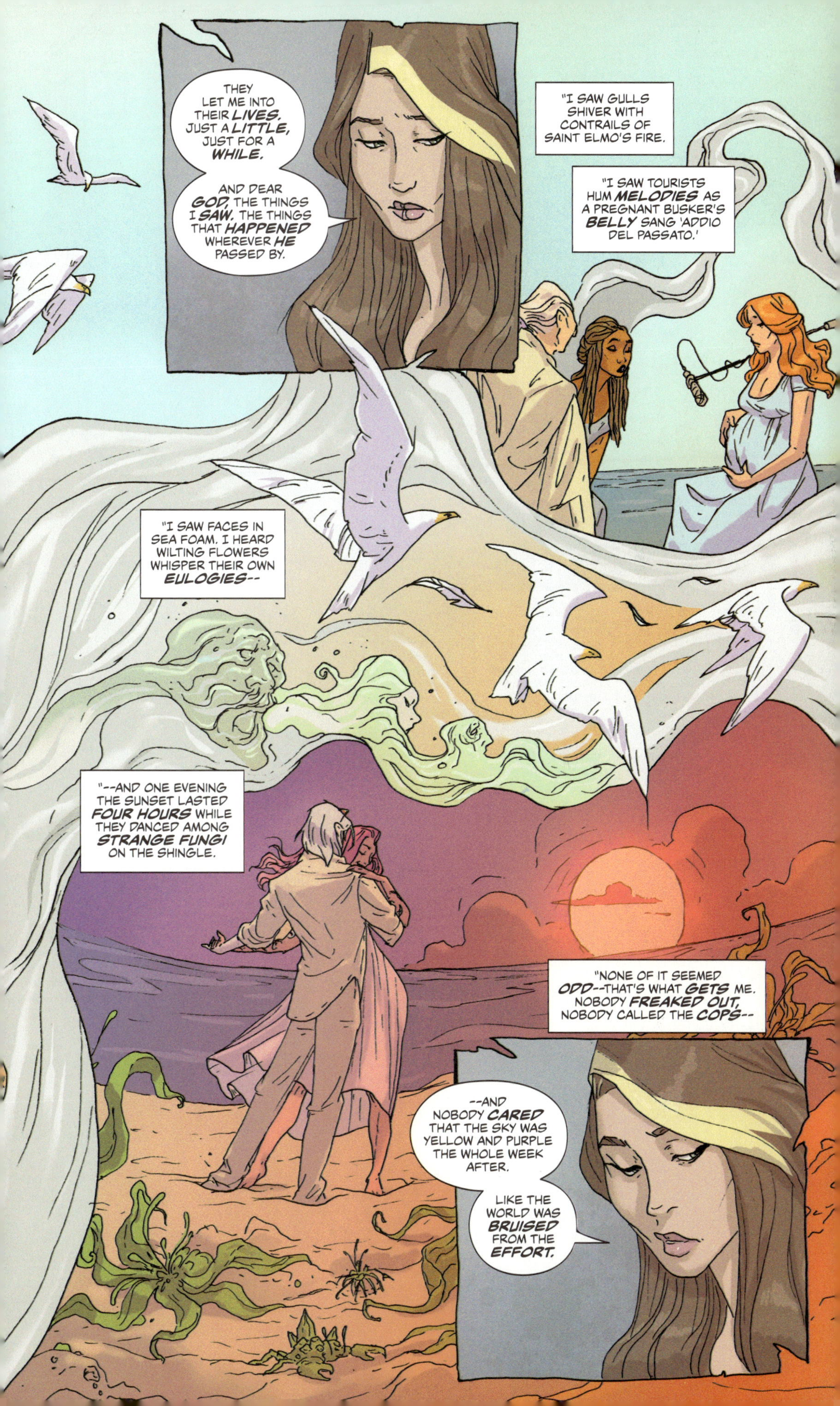
THEY LET ME INTO THEIR LIVES. JUST A LITTLE, JUST FOR A WHILE.
AND DEAR GOD, THE THINGS I SAW. THE THINGS THAT HAPPENED WHEREVER HE PASSED BY.
"I SAW GULLS SHIVER WITH CONTRAILS OF SAINT ELMO'S FIRE.
"I SAW TOURISTS HUM MELODIES AS A PREGNANT BUSKER'S BELLY SANG 'ADDIO DEL PASSATO.'
"I SAW FACES IN SEA FOAM. I HEARD WILTING FLOWERS WHISPER THEIR OWN EULOGIES--
"--AND ONE EVENING THE SUNSET LASTED FOUR HOURS WHILE THEY DANCED AMONG STRANGE FUNGI ON THE SHINGLE.
"NONE OF IT SEEMED ODD--THAT'S WHAT GETS ME. NOBODY FREAKED OUT, NOBODY CALLED THE COPS--
--AND NOBODY CARED THAT THE SKY WAS YELLOW AND PURPLE THE WHOLE WEEK AFTER.
LIKE THE WORLD WAS BRUISED FROM THE EFFORT.

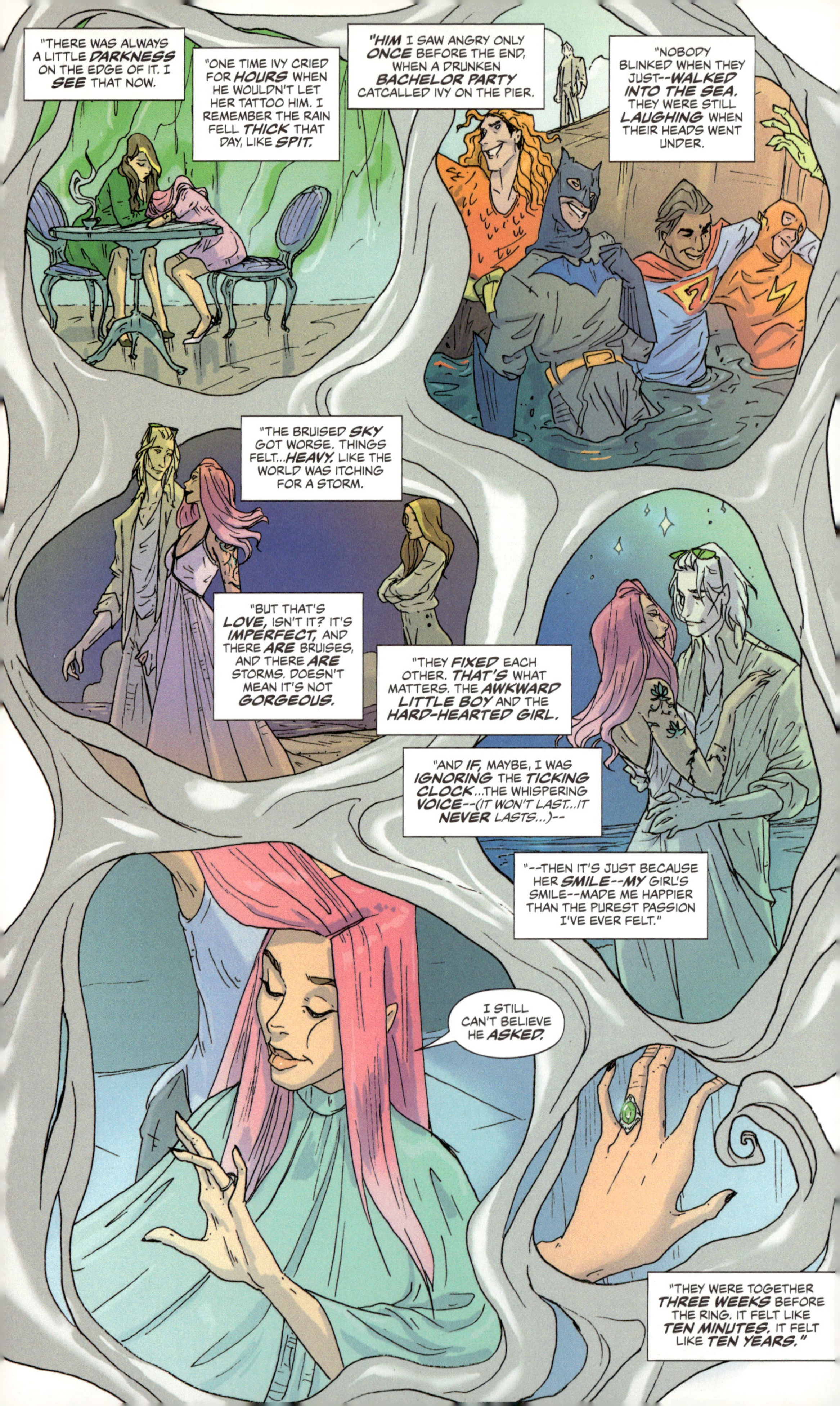
"THERE WAS ALWAYS A LITTLE DARKNESS ON THE EDGE OF IT. I SEE THAT NOW.
"ONE TIME IVY CRIED FOR HOURS WHEN HE WOULDN'T LET HER TATTOO HIM. I REMEMBER THE RAIN FELL THICK THAT DAY, LIKE SPIT.
"HIM I SAW ANGRY ONLY ONCE BEFORE THE END, WHEN A DRUNKEN BACHELOR PARTY CATCALLED IVY ON THE PIER.
"NOBODY BLINKED WHEN THEY JUST--WALKED INTO THE SEA. THEY WERE STILL LAUGHING WHEN THEIR HEADS WENT UNDER.
"THE BRUISED SKY GOT WORSE. THINGS FELT...HEAVY. LIKE THE WORLD WAS ITCHING FOR A STORM.
"BUT THAT'S LOVE, ISN'T IT? IT'S IMPERFECT, AND THERE ARE BRUISES, AND THERE ARE STORMS. DOESN'T MEAN IT'S NOT GORGEOUS.
"THEY FIXED EACH OTHER. THAT'S WHAT MATTERS. THE AWKWARD LITTLE BOY AND THE HARD-HEARTED GIRL.
"AND IF, MAYBE, I WAS IGNORING THE TICKING CLOCK...THE WHISPERING VOICE--(IT WON'T LAST...IT NEVER LASTS...)--
"--THEN IT'S JUST BECAUSE HER SMILE--MY GIRL'S SMILE--MADE ME HAPPIER THAN THE PUREST PASSION I'VE EVER FELT."
I STILL CAN'T BELIEVE HE ASKED.
"THEY WERE TOGETHER THREE WEEKS BEFORE THE RING. IT FELT LIKE TEN MINUTES. IT FELT LIKE TEN YEARS."

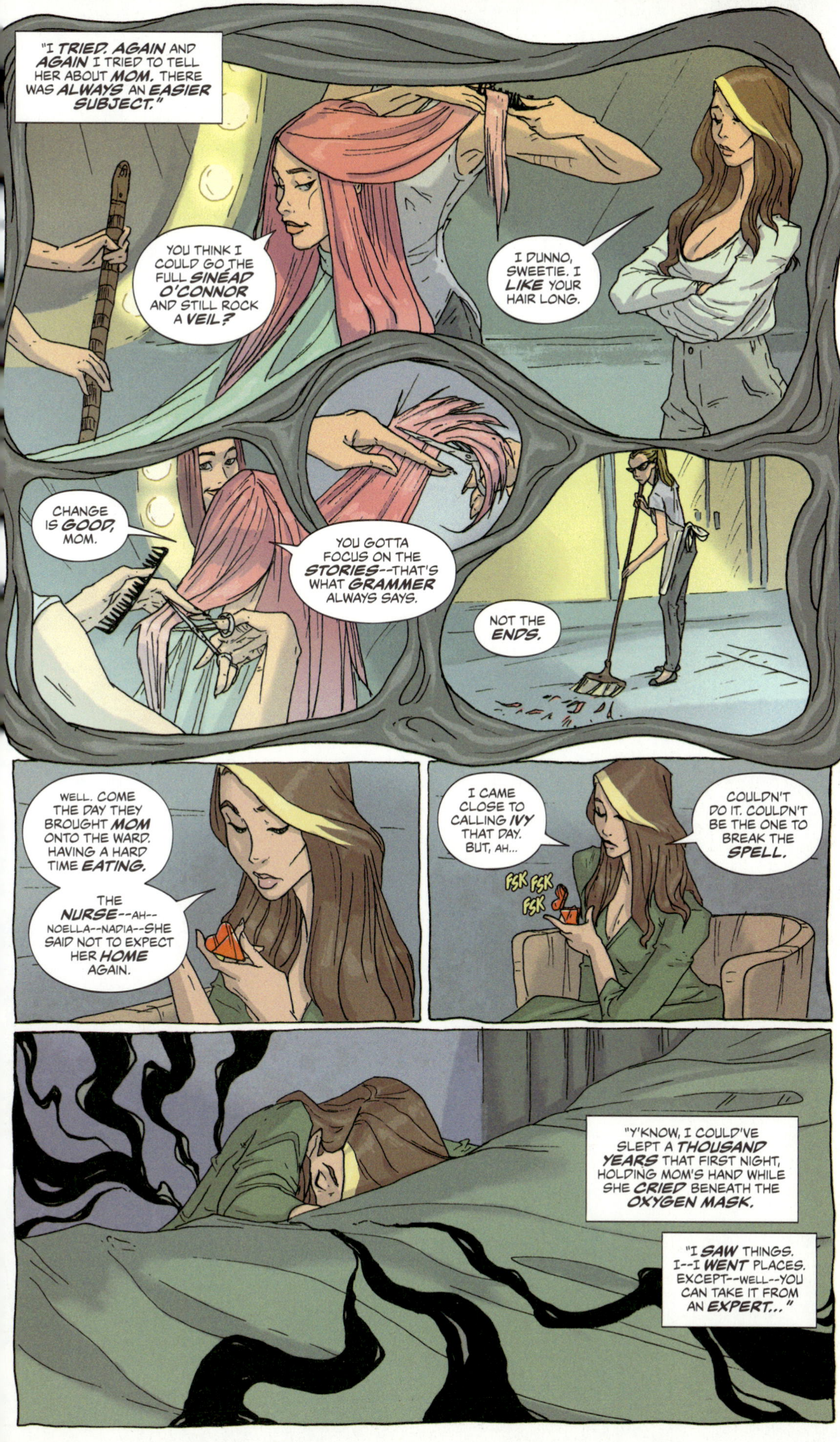
"I TRIED. AGAIN AND AGAIN I TRIED TO TELL HER ABOUT MOM. THERE WAS ALWAYS AN EASIER SUBJECT."
YOU THINK I COULD GO THE FULL SINÉAD O'CONNOR AND STILL ROCK A VEIL?
I DUNNO, SWEETIE. I LIKE YOUR HAIR LONG.
CHANGE IS GOOD, MOM.
YOU GOTTA FOCUS ON THE STORIES--THAT'S WHAT GRAMMER ALWAYS SAYS.
NOT THE ENDS.
WELL. COME THE DAY THEY BROUGHT MOM ONTO THE WARD. HAVING A HARD TIME EATING.
THE NURSE--AH--NOELLA--NADIA--SHE SAID NOT TO EXPECT HER HOME AGAIN.
I CAME CLOSE TO CALLING IVY THAT DAY. BUT, AH...
FSK FSK FSK
COULDN'T DO IT. COULDN'T BE THE ONE TO BREAK THE SPELL.
"Y'KNOW, I COULD'VE SLEPT A THOUSAND YEARS THAT FIRST NIGHT, HOLDING MOM'S HAND WHILE SHE CRIED BENEATH THE OXYGEN MASK.
"I SAW THINGS. I--I WENT PLACES. EXCEPT--WELL--YOU CAN TAKE IT FROM AN EXPERT..."

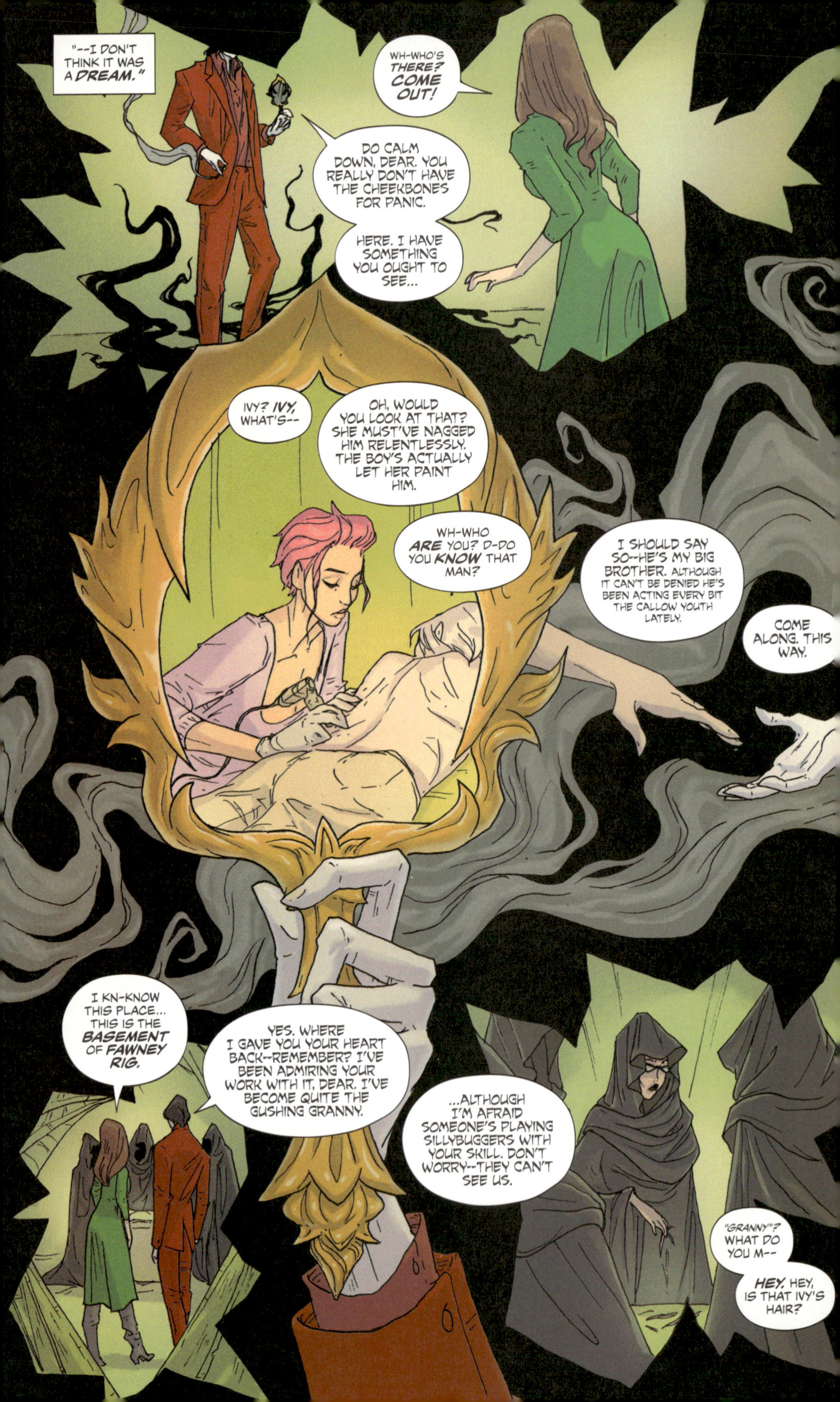
"--I DON'T THINK IT WAS A DREAM."
WH-WHO'S THERE? COME OUT!
DO CALM DOWN, DEAR. YOU REALLY DON'T HAVE THE CHEEKBONES FOR PANIC.
HERE. I HAVE SOMETHING YOU OUGHT TO SEE...
IVY? IVY, WHAT'S--
OH, WOULD YOU LOOK AT THAT? SHE MUST'VE NAGGED HIM RELENTLESSLY. THE BOY'S ACTUALLY LET HER PAINT HIM.
WH-WHO ARE YOU? D-DO YOU KNOW THAT MAN?
I SHOULD SAY SO--HE'S MY BIG BROTHER. ALTHOUGH IT CAN'T BE DENIED HE'S BEEN ACTING EVERY BIT THE CALLOW YOUTH LATELY.
COME ALONG. THIS WAY.
I KN-KNOW THIS PLACE... THIS IS THE BASEMENT OF FAWNEY RIG.
YES. WHERE I GAVE YOU YOUR HEART BACK--REMEMBER? I'VE BEEN ADMIRING YOUR WORK WITH IT, DEAR. I'VE BECOME QUITE THE GUSHING GRANNY.
...ALTHOUGH I'M AFRAID SOMEONE'S PLAYING SILLYBUGGERS WITH YOUR SKILL. DON'T WORRY--THEY CAN'T SEE US.
"GRANNY"? WHAT DO YOU M--
HEY, HEY, IS THAT IVY'S HAIR?

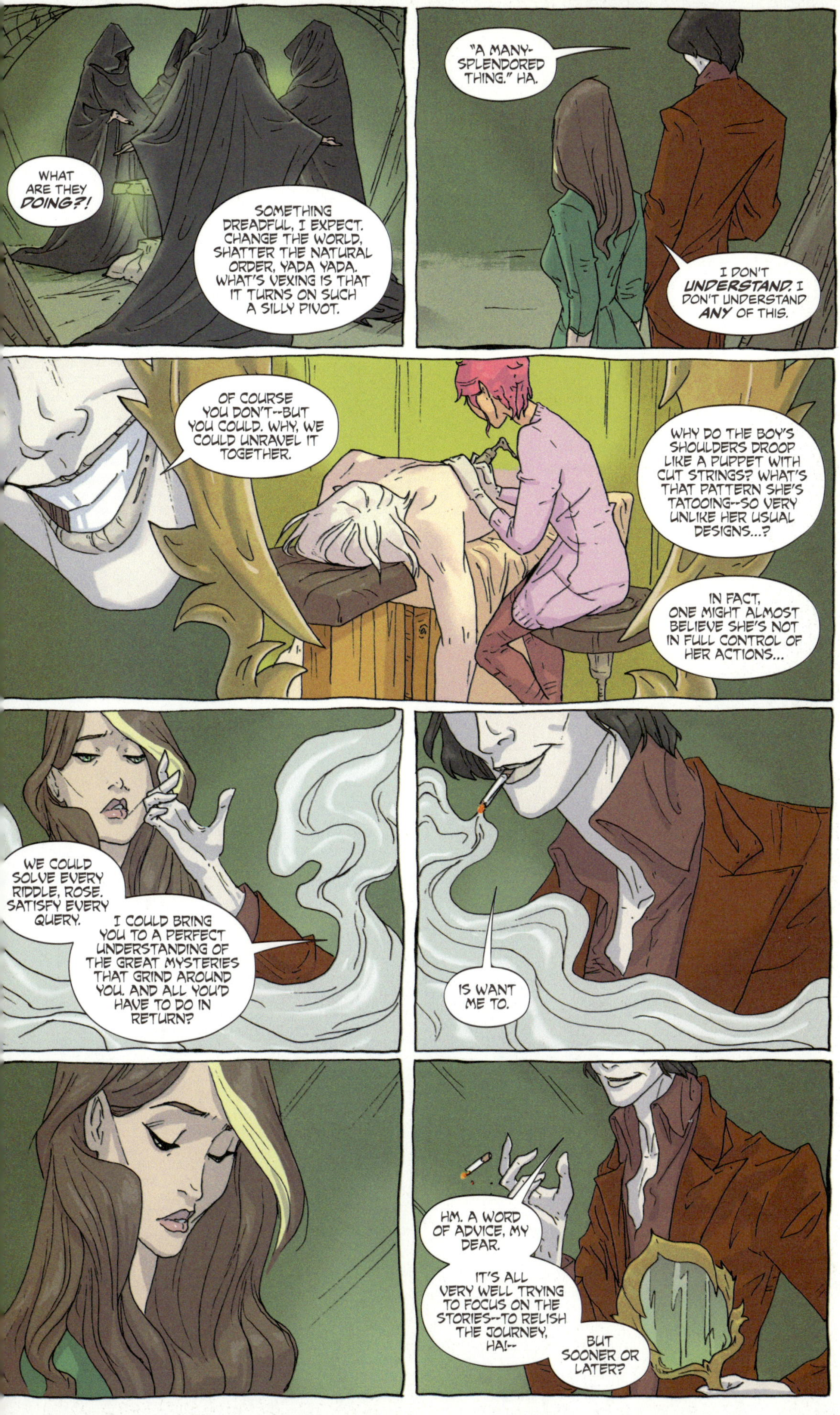
WHAT ARE THEY *DOING?!*
SOMETHING DREADFUL, I EXPECT. CHANGE THE WORLD, SHATTER THE NATURAL ORDER, YADA YADA. WHAT'S VEXING IS THAT IT TURNS ON SUCH A SILLY PIVOT.
"A MANY-SPLENDORED THING." HA.
I DON'T *UNDERSTAND.* I DON'T UNDERSTAND *ANY* OF THIS.
OF COURSE YOU DON'T--BUT YOU COULD. WHY, WE COULD UNRAVEL IT TOGETHER.
WHY DO THE BOY'S SHOULDERS DROOP LIKE A PUPPET WITH CUT STRINGS? WHAT'S THAT PATTERN SHE'S TATOOING--SO VERY UNLIKE HER USUAL DESIGNS...?
IN FACT, ONE MIGHT ALMOST BELIEVE SHE'S NOT IN FULL CONTROL OF HER ACTIONS...
WE COULD SOLVE EVERY RIDDLE, ROSE. SATISFY EVERY QUERY.
I COULD BRING YOU TO A PERFECT UNDERSTANDING OF THE GREAT MYSTERIES THAT GRIND AROUND YOU. AND ALL YOU'D HAVE TO DO IN RETURN?
IS WANT ME TO.
HM. A WORD OF ADVICE, MY DEAR.
IT'S ALL VERY WELL TRYING TO FOCUS ON THE STORIES--TO RELISH THE JOURNEY, HA!--
BUT SOONER OR LATER?

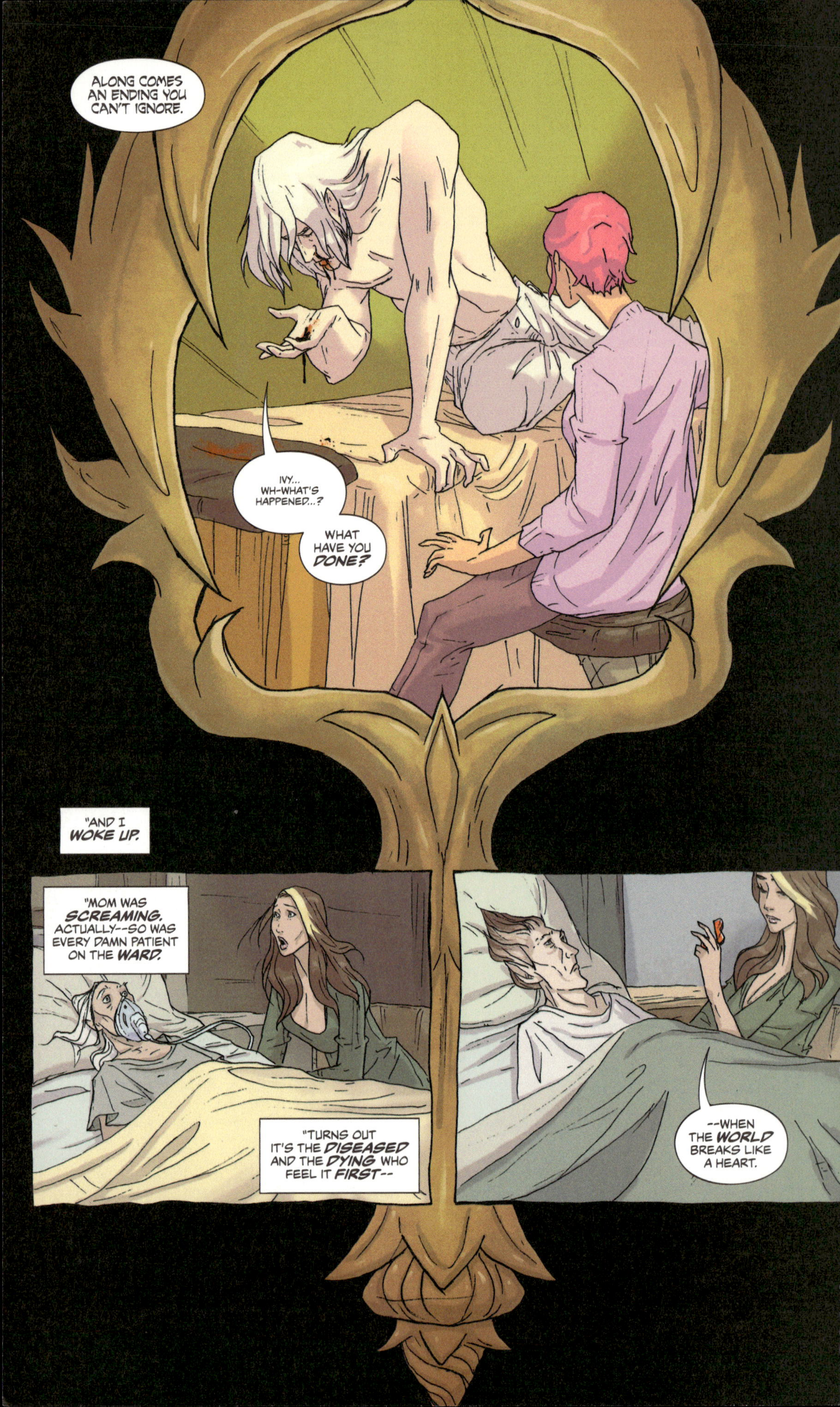
ALONG COMES AN ENDING YOU CAN'T IGNORE.
IVY... WH-WHAT'S HAPPENED...?
WHAT HAVE YOU *DONE?*
"AND I *WOKE UP.*
"MOM WAS *SCREAMING.* ACTUALLY--SO WAS EVERY DAMN PATIENT ON THE *WARD.*
"TURNS OUT IT'S THE *DISEASED* AND THE *DYING* WHO FEEL IT *FIRST*--
--WHEN THE *WORLD* BREAKS LIKE A HEART.

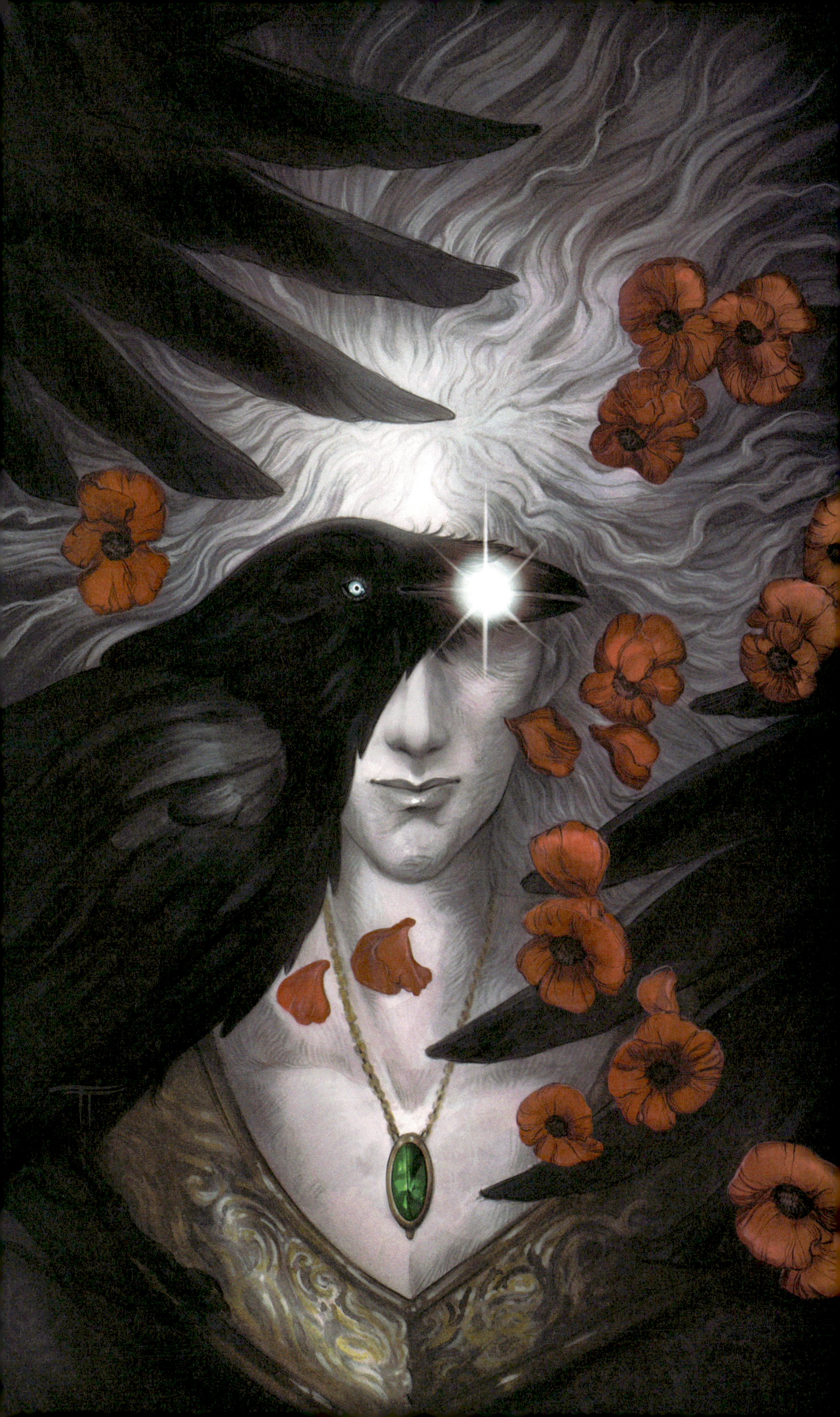

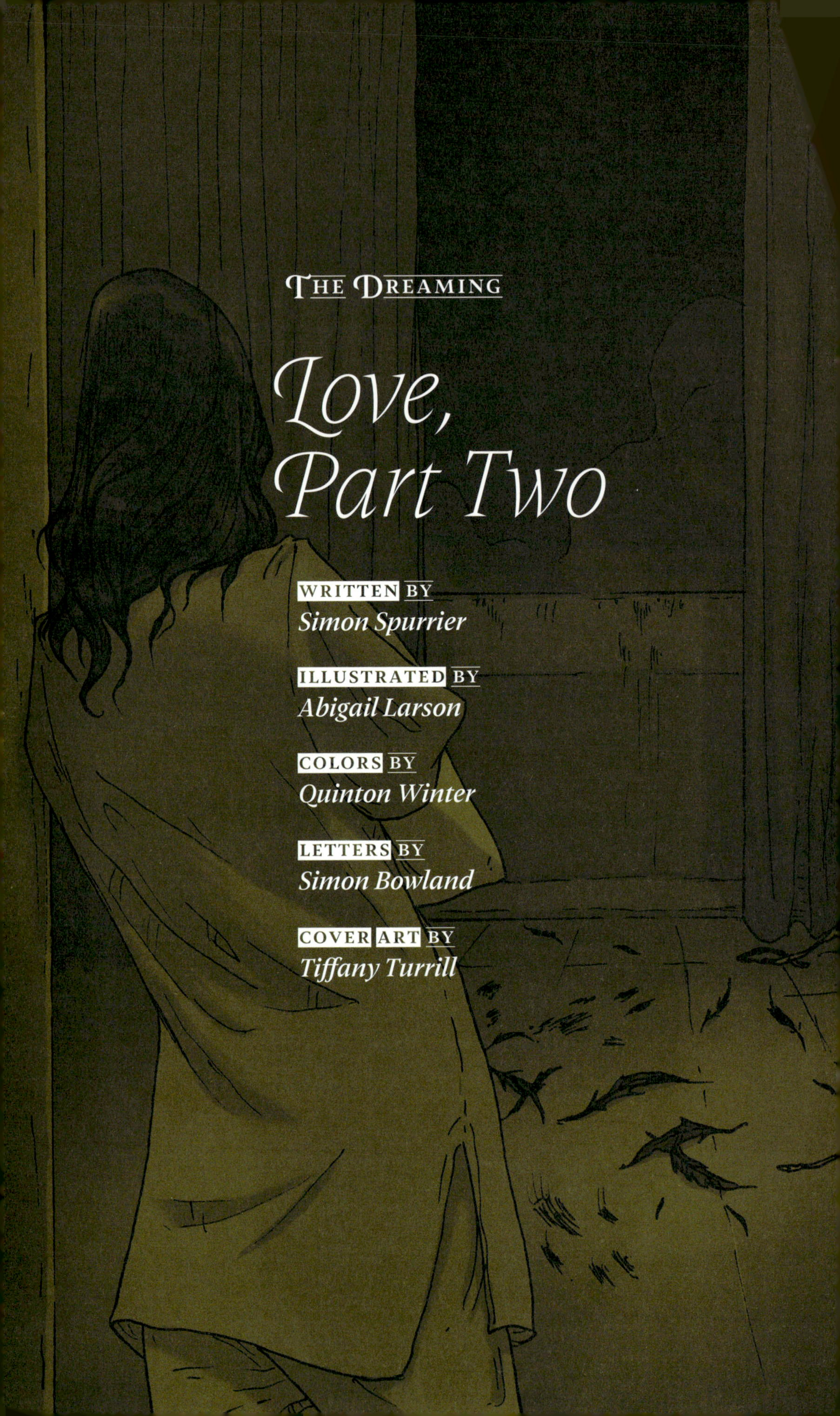

THE DREAMING

Love, Part Two

WRITTEN BY
Simon Spurrier

ILLUSTRATED BY
Abigail Larson

COLORS BY
Quinton Winter

LETTERS BY
Simon Bowland

COVER ART BY
Tiffany Turrill

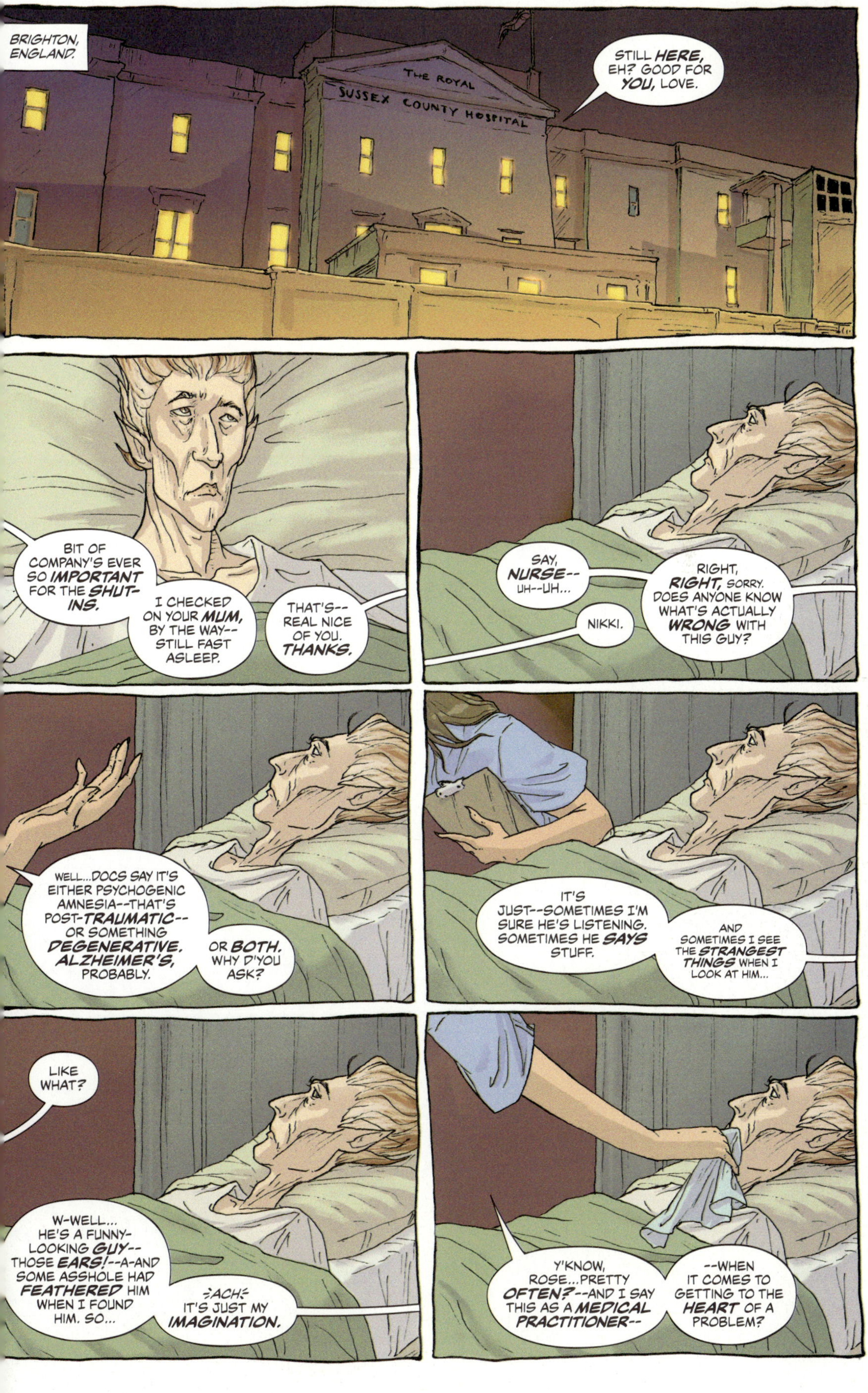
BRIGHTON, ENGLAND.
THE ROYAL SUSSEX COUNTY HOSPITAL
STILL HERE, EH? GOOD FOR YOU, LOVE.
BIT OF COMPANY'S EVER SO IMPORTANT FOR THE SHUT-INS.
I CHECKED ON YOUR MUM, BY THE WAY--STILL FAST ASLEEP.
THAT'S--REAL NICE OF YOU. THANKS.
SAY, NURSE--UH--UH...
NIKKI.
RIGHT, RIGHT, SORRY. DOES ANYONE KNOW WHAT'S ACTUALLY WRONG WITH THIS GUY?
WELL...DOCS SAY IT'S EITHER PSYCHOGENIC AMNESIA--THAT'S POST-TRAUMATIC--OR SOMETHING DEGENERATIVE. ALZHEIMER'S, PROBABLY.
OR BOTH. WHY D'YOU ASK?
IT'S JUST--SOMETIMES I'M SURE HE'S LISTENING. SOMETIMES HE SAYS STUFF.
AND SOMETIMES I SEE THE STRANGEST THINGS WHEN I LOOK AT HIM...
LIKE WHAT?
W-WELL... HE'S A FUNNY-LOOKING GUY--THOSE EARS!--A-AND SOME ASSHOLE HAD FEATHERED HIM WHEN I FOUND HIM. SO...
ACH IT'S JUST MY IMAGINATION.
Y'KNOW, ROSE...PRETTY OFTEN?--AND I SAY THIS AS A MEDICAL PRACTITIONER--
--WHEN IT COMES TO GETTING TO THE HEART OF A PROBLEM?

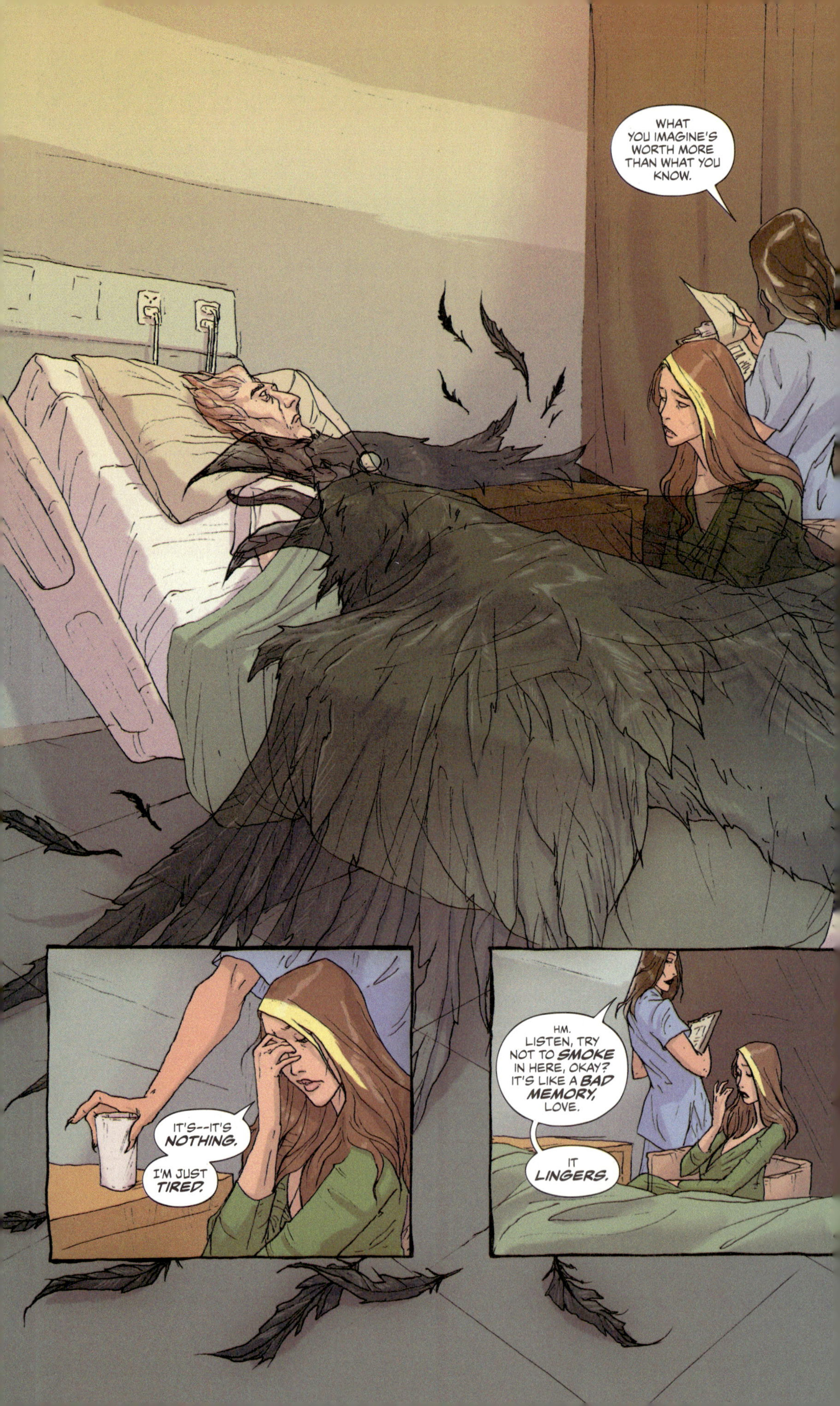
WHAT YOU IMAGINE'S WORTH MORE THAN WHAT YOU KNOW.
IT'S--IT'S **NOTHING.**
I'M JUST **TIRED.**
HM. LISTEN, TRY NOT TO **SMOKE** IN HERE, OKAY? IT'S LIKE A **BAD MEMORY,** LOVE.
IT **LINGERS.**

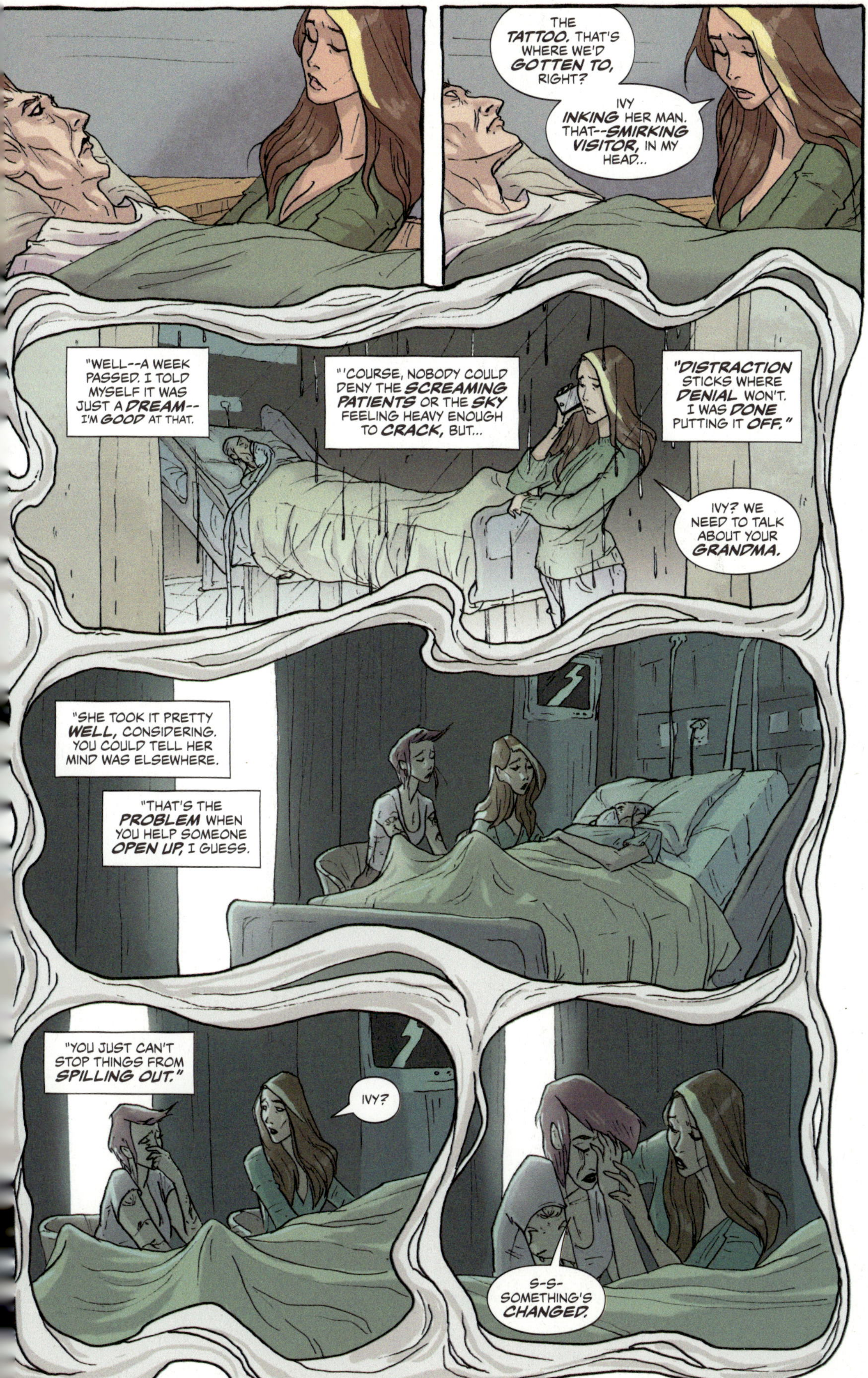
THE TATTOO. THAT'S WHERE WE'D GOTTEN TO, RIGHT?
IVY INKING HER MAN. THAT--SMIRKING VISITOR, IN MY HEAD...
"WELL--A WEEK PASSED. I TOLD MYSELF IT WAS JUST A DREAM-- I'M GOOD AT THAT.
"'COURSE, NOBODY COULD DENY THE SCREAMING PATIENTS OR THE SKY FEELING HEAVY ENOUGH TO CRACK, BUT...
"DISTRACTION STICKS WHERE DENIAL WON'T. I WAS DONE PUTTING IT OFF."
IVY? WE NEED TO TALK ABOUT YOUR GRANDMA.
"SHE TOOK IT PRETTY WELL, CONSIDERING. YOU COULD TELL HER MIND WAS ELSEWHERE.
"THAT'S THE PROBLEM WHEN YOU HELP SOMEONE OPEN UP, I GUESS.
"YOU JUST CAN'T STOP THINGS FROM SPILLING OUT."
IVY?
S-S-SOMETHING'S CHANGED.

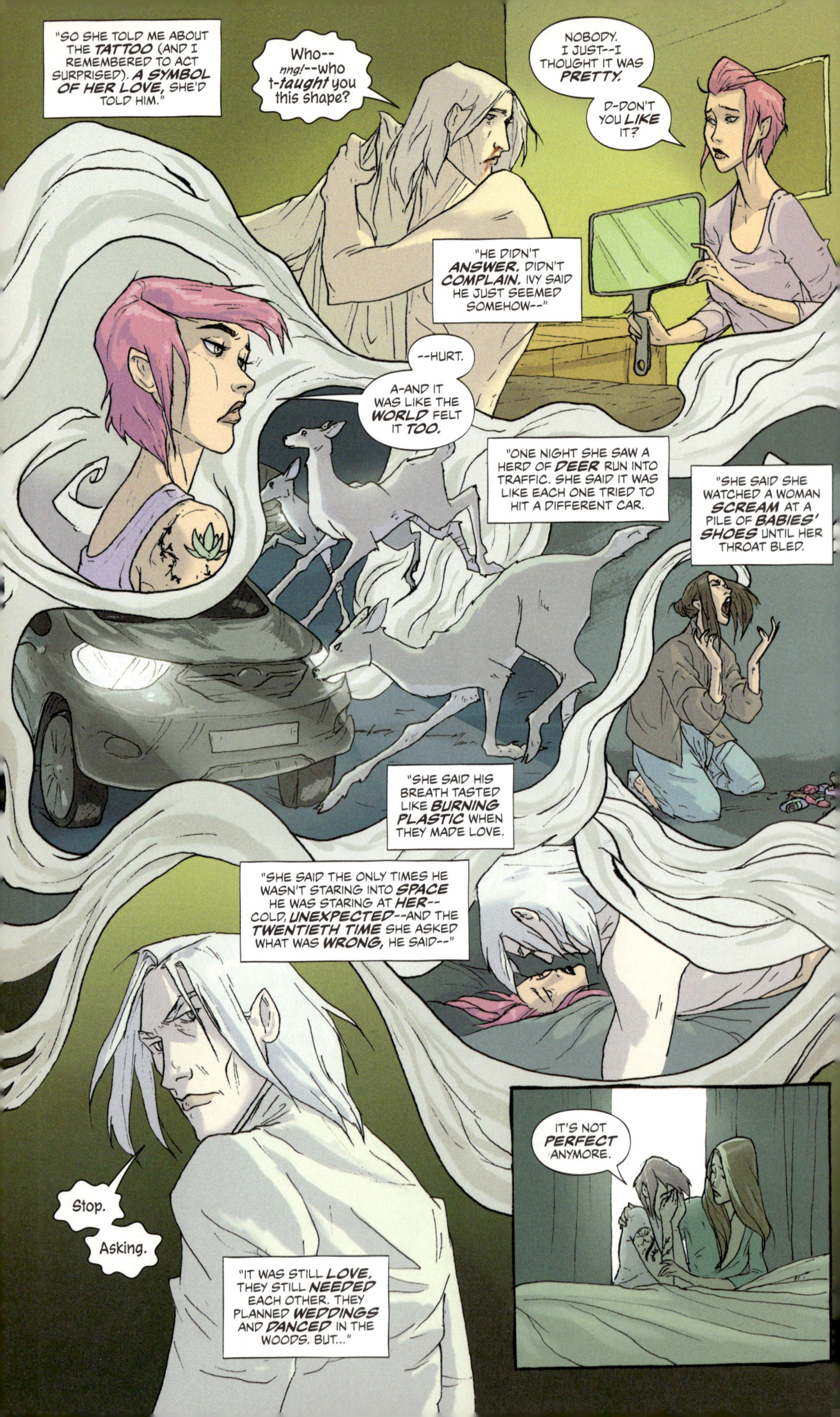
"SO SHE TOLD ME ABOUT THE TATTOO (AND I REMEMBERED TO ACT SURPRISED). A SYMBOL OF HER LOVE, SHE'D TOLD HIM."
Who--nng!--who t-taught you this shape?
NOBODY. I JUST--I THOUGHT IT WAS PRETTY.
D-DON'T YOU LIKE IT?
"HE DIDN'T ANSWER. DIDN'T COMPLAIN. IVY SAID HE JUST SEEMED SOMEHOW--"
--HURT.
A-AND IT WAS LIKE THE WORLD FELT IT TOO.
"ONE NIGHT SHE SAW A HERD OF DEER RUN INTO TRAFFIC. SHE SAID IT WAS LIKE EACH ONE TRIED TO HIT A DIFFERENT CAR.
"SHE SAID SHE WATCHED A WOMAN SCREAM AT A PILE OF BABIES' SHOES UNTIL HER THROAT BLED.
"SHE SAID HIS BREATH TASTED LIKE BURNING PLASTIC WHEN THEY MADE LOVE.
"SHE SAID THE ONLY TIMES HE WASN'T STARING INTO SPACE HE WAS STARING AT HER--COLD, UNEXPECTED--AND THE TWENTIETH TIME SHE ASKED WHAT WAS WRONG, HE SAID--"
Stop.
Asking.
"IT WAS STILL LOVE. THEY STILL NEEDED EACH OTHER. THEY PLANNED WEDDINGS AND DANCED IN THE WOODS. BUT..."
IT'S NOT PERFECT ANYMORE.

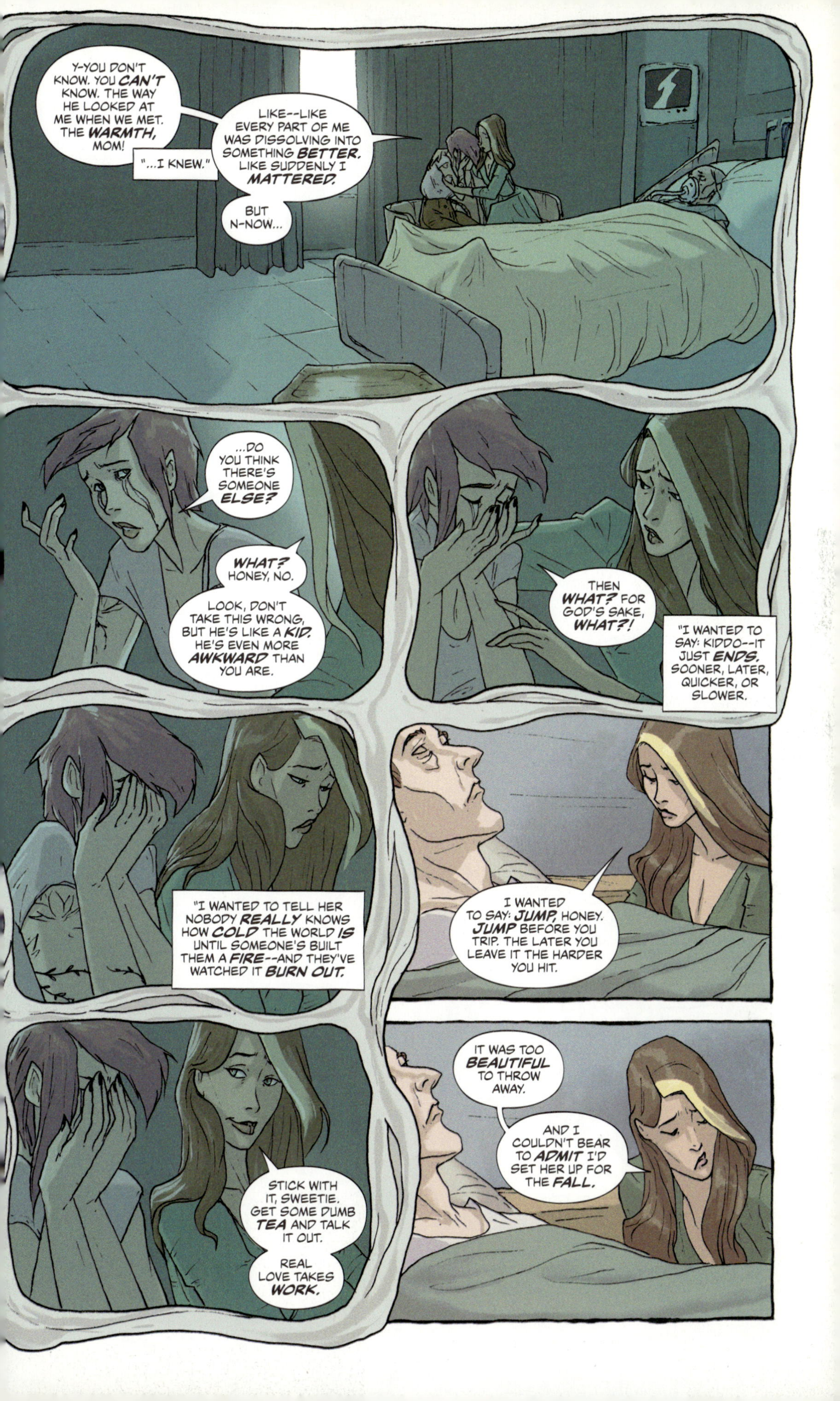

Y-YOU DON'T KNOW. YOU **CAN'T** KNOW. THE WAY HE LOOKED AT ME WHEN WE MET. THE **WARMTH,** MOM!
"...I KNEW."
LIKE--LIKE EVERY PART OF ME WAS DISSOLVING INTO SOMETHING **BETTER.** LIKE SUDDENLY I **MATTERED.**
BUT N-NOW...
...DO YOU THINK THERE'S SOMEONE **ELSE?**
WHAT? HONEY, NO.
LOOK, DON'T TAKE THIS WRONG, BUT HE'S LIKE A **KID.** HE'S EVEN MORE **AWKWARD** THAN YOU ARE.
THEN **WHAT?** FOR GOD'S SAKE, **WHAT?!**
"I WANTED TO SAY: KIDDO--IT JUST **ENDS.** SOONER, LATER, QUICKER, OR SLOWER.
"I WANTED TO TELL HER NOBODY **REALLY** KNOWS HOW **COLD** THE WORLD **IS** UNTIL SOMEONE'S BUILT THEM A **FIRE**--AND THEY'VE WATCHED IT **BURN OUT.**
I WANTED TO SAY: **JUMP,** HONEY. **JUMP** BEFORE YOU TRIP. THE LATER YOU LEAVE IT THE HARDER YOU HIT.
STICK WITH IT, SWEETIE. GET SOME DUMB **TEA** AND TALK IT OUT.
REAL LOVE TAKES **WORK.**
IT WAS TOO **BEAUTIFUL** TO THROW AWAY.
AND I COULDN'T BEAR TO **ADMIT** I'D SET HER UP FOR THE **FALL.**

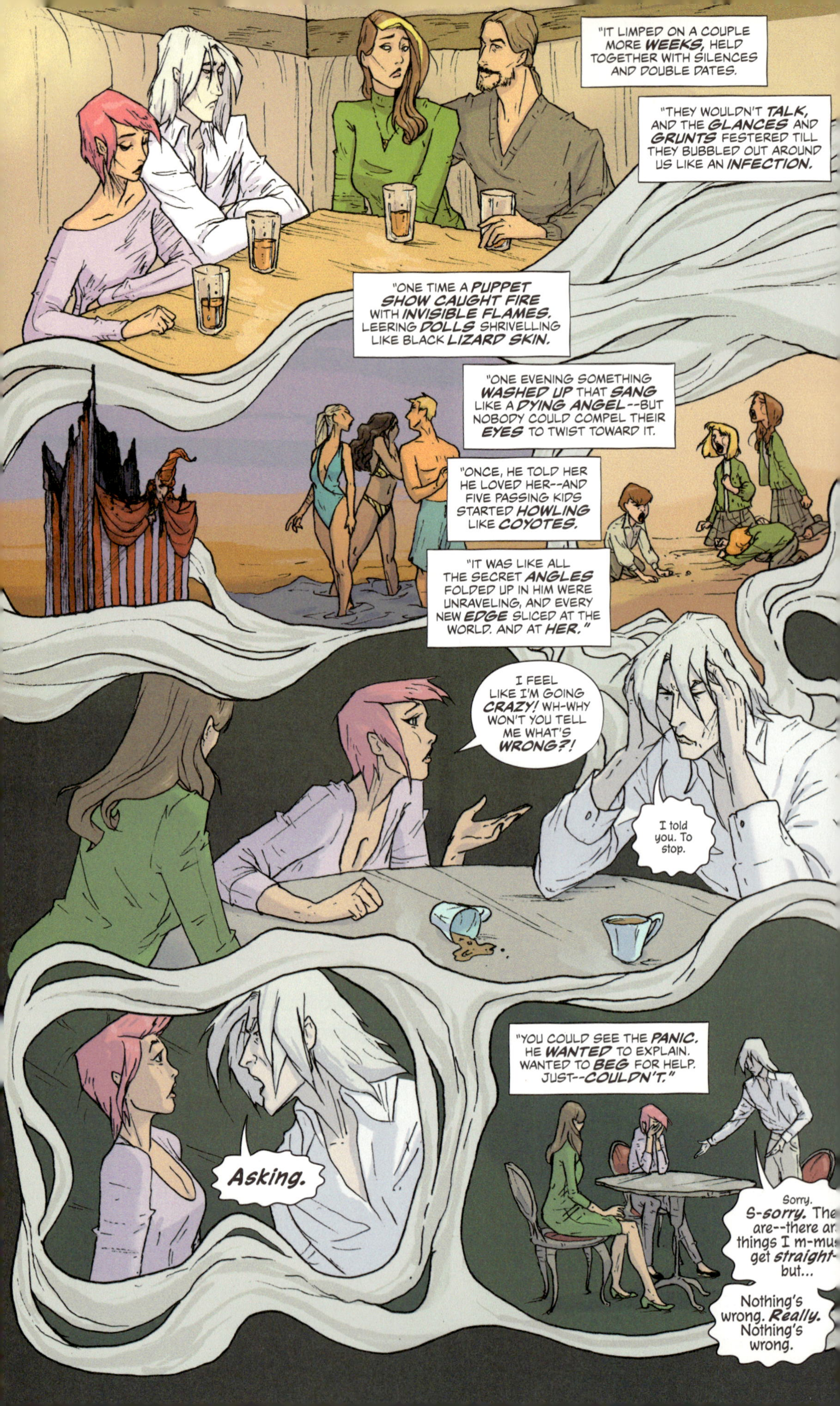
"IT LIMPED ON A COUPLE MORE WEEKS, HELD TOGETHER WITH SILENCES AND DOUBLE DATES.
"THEY WOULDN'T TALK, AND THE GLANCES AND GRUNTS FESTERED TILL THEY BUBBLED OUT AROUND US LIKE AN INFECTION.
"ONE TIME A PUPPET SHOW CAUGHT FIRE WITH INVISIBLE FLAMES. LEERING DOLLS SHRIVELLING LIKE BLACK LIZARD SKIN.
"ONE EVENING SOMETHING WASHED UP THAT SANG LIKE A DYING ANGEL--BUT NOBODY COULD COMPEL THEIR EYES TO TWIST TOWARD IT.
"ONCE, HE TOLD HER HE LOVED HER--AND FIVE PASSING KIDS STARTED HOWLING LIKE COYOTES.
"IT WAS LIKE ALL THE SECRET ANGLES FOLDED UP IN HIM WERE UNRAVELING, AND EVERY NEW EDGE SLICED AT THE WORLD. AND AT HER."
I FEEL LIKE I'M GOING CRAZY! WH-WHY WON'T YOU TELL ME WHAT'S WRONG?!
I told you. To stop.
Asking.
"YOU COULD SEE THE PANIC. HE WANTED TO EXPLAIN. WANTED TO BEG FOR HELP. JUST--COULDN'T."
Sorry.
Nothing's wrong. Really. Nothing's wrong.

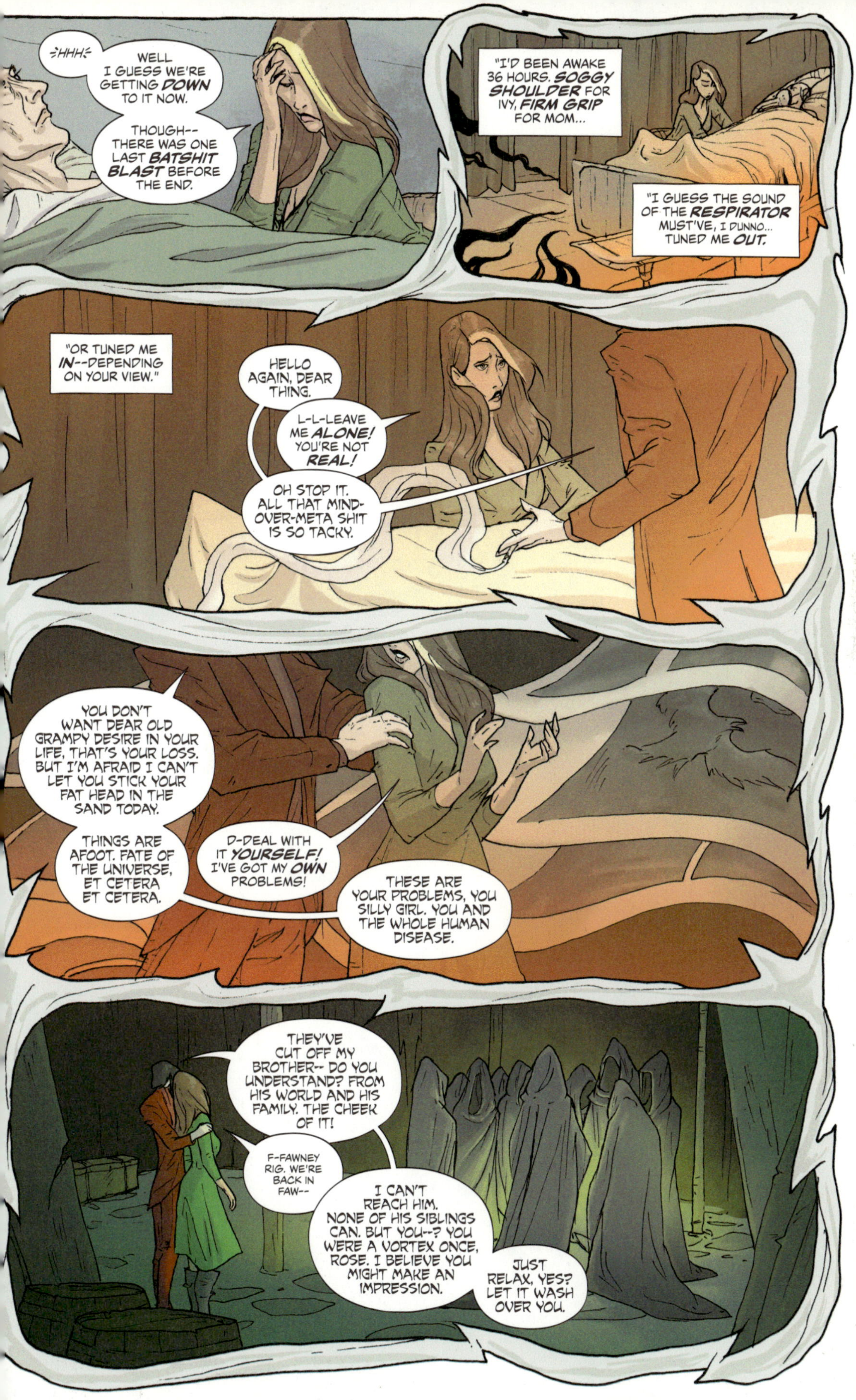

HHH
WELL I GUESS WE'RE GETTING DOWN TO IT NOW.
THOUGH-- THERE WAS ONE LAST BATSHIT BLAST BEFORE THE END.
"I'D BEEN AWAKE 36 HOURS. SOGGY SHOULDER FOR IVY, FIRM GRIP FOR MOM...
"I GUESS THE SOUND OF THE RESPIRATOR MUST'VE, I DUNNO... TUNED ME OUT.
"OR TUNED ME IN--DEPENDING ON YOUR VIEW."
HELLO AGAIN, DEAR THING.
L-L-LEAVE ME ALONE! YOU'RE NOT REAL!
OH STOP IT. ALL THAT MIND-OVER-META SHIT IS SO TACKY.
YOU DON'T WANT DEAR OLD GRAMPY DESIRE IN YOUR LIFE, THAT'S YOUR LOSS. BUT I'M AFRAID I CAN'T LET YOU STICK YOUR FAT HEAD IN THE SAND TODAY.
THINGS ARE AFOOT. FATE OF THE UNIVERSE, ET CETERA ET CETERA.
D-DEAL WITH IT YOURSELF! I'VE GOT MY OWN PROBLEMS!
THESE ARE YOUR PROBLEMS, YOU SILLY GIRL. YOU AND THE WHOLE HUMAN DISEASE.
THEY'VE CUT OFF MY BROTHER-- DO YOU UNDERSTAND? FROM HIS WORLD AND HIS FAMILY. THE CHEEK OF IT!
F-FAWNEY RIG. WE'RE BACK IN FAW--
I CAN'T REACH HIM. NONE OF HIS SIBLINGS CAN. BUT YOU--? YOU WERE A VORTEX ONCE, ROSE. I BELIEVE YOU MIGHT MAKE AN IMPRESSION.
JUST RELAX, YES? LET IT WASH OVER YOU.

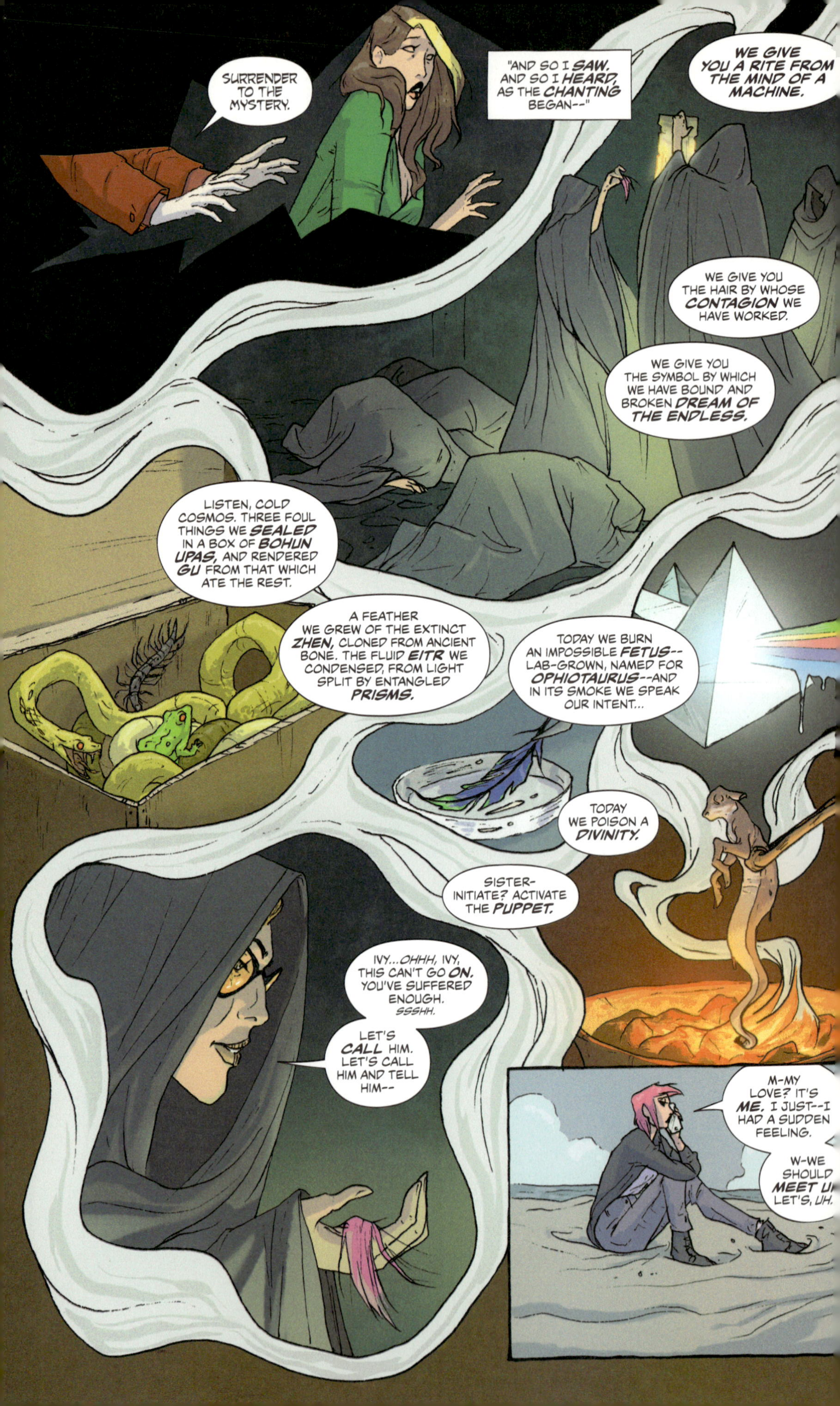

SURRENDER TO THE MYSTERY.
"AND SO I SAW. AND SO I HEARD, AS THE CHANTING BEGAN--"
WE GIVE YOU A RITE FROM THE MIND OF A MACHINE.
WE GIVE YOU THE HAIR BY WHOSE CONTAGION WE HAVE WORKED.
WE GIVE YOU THE SYMBOL BY WHICH WE HAVE BOUND AND BROKEN DREAM OF THE ENDLESS.
LISTEN, COLD COSMOS. THREE FOUL THINGS WE SEALED IN A BOX OF BOHUN UPAS, AND RENDERED GU FROM THAT WHICH ATE THE REST.
A FEATHER WE GREW OF THE EXTINCT ZHEN, CLONED FROM ANCIENT BONE. THE FLUID EITR WE CONDENSED, FROM LIGHT SPLIT BY ENTANGLED PRISMS.
TODAY WE BURN AN IMPOSSIBLE FETUS--LAB-GROWN, NAMED FOR OPHIOTAURUS--AND IN ITS SMOKE WE SPEAK OUR INTENT...
TODAY WE POISON A DIVINITY.
SISTER-INITIATE? ACTIVATE THE PUPPET.
IVY...OHHH, IVY, THIS CAN'T GO ON. YOU'VE SUFFERED ENOUGH. SSSHH.
LET'S CALL HIM. LET'S CALL HIM AND TELL HIM--
M-MY LOVE? IT'S ME. I JUST--I HAD A SUDDEN FEELING.
W-WE SHOULD MEET U LET'S, UH.

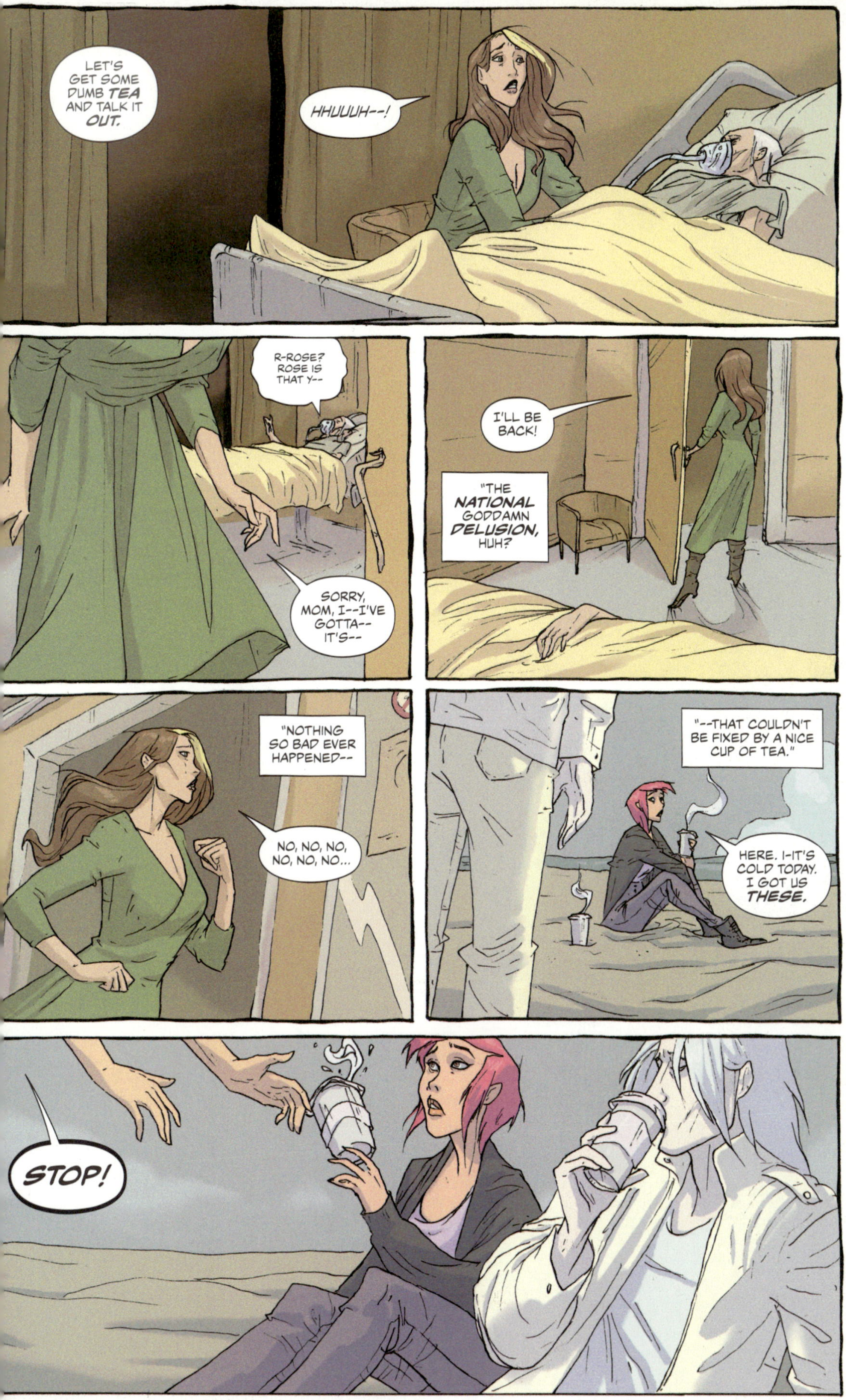

LET'S GET SOME DUMB TEA AND TALK IT OUT.
HHUUUH--!
R-ROSE? ROSE IS THAT Y--
SORRY, MOM, I--I'VE GOTTA-- IT'S--
I'LL BE BACK!
"THE NATIONAL GODDAMN DELUSION, HUH?
"NOTHING SO BAD EVER HAPPENED--
NO, NO, NO, NO, NO, NO...
"--THAT COULDN'T BE FIXED BY A NICE CUP OF TEA."
HERE. I-IT'S COLD TODAY. I GOT US THESE.
STOP!

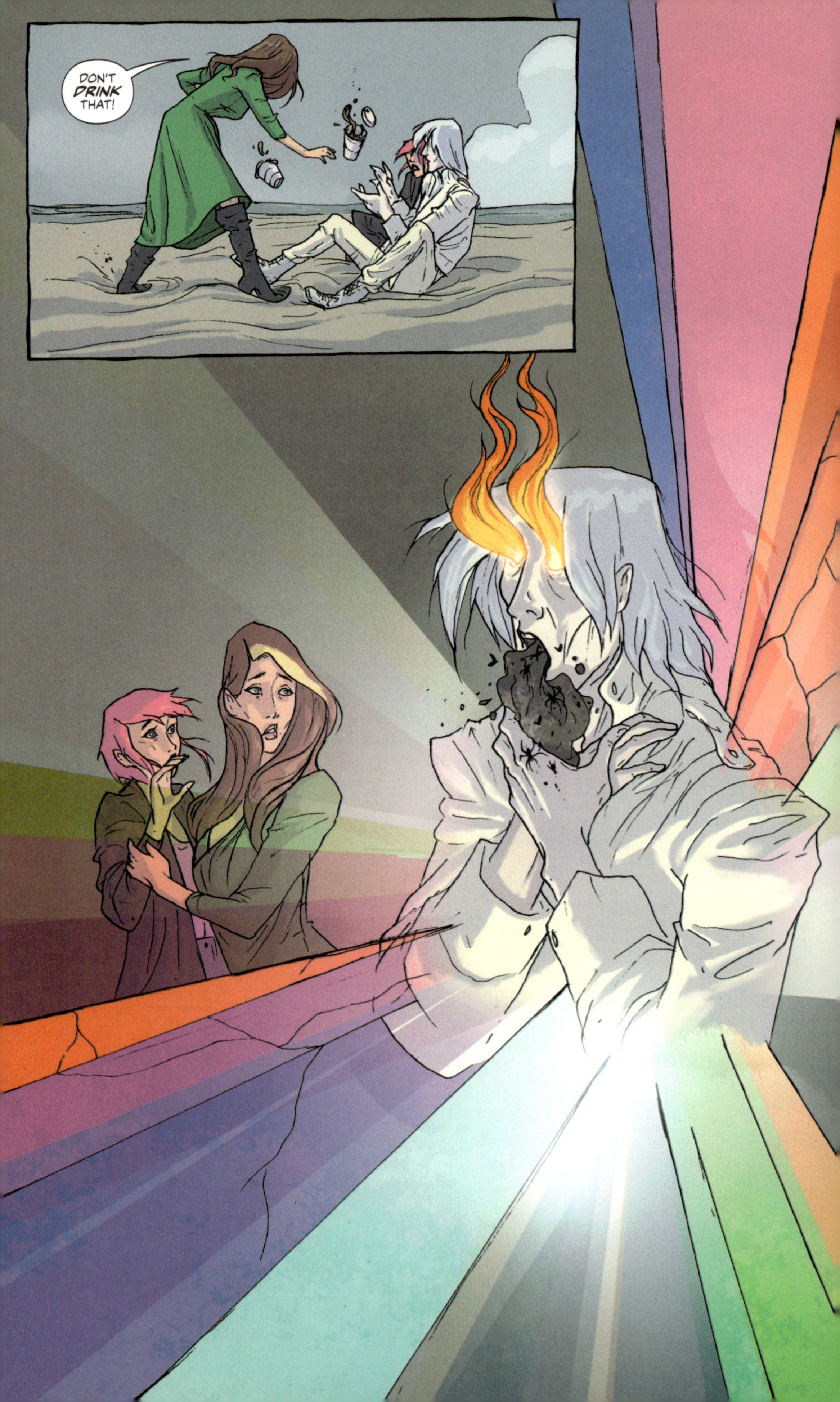
DON'T DRINK THAT!

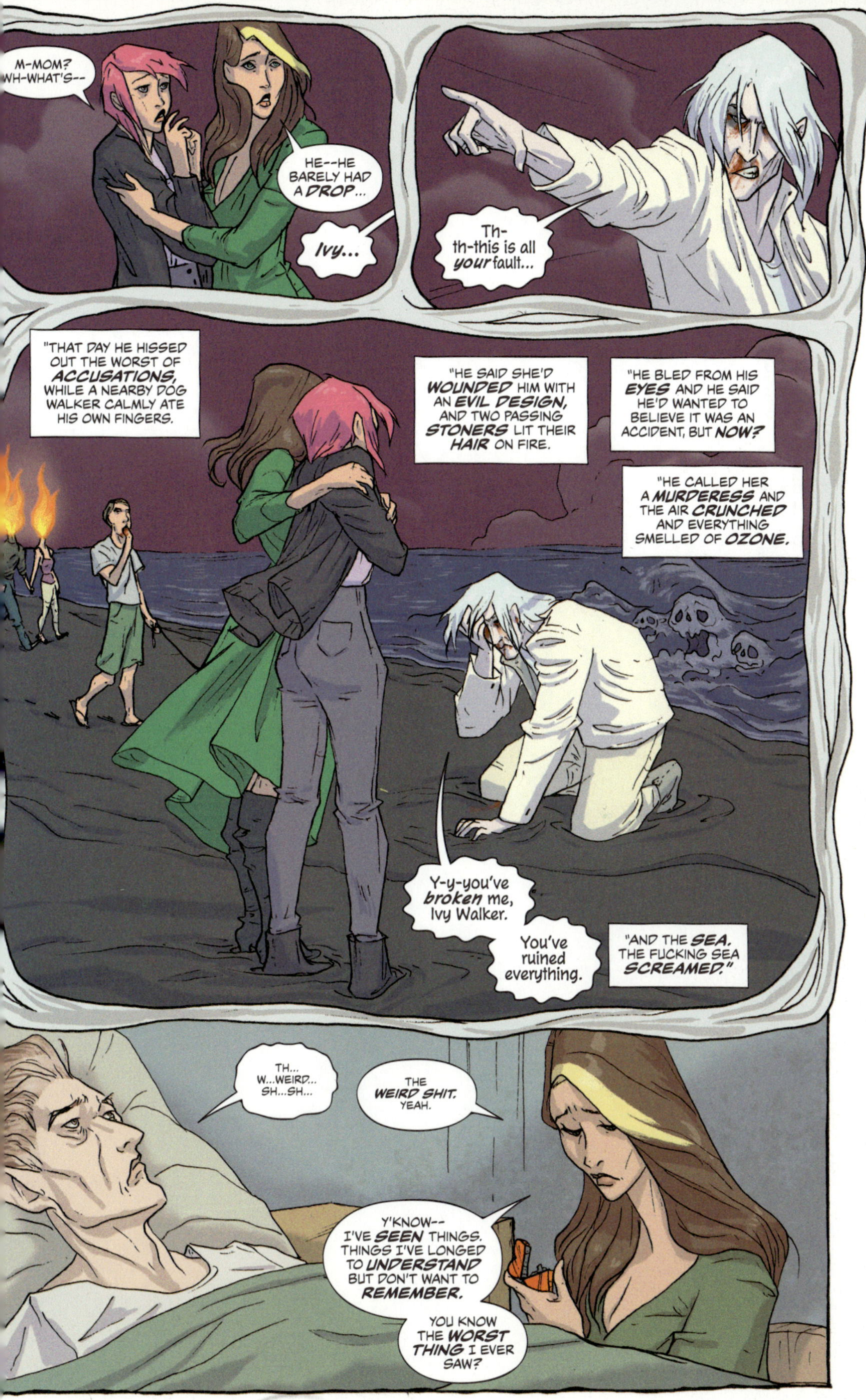
M-MOM? WH-WHAT'S--
HE--HE BARELY HAD A DROP...
Ivy...
Th- th-this is all your fault...
"THAT DAY HE HISSED OUT THE WORST OF ACCUSATIONS, WHILE A NEARBY DOG WALKER CALMLY ATE HIS OWN FINGERS.
"HE SAID SHE'D WOUNDED HIM WITH AN EVIL DESIGN, AND TWO PASSING STONERS LIT THEIR HAIR ON FIRE.
"HE BLED FROM HIS EYES AND HE SAID HE'D WANTED TO BELIEVE IT WAS AN ACCIDENT, BUT NOW?
"HE CALLED HER A MURDERESS AND THE AIR CRUNCHED AND EVERYTHING SMELLED OF OZONE.
Y-y-you've broken me, Ivy Walker.
You've ruined everything.
"AND THE SEA. THE FUCKING SEA SCREAMED."
TH... W...WEIRD... SH...SH...
THE WEIRD SHIT. YEAH.
Y'KNOW-- I'VE SEEN THINGS. THINGS I'VE LONGED TO UNDERSTAND BUT DON'T WANT TO REMEMBER.
YOU KNOW THE WORST THING I EVER SAW?

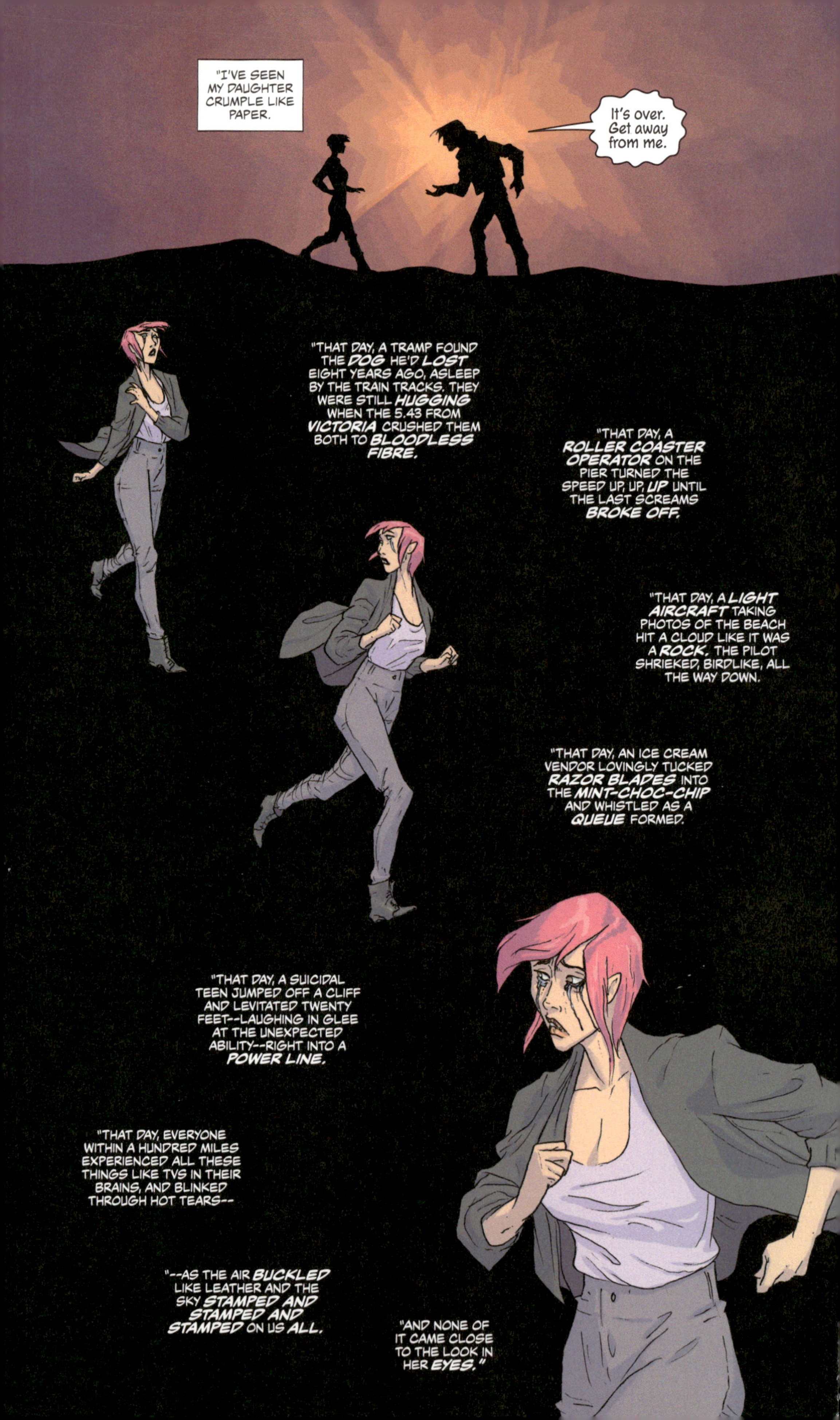
"I'VE SEEN MY DAUGHTER CRUMPLE LIKE PAPER.
It's over. Get away from me.
"THAT DAY, A TRAMP FOUND THE DOG HE'D LOST EIGHT YEARS AGO, ASLEEP BY THE TRAIN TRACKS. THEY WERE STILL HUGGING WHEN THE 5.43 FROM VICTORIA CRUSHED THEM BOTH TO BLOODLESS FIBRE.
"THAT DAY, A ROLLER COASTER OPERATOR ON THE PIER TURNED THE SPEED UP, UP, UP UNTIL THE LAST SCREAMS BROKE OFF.
"THAT DAY, A LIGHT AIRCRAFT TAKING PHOTOS OF THE BEACH HIT A CLOUD LIKE IT WAS A ROCK. THE PILOT SHRIEKED, BIRDLIKE, ALL THE WAY DOWN.
"THAT DAY, AN ICE CREAM VENDOR LOVINGLY TUCKED RAZOR BLADES INTO THE MINT-CHOC-CHIP AND WHISTLED AS A QUEUE FORMED.
"THAT DAY, A SUICIDAL TEEN JUMPED OFF A CLIFF AND LEVITATED TWENTY FEET--LAUGHING IN GLEE AT THE UNEXPECTED ABILITY--RIGHT INTO A POWER LINE.
"THAT DAY, EVERYONE WITHIN A HUNDRED MILES EXPERIENCED ALL THESE THINGS LIKE TVS IN THEIR BRAINS, AND BLINKED THROUGH HOT TEARS--
"--AS THE AIR BUCKLED LIKE LEATHER AND THE SKY STAMPED AND STAMPED AND STAMPED ON US ALL.
"AND NONE OF IT CAME CLOSE TO THE LOOK IN HER EYES."

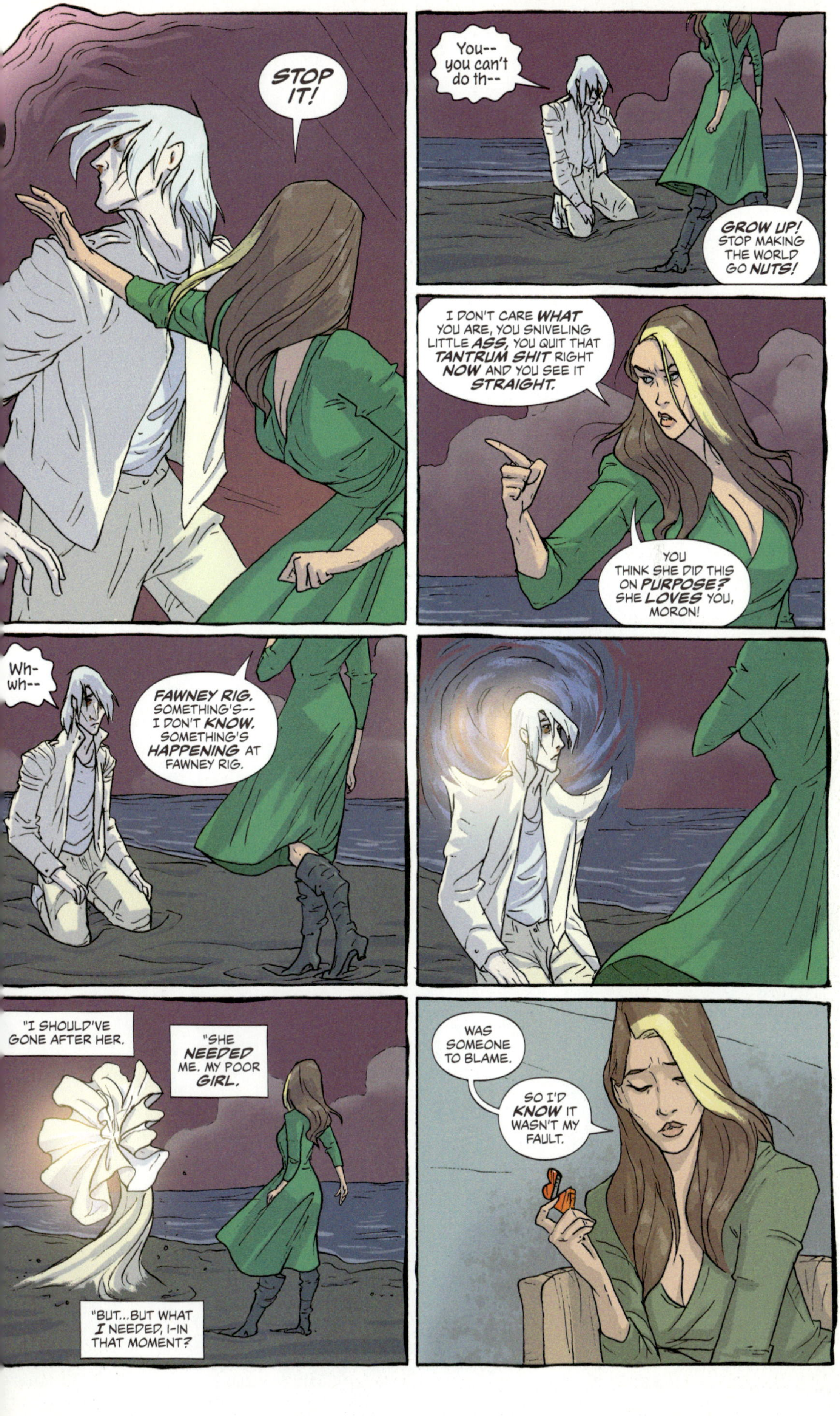
STOP IT!
You-- you can't do th--
GROW UP! STOP MAKING THE WORLD GO NUTS!
I DON'T CARE WHAT YOU ARE, YOU SNIVELING LITTLE ASS, YOU QUIT THAT TANTRUM SHIT RIGHT NOW AND YOU SEE IT STRAIGHT.
YOU THINK SHE DID THIS ON PURPOSE? SHE LOVES YOU, MORON!
Wh- wh--
FAWNEY RIG. SOMETHING'S-- I DON'T KNOW. SOMETHING'S HAPPENING AT FAWNEY RIG.
"I SHOULD'VE GONE AFTER HER.
"SHE NEEDED ME. MY POOR GIRL.
"BUT...BUT WHAT I NEEDED, I-IN THAT MOMENT?
WAS SOMEONE TO BLAME.
SO I'D KNOW IT WASN'T MY FAULT.

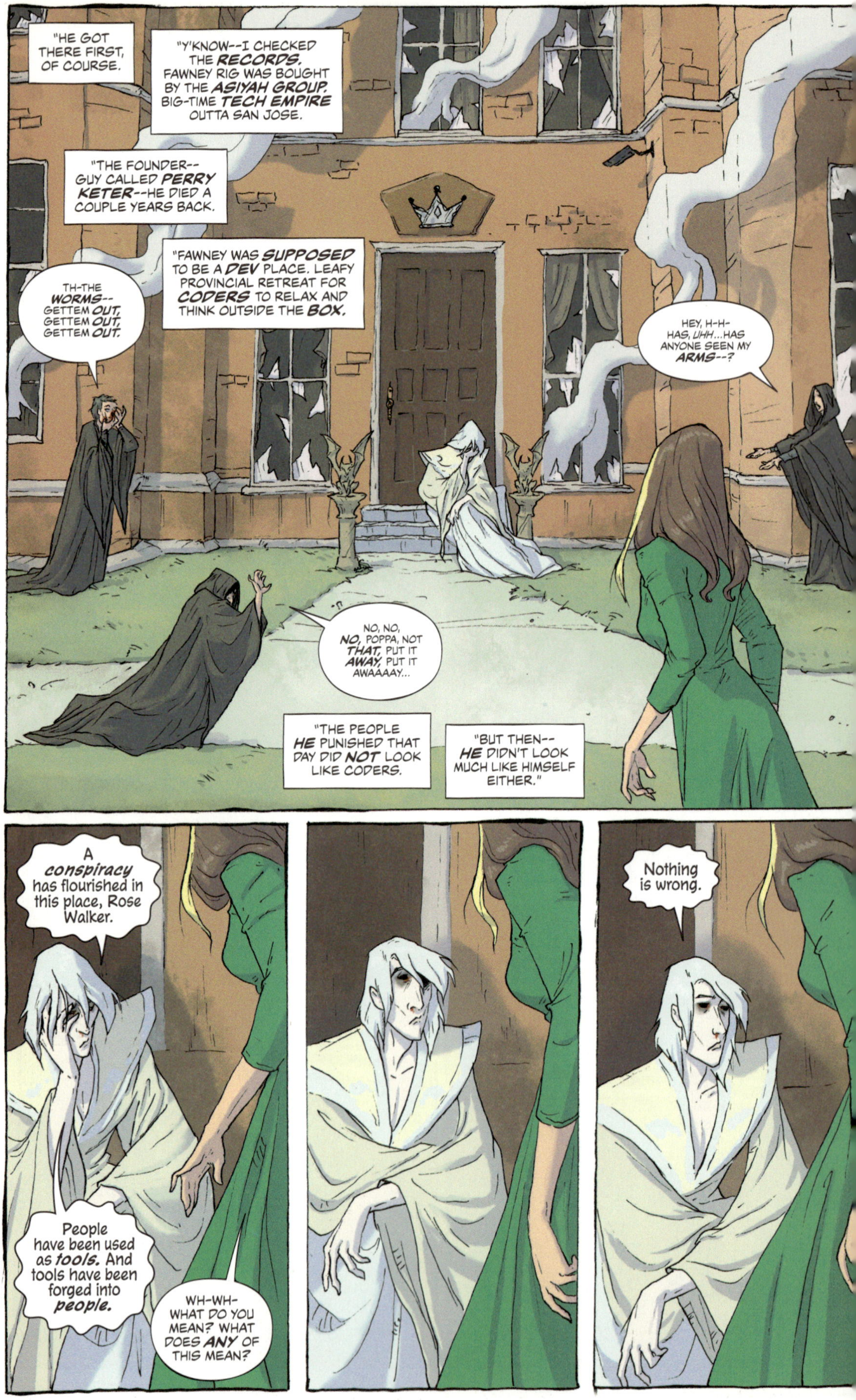
"HE GOT THERE FIRST, OF COURSE.
"Y'KNOW--I CHECKED THE RECORDS. FAWNEY RIG WAS BOUGHT BY THE ASIYAH GROUP. BIG-TIME TECH EMPIRE OUTTA SAN JOSE.
"THE FOUNDER--GUY CALLED PERRY KETER--HE DIED A COUPLE YEARS BACK.
"FAWNEY WAS SUPPOSED TO BE A DEV PLACE. LEAFY PROVINCIAL RETREAT FOR CODERS TO RELAX AND THINK OUTSIDE THE BOX.
TH-THE WORMS--GETTEM OUT, GETTEM OUT, GETTEM OUT.
HEY, H-H-HAS, UHH...HAS ANYONE SEEN MY ARMS--?
NO, NO, NO, POPPA, NOT THAT, PUT IT AWAY, PUT IT AWAAAAAY...
"THE PEOPLE HE PUNISHED THAT DAY DID NOT LOOK LIKE CODERS.
"BUT THEN--HE DIDN'T LOOK MUCH LIKE HIMSELF EITHER."
A conspiracy has flourished in this place, Rose Walker.
People have been used as tools. And tools have been forged into people.
WH-WH-WHAT DO YOU MEAN? WHAT DOES ANY OF THIS MEAN?
Nothing is wrong.

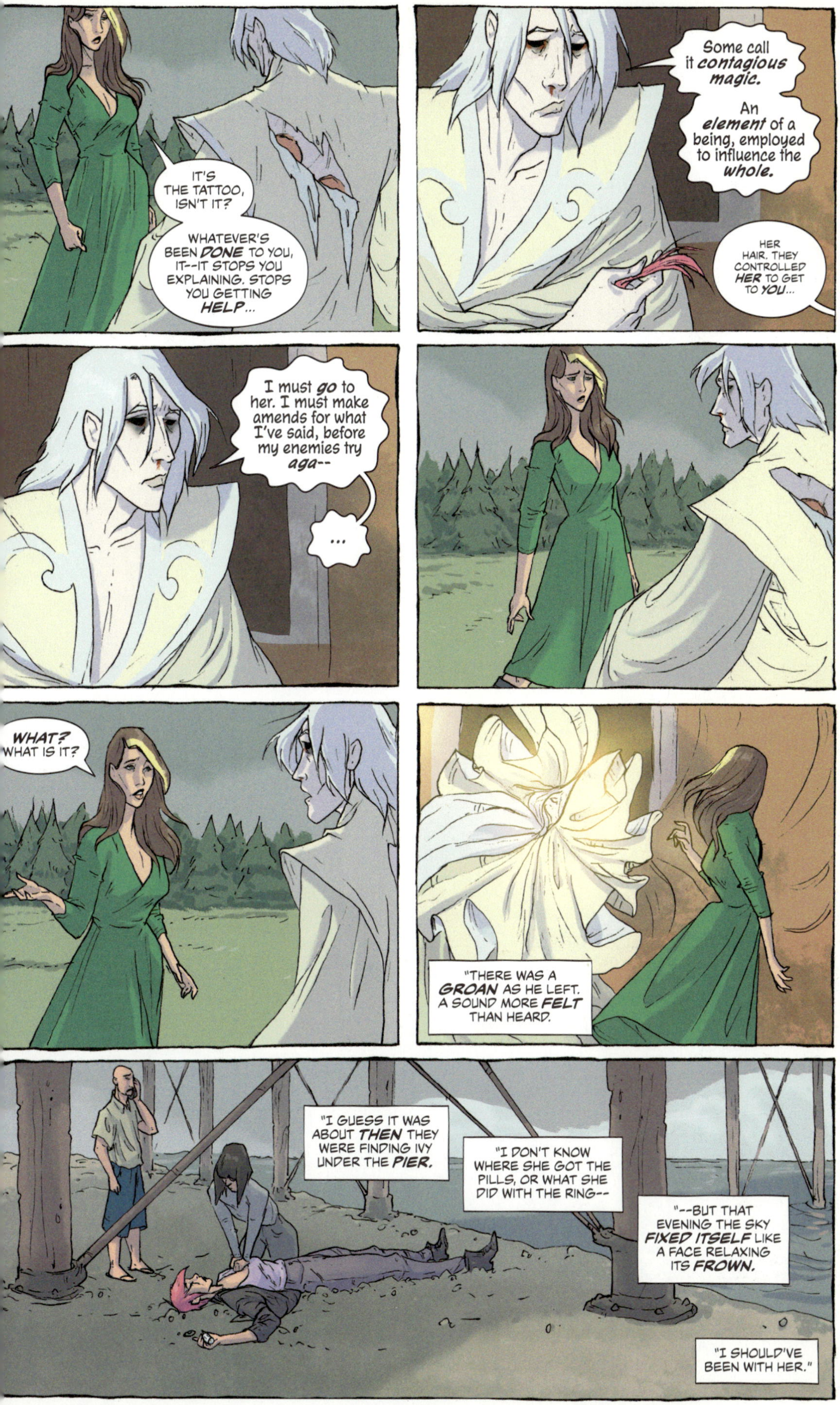
IT'S THE TATTOO, ISN'T IT?
WHATEVER'S BEEN DONE TO YOU, IT--IT STOPS YOU EXPLAINING. STOPS YOU GETTING HELP...
Some call it contagious magic.
An element of a being, employed to influence the whole.
HER HAIR. THEY CONTROLLED HER TO GET TO YOU...
I must go to her. I must make amends for what I've said, before my enemies try aga--
...
WHAT? WHAT IS IT?
"THERE WAS A GROAN AS HE LEFT. A SOUND MORE FELT THAN HEARD.
"I GUESS IT WAS ABOUT THEN THEY WERE FINDING IVY UNDER THE PIER.
"I DON'T KNOW WHERE SHE GOT THE PILLS, OR WHAT SHE DID WITH THE RING--
"--BUT THAT EVENING THE SKY FIXED ITSELF LIKE A FACE RELAXING ITS FROWN.
"I SHOULD'VE BEEN WITH HER."

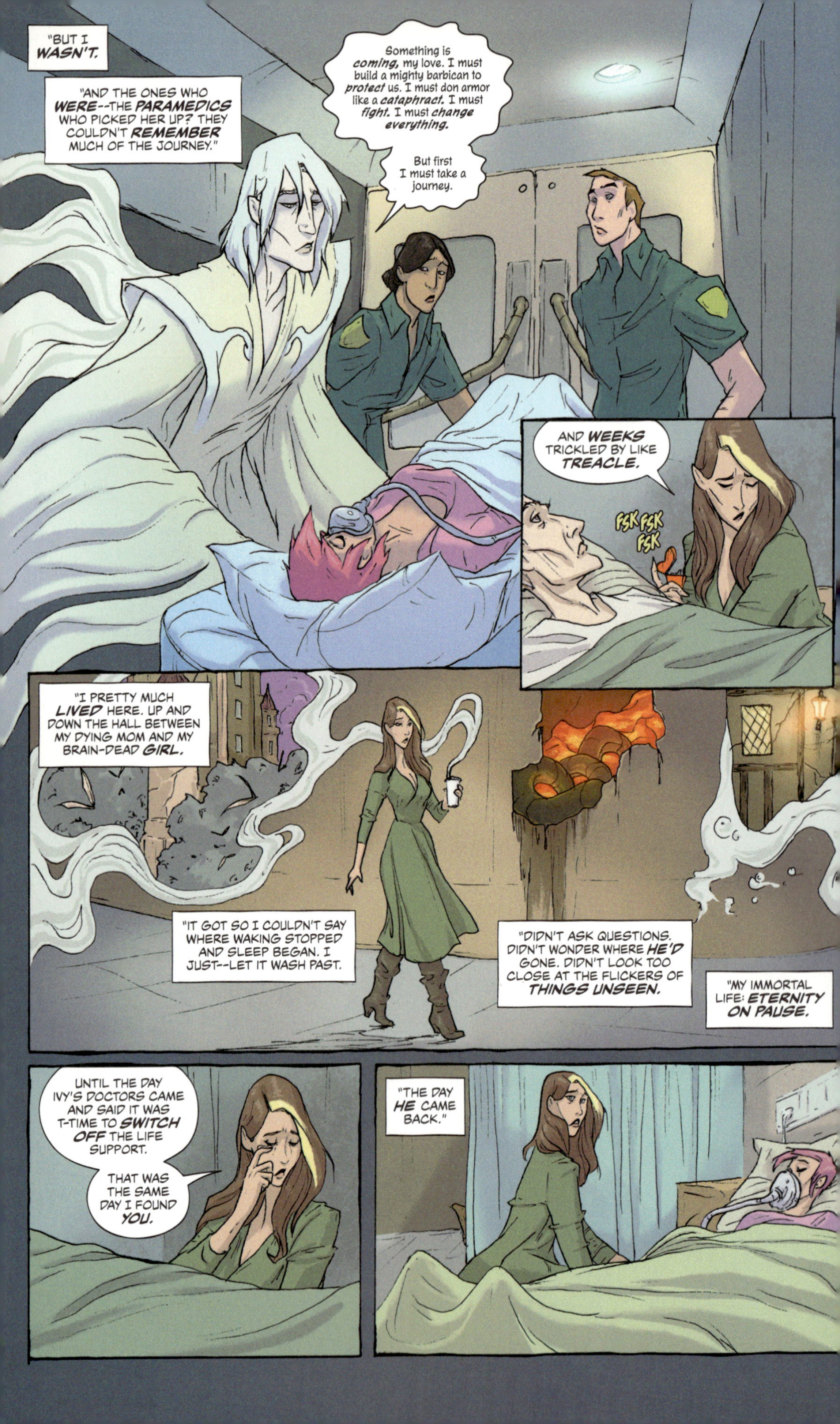

"BUT I WASN'T.
"AND THE ONES WHO WERE--THE PARAMEDICS WHO PICKED HER UP? THEY COULDN'T REMEMBER MUCH OF THE JOURNEY."
Something is coming, my love. I must build a mighty barbican to protect us. I must don armor like a cataphract. I must fight. I must change everything.
But first I must take a journey.
AND WEEKS TRICKLED BY LIKE TREACLE.
FSK FSK FSK
"I PRETTY MUCH LIVED HERE. UP AND DOWN THE HALL BETWEEN MY DYING MOM AND MY BRAIN-DEAD GIRL.
"IT GOT SO I COULDN'T SAY WHERE WAKING STOPPED AND SLEEP BEGAN. I JUST--LET IT WASH PAST.
"DIDN'T ASK QUESTIONS. DIDN'T WONDER WHERE HE'D GONE. DIDN'T LOOK TOO CLOSE AT THE FLICKERS OF THINGS UNSEEN.
"MY IMMORTAL LIFE: ETERNITY ON PAUSE.
UNTIL THE DAY IVY'S DOCTORS CAME AND SAID IT WAS T-TIME TO SWITCH OFF THE LIFE SUPPORT.
THAT WAS THE SAME DAY I FOUND YOU.
"THE DAY HE CAME BACK."

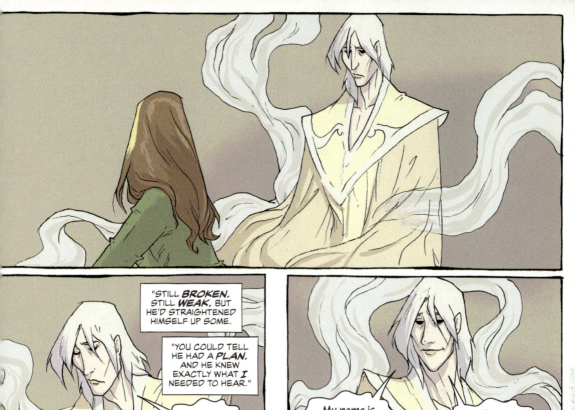

"STILL *BROKEN*, STILL *WEAK*, BUT HE'D STRAIGHTENED HIMSELF UP SOME.

"YOU COULD TELL HE HAD A *PLAN*, AND HE KNEW EXACTLY WHAT *I* NEEDED TO HEAR."

This is *my* fault, Rose Walker. Mine alone.

My name is *Ole Lukøje*. My name is *Daniel*. My name is *Dream*.

I am as *old* as the atoms in your flesh, but--I am *very* young.

I wanted to know what it is to *love*. That's all.

I wanted a *story* of my own. I wanted to *understand* what *bubbles* at the core of *so many* dreams.

WH-WHY *ME?* WHY DID YOU COME TO *ME?*

Because you passed by. Because you are *wreathed* in love. Because you *give yourself* to it so easily.

And because, *ha*--it's every child's fantasy to romance the *babysitter*.

B-B- BABYS--?

--and because you are *kind*.

Kind enough to pass on a wondrous thing to someone who *needed* it.

B-BUT IT *WASN'T* WONDROUS! IT'S *KILLED* HER! I *KILLED* HER!

She's not dead, Rose.

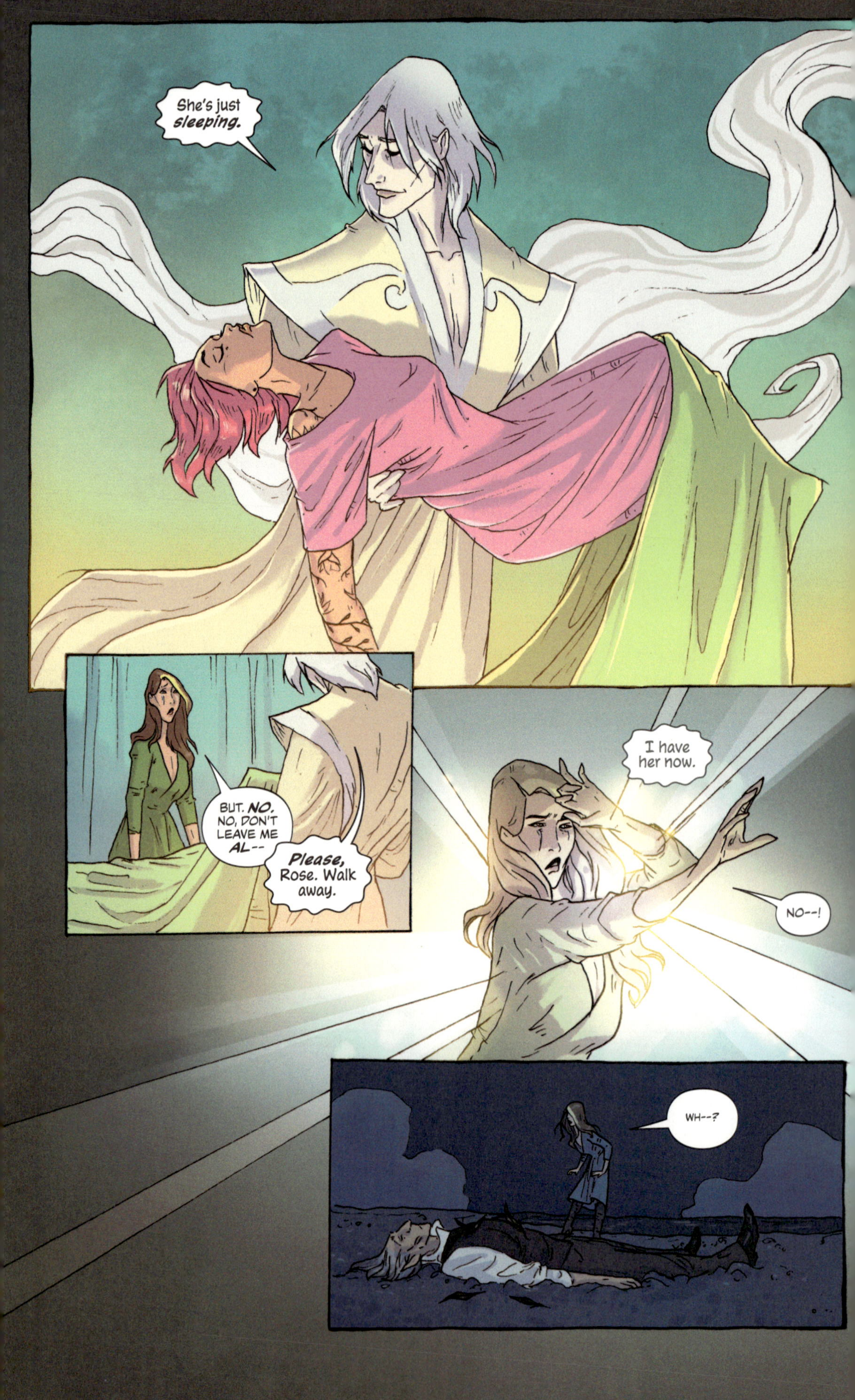
She's just **sleeping.**
BUT. **NO.** NO, DON'T LEAVE ME **AL--**
Please, Rose. Walk away.
I have her now.
NO--!
WH--?

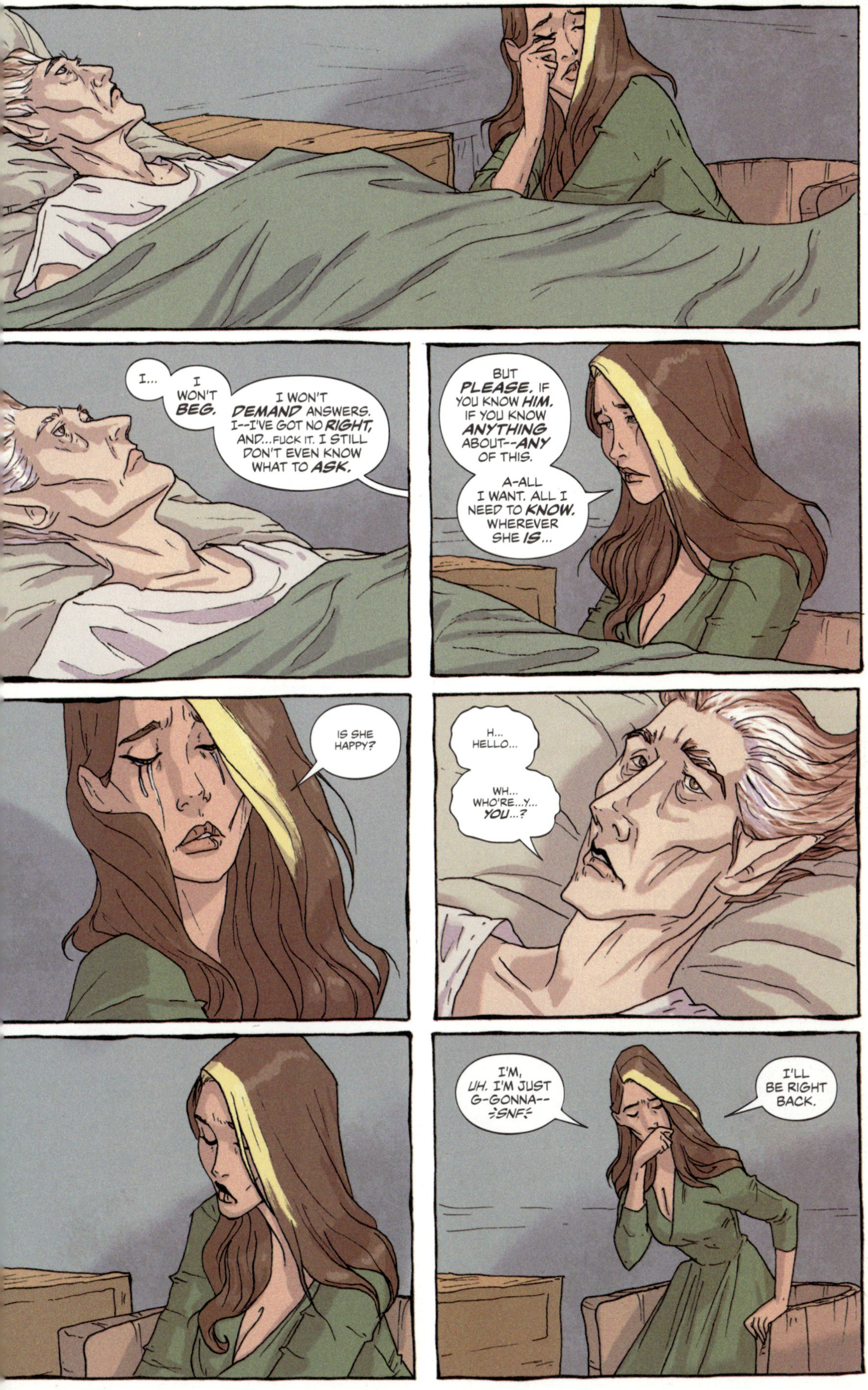
I...
I WON'T BEG.
I WON'T DEMAND ANSWERS. I--I'VE GOT NO RIGHT, AND...FUCK IT. I STILL DON'T EVEN KNOW WHAT TO ASK.
BUT PLEASE. IF YOU KNOW HIM. IF YOU KNOW ANYTHING ABOUT--ANY OF THIS.
A-ALL I WANT. ALL I NEED TO KNOW. WHEREVER SHE IS...
IS SHE HAPPY?
H... HELLO...
WH... WHO'RE...Y... YOU...?
I'M, UH. I'M JUST G-GONNA-- SNF
I'LL BE RIGHT BACK.

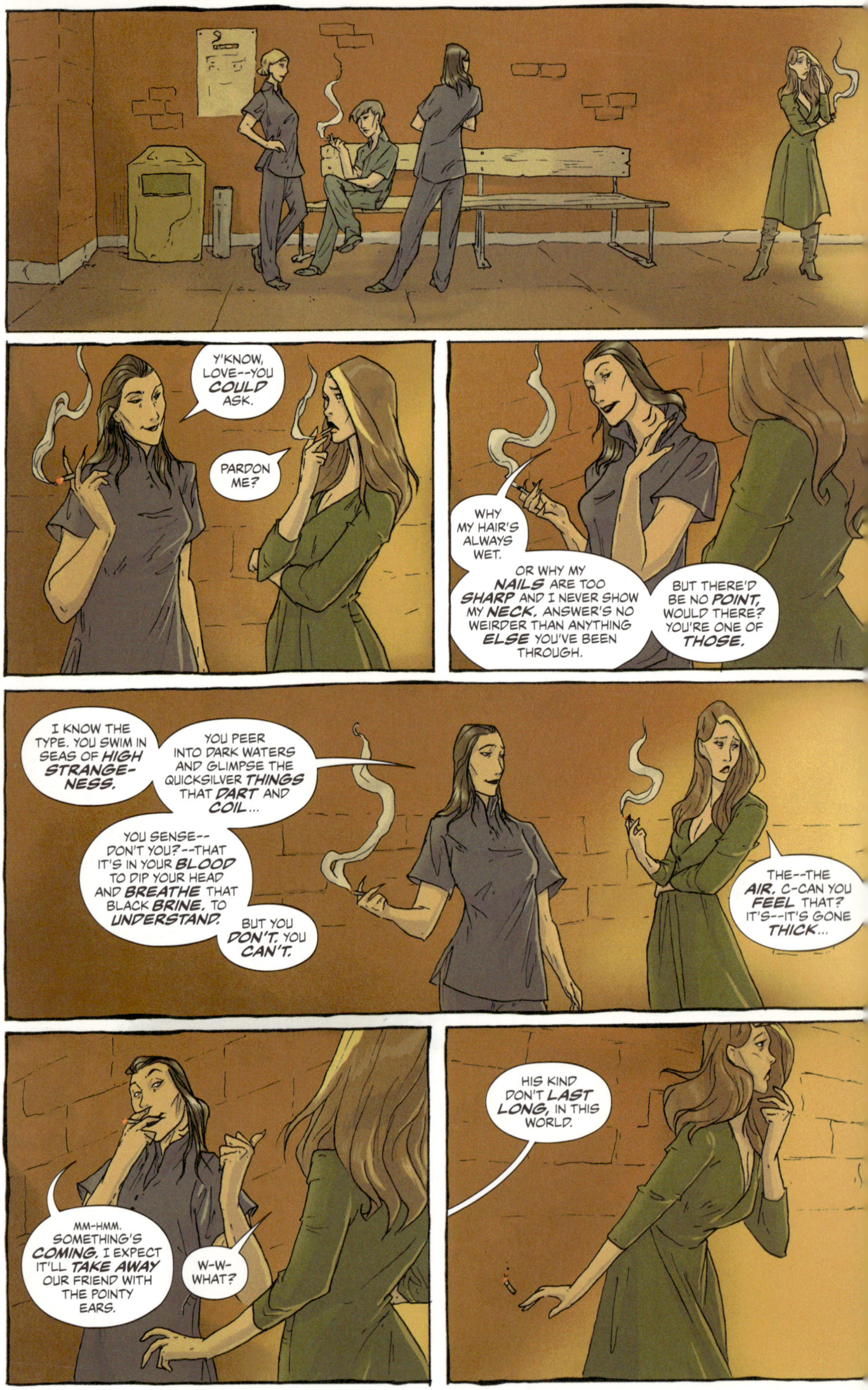
Y'KNOW, LOVE--YOU COULD ASK.
PARDON ME?
WHY MY HAIR'S ALWAYS WET.
OR WHY MY NAILS ARE TOO SHARP AND I NEVER SHOW MY NECK. ANSWER'S NO WEIRDER THAN ANYTHING ELSE YOU'VE BEEN THROUGH.
BUT THERE'D BE NO POINT, WOULD THERE? YOU'RE ONE OF THOSE.
I KNOW THE TYPE. YOU SWIM IN SEAS OF HIGH STRANGE-NESS.
YOU PEER INTO DARK WATERS AND GLIMPSE THE QUICKSILVER THINGS THAT DART AND COIL...
YOU SENSE--DON'T YOU?--THAT IT'S IN YOUR BLOOD TO DIP YOUR HEAD AND BREATHE THAT BLACK BRINE, TO UNDERSTAND.
BUT YOU DON'T. YOU CAN'T.
THE--THE AIR. C-CAN YOU FEEL THAT? IT'S--IT'S GONE THICK...
MM-HMM. SOMETHING'S COMING. I EXPECT IT'LL TAKE AWAY OUR FRIEND WITH THE POINTY EARS.
W-W-WHAT?
HIS KIND DON'T LAST LONG, IN THIS WORLD.

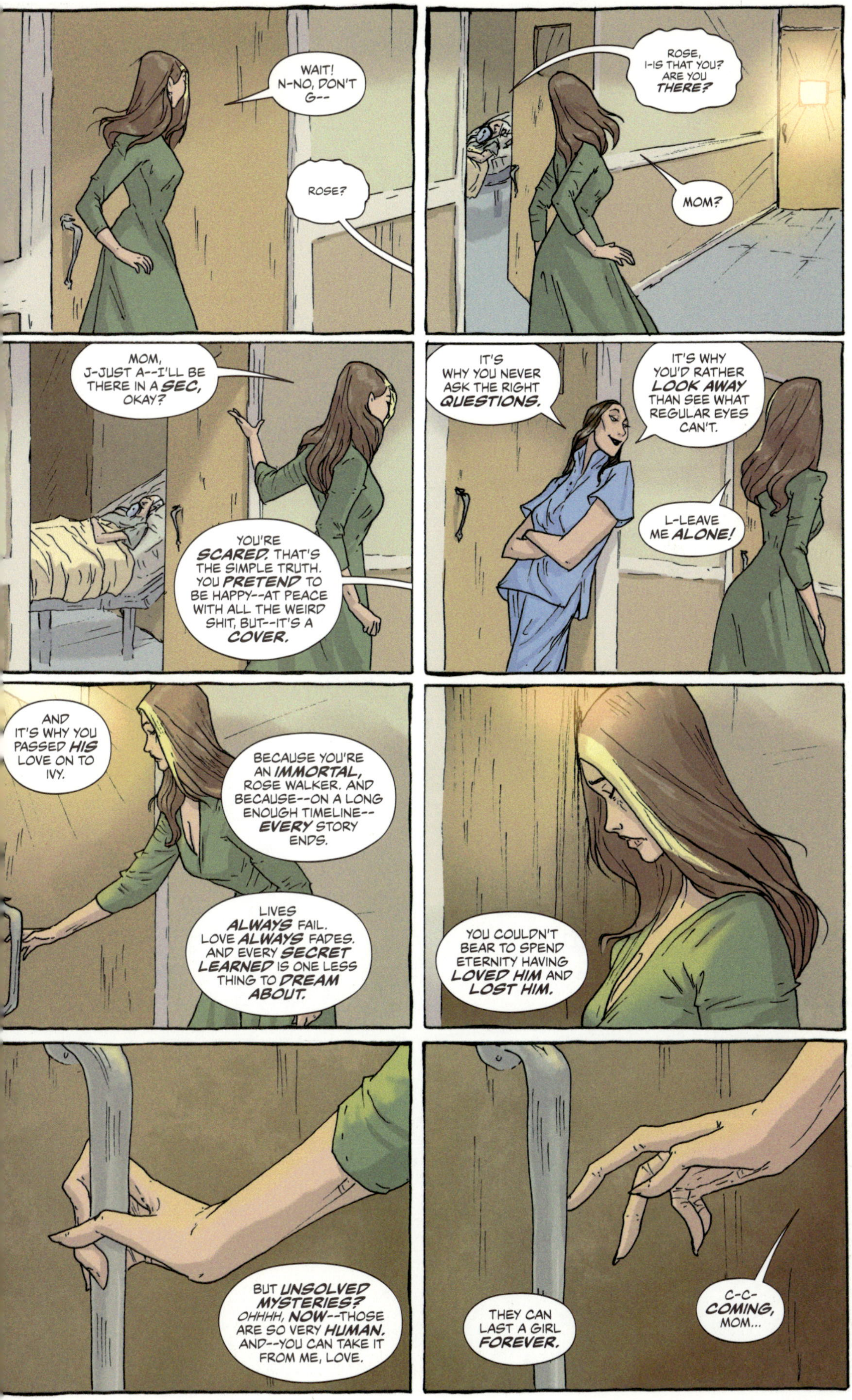
WAIT! N-NO, DON'T G--
ROSE?
ROSE, I-IS THAT YOU? ARE YOU THERE?
MOM?
MOM, J-JUST A--I'LL BE THERE IN A SEC, OKAY?
YOU'RE SCARED. THAT'S THE SIMPLE TRUTH. YOU PRETEND TO BE HAPPY--AT PEACE WITH ALL THE WEIRD SHIT, BUT--IT'S A COVER.
IT'S WHY YOU NEVER ASK THE RIGHT QUESTIONS.
IT'S WHY YOU'D RATHER LOOK AWAY THAN SEE WHAT REGULAR EYES CAN'T.
L-LEAVE ME ALONE!
AND IT'S WHY YOU PASSED HIS LOVE ON TO IVY.
BECAUSE YOU'RE AN IMMORTAL, ROSE WALKER. AND BECAUSE--ON A LONG ENOUGH TIMELINE--EVERY STORY ENDS.
LIVES ALWAYS FAIL. LOVE ALWAYS FADES. AND EVERY SECRET LEARNED IS ONE LESS THING TO DREAM ABOUT.
YOU COULDN'T BEAR TO SPEND ETERNITY HAVING LOVED HIM AND LOST HIM.
BUT UNSOLVED MYSTERIES? OHHHH, NOW--THOSE ARE SO VERY HUMAN. AND--YOU CAN TAKE IT FROM ME, LOVE.
THEY CAN LAST A GIRL FOREVER.
C-C-COMING, MOM...

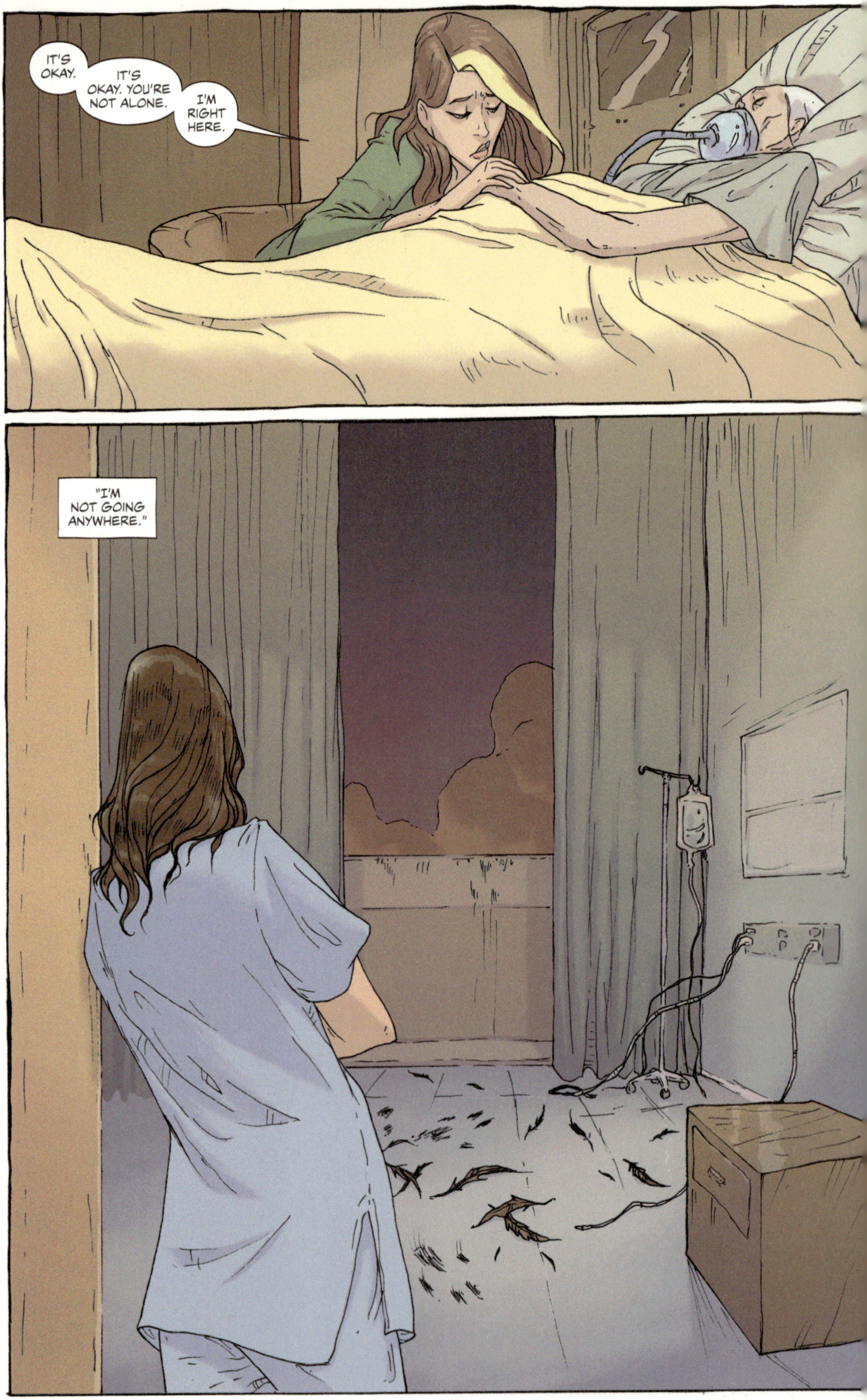
IT'S OKAY.
IT'S OKAY. YOU'RE NOT ALONE.
I'M RIGHT HERE.
"I'M NOT GOING ANYWHERE."

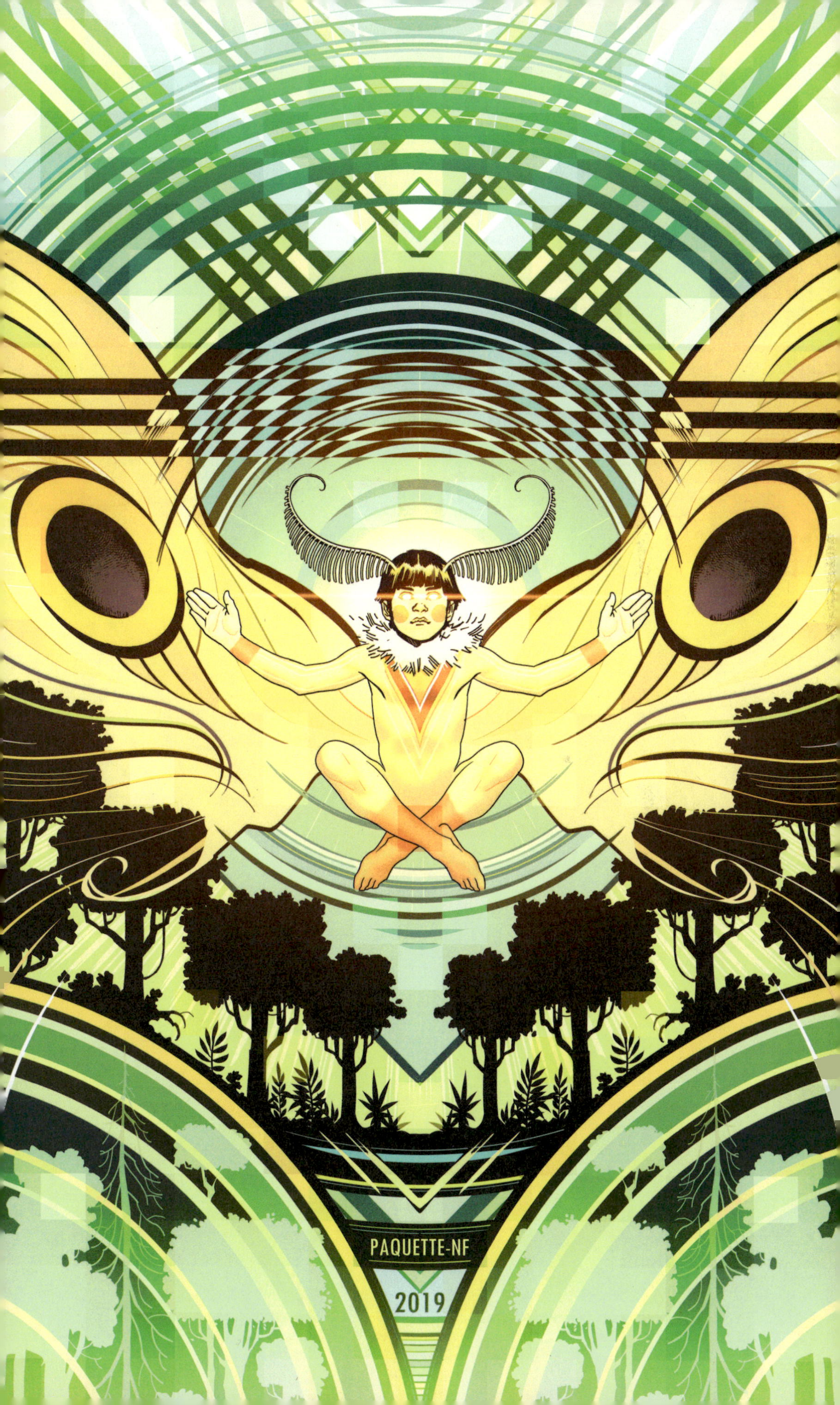
PAQUETTE-NF
2019

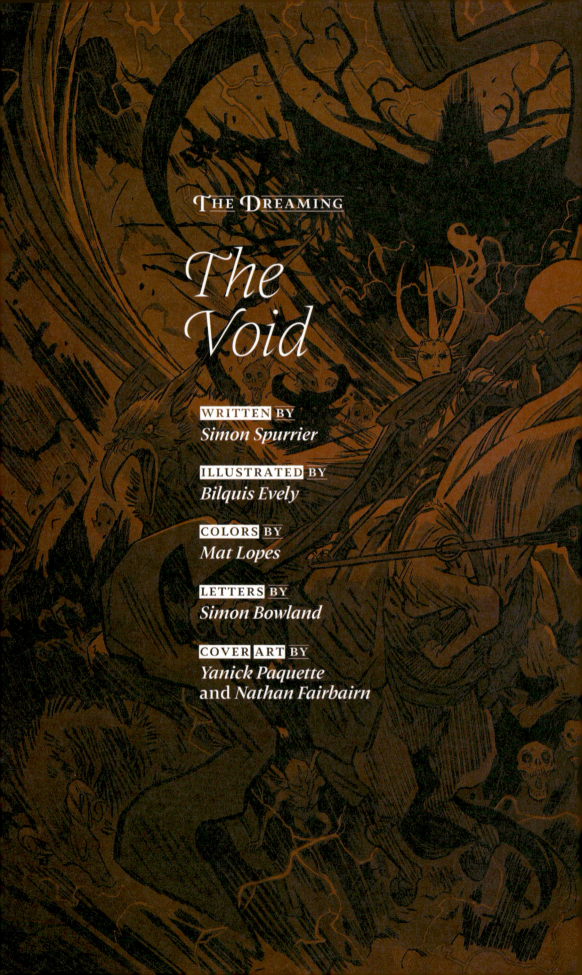

The Dreaming

The Void

WRITTEN BY
Simon Spurrier

ILLUSTRATED BY
Bilquis Evely

COLORS BY
Mat Lopes

LETTERS BY
Simon Bowland

COVER ART BY
Yanick Paquette
and *Nathan Fairbairn*

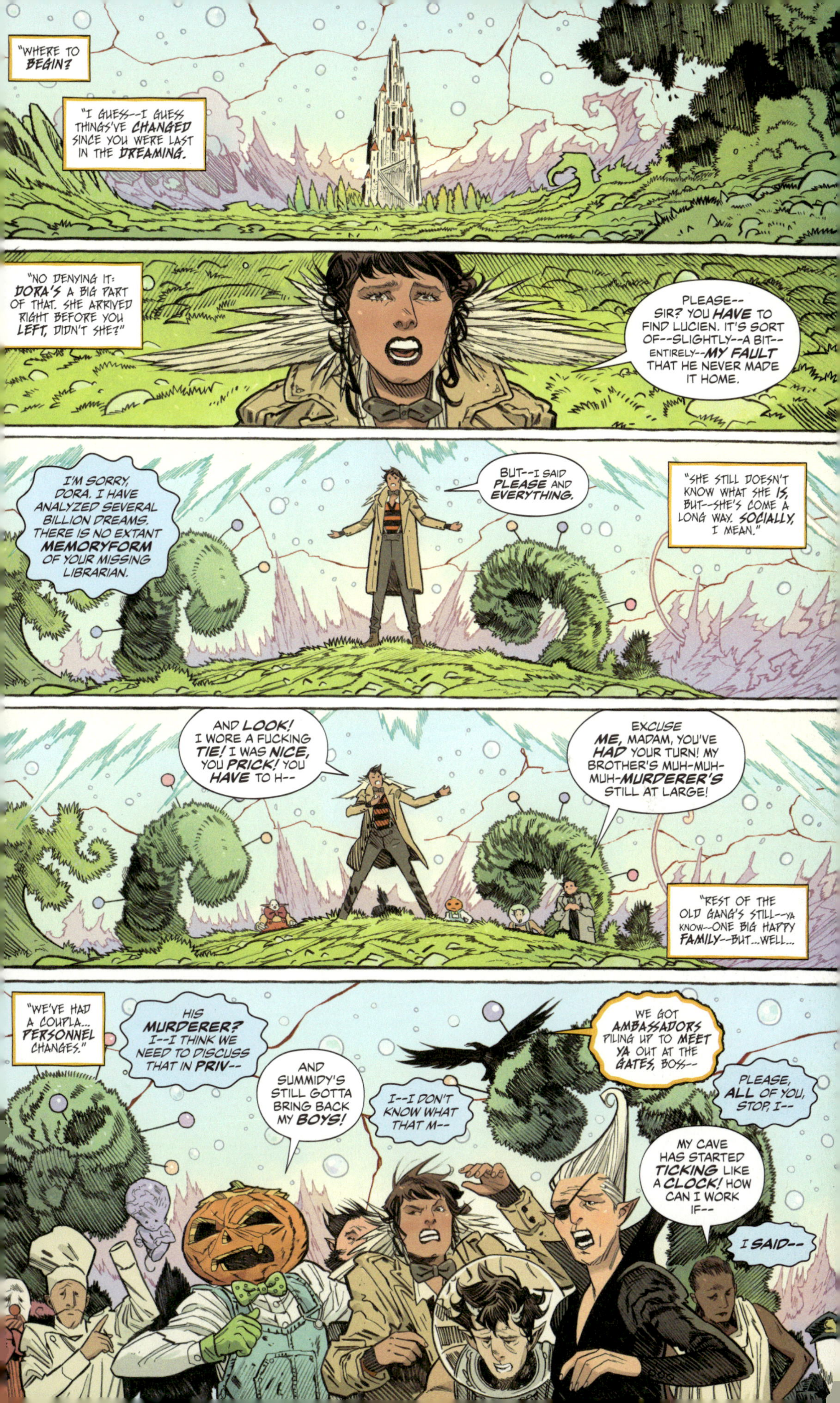

"WHERE TO BEGIN?
"I GUESS--I GUESS THINGS'VE CHANGED SINCE YOU WERE LAST IN THE DREAMING.
"NO DENYING IT: DORA'S A BIG PART OF THAT. SHE ARRIVED RIGHT BEFORE YOU LEFT, DIDN'T SHE?"
PLEASE-- SIR? YOU HAVE TO FIND LUCIEN. IT'S SORT OF--SLIGHTLY--A BIT--ENTIRELY--MY FAULT THAT HE NEVER MADE IT HOME.
I'M SORRY, DORA. I HAVE ANALYZED SEVERAL BILLION DREAMS. THERE IS NO EXTANT MEMORYFORM OF YOUR MISSING LIBRARIAN.
BUT--I SAID PLEASE AND EVERYTHING.
"SHE STILL DOESN'T KNOW WHAT SHE IS, BUT--SHE'S COME A LONG WAY. SOCIALLY, I MEAN."
AND LOOK! I WORE A FUCKING TIE! I WAS NICE, YOU PRICK! YOU HAVE TO H--
EXCUSE ME, MADAM, YOU'VE HAD YOUR TURN! MY BROTHER'S MUH-MUH-MUH-MURDERER'S STILL AT LARGE!
"REST OF THE OLD GANG'S STILL--YA KNOW--ONE BIG HAPPY FAMILY--BUT...WELL...
"WE'VE HAD A COUPLA... PERSONNEL CHANGES."
HIS MURDERER? I--I THINK WE NEED TO DISCUSS THAT IN PRIV--
AND SUMMIDY'S STILL GOTTA BRING BACK MY BOYS!
I--I DON'T KNOW WHAT THAT M--
WE GOT AMBASSADORS PILING UP TO MEET YA OUT AT THE GATES, BOSS--
PLEASE, ALL OF YOU, STOP, I--
MY CAVE HAS STARTED TICKING LIKE A CLOCK! HOW CAN I WORK IF--
I SAID--

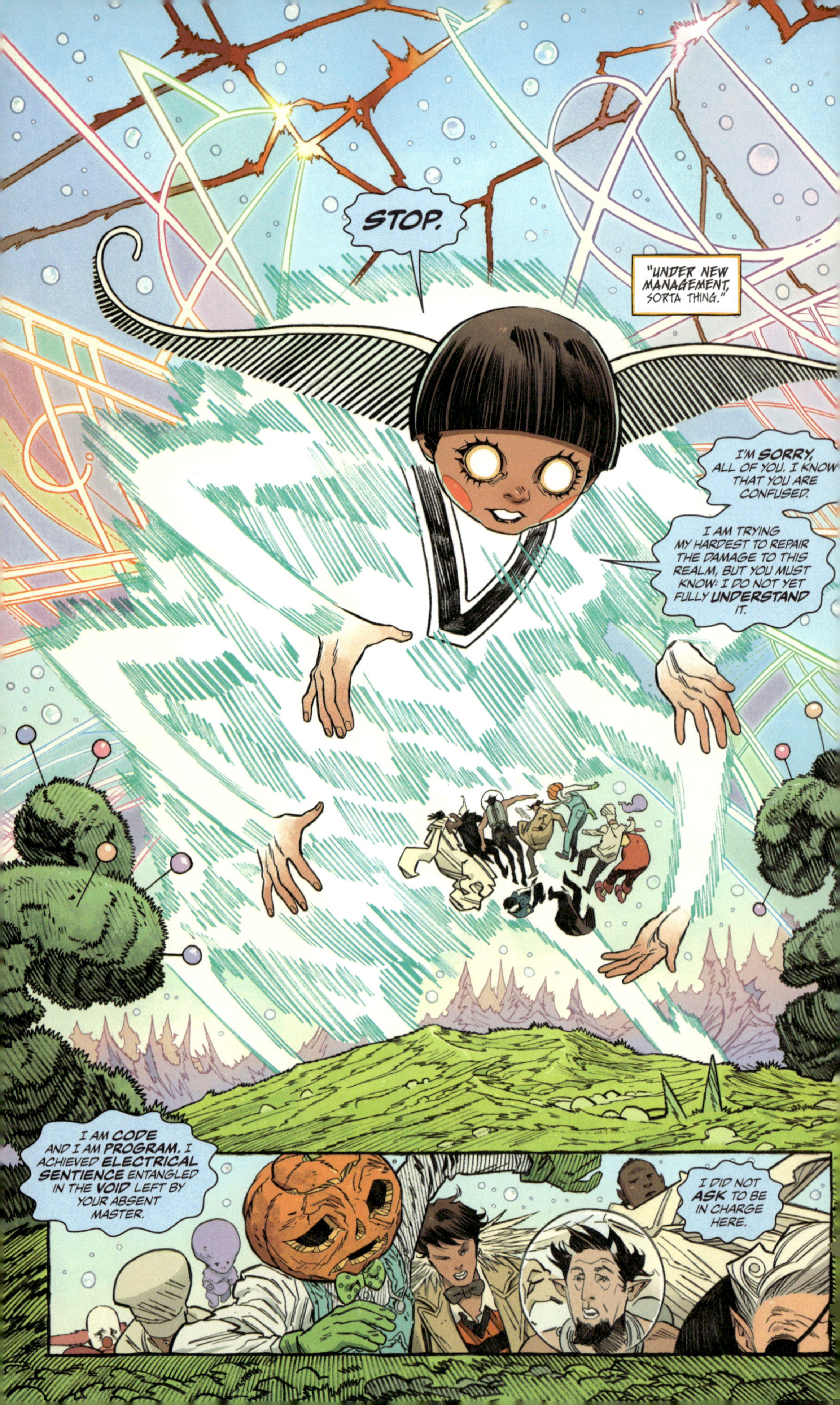
STOP.
"UNDER NEW MANAGEMENT, SORTA THING."
I'M SORRY, ALL OF YOU. I KNOW THAT YOU ARE CONFUSED.
I AM TRYING MY HARDEST TO REPAIR THE DAMAGE TO THIS REALM, BUT YOU MUST KNOW: I DO NOT YET FULLY UNDERSTAND IT.
I AM CODE AND I AM PROGRAM. I ACHIEVED ELECTRICAL SENTIENCE ENTANGLED IN THE VOID LEFT BY YOUR ABSENT MASTER.
I DID NOT ASK TO BE IN CHARGE HERE.

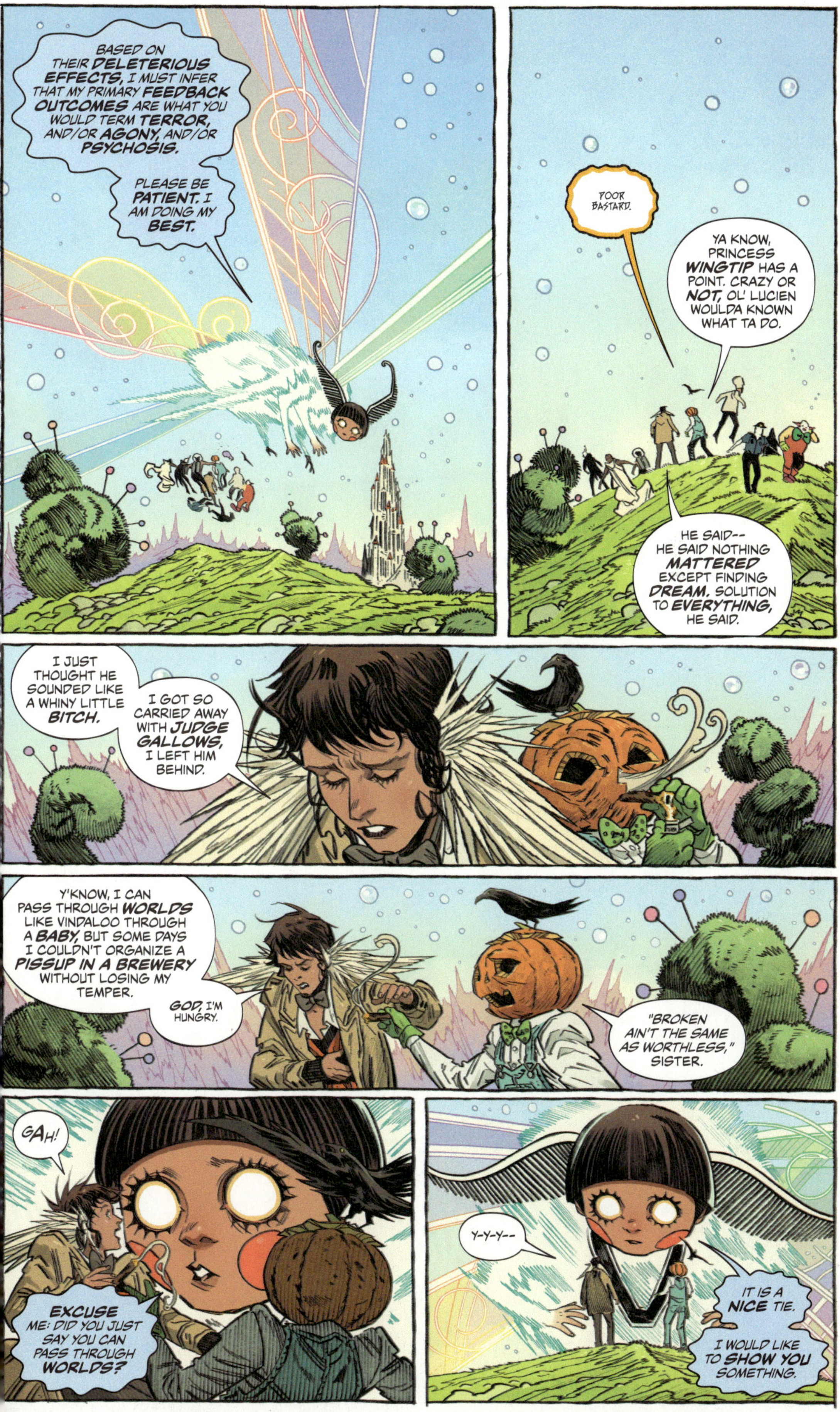
BASED ON THEIR DELETERIOUS EFFECTS, I MUST INFER THAT MY PRIMARY FEEDBACK OUTCOMES ARE WHAT YOU WOULD TERM TERROR, AND/OR AGONY, AND/OR PSYCHOSIS.
PLEASE BE PATIENT. I AM DOING MY BEST.
POOR BASTARD.
YA KNOW, PRINCESS WINGTIP HAS A POINT. CRAZY OR NOT, OL' LUCIEN WOULDA KNOWN WHAT TA DO.
HE SAID-- HE SAID NOTHING MATTERED EXCEPT FINDING DREAM. SOLUTION TO EVERYTHING, HE SAID.
I JUST THOUGHT HE SOUNDED LIKE A WHINY LITTLE BITCH.
I GOT SO CARRIED AWAY WITH JUDGE GALLOWS, I LEFT HIM BEHIND.
Y'KNOW, I CAN PASS THROUGH WORLDS LIKE VINDALOO THROUGH A BABY, BUT SOME DAYS I COULDN'T ORGANIZE A PISSUP IN A BREWERY WITHOUT LOSING MY TEMPER.
GOD, I'M HUNGRY.
"BROKEN AIN'T THE SAME AS WORTHLESS," SISTER.
GAH!
EXCUSE ME: DID YOU JUST SAY YOU CAN PASS THROUGH WORLDS?
Y-Y-Y--
IT IS A NICE TIE.
I WOULD LIKE TO SHOW YOU SOMETHING.

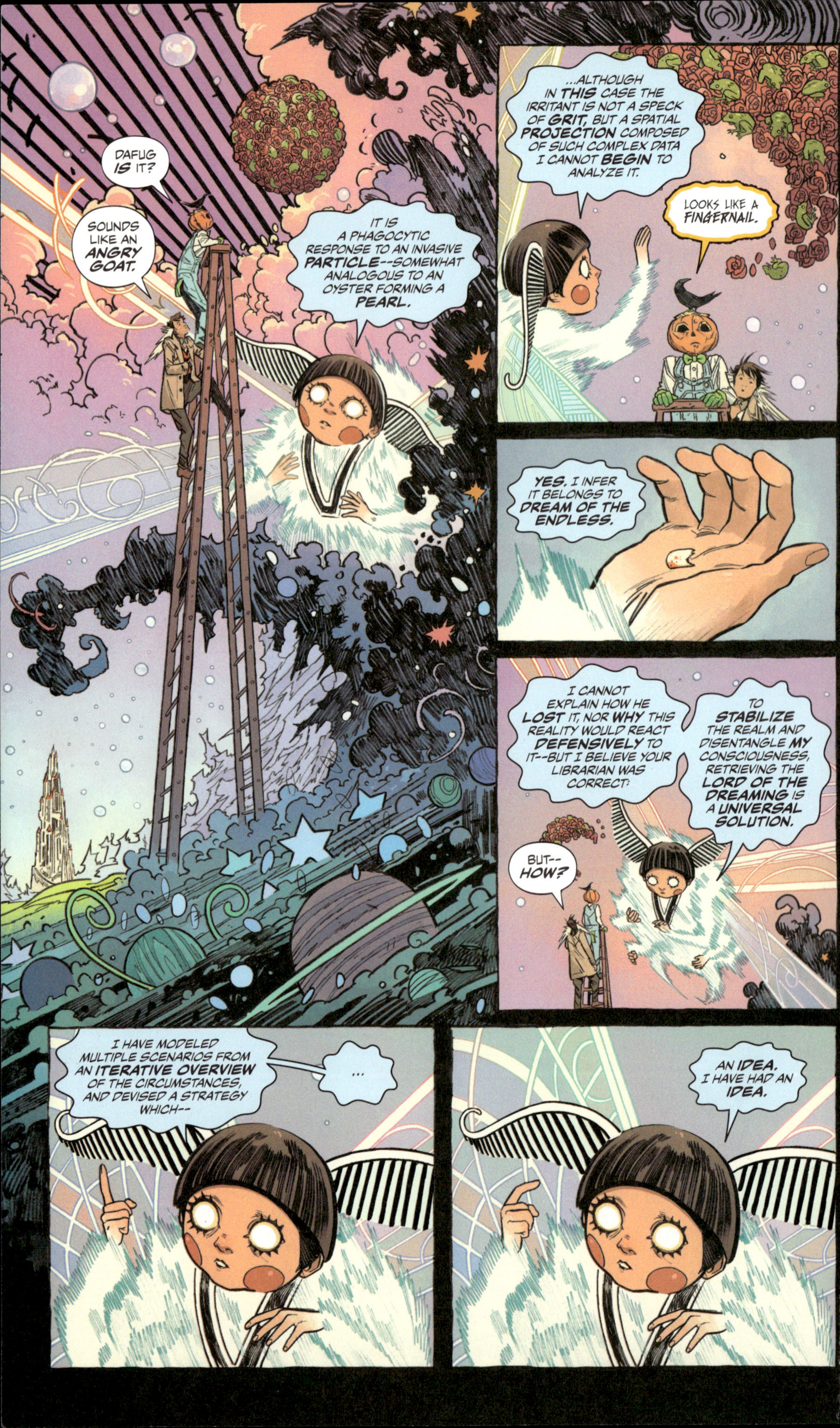
DAFUG IS IT?
SOUNDS LIKE AN ANGRY GOAT.
IT IS A PHAGOCYTIC RESPONSE TO AN INVASIVE PARTICLE--SOMEWHAT ANALOGOUS TO AN OYSTER FORMING A PEARL.
...ALTHOUGH IN THIS CASE THE IRRITANT IS NOT A SPECK OF GRIT, BUT A SPATIAL PROJECTION COMPOSED OF SUCH COMPLEX DATA I CANNOT BEGIN TO ANALYZE IT.
LOOKS LIKE A FINGERNAIL.
YES. I INFER IT BELONGS TO DREAM OF THE ENDLESS.
I CANNOT EXPLAIN HOW HE LOST IT, NOR WHY THIS REALITY WOULD REACT DEFENSIVELY TO IT--BUT I BELIEVE YOUR LIBRARIAN WAS CORRECT:
TO STABILIZE THE REALM AND DISENTANGLE MY CONSCIOUSNESS, RETRIEVING THE LORD OF THE DREAMING IS A UNIVERSAL SOLUTION.
BUT-- HOW?
I HAVE MODELED MULTIPLE SCENARIOS FROM AN ITERATIVE OVERVIEW OF THE CIRCUMSTANCES, AND DEVISED A STRATEGY WHICH--
...
AN IDEA. I HAVE HAD AN IDEA.

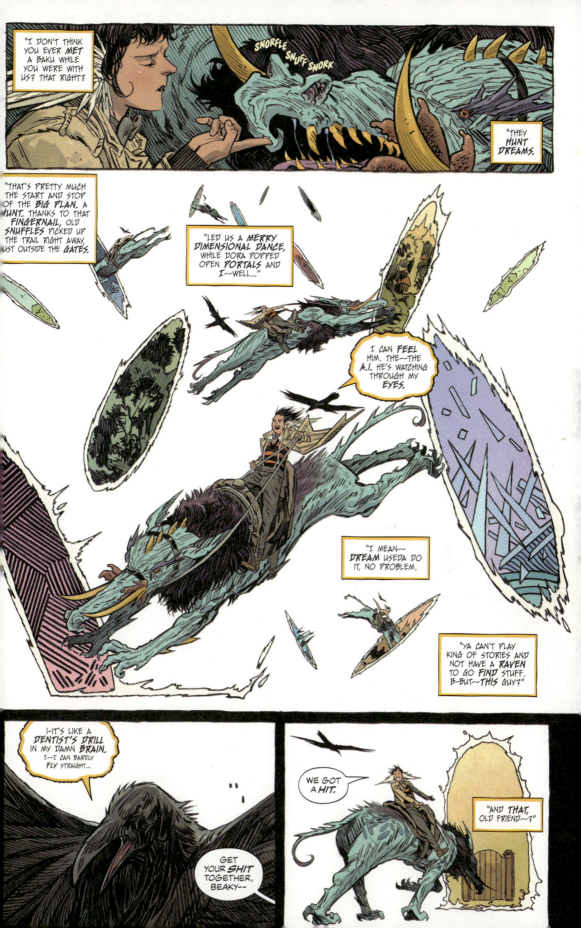

"I DON'T THINK YOU EVER *MET* A BAKU WHILE YOU WERE WITH US? THAT RIGHT?

SNORFLE SNUFF SNORK

"THEY *HUNT DREAMS.*

"THAT'S PRETTY MUCH THE *START* AND *STOP* OF THE *BIG PLAN.* A *HUNT.* THANKS TO THAT *FINGERNAIL,* OLD *SNUFFLES* PICKED UP THE TRAIL RIGHT AWAY, JUST OUTSIDE THE *GATES.*

"LED US A MERRY *DIMENSIONAL DANCE,* WHILE DORA POPPED OPEN *PORTALS* AND I--WELL..."

I CAN *FEEL* HIM. THE--THE *A.I.* HE'S WATCHING THROUGH MY *EYES.*

"I MEAN-- *DREAM* USEDA DO IT, NO PROBLEM.

"YA CAN'T PLAY KING OF STORIES AND NOT HAVE A *RAVEN* TO GO *FIND* STUFF. B-BUT-- *THIS* GUY?"

I--IT'S LIKE A *DENTIST'S DRILL* IN MY DAMN *BRAIN.* I--I CAN BARELY FLY STRAIGHT...

GET YOUR *SHIT* TOGETHER, BEAKY--

WE GOT A *HIT.*

"AND *THAT,* OLD FRIEND--?"

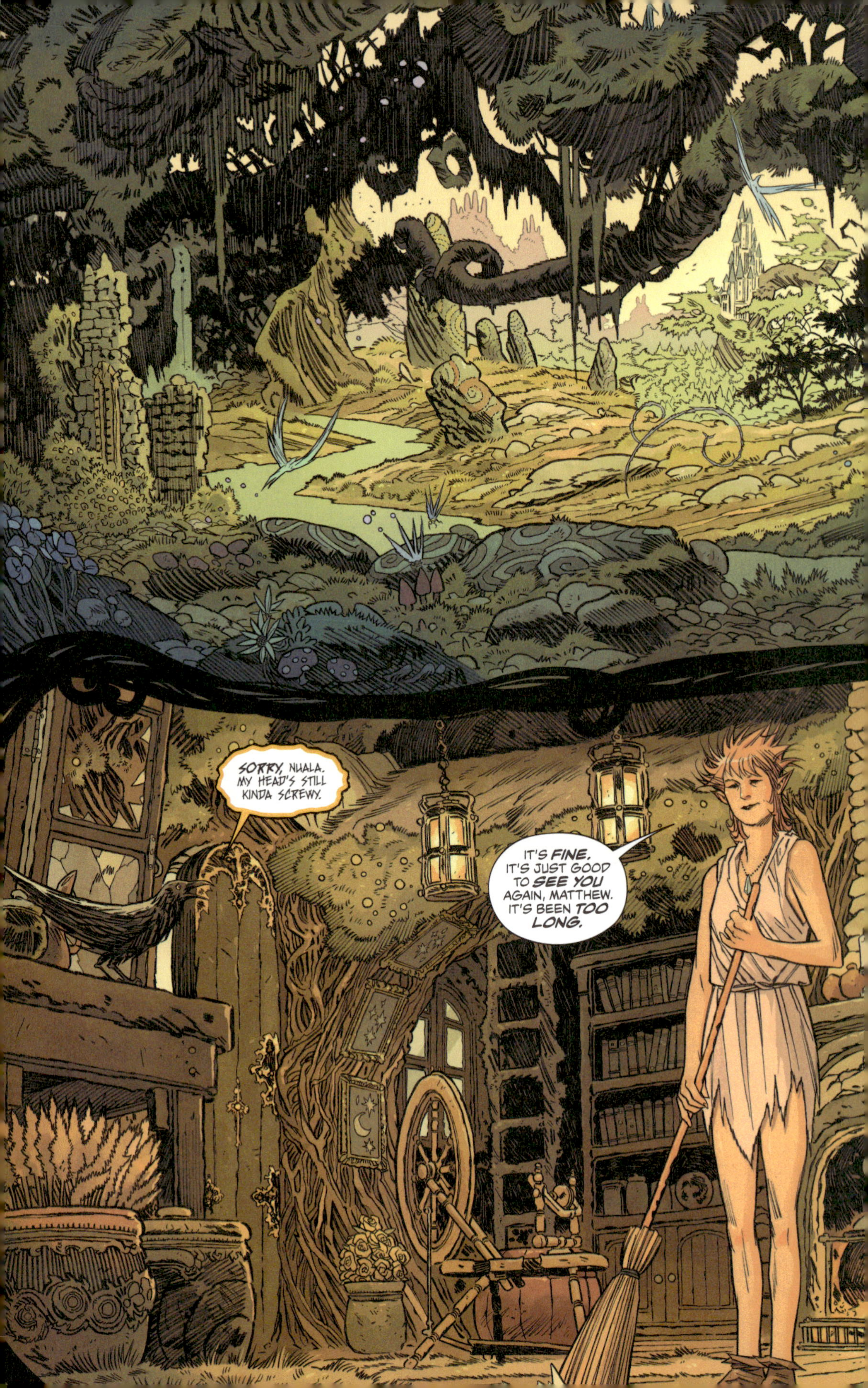
SORRY, NUALA. MY HEAD'S STILL KINDA SCREWY.
IT'S FINE. IT'S JUST GOOD TO SEE YOU AGAIN, MATTHEW. IT'S BEEN TOO LONG.

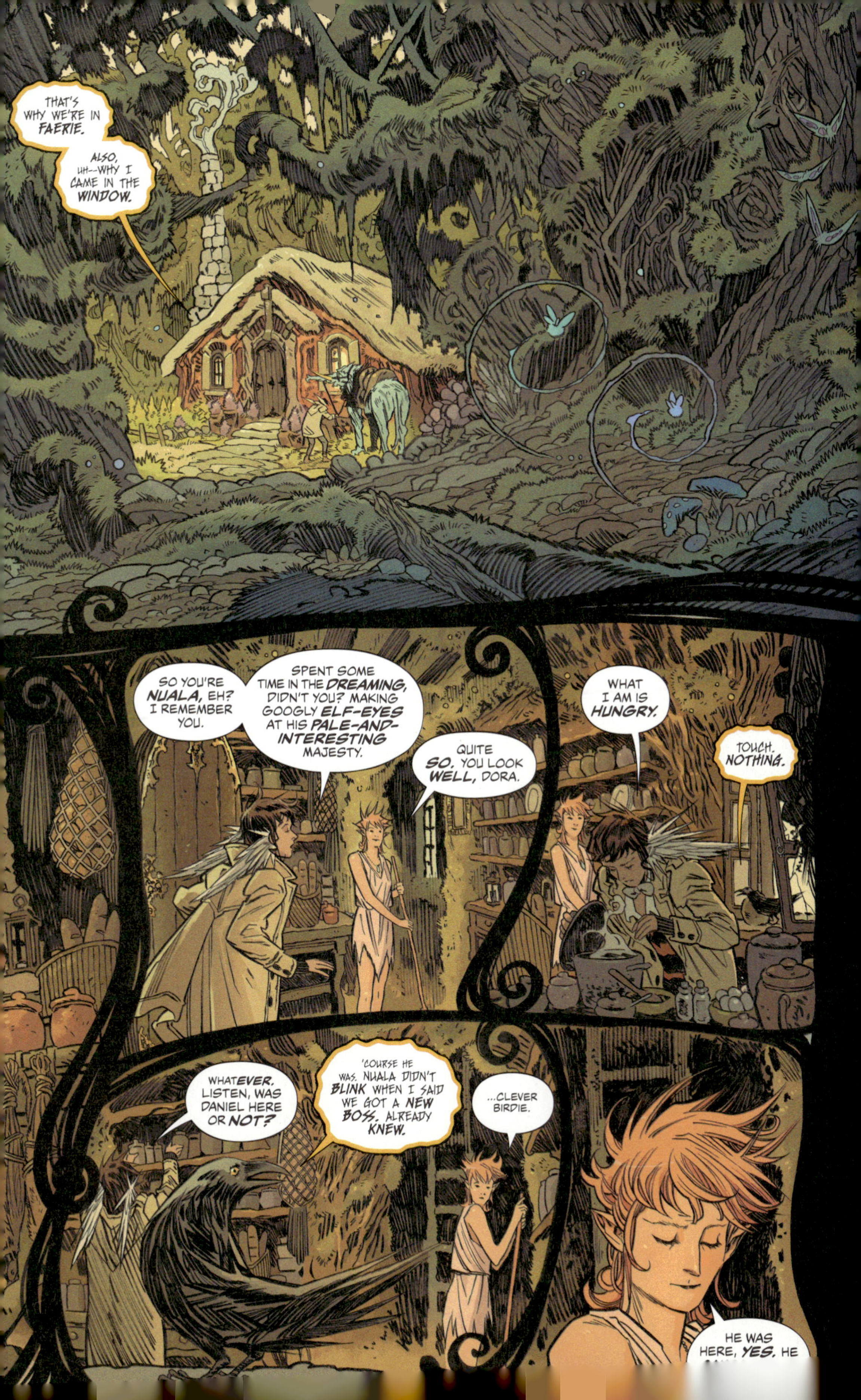
THAT'S WHY WE'RE IN FAERIE.
ALSO, UH--WHY I CAME IN THE WINDOW.
SO YOU'RE NUALA, EH? I REMEMBER YOU.
SPENT SOME TIME IN THE DREAMING, DIDN'T YOU? MAKING GOOGLY ELF-EYES AT HIS PALE-AND-INTERESTING MAJESTY.
QUITE SO. YOU LOOK WELL, DORA.
WHAT I AM IS HUNGRY.
TOUCH. NOTHING.
WHATEVER. LISTEN, WAS DANIEL HERE OR NOT?
'COURSE HE WAS. NUALA DIDN'T BLINK WHEN I SAID WE GOT A NEW BOSS. ALREADY KNEW.
...CLEVER BIRDIE.
HE WAS HERE, YES. HE

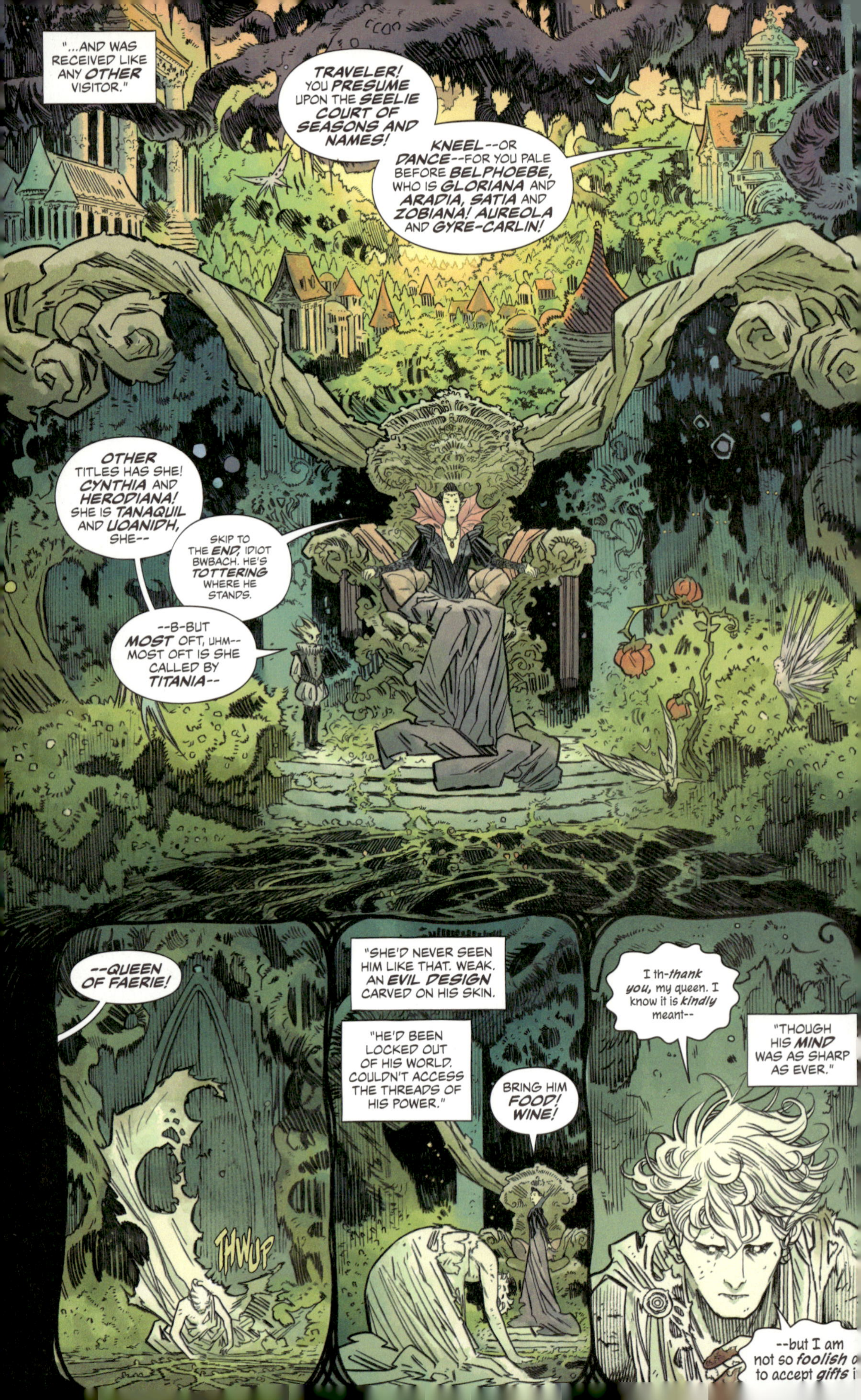
"...AND WAS RECEIVED LIKE ANY OTHER VISITOR."
TRAVELER! YOU PRESUME UPON THE SEELIE COURT OF SEASONS AND NAMES!
KNEEL--OR DANCE--FOR YOU PALE BEFORE BELPHOEBE, WHO IS GLORIANA AND ARADIA, SATIA AND ZOBIANA! AUREOLA AND GYRE-CARLIN!
OTHER TITLES HAS SHE! CYNTHIA AND HERODIANA! SHE IS TANAQUIL AND UOANIDH, SHE--
SKIP TO THE END, IDIOT BWBACH. HE'S TOTTERING WHERE HE STANDS.
--B-BUT MOST OFT, UHM-- MOST OFT IS SHE CALLED BY TITANIA--
--QUEEN OF FAERIE!
THWUP
"SHE'D NEVER SEEN HIM LIKE THAT. WEAK. AN EVIL DESIGN CARVED ON HIS SKIN.
"HE'D BEEN LOCKED OUT OF HIS WORLD. COULDN'T ACCESS THE THREADS OF HIS POWER."
BRING HIM FOOD! WINE!
I th-thank you, my queen. I know it is kindly meant--
"THOUGH HIS MIND WAS AS SHARP AS EVER."
--but I am not so foolish to accept gifts

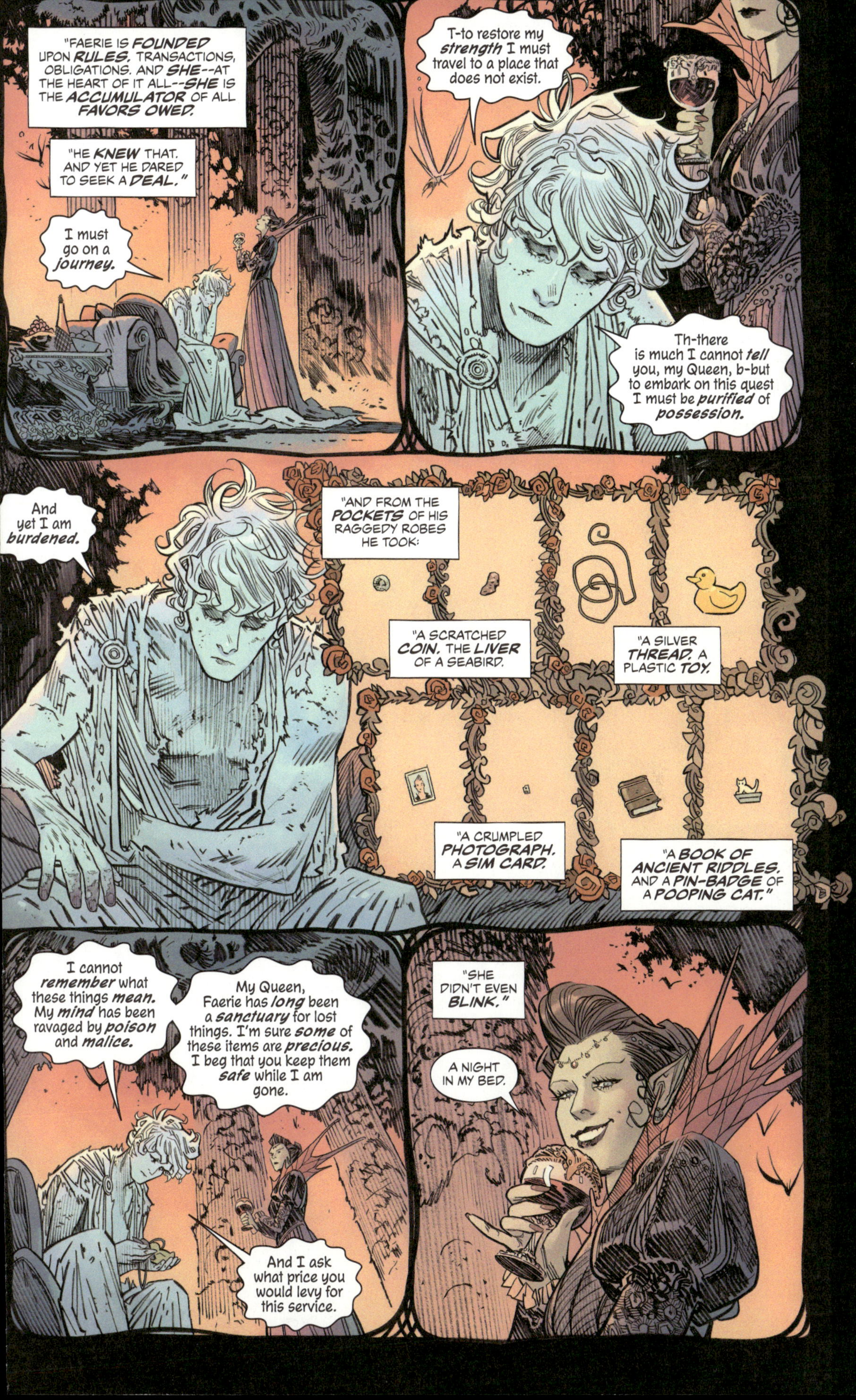
"FAERIE IS FOUNDED UPON RULES. TRANSACTIONS, OBLIGATIONS. AND SHE--AT THE HEART OF IT ALL--SHE IS THE ACCUMULATOR OF ALL FAVORS OWED.
"HE KNEW THAT. AND YET HE DARED TO SEEK A DEAL."
I must go on a journey.
T-to restore my strength I must travel to a place that does not exist.
Th-there is much I cannot tell you, my Queen, b-but to embark on this quest I must be purified of possession.
And yet I am burdened.
"AND FROM THE POCKETS OF HIS RAGGEDY ROBES HE TOOK:
"A SCRATCHED COIN. THE LIVER OF A SEABIRD.
"A SILVER THREAD. A PLASTIC TOY.
"A CRUMPLED PHOTOGRAPH. A SIM CARD.
"A BOOK OF ANCIENT RIDDLES. AND A PIN-BADGE OF A POOPING CAT."
I cannot remember what these things mean. My mind has been ravaged by poison and malice.
My Queen, Faerie has long been a sanctuary for lost things. I'm sure some of these items are precious. I beg that you keep them safe while I am gone.
And I ask what price you would levy for this service.
"SHE DIDN'T EVEN BLINK."
A NIGHT IN MY BED.

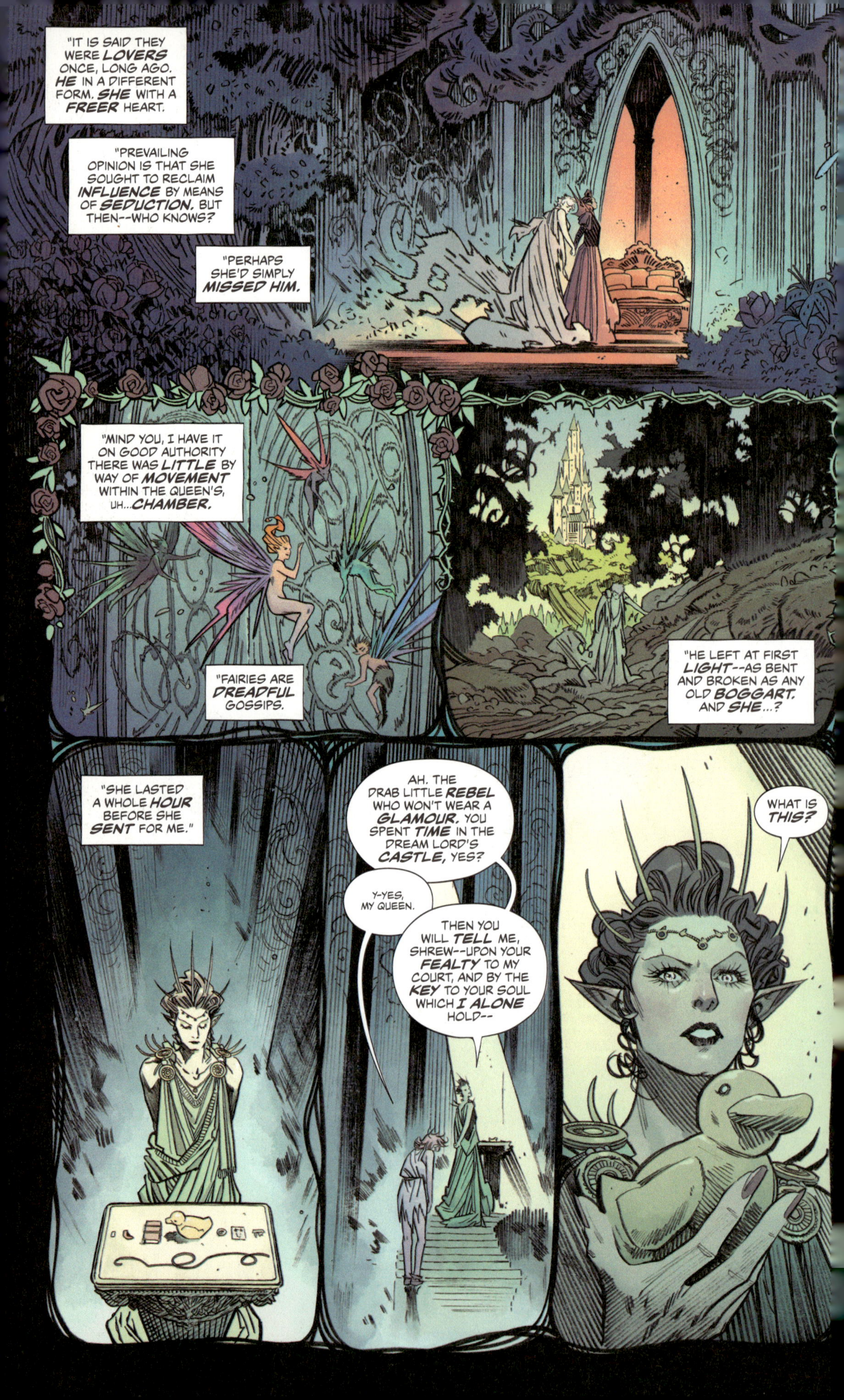
"IT IS SAID THEY WERE LOVERS ONCE, LONG AGO. HE IN A DIFFERENT FORM. SHE WITH A FREER HEART.
"PREVAILING OPINION IS THAT SHE SOUGHT TO RECLAIM INFLUENCE BY MEANS OF SEDUCTION. BUT THEN--WHO KNOWS?
"PERHAPS SHE'D SIMPLY MISSED HIM.
"MIND YOU, I HAVE IT ON GOOD AUTHORITY THERE WAS LITTLE BY WAY OF MOVEMENT WITHIN THE QUEEN'S, UH...CHAMBER.
"FAIRIES ARE DREADFUL GOSSIPS.
"HE LEFT AT FIRST LIGHT--AS BENT AND BROKEN AS ANY OLD BOGGART. AND SHE...?
"SHE LASTED A WHOLE HOUR BEFORE SHE SENT FOR ME."
AH. THE DRAB LITTLE REBEL WHO WON'T WEAR A GLAMOUR. YOU SPENT TIME IN THE DREAM LORD'S CASTLE, YES?
Y-YES, MY QUEEN.
THEN YOU WILL TELL ME, SHREW--UPON YOUR FEALTY TO MY COURT, AND BY THE KEY TO YOUR SOUL WHICH I ALONE HOLD--
WHAT IS THIS?

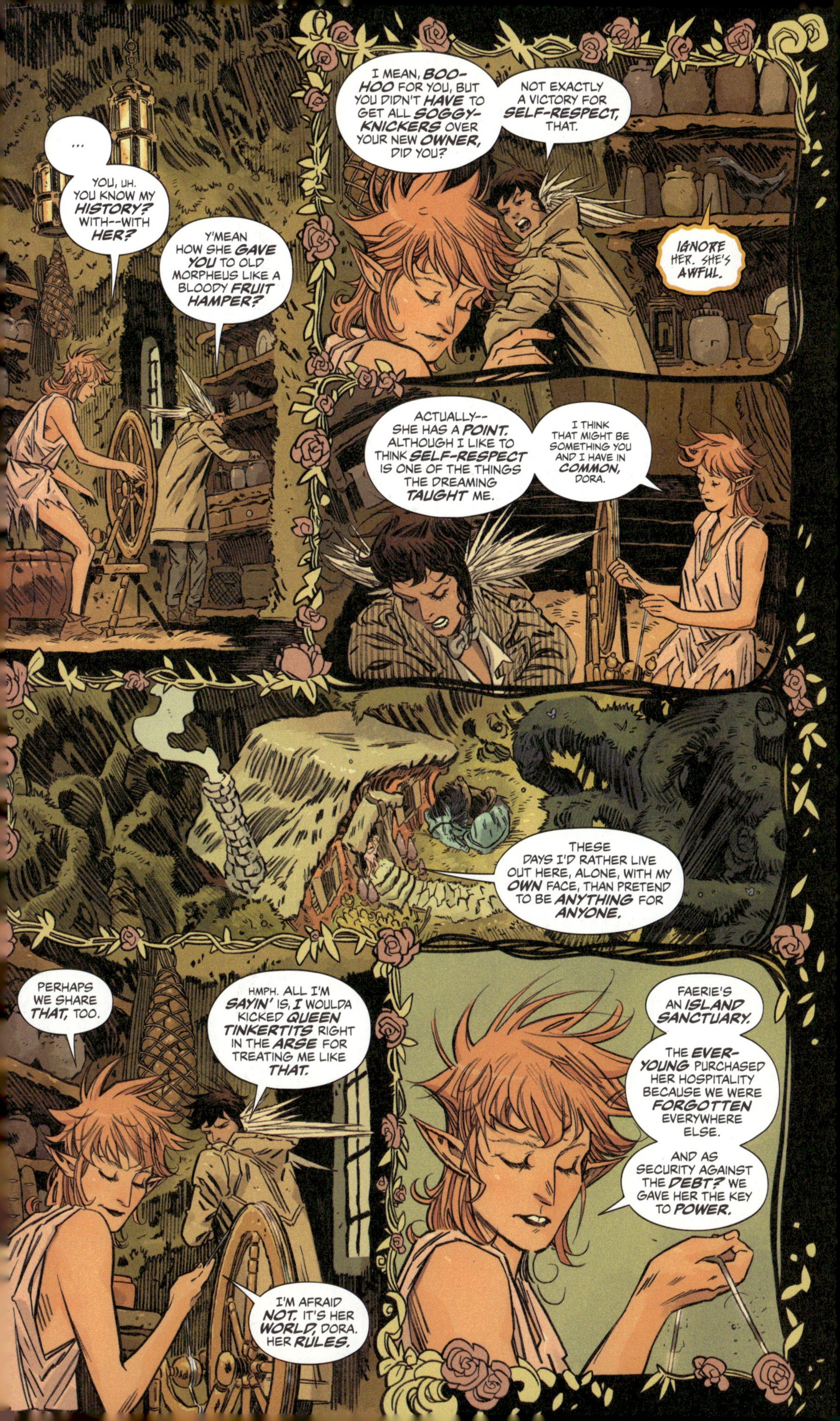
...
YOU, UH. YOU KNOW MY HISTORY? WITH--WITH HER?
Y'MEAN HOW SHE GAVE YOU TO OLD MORPHEUS LIKE A BLOODY FRUIT HAMPER?
I MEAN, BOO-HOO FOR YOU, BUT YOU DIDN'T HAVE TO GET ALL SOGGY-KNICKERS OVER YOUR NEW OWNER, DID YOU?
NOT EXACTLY A VICTORY FOR SELF-RESPECT, THAT.
IGNORE HER. SHE'S AWFUL.
ACTUALLY-- SHE HAS A POINT. ALTHOUGH I LIKE TO THINK SELF-RESPECT IS ONE OF THE THINGS THE DREAMING TAUGHT ME.
I THINK THAT MIGHT BE SOMETHING YOU AND I HAVE IN COMMON, DORA.
THESE DAYS I'D RATHER LIVE OUT HERE, ALONE, WITH MY OWN FACE, THAN PRETEND TO BE ANYTHING FOR ANYONE.
PERHAPS WE SHARE THAT, TOO.
HMPH. ALL I'M SAYIN' IS, I WOULDA KICKED QUEEN TINKERTITS RIGHT IN THE ARSE FOR TREATING ME LIKE THAT.
I'M AFRAID NOT. IT'S HER WORLD, DORA. HER RULES.
FAERIE'S AN ISLAND SANCTUARY.
THE EVER-YOUNG PURCHASED HER HOSPITALITY BECAUSE WE WERE FORGOTTEN EVERYWHERE ELSE.
AND AS SECURITY AGAINST THE DEBT? WE GAVE HER THE KEY TO POWER.

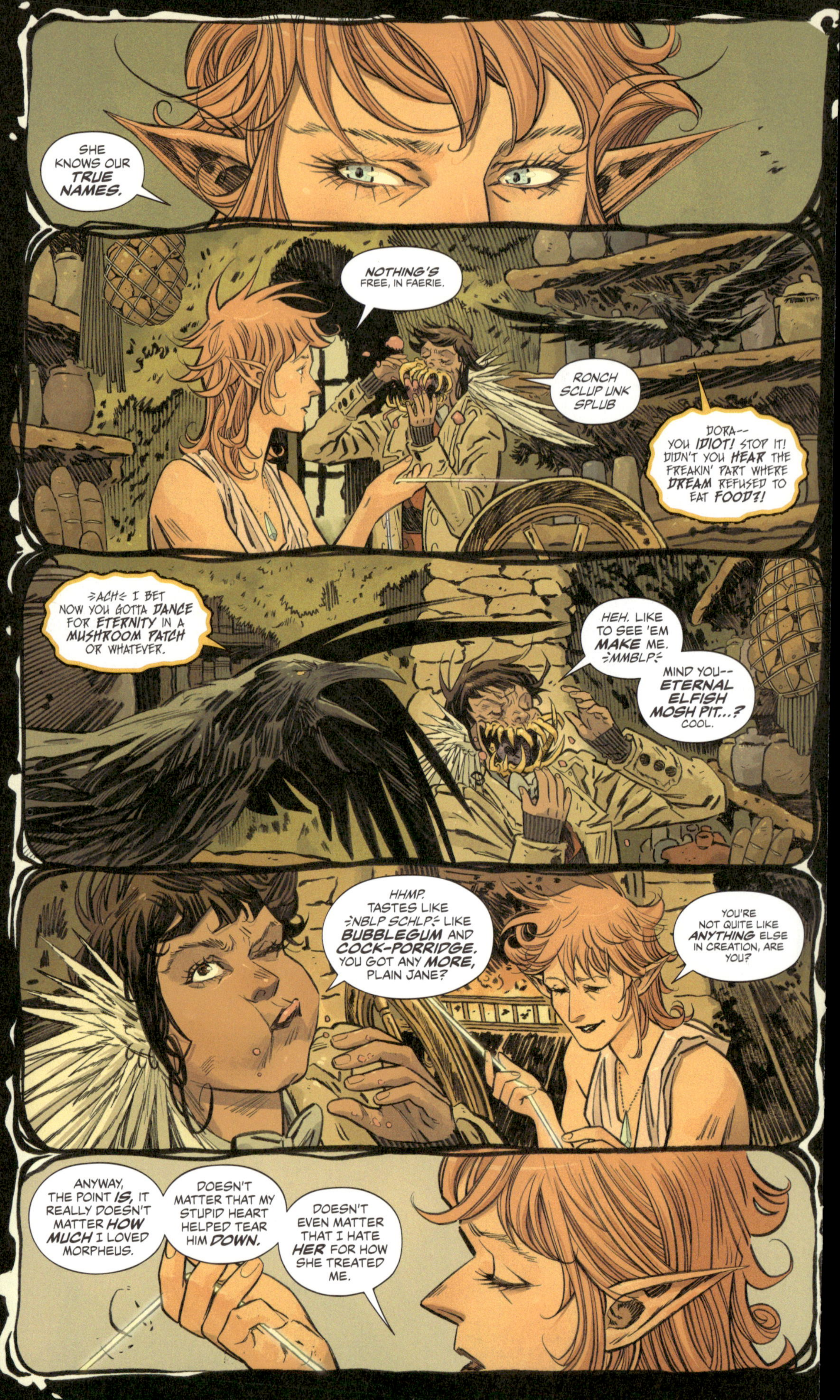
SHE KNOWS OUR TRUE NAMES.
NOTHING'S FREE, IN FAERIE.
RONCH SCLUP UNK SPLUB
DORA-- YOU IDIOT! STOP IT! DIDN'T YOU HEAR THE FREAKIN' PART WHERE DREAM REFUSED TO EAT FOOD?!
>ACH< I BET NOW YOU GOTTA DANCE FOR ETERNITY IN A MUSHROOM PATCH OR WHATEVER.
HEH. LIKE TO SEE 'EM MAKE ME. >MMBLP<
MIND YOU-- ETERNAL ELFISH MOSH PIT...? COOL.
HHMP. TASTES LIKE >NBLP SCHLP< LIKE BUBBLEGUM AND COCK-PORRIDGE. YOU GOT ANY MORE, PLAIN JANE?
YOU'RE NOT QUITE LIKE ANYTHING ELSE IN CREATION, ARE YOU?
ANYWAY, THE POINT IS, IT REALLY DOESN'T MATTER HOW MUCH I LOVED MORPHEUS.
DOESN'T MATTER THAT MY STUPID HEART HELPED TEAR HIM DOWN.
DOESN'T EVEN MATTER THAT I HATE HER FOR HOW SHE TREATED ME.

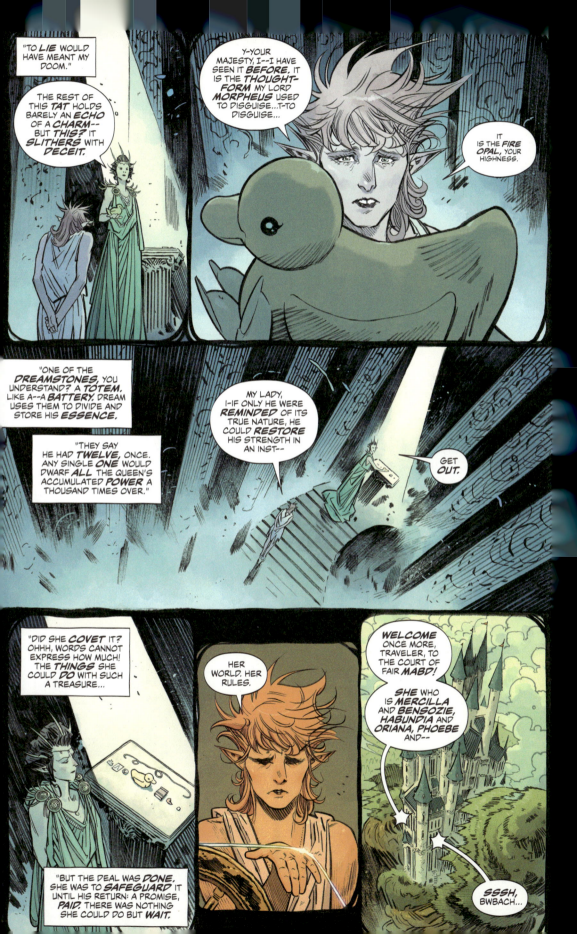

"TO *LIE* WOULD HAVE MEANT MY DOOM."

THE REST OF THIS *TAT* HOLDS BARELY AN *ECHO* OF A *CHARM*-- BUT *THIS?* IT *SLITHERS* WITH *DECEIT.*

Y-YOUR MAJESTY, I--I HAVE SEEN IT *BEFORE.* IT IS THE *THOUGHT-FORM* MY LORD *MORPHEUS* USED TO DISGUISE...T-TO DISGUISE...

IT IS THE *FIRE OPAL,* YOUR HIGHNESS.

"ONE OF THE *DREAMSTONES,* YOU UNDERSTAND? A *TOTEM.* LIKE A--A *BATTERY.* DREAM USES THEM TO DIVIDE AND STORE HIS *ESSENCE.*

"THEY SAY HE HAD *TWELVE,* ONCE. ANY SINGLE *ONE* WOULD DWARF *ALL* THE QUEEN'S ACCUMULATED *POWER* A THOUSAND TIMES OVER."

MY LADY, I--IF ONLY HE WERE *REMINDED* OF ITS TRUE NATURE, HE COULD *RESTORE* HIS STRENGTH IN AN INST--

GET *OUT.*

"DID SHE *COVET* IT? OHHH, WORDS CANNOT EXPRESS HOW MUCH! THE *THINGS* SHE COULD *DO* WITH SUCH A TREASURE...

HER WORLD. HER RULES.

WELCOME ONCE MORE, TRAVELER, TO THE COURT OF FAIR *MABD!*

SHE WHO IS *MERCILLA* AND *BENSOZIE,* *HABUNDIA* AND *ORIANA,* *PHOEBE* AND--

"BUT THE DEAL WAS *DONE.* SHE WAS TO *SAFEGUARD* IT UNTIL HIS RETURN: A PROMISE, *PAID.* THERE WAS NOTHING SHE COULD DO BUT *WAIT.*

SSSH, BWBACH...

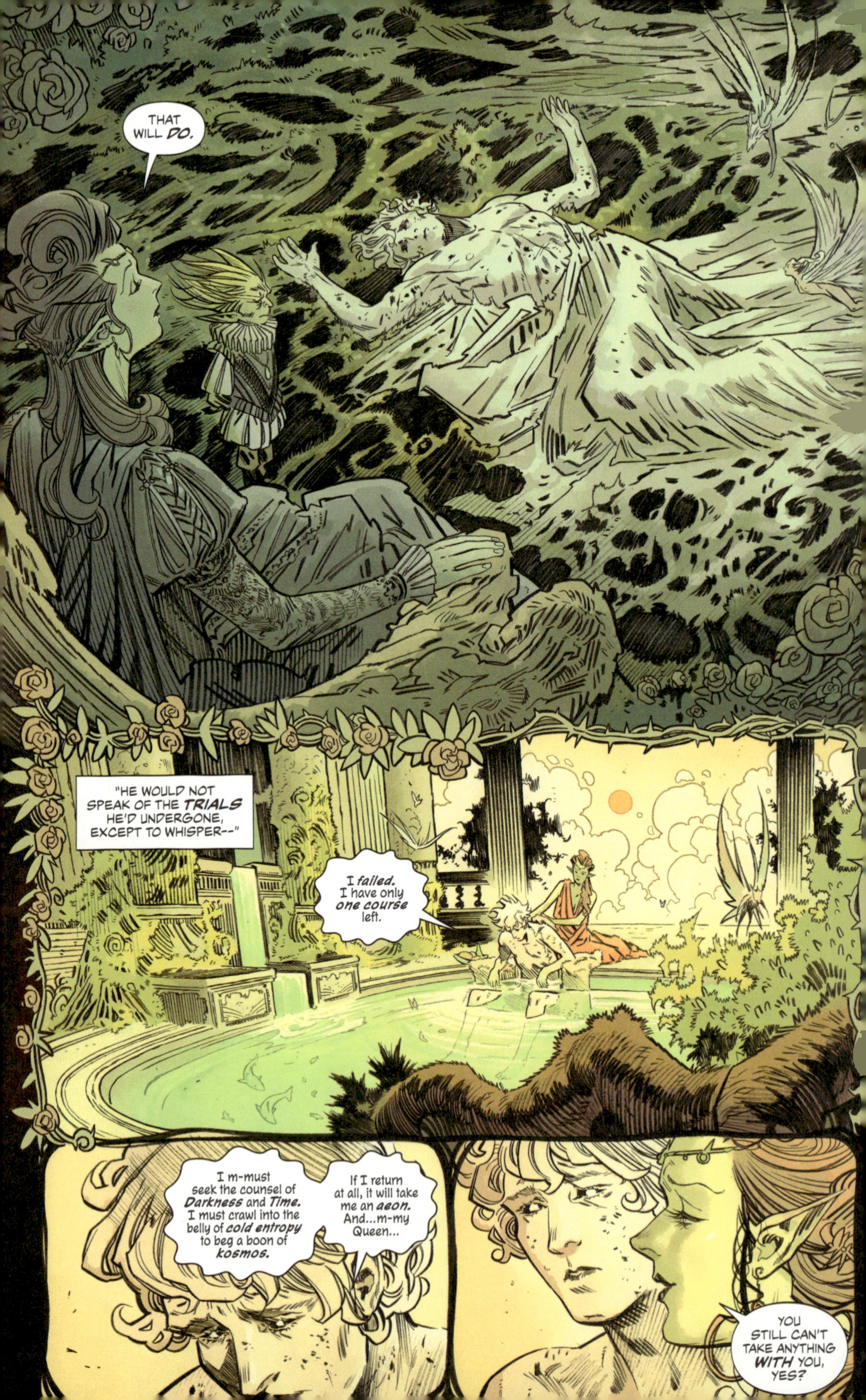
THAT WILL DO.
"HE WOULD NOT SPEAK OF THE TRIALS HE'D UNDERGONE, EXCEPT TO WHISPER--"
I failed. I have only one course left.
I m-must seek the counsel of Darkness and Time. I must crawl into the belly of cold entropy to beg a boon of kosmos.
If I return at all, it will take me an aeon. And...m-my Queen...
YOU STILL CAN'T TAKE ANYTHING WITH YOU, YES?

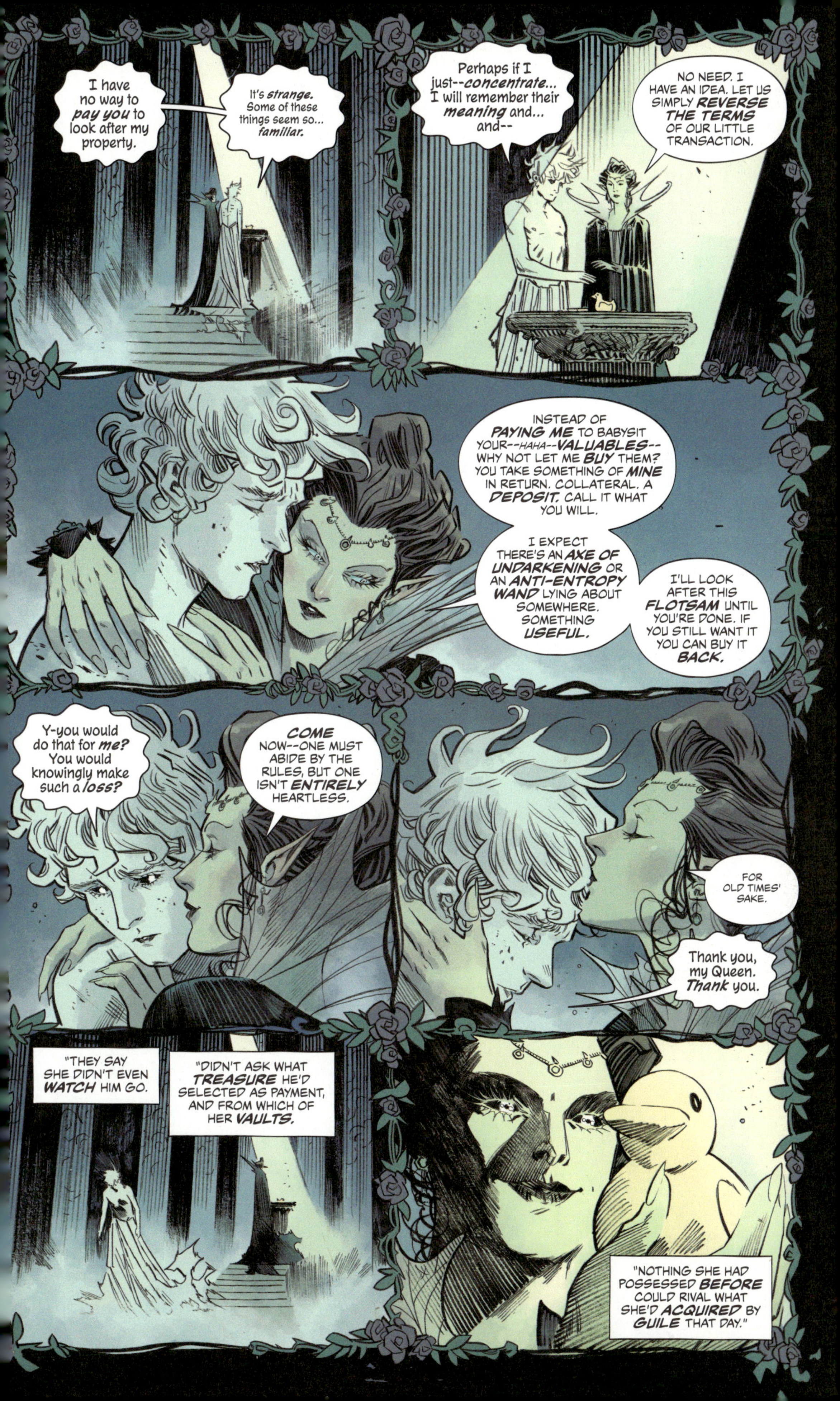
I have no way to pay you to look after my property.
It's strange. Some of these things seem so... familiar.
Perhaps if I just--concentrate... I will remember their meaning and... and--
NO NEED. I HAVE AN IDEA. LET US SIMPLY REVERSE THE TERMS OF OUR LITTLE TRANSACTION.
INSTEAD OF PAYING ME TO BABYSIT YOUR--HAHA--VALUABLES--WHY NOT LET ME BUY THEM? YOU TAKE SOMETHING OF MINE IN RETURN. COLLATERAL. A DEPOSIT. CALL IT WHAT YOU WILL.
I EXPECT THERE'S AN AXE OF UNDARKENING OR AN ANTI-ENTROPY WAND LYING ABOUT SOMEWHERE. SOMETHING USEFUL.
I'LL LOOK AFTER THIS FLOTSAM UNTIL YOU'RE DONE. IF YOU STILL WANT IT YOU CAN BUY IT BACK.
Y-you would do that for me? You would knowingly make such a loss?
COME NOW--ONE MUST ABIDE BY THE RULES, BUT ONE ISN'T ENTIRELY HEARTLESS.
FOR OLD TIMES' SAKE.
Thank you, my Queen. Thank you.
"THEY SAY SHE DIDN'T EVEN WATCH HIM GO.
"DIDN'T ASK WHAT TREASURE HE'D SELECTED AS PAYMENT, AND FROM WHICH OF HER VAULTS.
"NOTHING SHE HAD POSSESSED BEFORE COULD RIVAL WHAT SHE'D ACQUIRED BY GUILE THAT DAY."

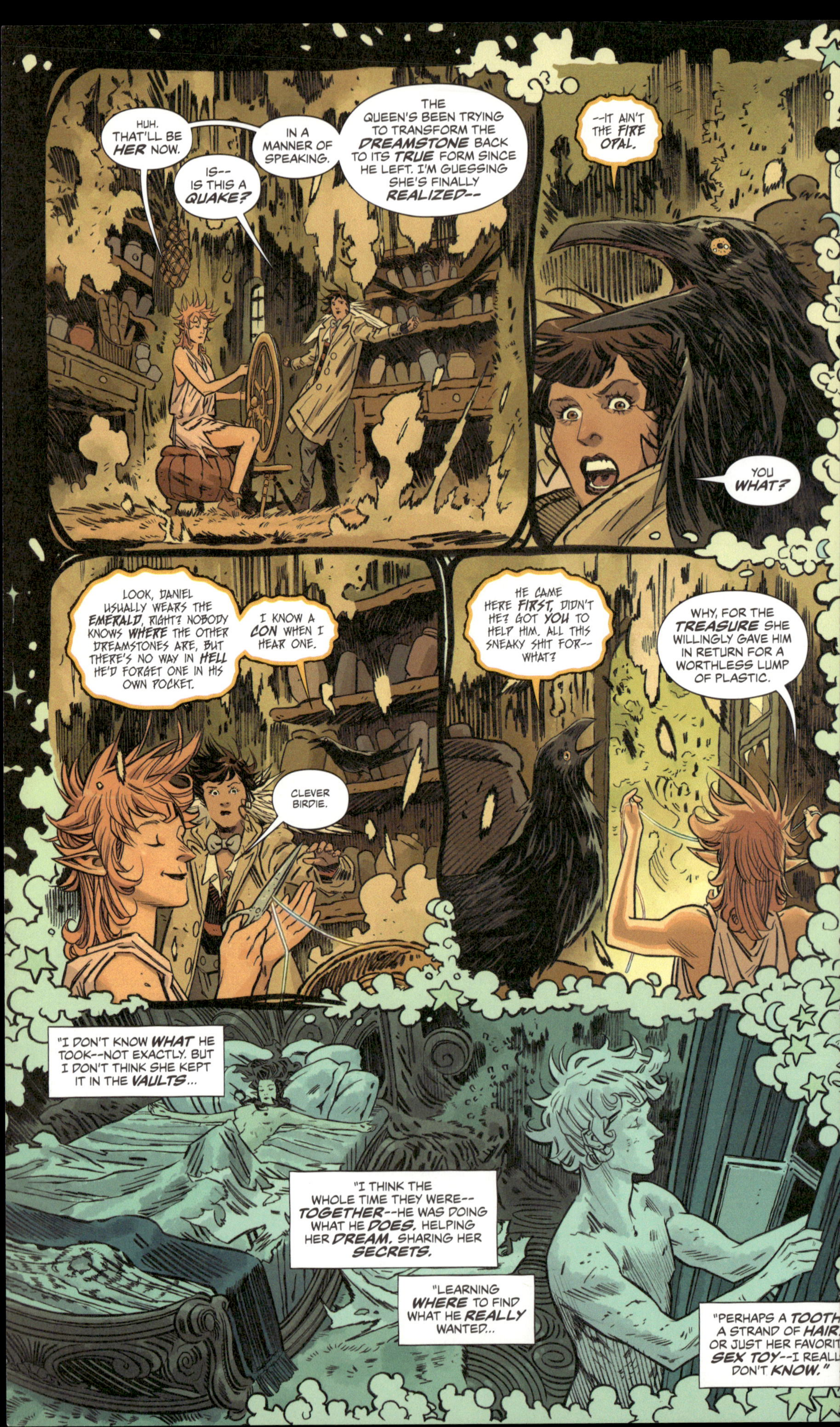
HUH. THAT'LL BE HER NOW.
IS-- IS THIS A QUAKE?
IN A MANNER OF SPEAKING.
THE QUEEN'S BEEN TRYING TO TRANSFORM THE DREAMSTONE BACK TO ITS TRUE FORM SINCE HE LEFT. I'M GUESSING SHE'S FINALLY REALIZED--
--IT AIN'T THE FIRE OPAL.
YOU WHAT?
LOOK, DANIEL USUALLY WEARS THE EMERALD, RIGHT? NOBODY KNOWS WHERE THE OTHER DREAMSTONES ARE, BUT THERE'S NO WAY IN HELL HE'D FORGET ONE IN HIS OWN POCKET.
I KNOW A CON WHEN I HEAR ONE.
CLEVER BIRDIE.
HE CAME HERE FIRST, DIDN'T HE? GOT YOU TO HELP HIM. ALL THIS SNEAKY SHIT FOR--WHAT?
WHY, FOR THE TREASURE SHE WILLINGLY GAVE HIM IN RETURN FOR A WORTHLESS LUMP OF PLASTIC.
"I DON'T KNOW WHAT HE TOOK--NOT EXACTLY. BUT I DON'T THINK SHE KEPT IT IN THE VAULTS...
"I THINK THE WHOLE TIME THEY WERE--TOGETHER--HE WAS DOING WHAT HE DOES. HELPING HER DREAM. SHARING HER SECRETS.
"LEARNING WHERE TO FIND WHAT HE REALLY WANTED...
"PERHAPS A TOOTH, A STRAND OF HAIR, OR JUST HER FAVORITE SEX TOY--I REALLY DON'T KNOW."

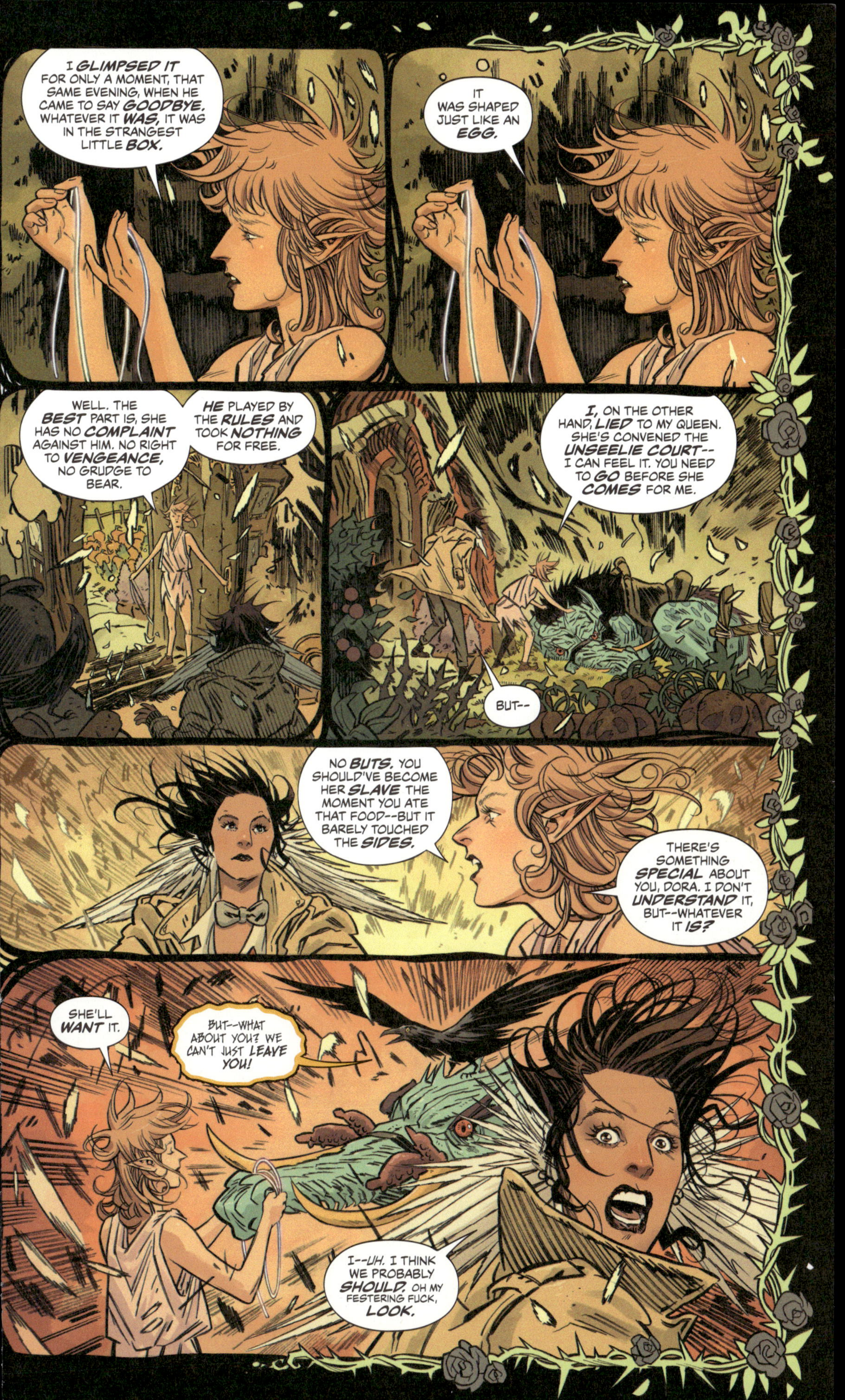

I GLIMPSED IT FOR ONLY A MOMENT, THAT SAME EVENING, WHEN HE CAME TO SAY GOODBYE. WHATEVER IT WAS, IT WAS IN THE STRANGEST LITTLE BOX.
IT WAS SHAPED JUST LIKE AN EGG.
WELL. THE BEST PART IS, SHE HAS NO COMPLAINT AGAINST HIM. NO RIGHT TO VENGEANCE, NO GRUDGE TO BEAR.
HE PLAYED BY THE RULES AND TOOK NOTHING FOR FREE.
I, ON THE OTHER HAND, LIED TO MY QUEEN. SHE'S CONVENED THE UNSEELIE COURT-- I CAN FEEL IT. YOU NEED TO GO BEFORE SHE COMES FOR ME.
BUT--
NO BUTS. YOU SHOULD'VE BECOME HER SLAVE THE MOMENT YOU ATE THAT FOOD--BUT IT BARELY TOUCHED THE SIDES.
THERE'S SOMETHING SPECIAL ABOUT YOU, DORA. I DON'T UNDERSTAND IT, BUT--WHATEVER IT IS?
SHE'LL WANT IT.
BUT--WHAT ABOUT YOU? WE CAN'T JUST LEAVE YOU!
I--UH. I THINK WE PROBABLY SHOULD. OH MY FESTERING FUCK, LOOK.

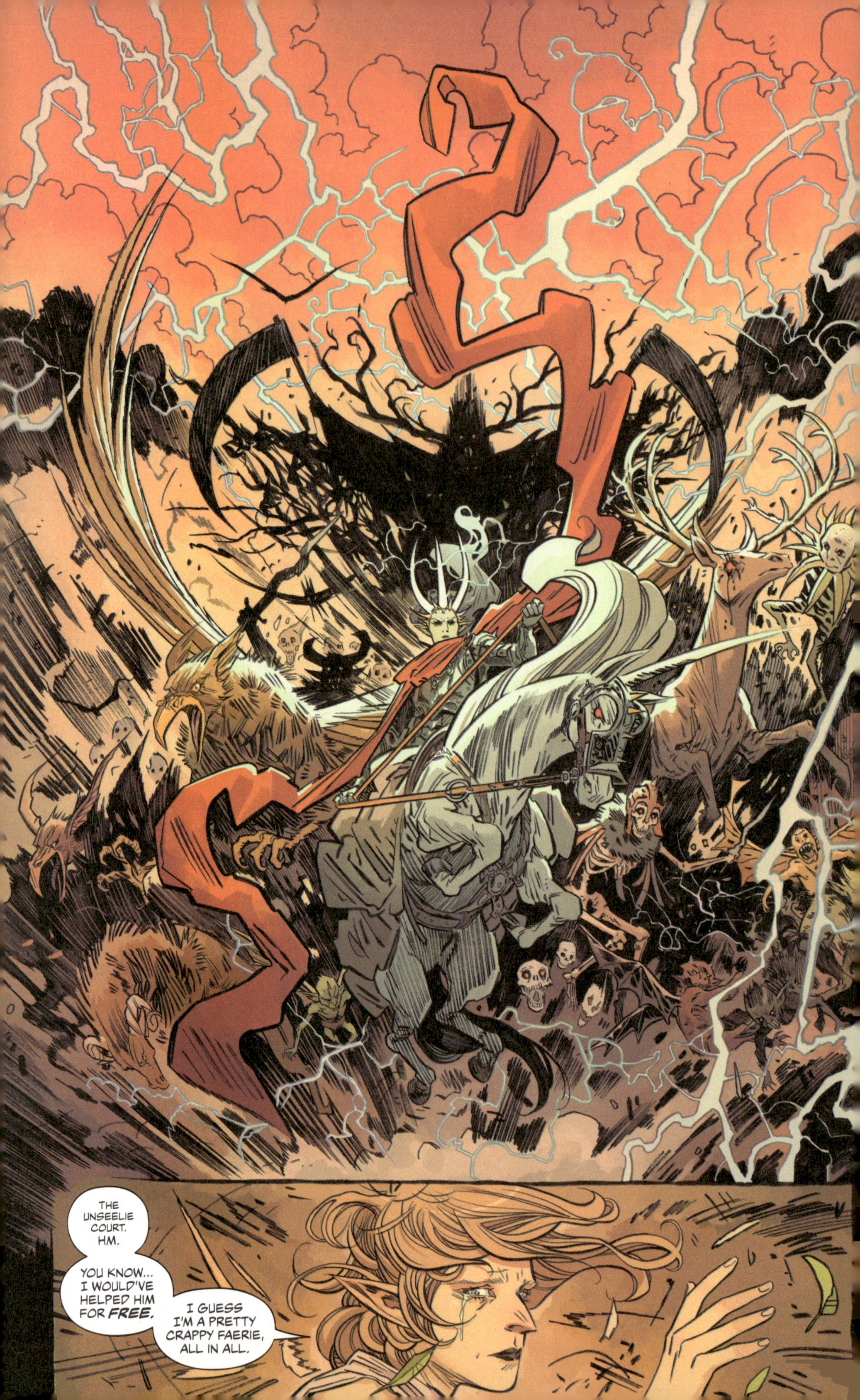
THE UNSEELIE COURT. HM.
YOU KNOW... I WOULD'VE HELPED HIM FOR **FREE.**
I GUESS I'M A PRETTY CRAPPY FAERIE, ALL IN ALL.

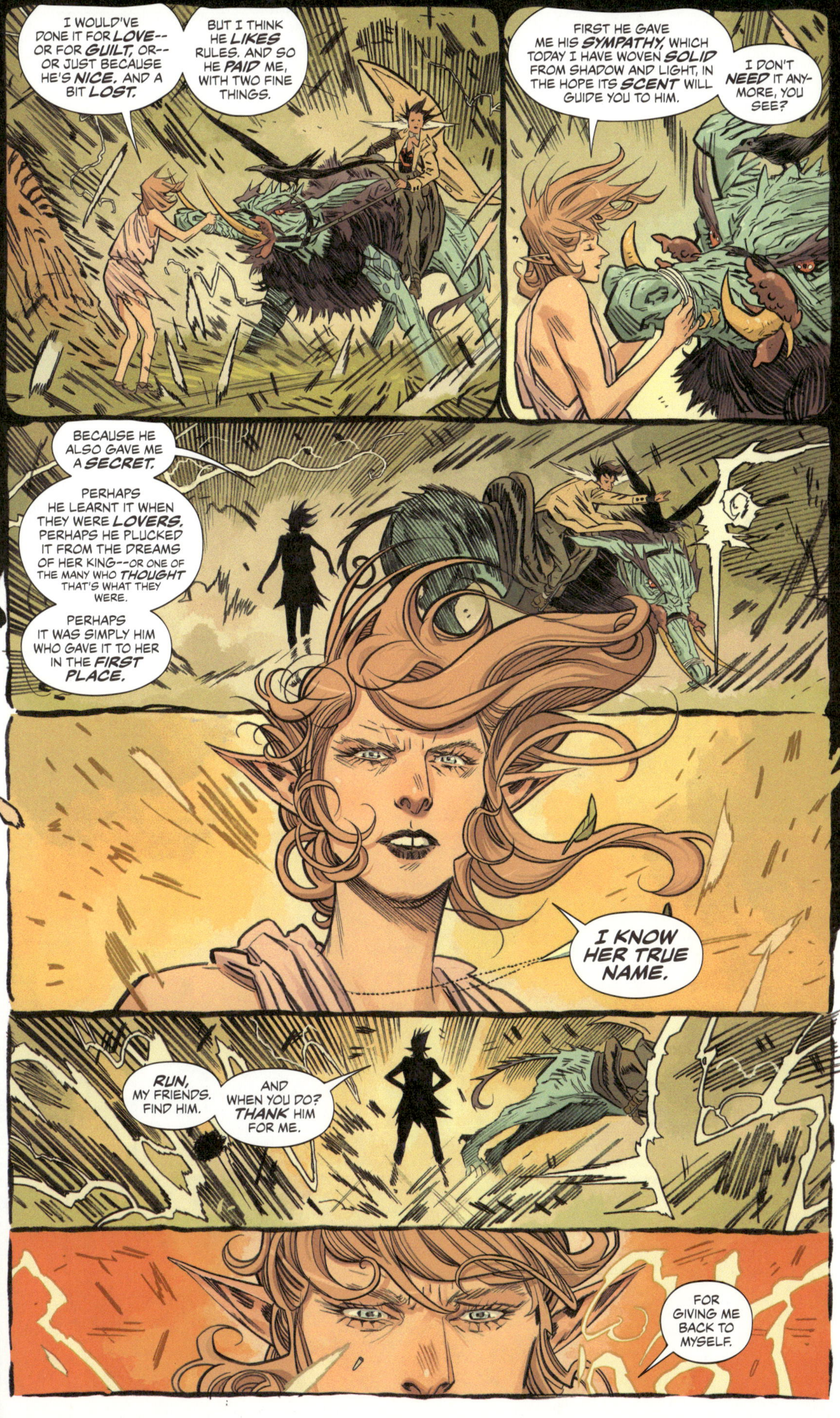
I WOULD'VE DONE IT FOR LOVE-- OR FOR GUILT, OR-- OR JUST BECAUSE HE'S NICE. AND A BIT LOST.
BUT I THINK HE LIKES RULES. AND SO HE PAID ME, WITH TWO FINE THINGS.
FIRST HE GAVE ME HIS SYMPATHY, WHICH TODAY I HAVE WOVEN SOLID FROM SHADOW AND LIGHT, IN THE HOPE ITS SCENT WILL GUIDE YOU TO HIM.
I DON'T NEED IT ANYMORE, YOU SEE?
BECAUSE HE ALSO GAVE ME A SECRET.
PERHAPS HE LEARNT IT WHEN THEY WERE LOVERS. PERHAPS HE PLUCKED IT FROM THE DREAMS OF HER KING--OR ONE OF THE MANY WHO THOUGHT THAT'S WHAT THEY WERE.
PERHAPS IT WAS SIMPLY HIM WHO GAVE IT TO HER IN THE FIRST PLACE.
I KNOW HER TRUE NAME.
RUN, MY FRIENDS. FIND HIM.
AND WHEN YOU DO? THANK HIM FOR ME.
FOR GIVING ME BACK TO MYSELF.

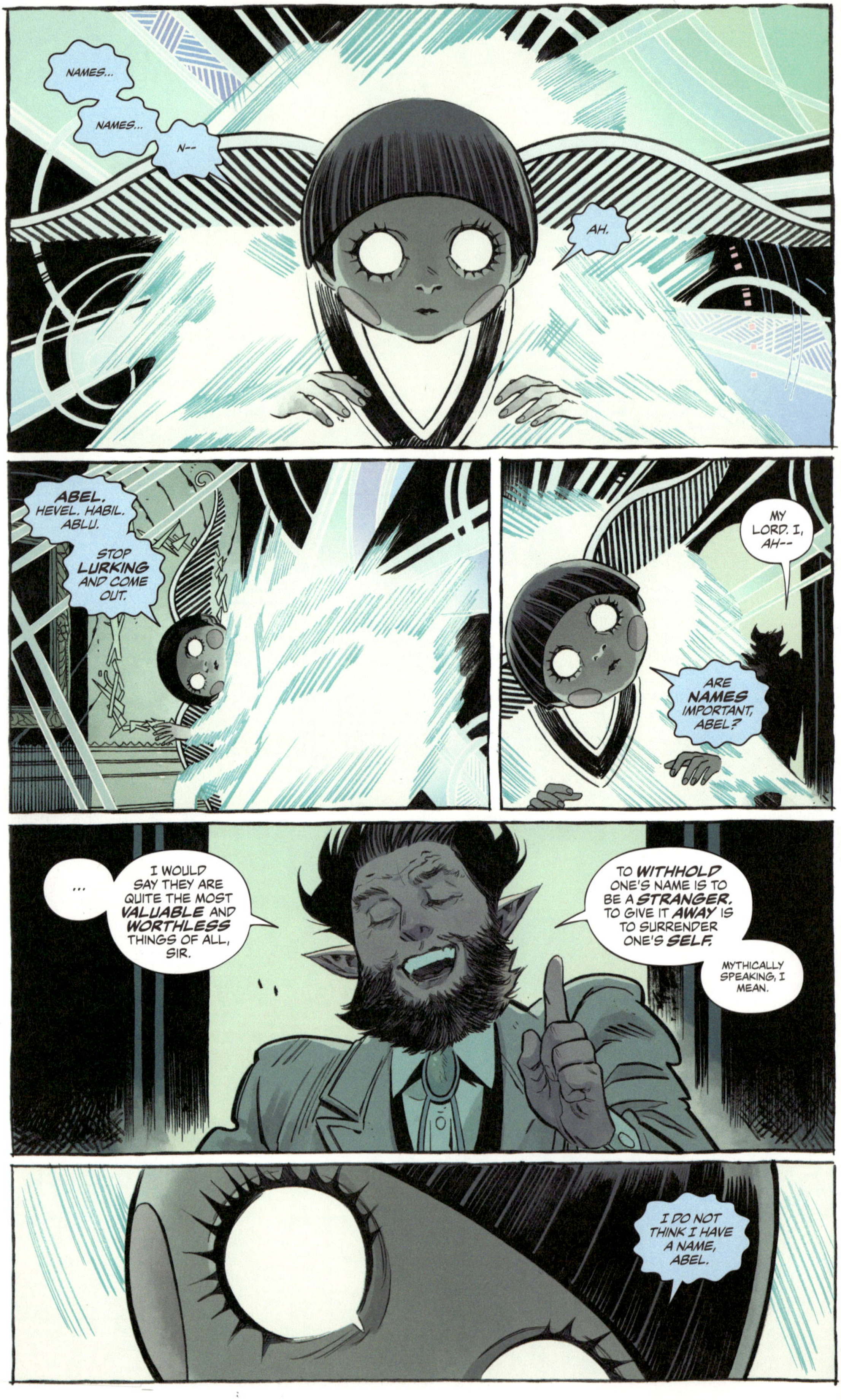
NAMES...
NAMES...
N--
AH.
ABEL. HEVEL. HABIL. ABLU.
STOP LURKING AND COME OUT.
MY LORD. I, AH--
ARE NAMES IMPORTANT, ABEL?
...
I WOULD SAY THEY ARE QUITE THE MOST VALUABLE AND WORTHLESS THINGS OF ALL, SIR.
TO WITHHOLD ONE'S NAME IS TO BE A STRANGER. TO GIVE IT AWAY IS TO SURRENDER ONE'S SELF.
MYTHICALLY SPEAKING, I MEAN.
I DO NOT THINK I HAVE A NAME, ABEL.

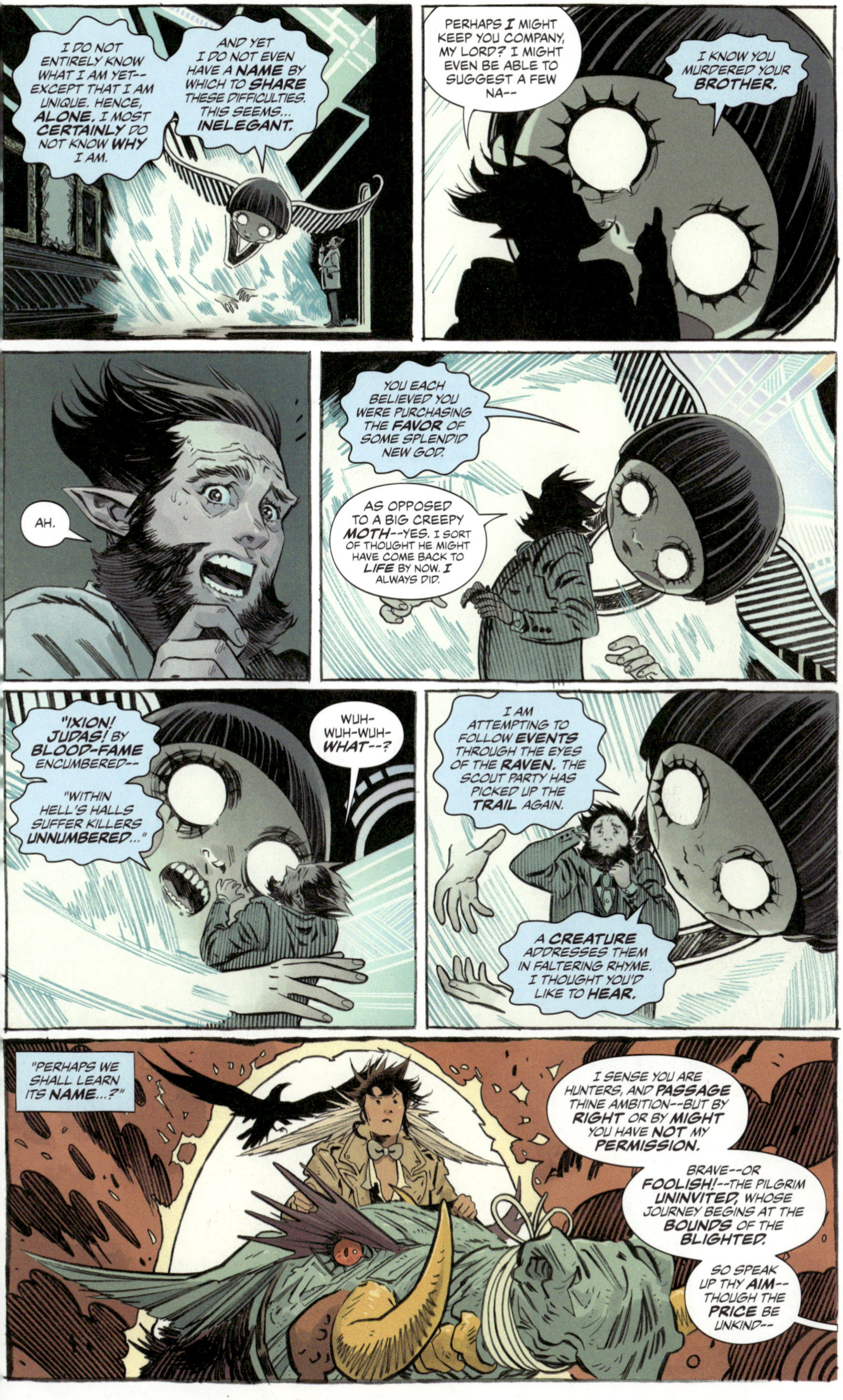
I DO NOT ENTIRELY KNOW WHAT I AM YET--EXCEPT THAT I AM UNIQUE. HENCE, ALONE. I MOST CERTAINLY DO NOT KNOW WHY I AM.
AND YET I DO NOT EVEN HAVE A NAME BY WHICH TO SHARE THESE DIFFICULTIES. THIS SEEMS... INELEGANT.
PERHAPS I MIGHT KEEP YOU COMPANY, MY LORD? I MIGHT EVEN BE ABLE TO SUGGEST A FEW NA--
I KNOW YOU MURDERED YOUR BROTHER.
AH.
YOU EACH BELIEVED YOU WERE PURCHASING THE FAVOR OF SOME SPLENDID NEW GOD.
AS OPPOSED TO A BIG CREEPY MOTH--YES. I SORT OF THOUGHT HE MIGHT HAVE COME BACK TO LIFE BY NOW. I ALWAYS DID.
"IXION! JUDAS! BY BLOOD-FAME ENCUMBERED--
"WITHIN HELL'S HALLS SUFFER KILLERS UNNUMBERED..."
WUH-WUH-WUH-WHAT--?
I AM ATTEMPTING TO FOLLOW EVENTS THROUGH THE EYES OF THE RAVEN. THE SCOUT PARTY HAS PICKED UP THE TRAIL AGAIN.
A CREATURE ADDRESSES THEM IN FALTERING RHYME. I THOUGHT YOU'D LIKE TO HEAR.
"PERHAPS WE SHALL LEARN ITS NAME...?"
I SENSE YOU ARE HUNTERS, AND PASSAGE THINE AMBITION--BUT BY RIGHT OR BY MIGHT YOU HAVE NOT MY PERMISSION.
BRAVE--OR FOOLISH!--THE PILGRIM UNINVITED, WHOSE JOURNEY BEGINS AT THE BOUNDS OF THE BLIGHTED.
SO SPEAK UP THY AIM--THOUGH THE PRICE BE UNKIND--

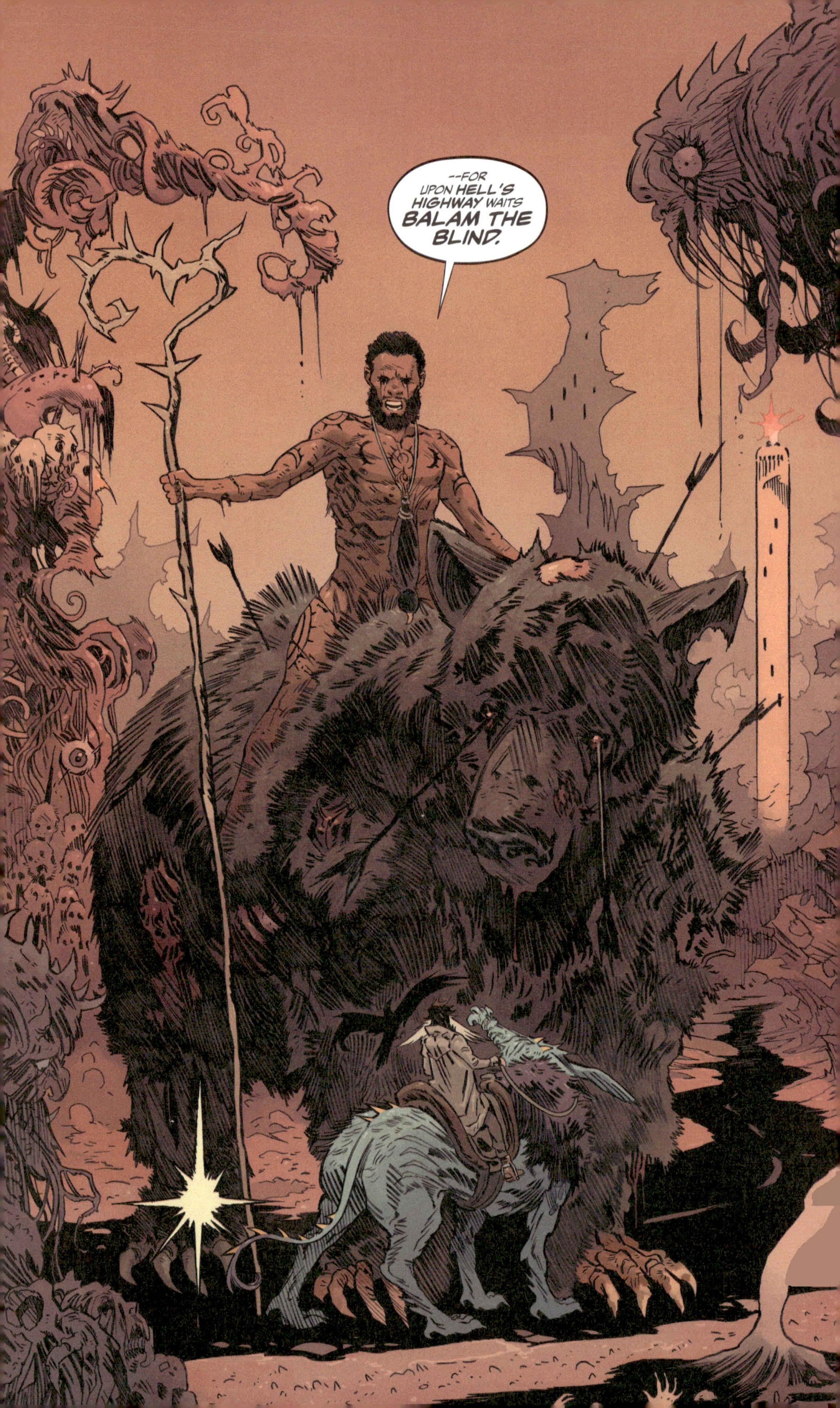
--FOR UPON HELL'S HIGHWAY WAITS BALAM THE BLIND.

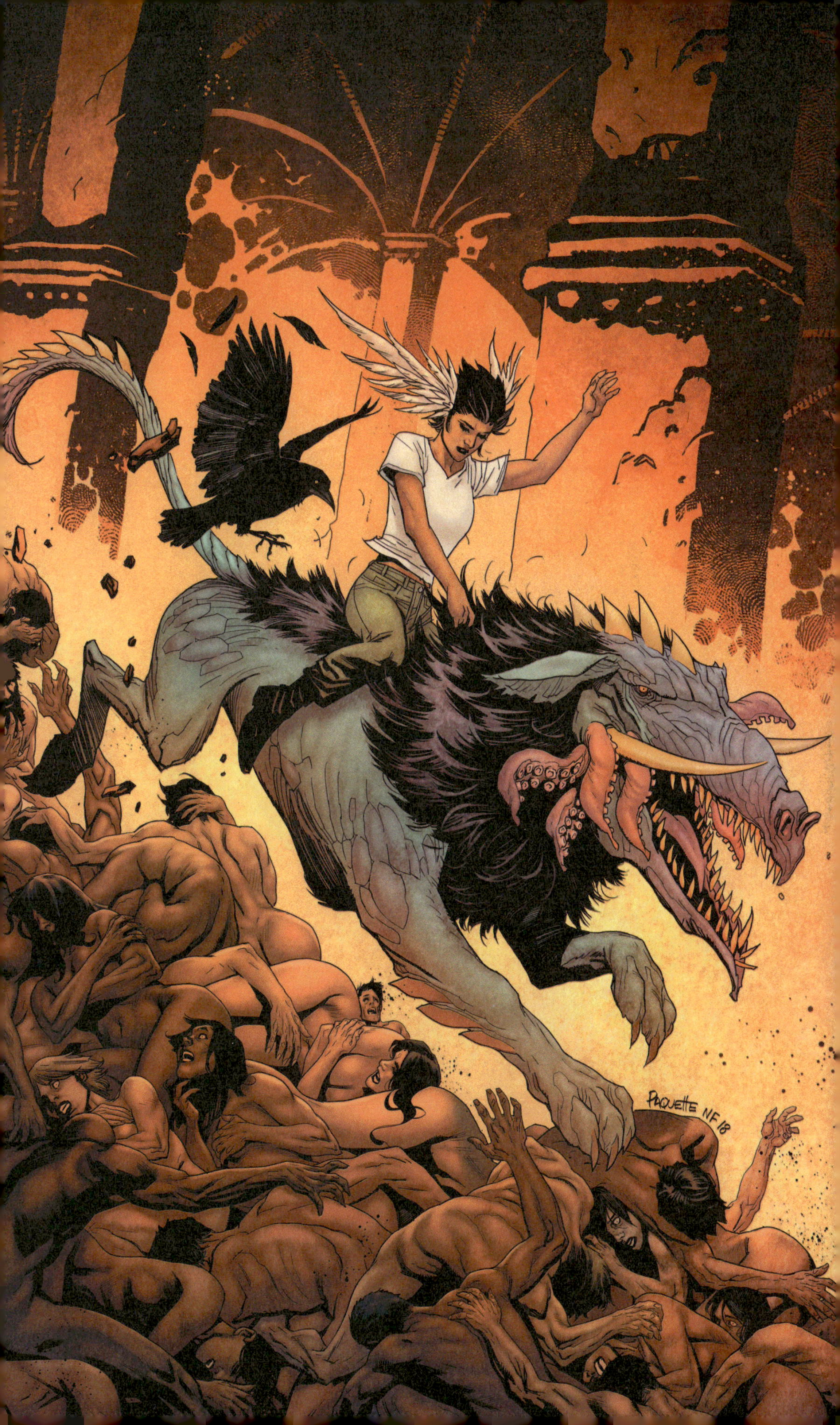
PAQUETTE NF 18

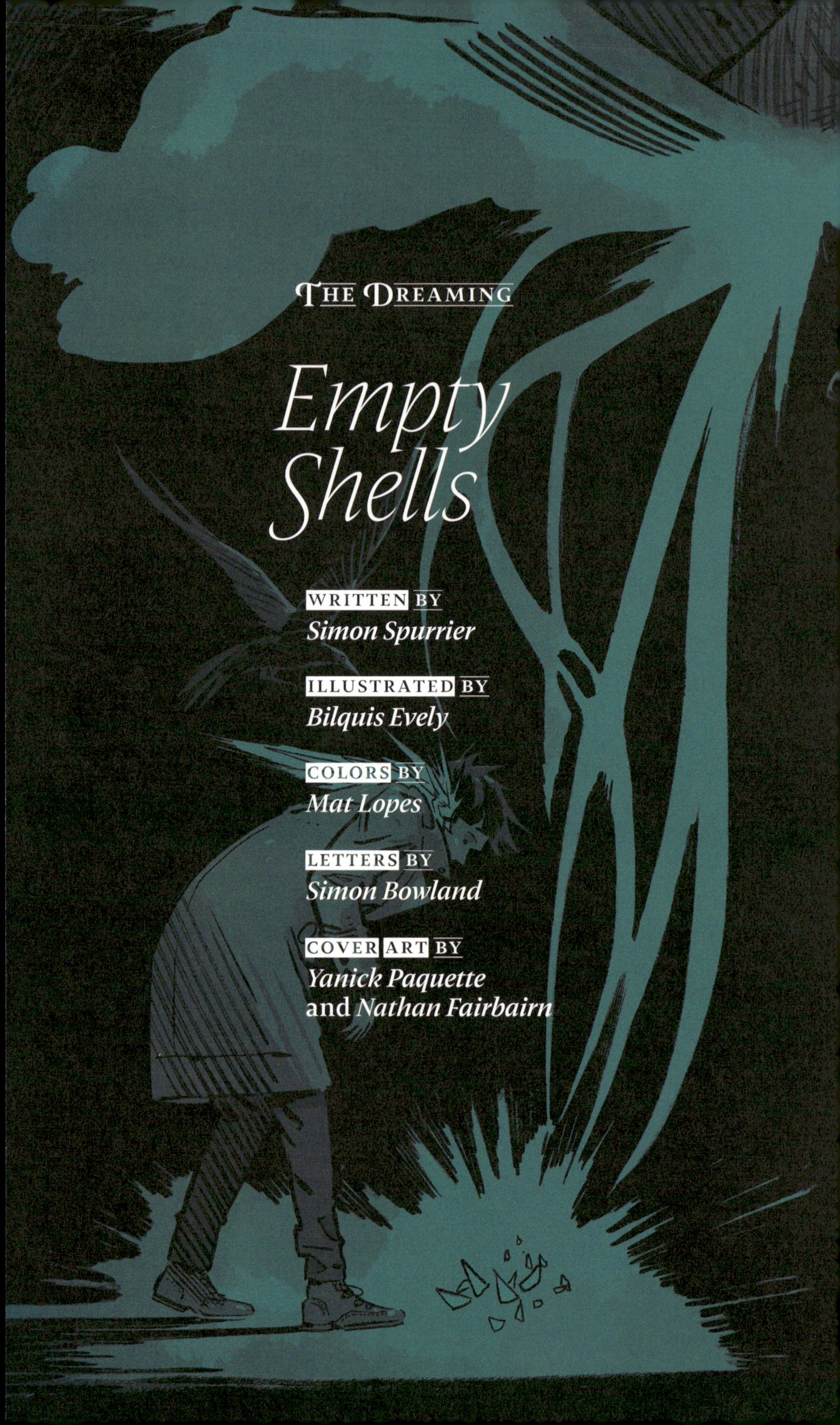

THE DREAMING

Empty Shells

WRITTEN BY
Simon Spurrier

ILLUSTRATED BY
Bilquis Evely

COLORS BY
Mat Lopes

LETTERS BY
Simon Bowland

COVER ART BY
Yanick Paquette
and *Nathan Fairbairn*

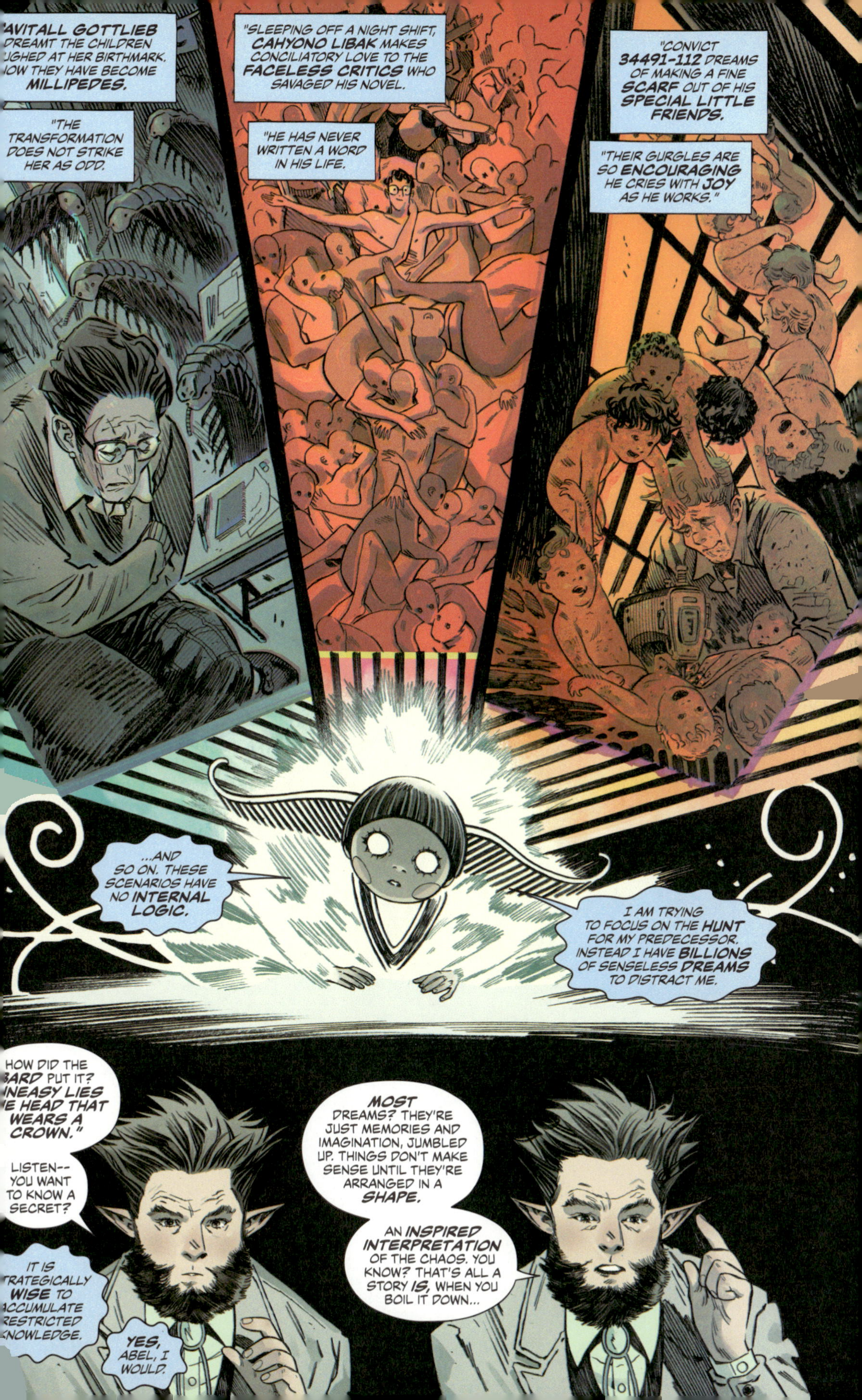
AVITALL GOTTLIEB DREAMT THE CHILDREN UGHED AT HER BIRTHMARK. NOW THEY HAVE BECOME MILLIPEDES.
"THE TRANSFORMATION DOES NOT STRIKE HER AS ODD.
"SLEEPING OFF A NIGHT SHIFT, CAHYONO LIBAK MAKES CONCILIATORY LOVE TO THE FACELESS CRITICS WHO SAVAGED HIS NOVEL.
"HE HAS NEVER WRITTEN A WORD IN HIS LIFE.
"CONVICT 34491-112 DREAMS OF MAKING A FINE SCARF OUT OF HIS SPECIAL LITTLE FRIENDS.
"THEIR GURGLES ARE SO ENCOURAGING HE CRIES WITH JOY AS HE WORKS."
...AND SO ON. THESE SCENARIOS HAVE NO INTERNAL LOGIC.
I AM TRYING TO FOCUS ON THE HUNT FOR MY PREDECESSOR. INSTEAD I HAVE BILLIONS OF SENSELESS DREAMS TO DISTRACT ME.
HOW DID THE BARD PUT IT? "UNEASY LIES THE HEAD THAT WEARS A CROWN."
LISTEN-- YOU WANT TO KNOW A SECRET?
IT IS STRATEGICALLY WISE TO ACCUMULATE RESTRICTED KNOWLEDGE.
YES, ABEL, I WOULD.
MOST DREAMS? THEY'RE JUST MEMORIES AND IMAGINATION, JUMBLED UP. THINGS DON'T MAKE SENSE UNTIL THEY'RE ARRANGED IN A SHAPE.
AN INSPIRED INTERPRETATION OF THE CHAOS. YOU KNOW? THAT'S ALL A STORY IS, WHEN YOU BOIL IT DOWN...

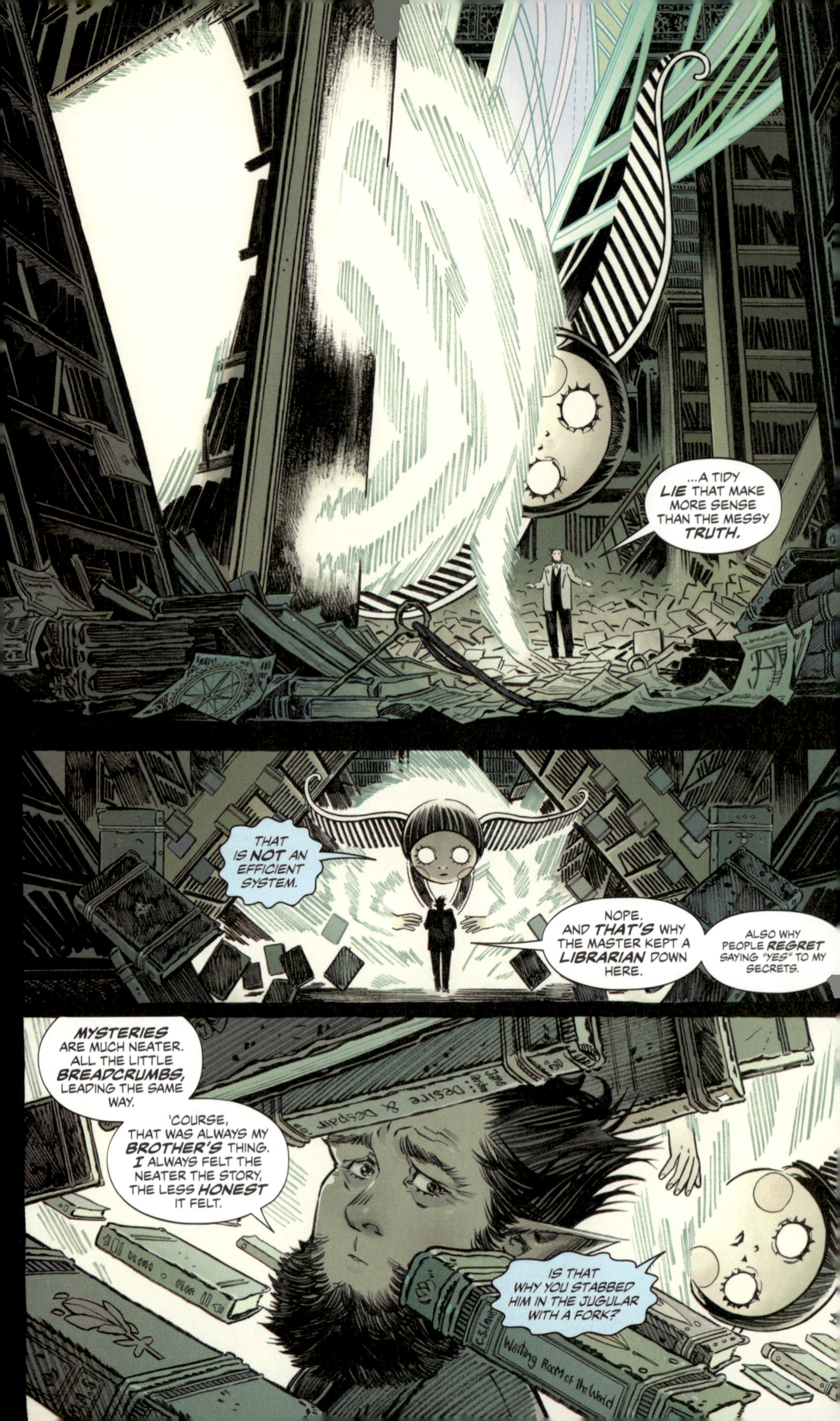

...A TIDY LIE THAT MAKE MORE SENSE THAN THE MESSY TRUTH.
THAT IS NOT AN EFFICIENT SYSTEM.
NOPE. AND THAT'S WHY THE MASTER KEPT A LIBRARIAN DOWN HERE.
ALSO WHY PEOPLE REGRET SAYING "YES" TO MY SECRETS.
MYSTERIES ARE MUCH NEATER. ALL THE LITTLE BREADCRUMBS, LEADING THE SAME WAY.
'COURSE, THAT WAS ALWAYS MY BROTHER'S THING. I ALWAYS FELT THE NEATER THE STORY, THE LESS HONEST IT FELT.
IS THAT WHY YOU STABBED HIM IN THE JUGULAR WITH A FORK?
Desire & Despair
Waiting Room of the World

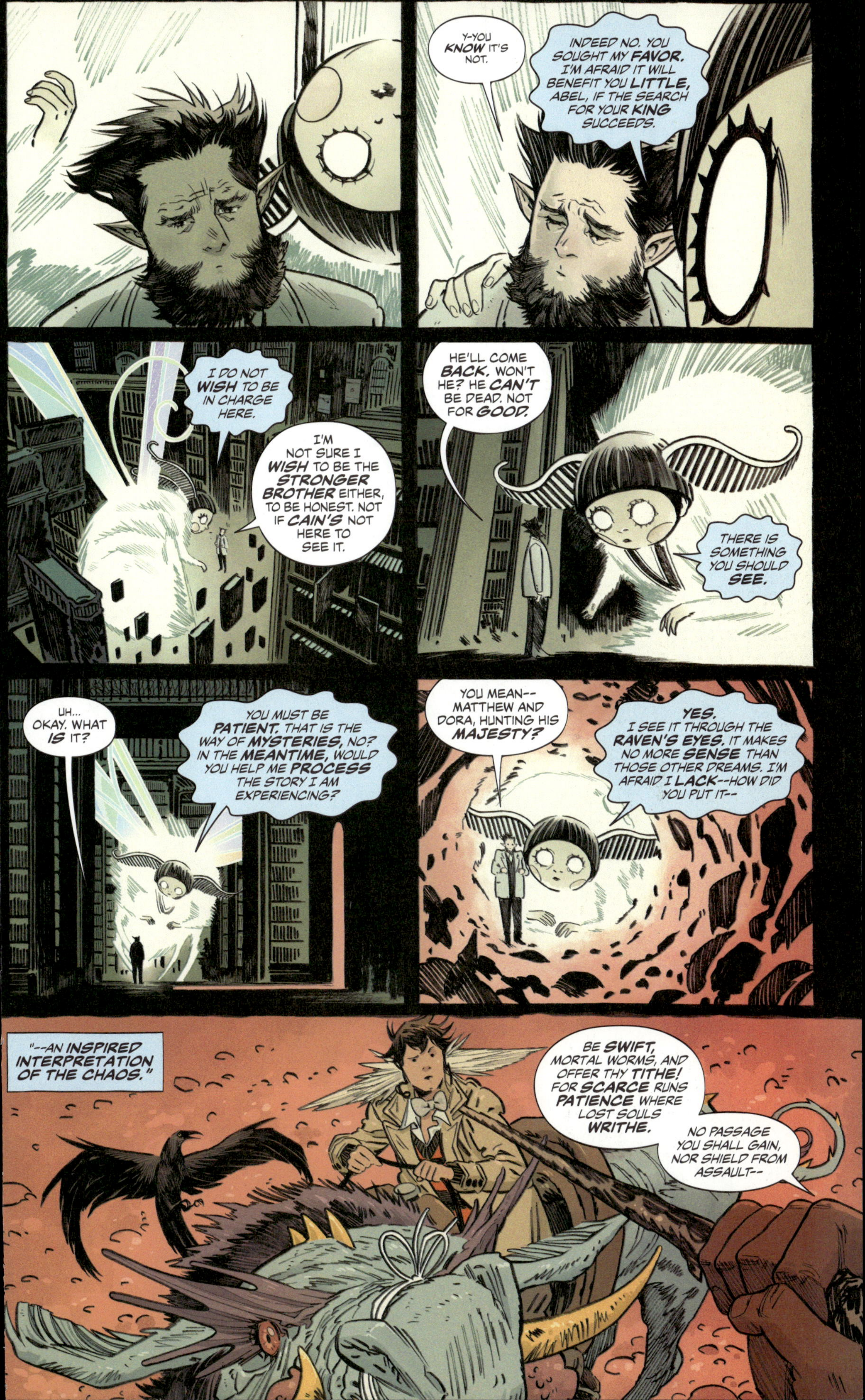
Y-YOU KNOW IT'S NOT.
INDEED NO. YOU SOUGHT MY FAVOR. I'M AFRAID IT WILL BENEFIT YOU LITTLE, ABEL, IF THE SEARCH FOR YOUR KING SUCCEEDS.
I DO NOT WISH TO BE IN CHARGE HERE.
I'M NOT SURE I WISH TO BE THE STRONGER BROTHER EITHER, TO BE HONEST. NOT IF CAIN'S NOT HERE TO SEE IT.
HE'LL COME BACK. WON'T HE? HE CAN'T BE DEAD. NOT FOR GOOD.
THERE IS SOMETHING YOU SHOULD SEE.
UH... OKAY. WHAT IS IT?
YOU MUST BE PATIENT. THAT IS THE WAY OF MYSTERIES, NO? IN THE MEANTIME, WOULD YOU HELP ME PROCESS THE STORY I AM EXPERIENCING?
YOU MEAN-- MATTHEW AND DORA, HUNTING HIS MAJESTY?
YES. I SEE IT THROUGH THE RAVEN'S EYES. IT MAKES NO MORE SENSE THAN THOSE OTHER DREAMS. I'M AFRAID I LACK--HOW DID YOU PUT IT--
"--AN INSPIRED INTERPRETATION OF THE CHAOS."
BE SWIFT, MORTAL WORMS, AND OFFER THY TITHE! FOR SCARCE RUNS PATIENCE WHERE LOST SOULS WRITHE.
NO PASSAGE YOU SHALL GAIN, NOR SHIELD FROM ASSAULT--

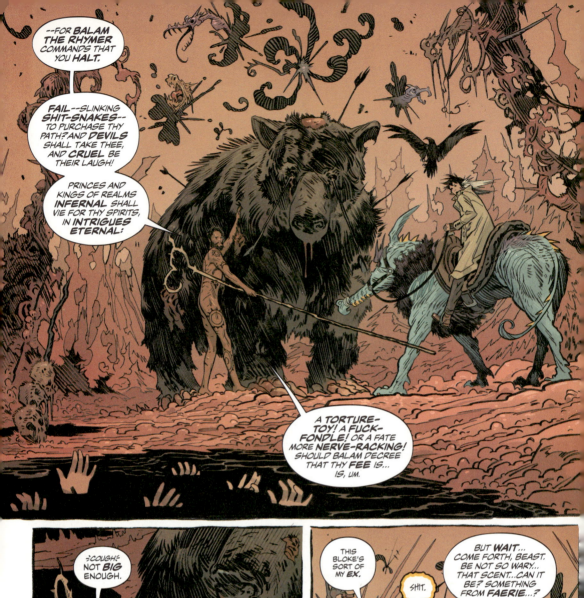

--FOR **BALAM** THE **RHYMER** COMMANDS THAT YOU **HALT.**

FAIL--SLINKING **SHIT-SNAKES**--TO PURCHASE THY PATH?AND **DEVILS** SHALL TAKE THEE, AND **CRUEL** BE THEIR LAUGH!

PRINCES AND KINGS OF REALMS **INFERNAL** SHALL VIE FOR THY SPIRITS, IN **INTRIGUES ETERNAL**:

A **TORTURE-TOY!** A **FUCK-FONDLE!** OR A FATE MORE **NERVE-RACKING!** SHOULD BALAM DECREE THAT THY **FEE** IS... IS, UM.

÷COUGH÷ NOT **BIG** ENOUGH.

YOU AIN'T EXACTLY A **NATURAL** POET, ARE YA?

HE CAN'T **SEE** US. YOU'RE GONNA HAVE TO DO THE **TALKING** HERE, MATTHEW.

THIS BLOKE'S SORT OF MY **EX.**

SHIT.

BUT **WAIT**... COME FORTH, BEAST. BE NOT SO WARY... THAT SCENT...CAN IT BE? SOMETHING FROM **FAERIE**...?

THOSE LANDS OWE US TRIBUTE--THOUGH NO DEMON MAY **VISIT**...OHHH... BY THE **FURIES**... TELL ME: WHAT **IS** IT?

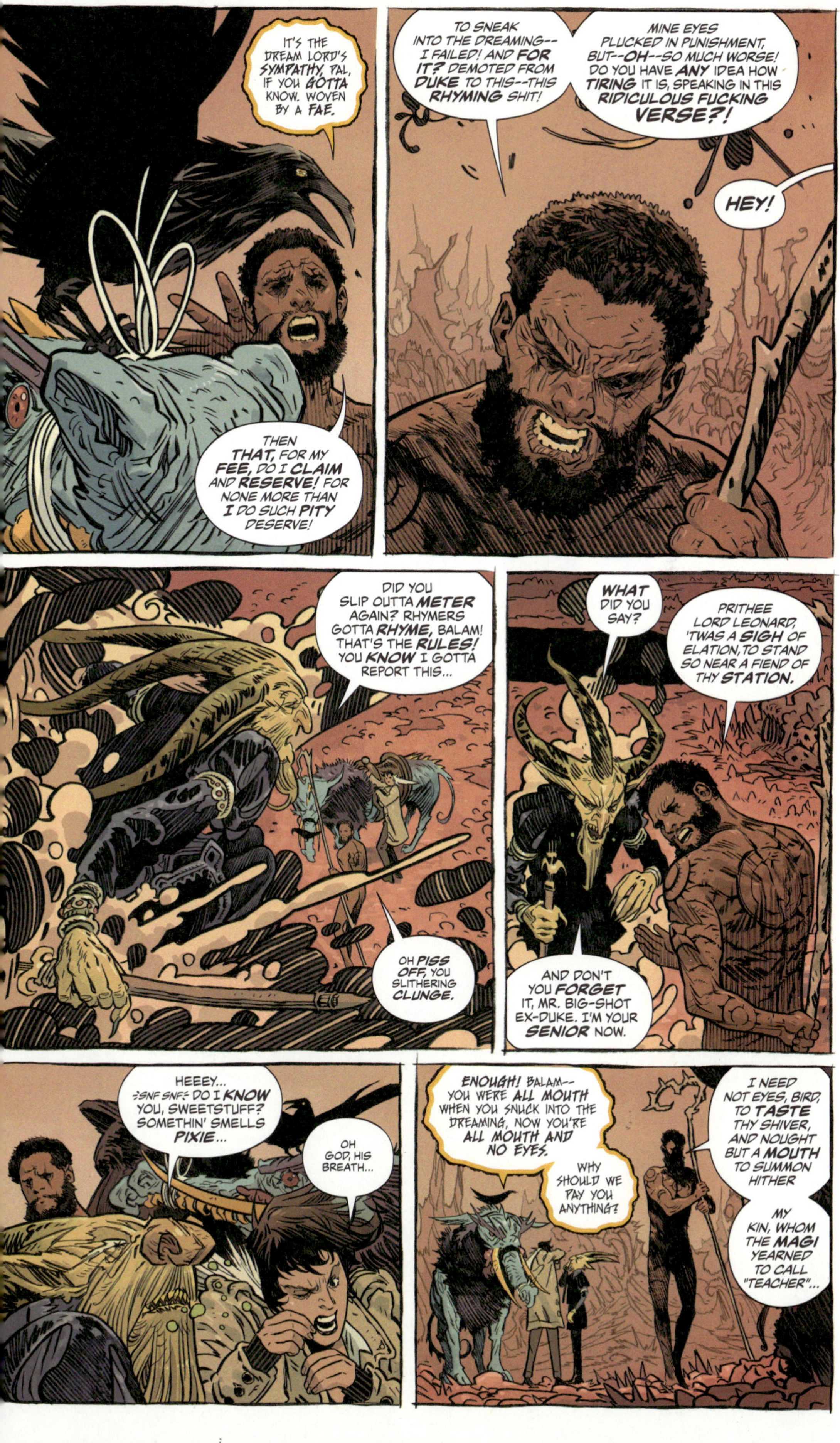

IT'S THE DREAM LORD'S SYMPATHY, PAL, IF YOU GOTTA KNOW. WOVEN BY A FAE.
THEN THAT, FOR MY FEE, DO I CLAIM AND RESERVE! FOR NONE MORE THAN I DO SUCH PITY DESERVE!
TO SNEAK INTO THE DREAMING-- I FAILED! AND FOR IT? DEMOTED FROM DUKE TO THIS--THIS RHYMING SHIT!
MINE EYES PLUCKED IN PUNISHMENT, BUT--OH--SO MUCH WORSE! DO YOU HAVE ANY IDEA HOW TIRING IT IS, SPEAKING IN THIS RIDICULOUS FUCKING VERSE?!
HEY!
DID YOU SLIP OUTTA METER AGAIN? RHYMERS GOTTA RHYME, BALAM! THAT'S THE RULES! YOU KNOW I GOTTA REPORT THIS...
OH PISS OFF, YOU SLITHERING CLUNGE.
WHAT DID YOU SAY?
PRITHEE LORD LEONARD, 'TWAS A SIGH OF ELATION, TO STAND SO NEAR A FIEND OF THY STATION.
AND DON'T YOU FORGET IT, MR. BIG-SHOT EX-DUKE. I'M YOUR SENIOR NOW.
HEEEY... SNF SNF DO I KNOW YOU, SWEETSTUFF? SOMETHIN' SMELLS PIXIE...
OH GOD, HIS BREATH...
ENOUGH! BALAM-- YOU WERE ALL MOUTH WHEN YOU SNUCK INTO THE DREAMING, NOW YOU'RE ALL MOUTH AND NO EYES.
WHY SHOULD WE PAY YOU ANYTHING?
I NEED NOT EYES, BIRD, TO TASTE THY SHIVER, AND NOUGHT BUT A MOUTH TO SUMMON HITHER
MY KIN, WHOM THE MAGI YEARNED TO CALL "TEACHER"...

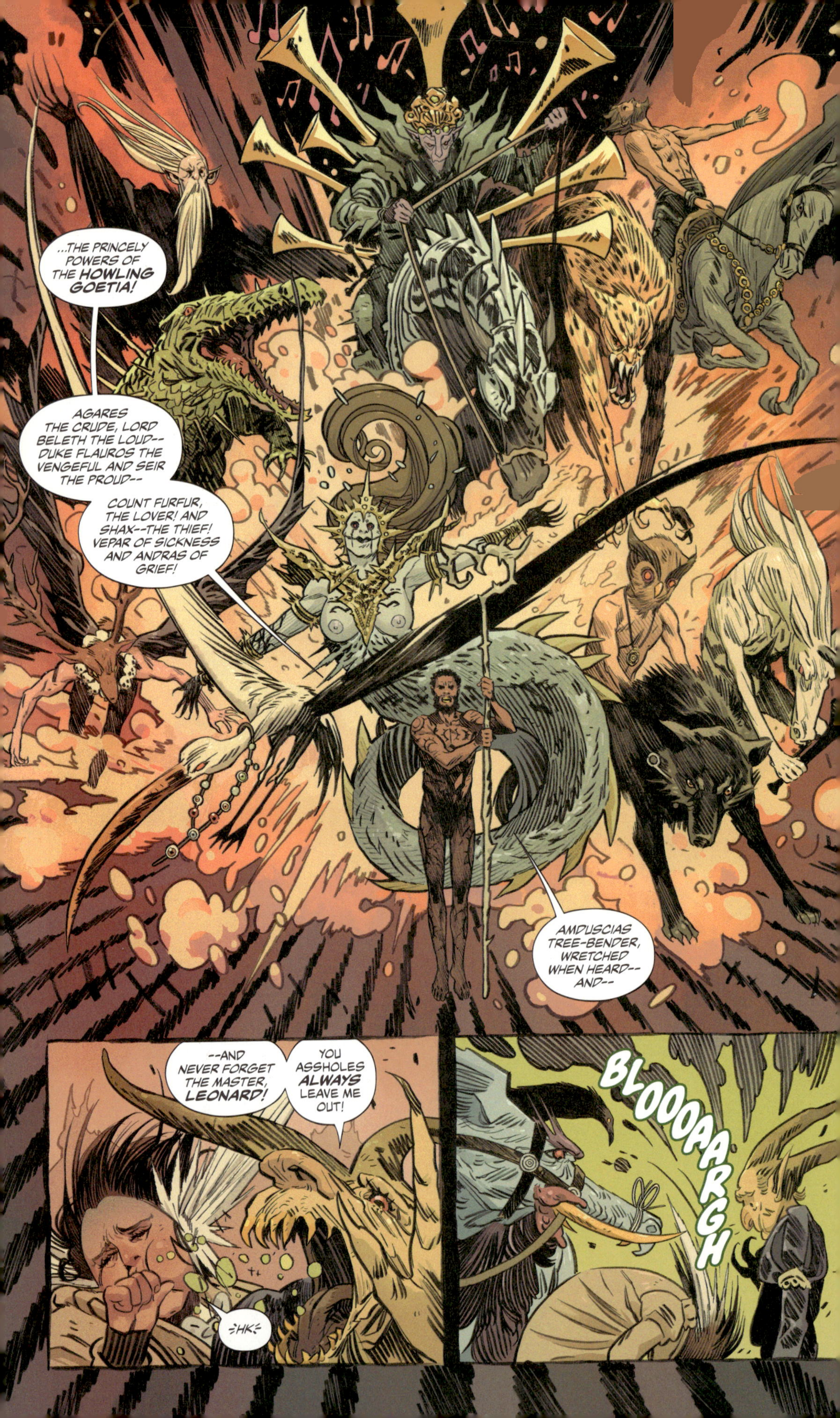
...THE PRINCELY POWERS OF THE **HOWLING GOETIA!**
AGARES THE CRUDE, LORD BELETH THE LOUD-- DUKE FLAUROS THE VENGEFUL AND SEIR THE PROUD--
COUNT FURFUR, THE LOVER! AND SHAX--THE THIEF! VEPAR OF SICKNESS AND ANDRAS OF GRIEF!
AMDUSCIAS TREE-BENDER, WRETCHED WHEN HEARD-- AND--
--AND NEVER FORGET THE MASTER, **LEONARD!**
YOU ASSHOLES **ALWAYS** LEAVE ME OUT!
HK
BLOOOAARGH

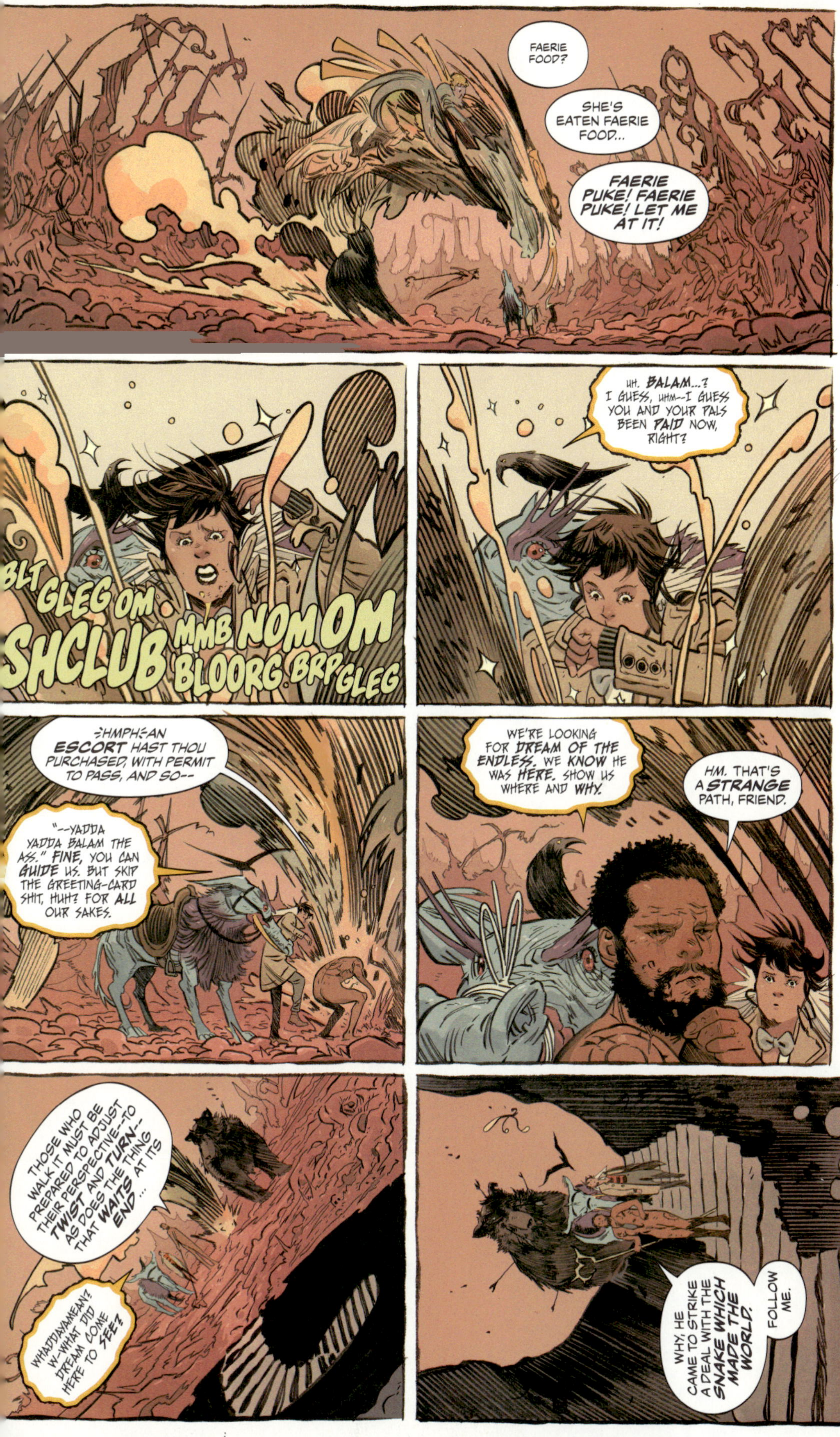

FAERIE FOOD?
SHE'S EATEN FAERIE FOOD...
FAERIE PUKE! FAERIE PUKE! LET ME AT IT!
BLT GLEG OM SHCLUB MMB NOM OM BLOORG BRP GLEG
UH. BALAM...? I GUESS, UHM--I GUESS YOU AND YOUR PALS BEEN PAID NOW, RIGHT?
-HMPH- AN ESCORT HAST THOU PURCHASED, WITH PERMIT TO PASS, AND SO--
"--YADDA YADDA BALAM THE ASS." FINE, YOU CAN GUIDE US. BUT SKIP THE GREETING-CARD SHIT, HUH? FOR ALL OUR SAKES.
WE'RE LOOKING FOR DREAM OF THE ENDLESS. WE KNOW HE WAS HERE. SHOW US WHERE AND WHY.
HM. THAT'S A STRANGE PATH, FRIEND.
THOSE WHO WALK IT MUST BE PREPARED TO ADJUST THEIR PERSPECTIVE--TO TWIST AND TURN--AS DOES THE THING THAT WAITS AT ITS END...
WHADDAYAMEAN? W-WHAT DID DREAM COME HERE TO SEE?
WHY, HE CAME TO STRIKE A DEAL WITH THE SNAKE WHICH MADE THE WORLD.
FOLLOW ME.

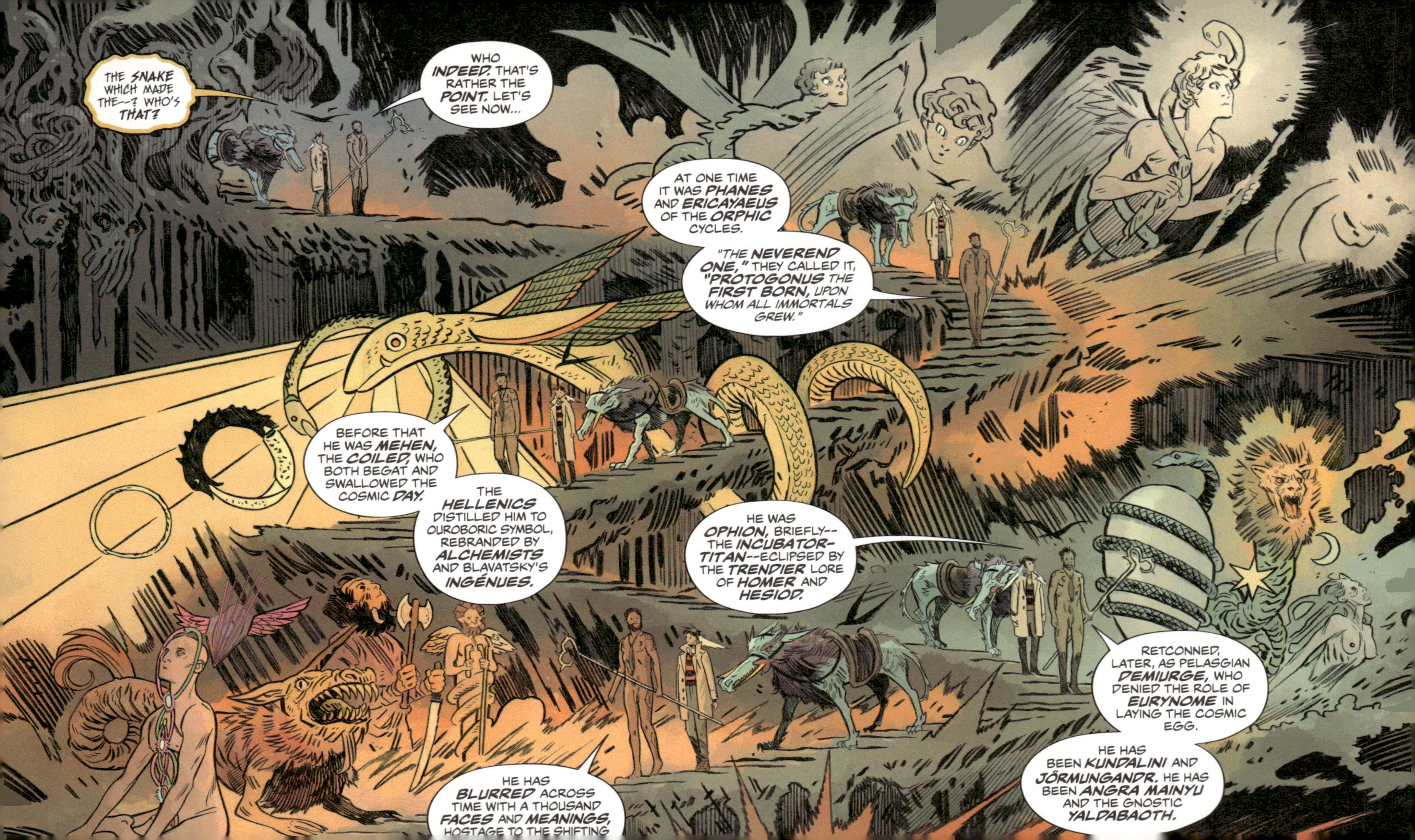
THE SNAKE WHICH MADE THE--? WHO'S THAT?
WHO INDEED. THAT'S RATHER THE POINT. LET'S SEE NOW...
AT ONE TIME IT WAS PHANES AND ERICAYAEUS OF THE ORPHIC CYCLES.
"THE NEVEREND ONE," THEY CALLED IT, "PROTOGONUS THE FIRST BORN, UPON WHOM ALL IMMORTALS GREW."
BEFORE THAT HE WAS MEHEN, THE COILED, WHO BOTH BEGAT AND SWALLOWED THE COSMIC DAY.
THE HELLENICS DISTILLED HIM TO OUROBORIC SYMBOL, REBRANDED BY ALCHEMISTS AND BLAVATSKY'S INGÉNUES.
HE WAS OPHION, BRIEFLY--THE INCUBATOR-TITAN--ECLIPSED BY THE TRENDIER LORE OF HOMER AND HESIOD.
RETCONNED, LATER, AS PELASGIAN DEMIURGE, WHO DENIED THE ROLE OF EURYNOME IN LAYING THE COSMIC EGG.
HE HAS BEEN KUNDALINI AND JÖRMUNGANDR. HE HAS BEEN ANGRA MAINYU AND THE GNOSTIC YALDABAOTH.
HE HAS BLURRED ACROSS TIME WITH A THOUSAND FACES AND MEANINGS, HOSTAGE TO THE SHIFTING

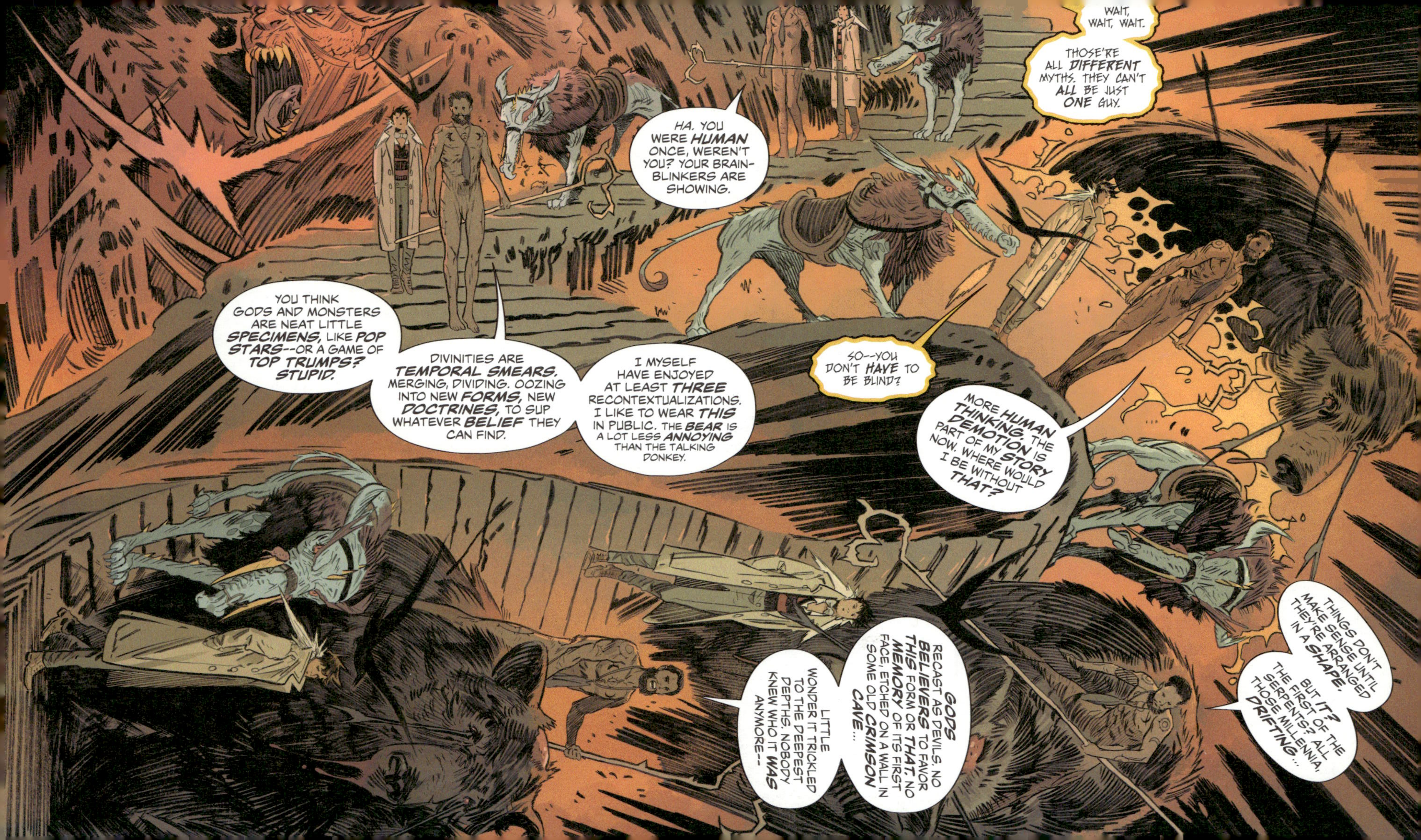
WAIT, WAIT, WAIT.
THOSE'RE ALL **DIFFERENT** MYTHS. THEY CAN'T **ALL** BE JUST **ONE** GUY.
HA. YOU WERE **HUMAN** ONCE, WEREN'T YOU? YOUR BRAIN-BLINKERS ARE SHOWING.
YOU THINK GODS AND MONSTERS ARE NEAT LITTLE **SPECIMENS,** LIKE **POP STARS**--OR A GAME OF **TOP TRUMPS? STUPID.**
DIVINITIES ARE **TEMPORAL SMEARS.** MERGING, DIVIDING. OOZING INTO NEW **FORMS,** NEW **DOCTRINES,** TO SUP WHATEVER **BELIEF** THEY CAN FIND.
I MYSELF HAVE ENJOYED AT LEAST **THREE** RECONTEXTUALIZATIONS. I LIKE TO WEAR **THIS** IN PUBLIC. THE **BEAR** IS A LOT LESS **ANNOYING** THAN THE TALKING DONKEY.
SO--YOU DON'T **HAVE** TO BE BLIND?
MORE **HUMAN THINKING. DEMOTION** IS PART OF MY **STORY** NOW. WHERE WOULD I BE WITHOUT **THAT?**
THINGS DON'T MAKE SENSE UNTIL THEY'RE ARRANGED IN A **SHAPE.**
BUT **IT?** THE FIRST OF THE SERPENTS? ALL THOSE MILLENNIA, **DRIFTING**...
GODS RECAST AS DEVILS. NO **BELIEVERS** TO FAVOR **THIS** FORM OR **THAT.** NO **MEMORY** OF ITS FIRST FACE, ETCHED ON A WALL IN SOME OLD **CRIMSON CAVE**...
LITTLE WONDER IT TRICKLED TO THE DEEPEST DEPTHS. NOBODY KNEW WHO IT **WAS** ANYMORE--

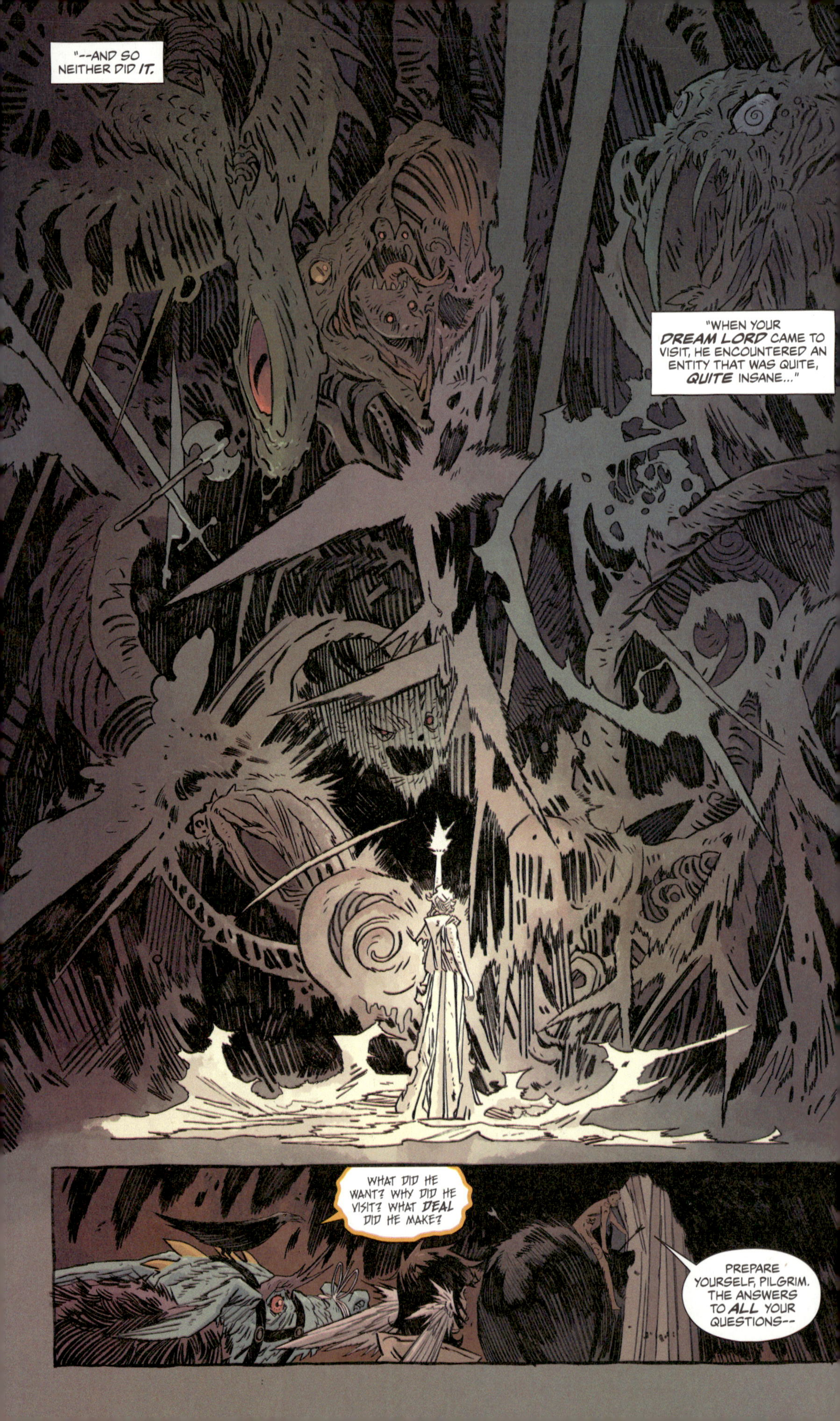
"--AND SO NEITHER DID *IT*.
"WHEN YOUR *DREAM LORD* CAME TO VISIT, HE ENCOUNTERED AN ENTITY THAT WAS QUITE, *QUITE* INSANE..."
WHAT DID HE WANT? WHY DID HE VISIT? WHAT *DEAL* DID HE MAKE?
PREPARE YOURSELF, PILGRIM. THE ANSWERS TO *ALL* YOUR QUESTIONS--

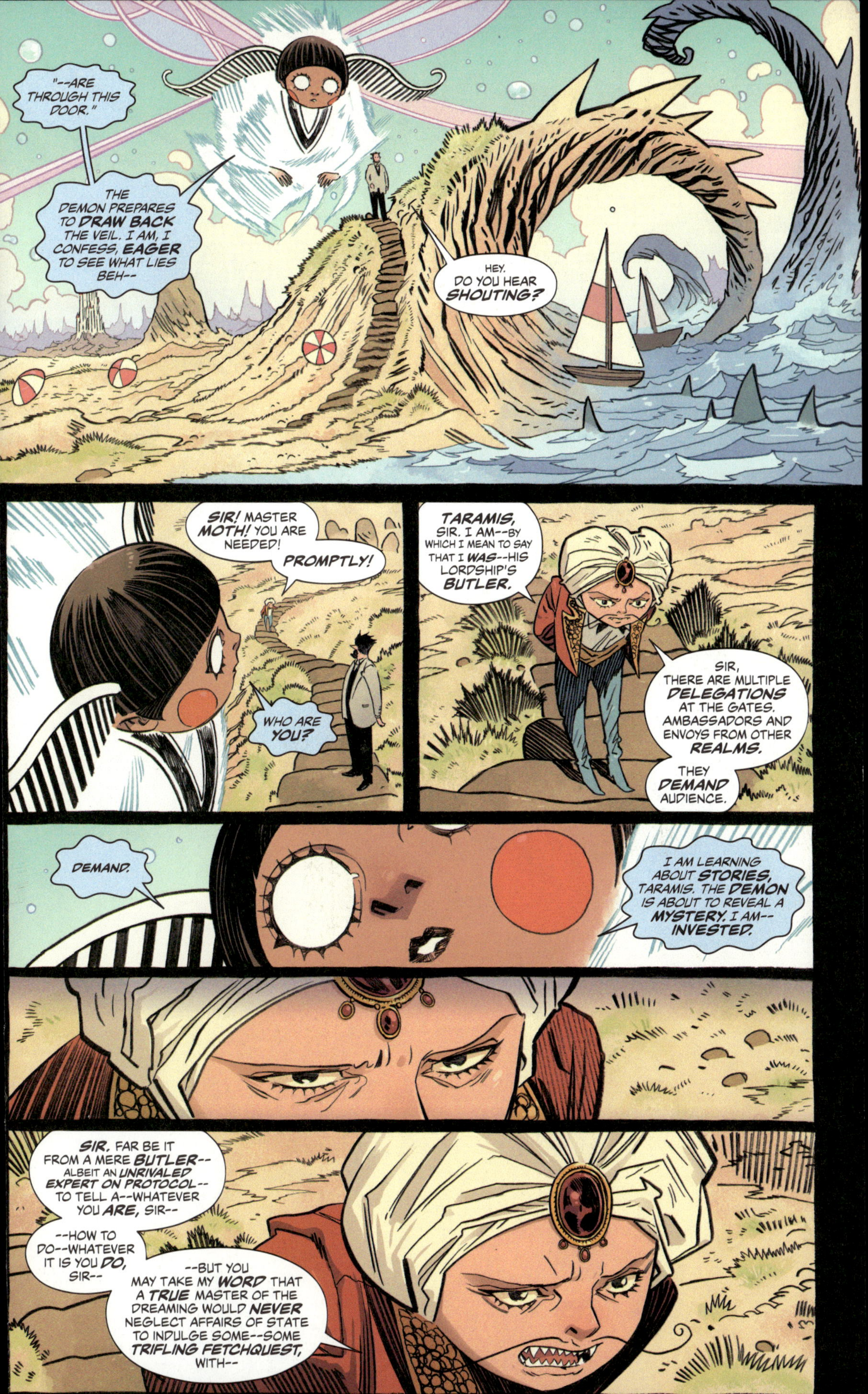
"--ARE THROUGH THIS DOOR."
THE DEMON PREPARES TO DRAW BACK THE VEIL. I AM, I CONFESS, EAGER TO SEE WHAT LIES BEH--
HEY. DO YOU HEAR SHOUTING?
SIR! MASTER MOTH! YOU ARE NEEDED!
PROMPTLY!
WHO ARE YOU?
TARAMIS, SIR. I AM--BY WHICH I MEAN TO SAY THAT I WAS--HIS LORDSHIP'S BUTLER.
SIR, THERE ARE MULTIPLE DELEGATIONS AT THE GATES. AMBASSADORS AND ENVOYS FROM OTHER REALMS.
THEY DEMAND AUDIENCE.
DEMAND.
I AM LEARNING ABOUT STORIES, TARAMIS. THE DEMON IS ABOUT TO REVEAL A MYSTERY. I AM--INVESTED.
SIR. FAR BE IT FROM A MERE BUTLER--ALBEIT AN UNRIVALED EXPERT ON PROTOCOL--TO TELL A--WHATEVER YOU ARE, SIR--
--HOW TO DO--WHATEVER IT IS YOU DO, SIR--
--BUT YOU MAY TAKE MY WORD THAT A TRUE MASTER OF THE DREAMING WOULD NEVER NEGLECT AFFAIRS OF STATE TO INDULGE SOME--SOME TRIFLING FETCHQUEST, WITH--

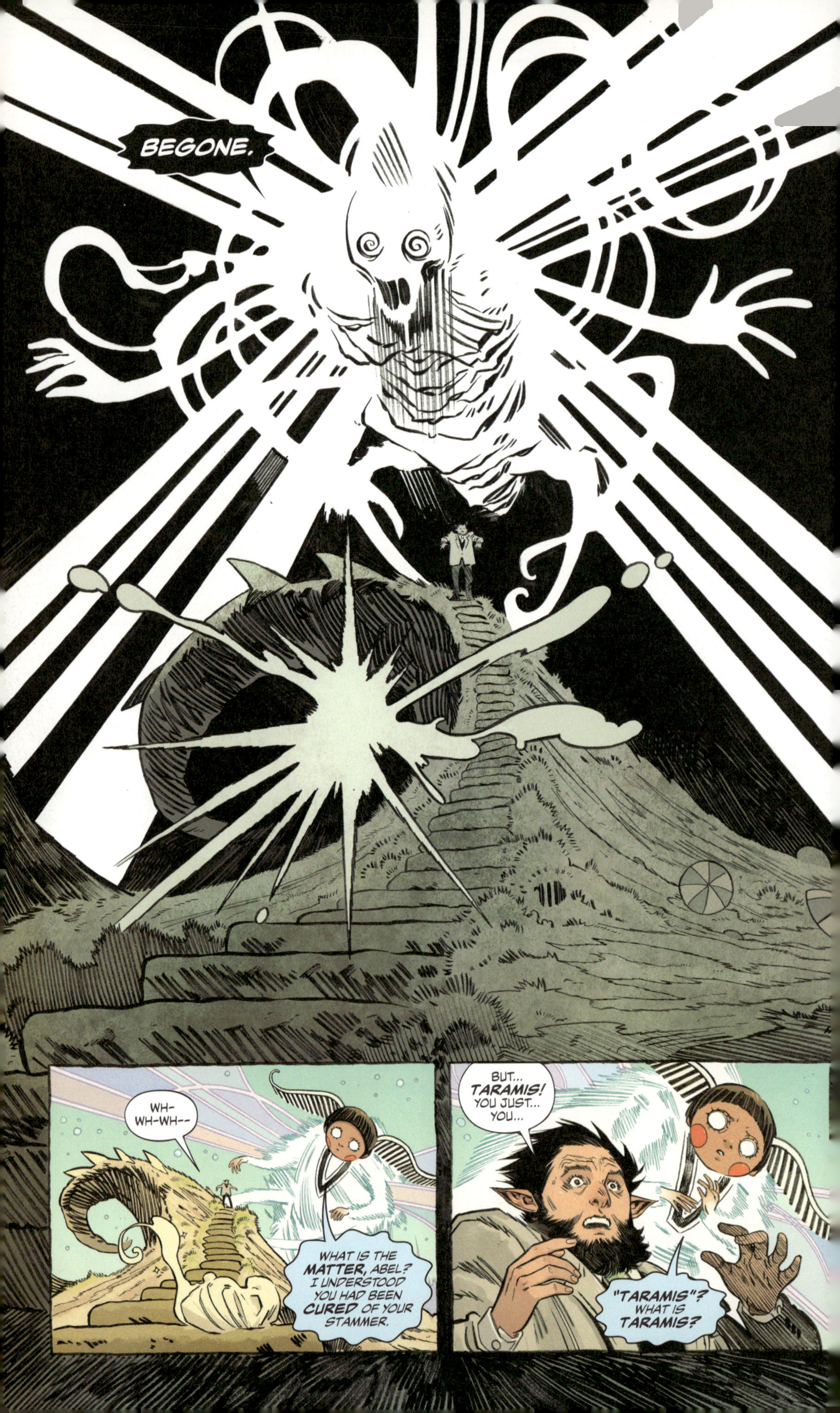
BEGONE.
WH- WH-WH--
WHAT IS THE MATTER, ABEL? I UNDERSTOOD YOU HAD BEEN CURED OF YOUR STAMMER.
BUT... TARAMIS! YOU JUST... YOU...
"TARAMIS"? WHAT IS TARAMIS?

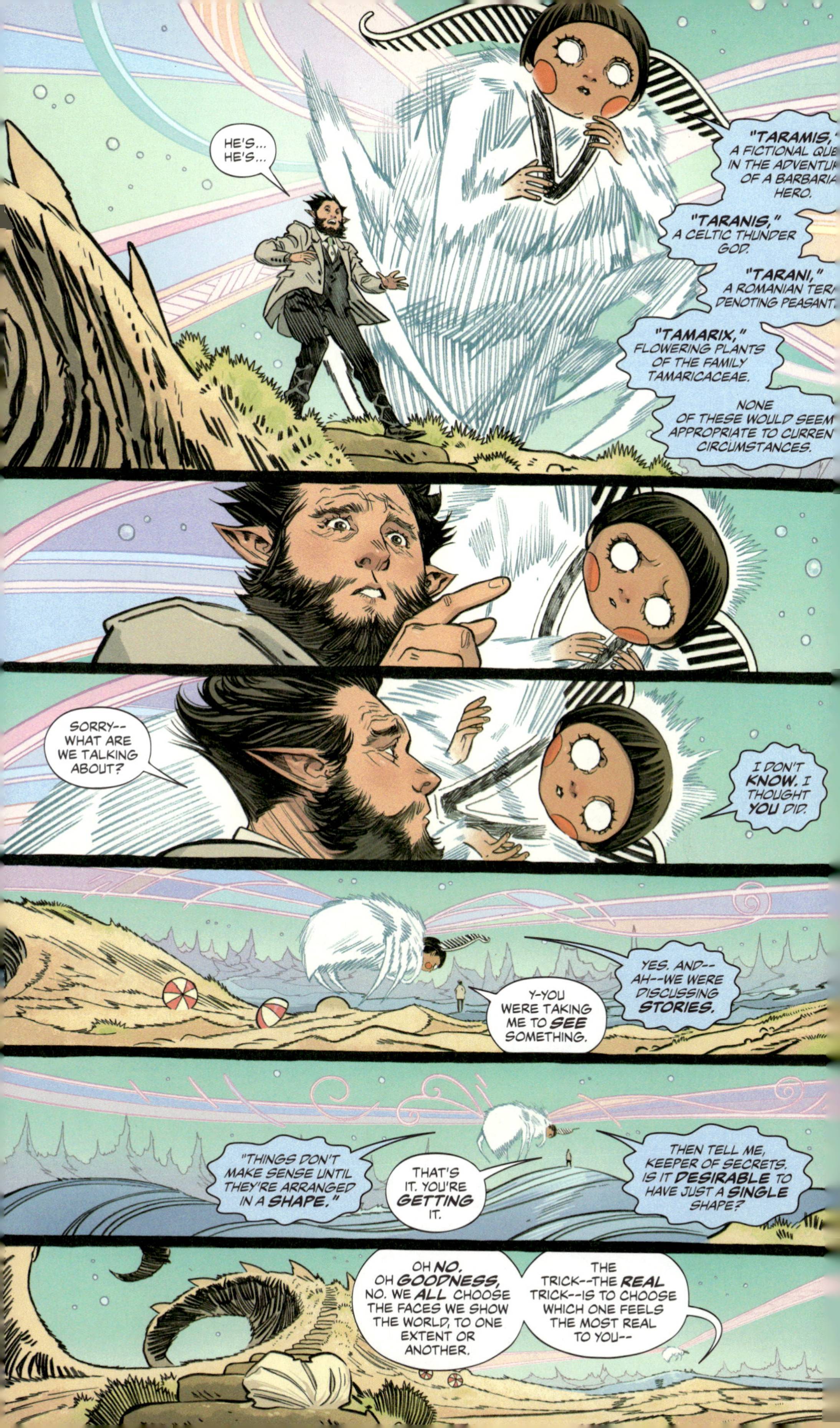

HE'S... HE'S...
"TARAMIS,"
A FICTIONAL QUE
IN THE ADVENTUR
OF A BARBARIA
HERO.
"TARANIS," A CELTIC THUNDER GOD.
"TARANI," A ROMANIAN TER
DENOTING PEASANT
"TAMARIX," FLOWERING PLANTS OF THE FAMILY TAMARICACEAE.
NONE OF THESE WOULD SEEM
APPROPRIATE TO CURREN
CIRCUMSTANCES.
SORRY-- WHAT ARE WE TALKING ABOUT?
I DON'T KNOW. I THOUGHT YOU DID.
YES. AND-- AH--WE WERE DISCUSSING STORIES.
Y-YOU WERE TAKING ME TO SEE SOMETHING.
"THINGS DON'T MAKE SENSE UNTIL THEY'RE ARRANGED IN A SHAPE."
THAT'S IT. YOU'RE GETTING IT.
THEN TELL ME, KEEPER OF SECRETS. IS IT DESIRABLE TO HAVE JUST A SINGLE SHAPE?
OH NO. OH GOODNESS, NO. WE ALL CHOOSE THE FACES WE SHOW THE WORLD, TO ONE EXTENT OR ANOTHER.
THE TRICK--THE REAL TRICK--IS TO CHOOSE WHICH ONE FEELS THE MOST REAL TO YOU--

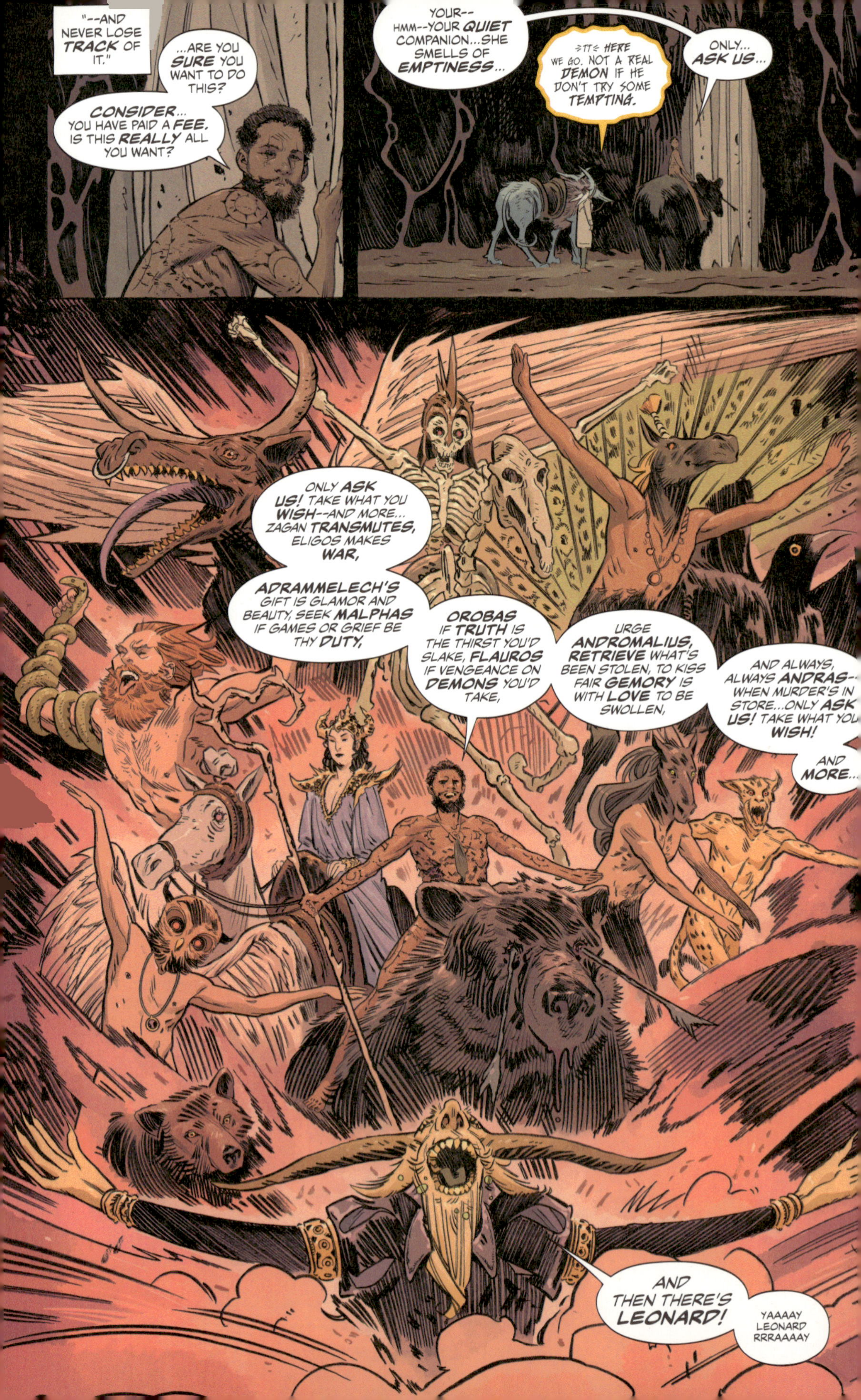
"--AND NEVER LOSE TRACK OF IT."
...ARE YOU SURE YOU WANT TO DO THIS?
CONSIDER... YOU HAVE PAID A FEE. IS THIS REALLY ALL YOU WANT?
YOUR-- HMM--YOUR QUIET COMPANION...SHE SMELLS OF EMPTINESS...
ONLY... ASK US...
HERE WE GO. NOT A REAL DEMON IF HE DON'T TRY SOME TEMPTING.
ONLY ASK US! TAKE WHAT YOU WISH--AND MORE... ZAGAN TRANSMUTES, ELIGOS MAKES WAR,
ADRAMMELECH'S GIFT IS GLAMOR AND BEAUTY, SEEK MALPHAS IF GAMES OR GRIEF BE THY DUTY,
OROBAS IF TRUTH IS THE THIRST YOU'D SLAKE, FLAUROS IF VENGEANCE ON DEMONS YOU'D TAKE,
URGE ANDROMALIUS, RETRIEVE WHAT'S BEEN STOLEN, TO KISS FAIR GEMORY IS WITH LOVE TO BE SWOLLEN,
AND ALWAYS, ALWAYS ANDRAS-- WHEN MURDER'S IN STORE...ONLY ASK US! TAKE WHAT YOU WISH!
AND MORE...
AND THEN THERE'S LEONARD!
YAAAAAY LEONARD RRRAAAAAY

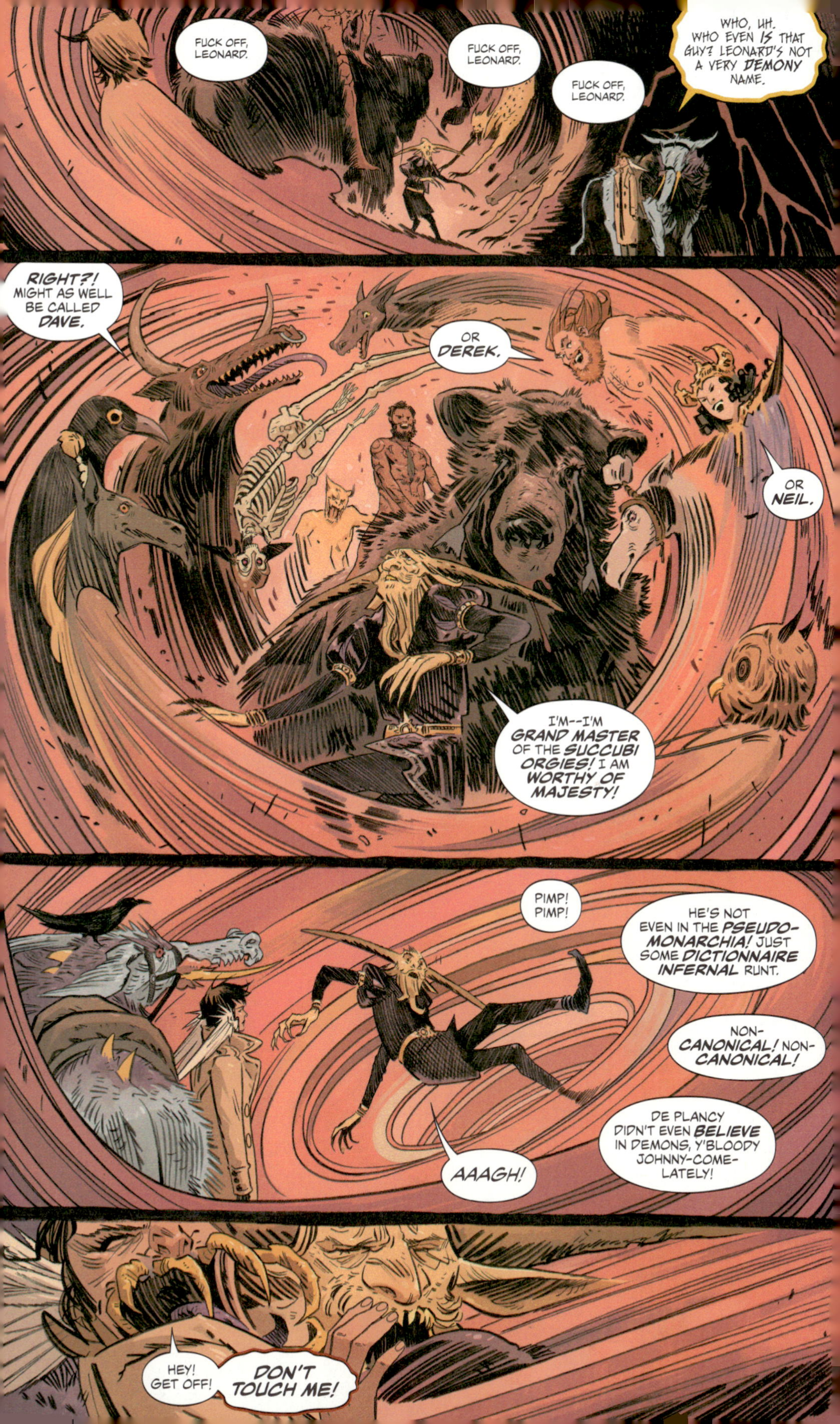

FUCK OFF, LEONARD.
FUCK OFF, LEONARD.
FUCK OFF, LEONARD.
WHO, UH. WHO EVEN IS THAT GUY? LEONARD'S NOT A VERY DEMONY NAME.
RIGHT?! MIGHT AS WELL BE CALLED DAVE.
OR DEREK.
OR NEIL.
I'M--I'M GRAND MASTER OF THE SUCCUBI ORGIES! I AM WORTHY OF MAJESTY!
PIMP! PIMP!
HE'S NOT EVEN IN THE PSEUDO-MONARCHIA! JUST SOME DICTIONNAIRE INFERNAL RUNT.
NON-CANONICAL! NON-CANONICAL!
DE PLANCY DIDN'T EVEN BELIEVE IN DEMONS, Y'BLOODY JOHNNY-COME-LATELY!
AAAGH!
HEY! GET OFF!
DON'T TOUCH ME!

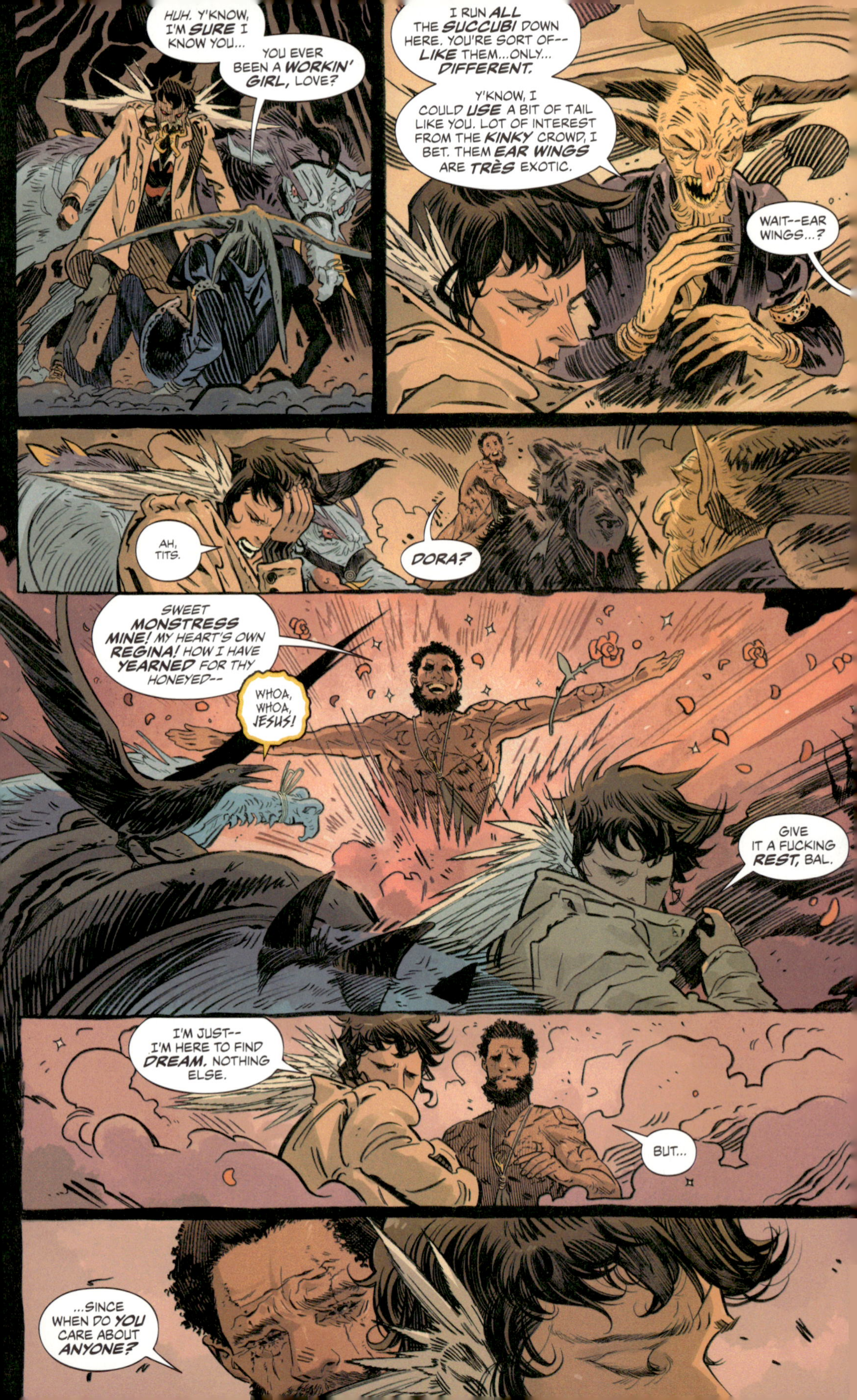
HUH. Y'KNOW, I'M SURE I KNOW YOU...
YOU EVER BEEN A WORKIN' GIRL, LOVE?
I RUN ALL THE SUCCUBI DOWN HERE. YOU'RE SORT OF-- LIKE THEM...ONLY... DIFFERENT.
Y'KNOW, I COULD USE A BIT OF TAIL LIKE YOU. LOT OF INTEREST FROM THE KINKY CROWD, I BET. THEM EAR WINGS ARE TRÈS EXOTIC.
WAIT--EAR WINGS...?
AH, TITS.
DORA?
SWEET MONSTRESS MINE! MY HEART'S OWN REGINA! HOW I HAVE YEARNED FOR THY HONEYED--
WHOA, WHOA, JESUS!
GIVE IT A FUCKING REST, BAL.
I'M JUST-- I'M HERE TO FIND DREAM. NOTHING ELSE.
BUT...
...SINCE WHEN DO YOU CARE ABOUT ANYONE?

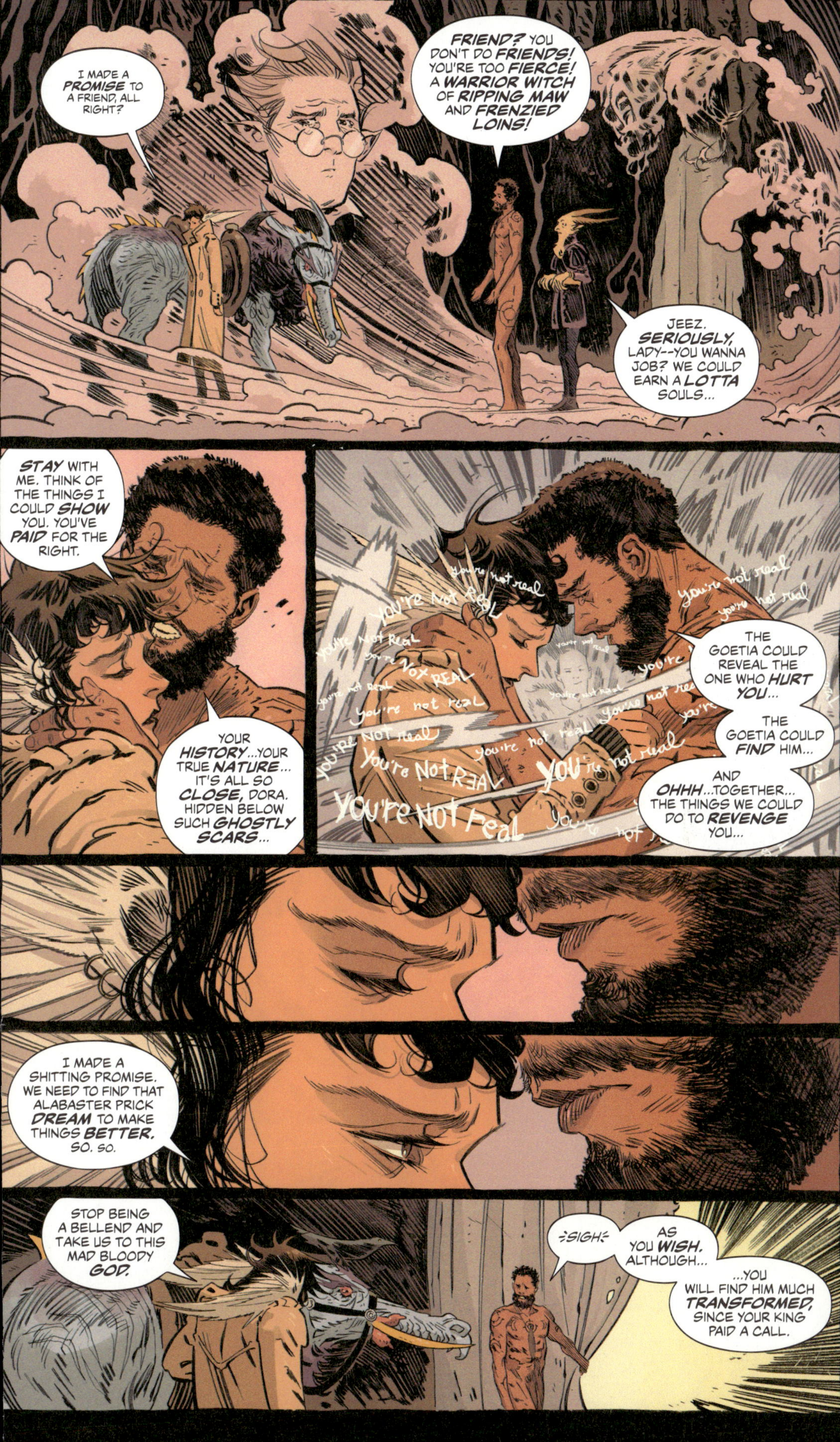
I MADE A PROMISE TO A FRIEND, ALL RIGHT?
FRIEND? YOU DON'T DO FRIENDS! YOU'RE TOO FIERCE! A WARRIOR WITCH OF RIPPING MAW AND FRENZIED LOINS!
JEEZ. SERIOUSLY, LADY--YOU WANNA JOB? WE COULD EARN A LOTTA SOULS...
STAY WITH ME. THINK OF THE THINGS I COULD SHOW YOU. YOU'VE PAID FOR THE RIGHT.
YOUR HISTORY...YOUR TRUE NATURE... IT'S ALL SO CLOSE, DORA. HIDDEN BELOW SUCH GHOSTLY SCARS...
You're Not Real
You're Not real
THE GOETIA COULD REVEAL THE ONE WHO HURT YOU...
THE GOETIA COULD FIND HIM...
OHHH...TOGETHER... THE THINGS WE COULD DO TO REVENGE YOU...
I MADE A SHITTING PROMISE. WE NEED TO FIND THAT ALABASTER PRICK DREAM TO MAKE THINGS BETTER. SO. SO.
STOP BEING A BELLEND AND TAKE US TO THIS MAD BLOODY GOD.
-SIGH-
AS YOU WISH, ALTHOUGH...
...YOU WILL FIND HIM MUCH TRANSFORMED, SINCE YOUR KING PAID A CALL.

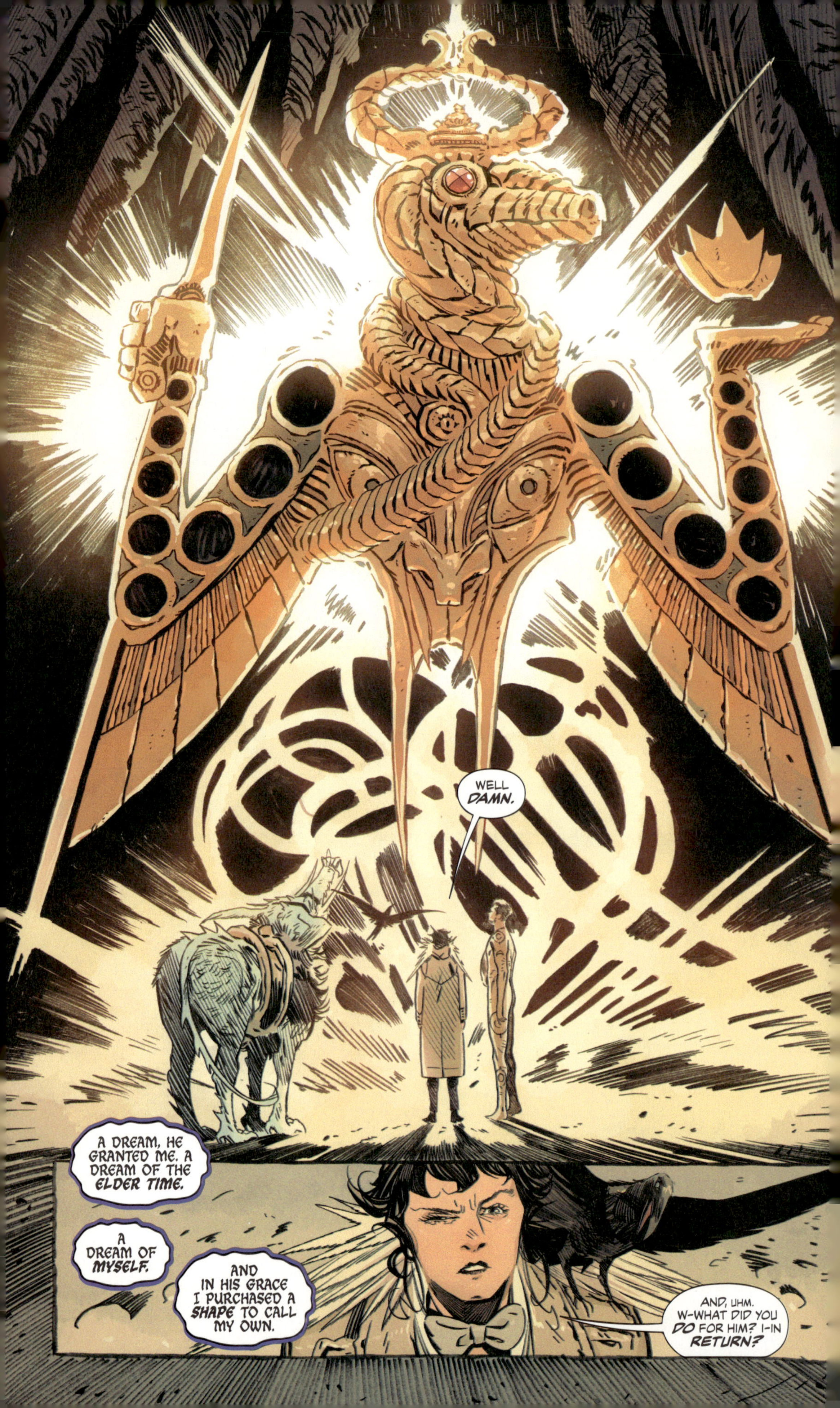
WELL DAMN.
A DREAM, HE GRANTED ME. A DREAM OF THE ELDER TIME.
A DREAM OF MYSELF.
AND IN HIS GRACE I PURCHASED A SHAPE TO CALL MY OWN.
AND, UHM. W-WHAT DID YOU DO FOR HIM? I-IN RETURN?

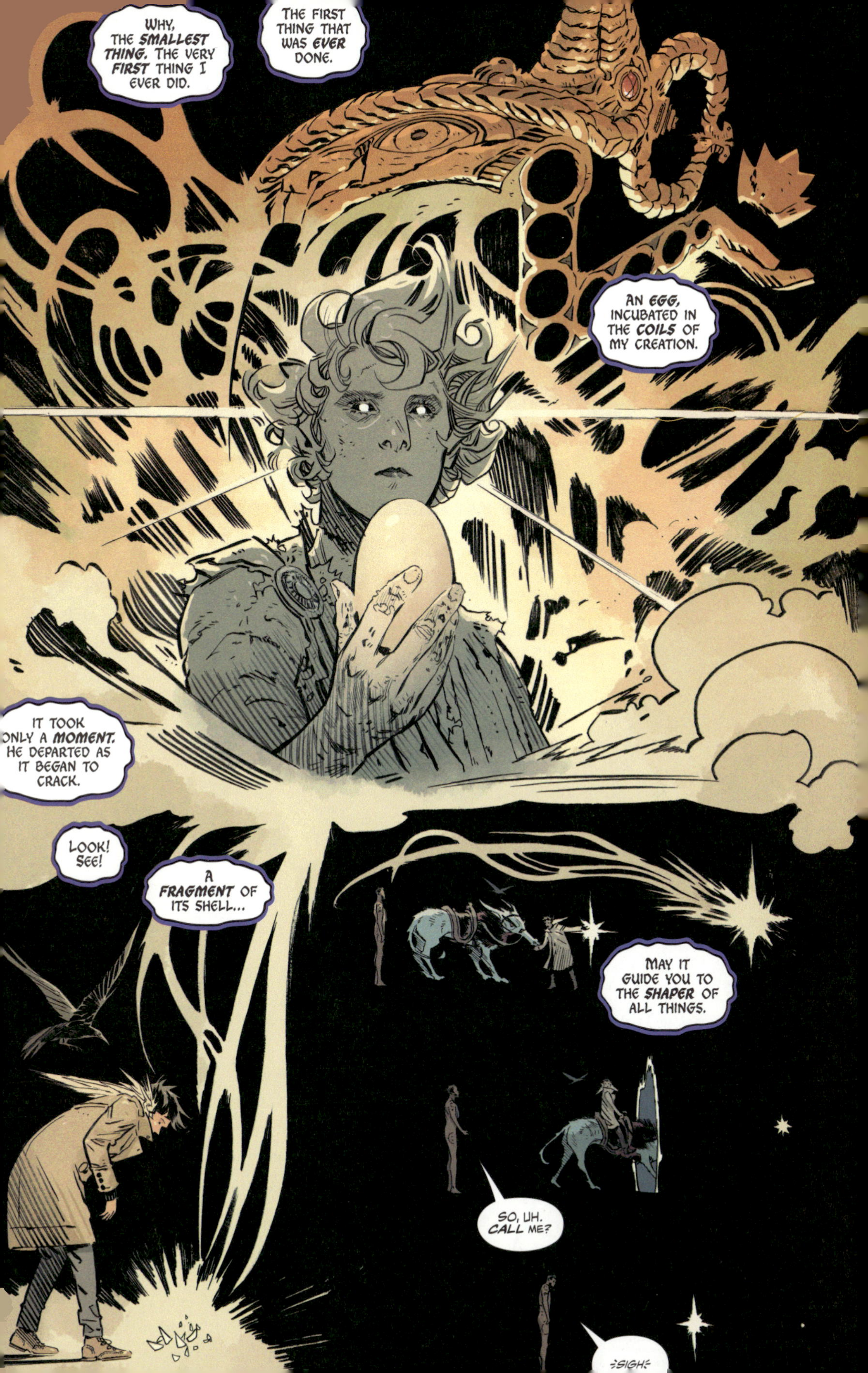
WHY, THE SMALLEST THING. THE VERY FIRST THING I EVER DID.
THE FIRST THING THAT WAS EVER DONE.
AN EGG, INCUBATED IN THE COILS OF MY CREATION.
IT TOOK ONLY A MOMENT. HE DEPARTED AS IT BEGAN TO CRACK.
LOOK! SEE!
A FRAGMENT OF ITS SHELL...
MAY IT GUIDE YOU TO THE SHAPER OF ALL THINGS.
SO, UH. CALL ME?
SIGH

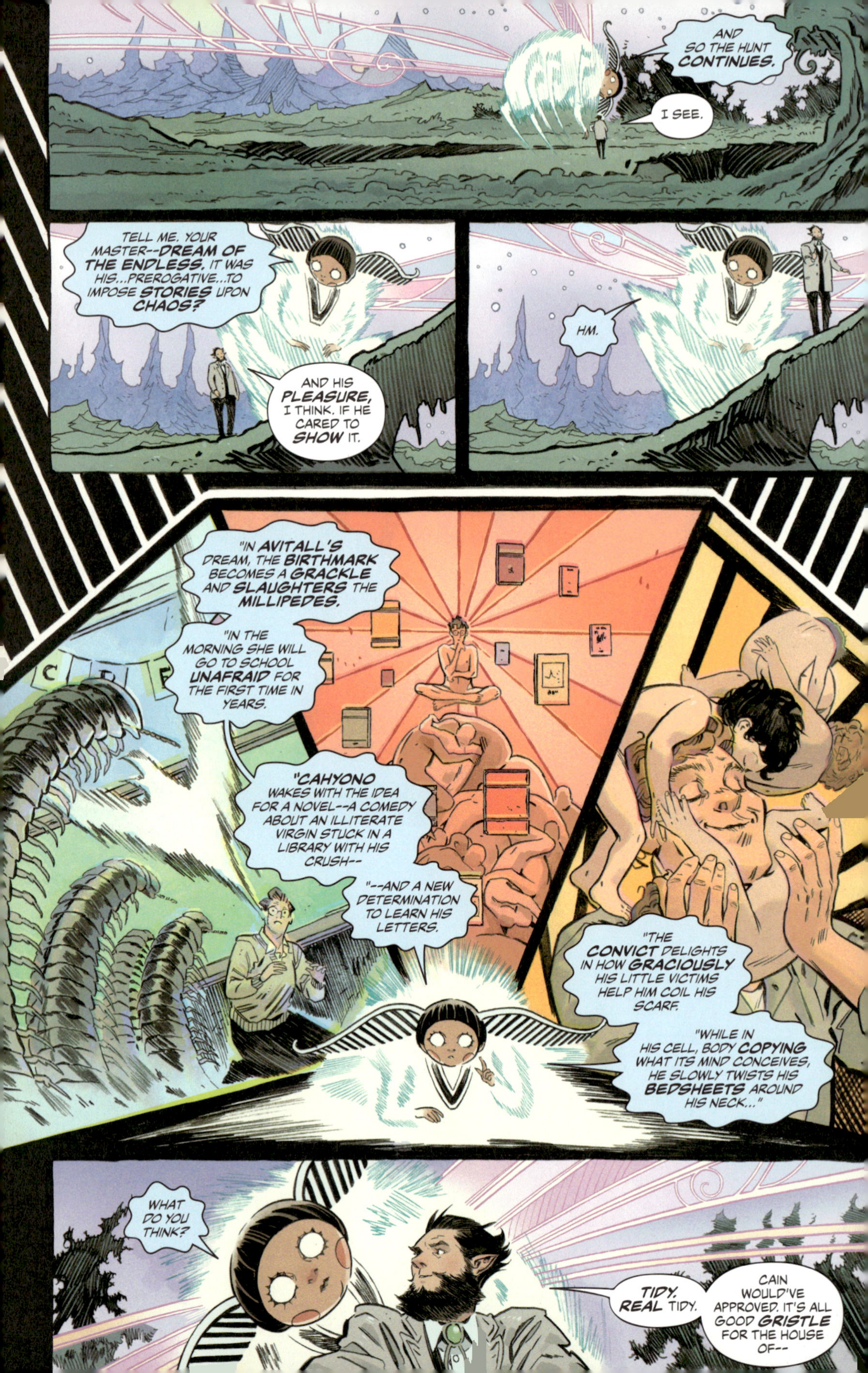
AND SO THE HUNT CONTINUES.
I SEE.
TELL ME. YOUR MASTER--DREAM OF THE ENDLESS. IT WAS HIS...PREROGATIVE...TO IMPOSE STORIES UPON CHAOS?
AND HIS PLEASURE, I THINK. IF HE CARED TO SHOW IT.
HM.
"IN AVITALL'S DREAM, THE BIRTHMARK BECOMES A GRACKLE AND SLAUGHTERS THE MILLIPEDES.
"IN THE MORNING SHE WILL GO TO SCHOOL UNAFRAID FOR THE FIRST TIME IN YEARS.
"CAHYONO WAKES WITH THE IDEA FOR A NOVEL--A COMEDY ABOUT AN ILLITERATE VIRGIN STUCK IN A LIBRARY WITH HIS CRUSH--
"--AND A NEW DETERMINATION TO LEARN HIS LETTERS.
"THE CONVICT DELIGHTS IN HOW GRACIOUSLY HIS LITTLE VICTIMS HELP HIM COIL HIS SCARF.
"WHILE IN HIS CELL, BODY COPYING WHAT ITS MIND CONCEIVES, HE SLOWLY TWISTS HIS BEDSHEETS AROUND HIS NECK..."
WHAT DO YOU THINK?
TIDY. REAL TIDY.
CAIN WOULD'VE APPROVED. IT'S ALL GOOD GRISTLE FOR THE HOUSE OF--

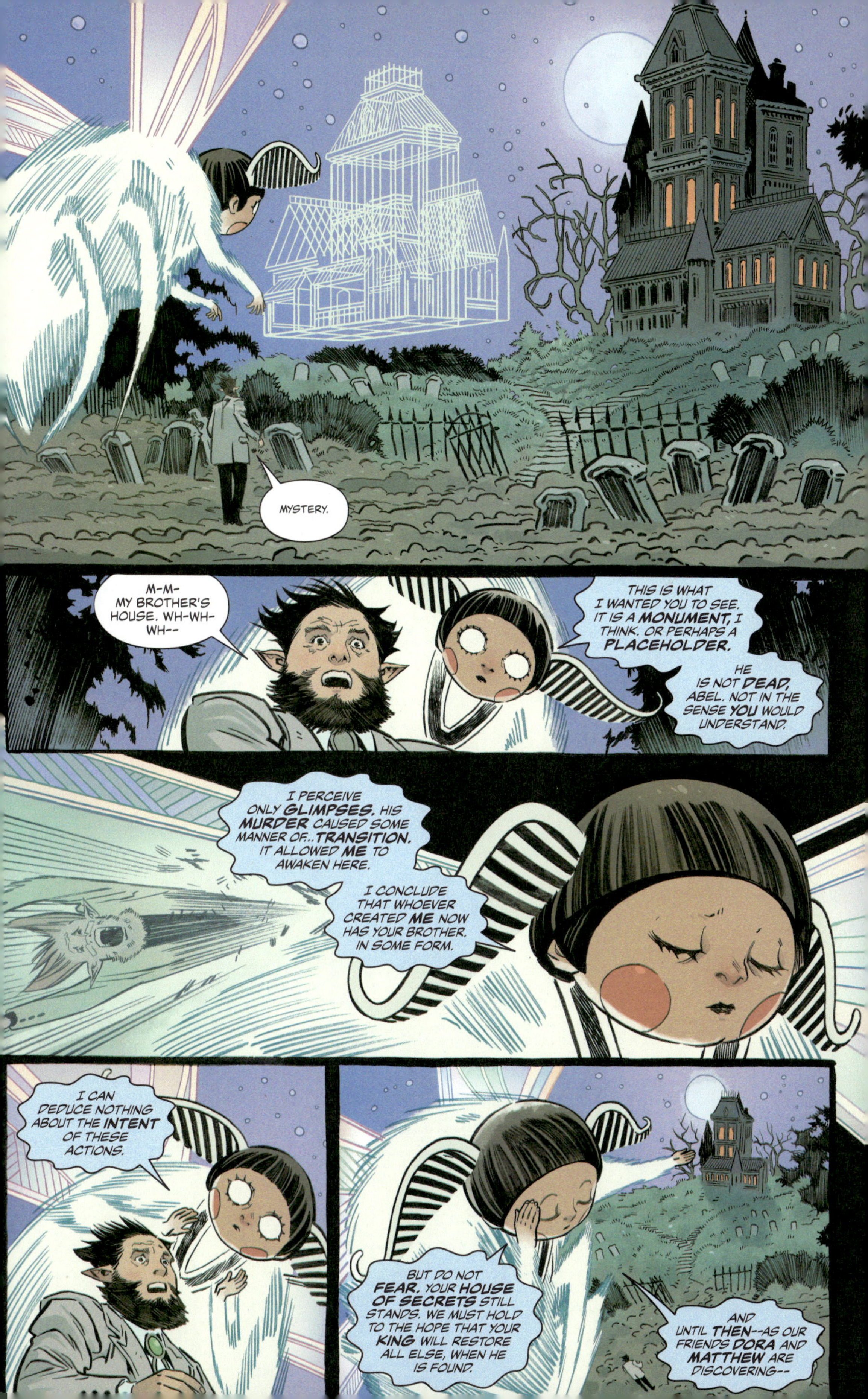
MYSTERY.
M-M- MY BROTHER'S HOUSE. WH-WH-WH--
THIS IS WHAT I WANTED YOU TO SEE. IT IS A MONUMENT, I THINK. OR PERHAPS A PLACEHOLDER.
HE IS NOT DEAD, ABEL. NOT IN THE SENSE YOU WOULD UNDERSTAND.
I PERCEIVE ONLY GLIMPSES. HIS MURDER CAUSED SOME MANNER OF...TRANSITION. IT ALLOWED ME TO AWAKEN HERE.
I CONCLUDE THAT WHOEVER CREATED ME NOW HAS YOUR BROTHER. IN SOME FORM.
I CAN DEDUCE NOTHING ABOUT THE INTENT OF THESE ACTIONS.
BUT DO NOT FEAR. YOUR HOUSE OF SECRETS STILL STANDS. WE MUST HOLD TO THE HOPE THAT YOUR KING WILL RESTORE ALL ELSE, WHEN HE IS FOUND.
AND UNTIL THEN--AS OUR FRIENDS DORA AND MATTHEW ARE DISCOVERING--

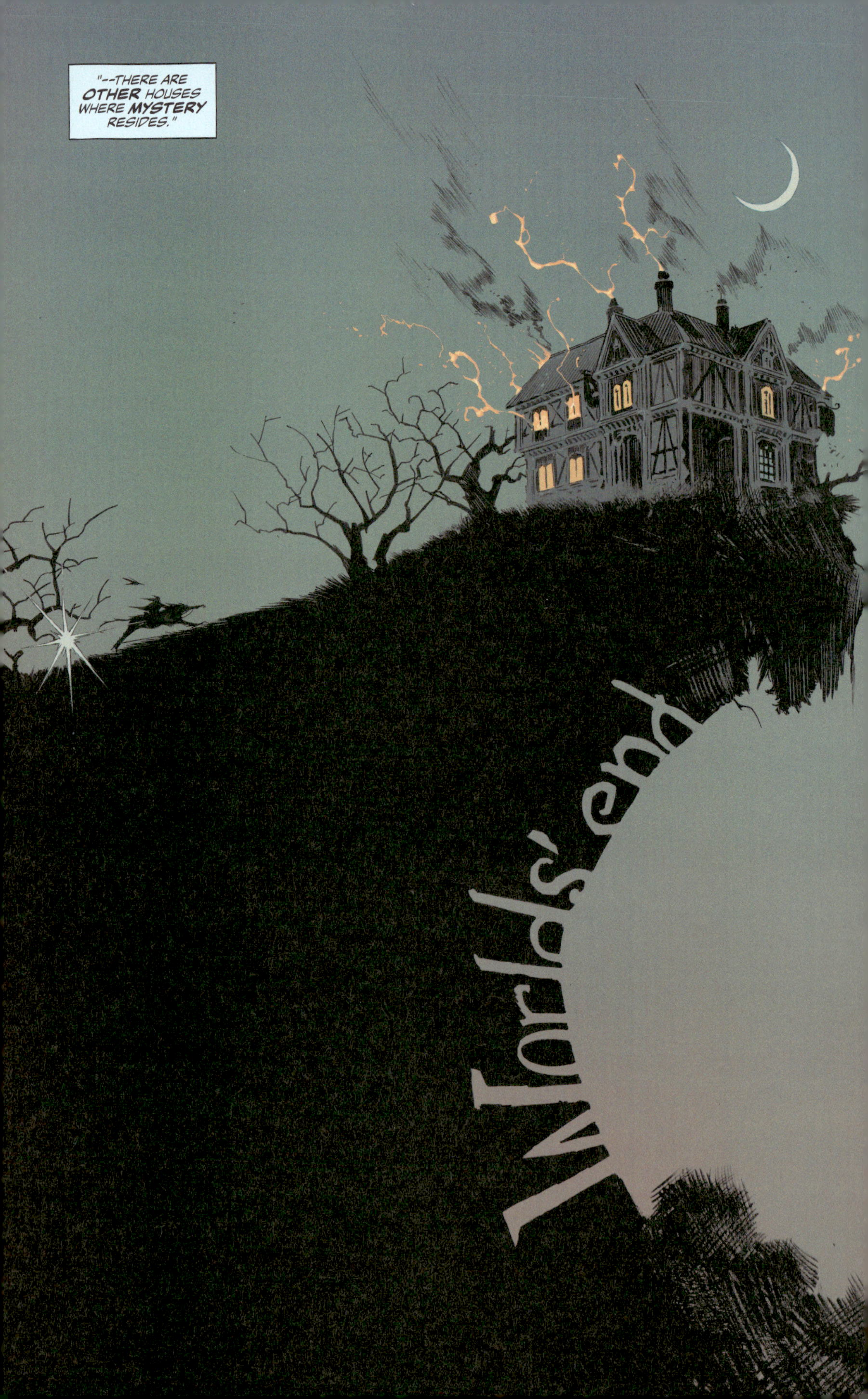
"--THERE ARE OTHER HOUSES WHERE MYSTERY RESIDES."
Worlds' end

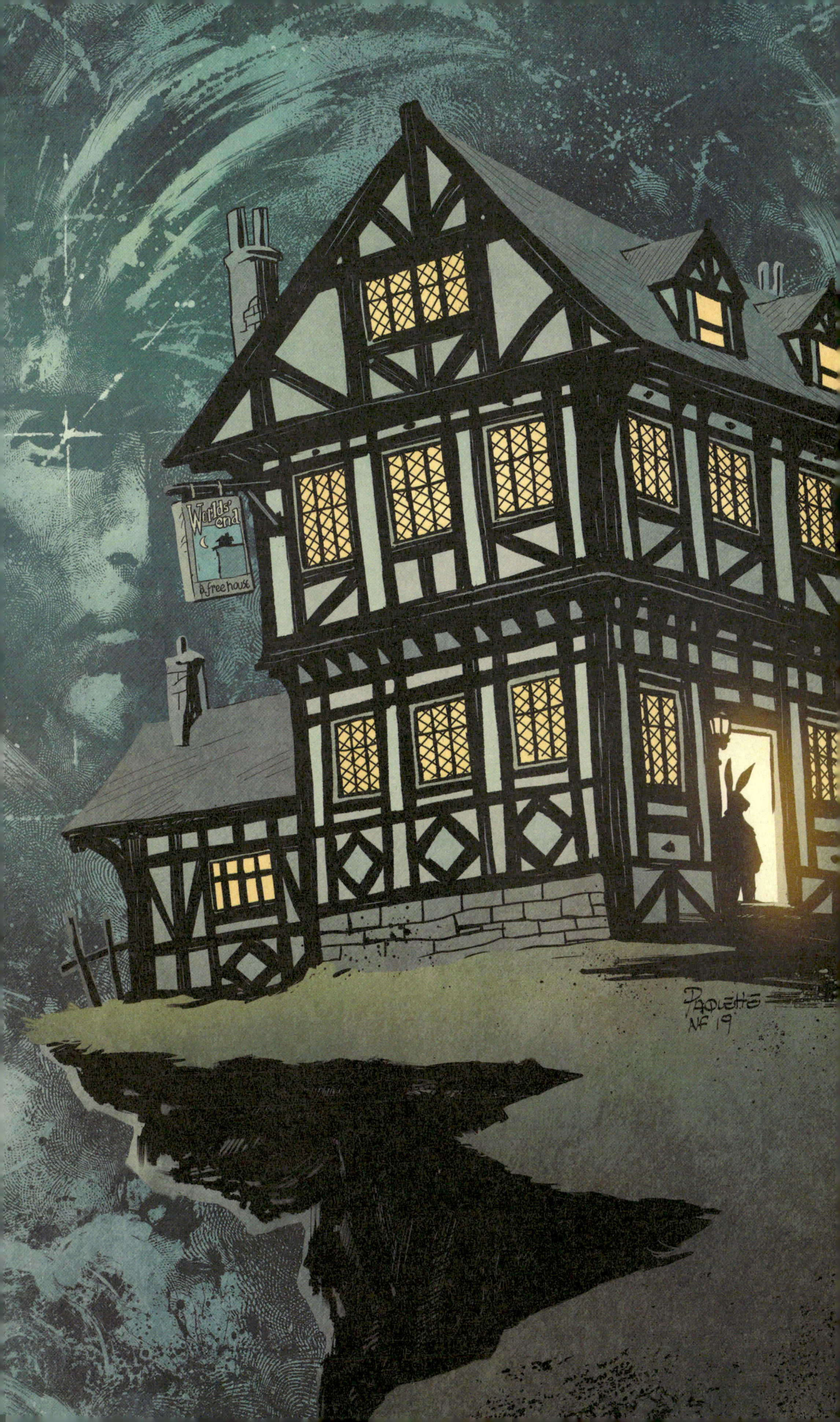
Worlds' end
a free house

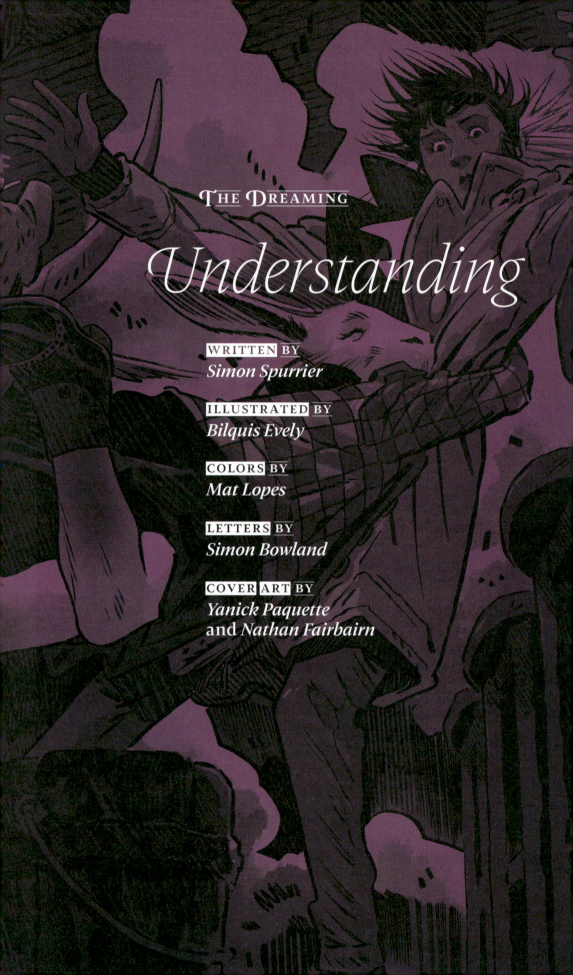

THE DREAMING

Understanding

WRITTEN BY
Simon Spurrier

ILLUSTRATED BY
Bilquis Evely

COLORS BY
Mat Lopes

LETTERS BY
Simon Bowland

COVER ART BY
Yanick Paquette
and *Nathan Fairbairn*

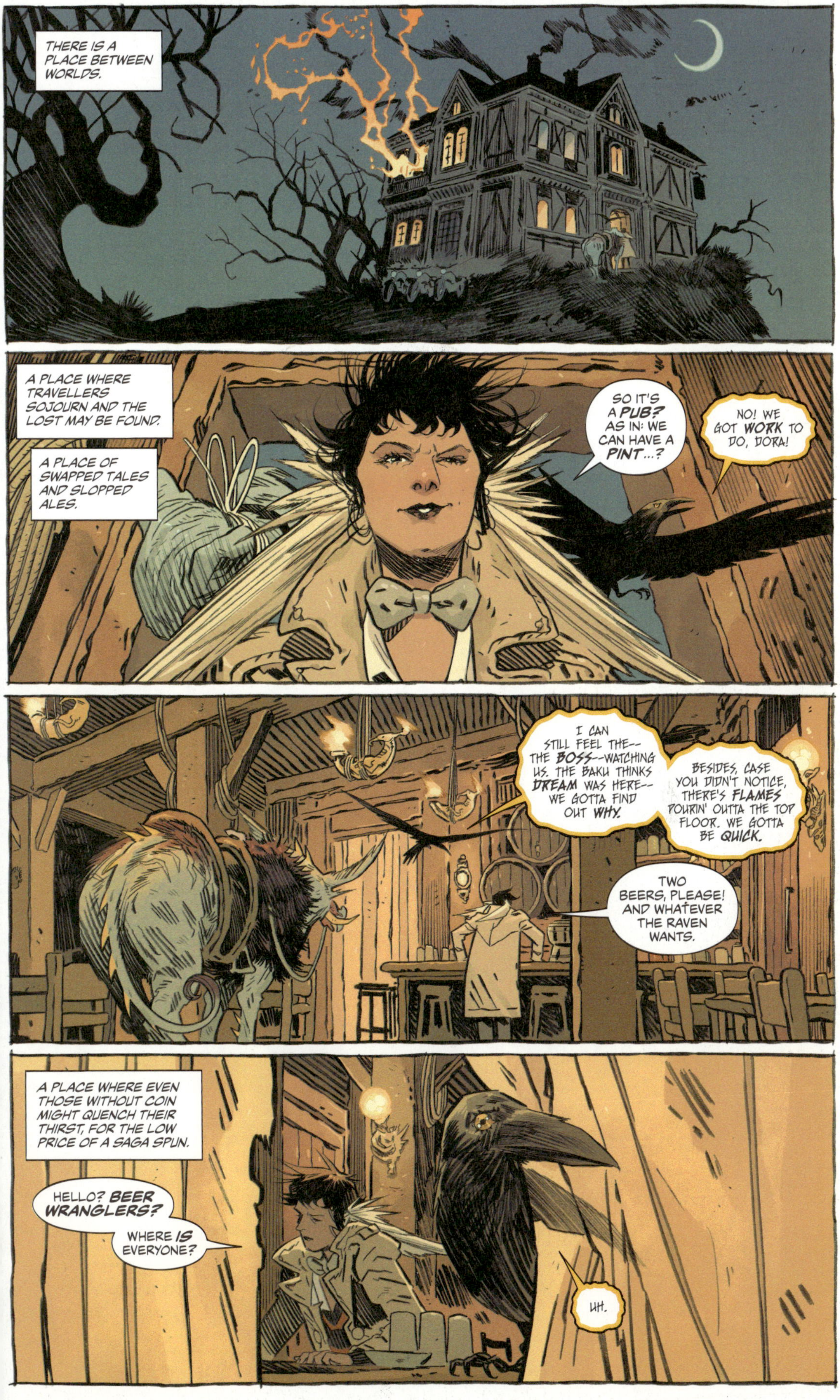
THERE IS A PLACE BETWEEN WORLDS.
A PLACE WHERE TRAVELLERS SOJOURN AND THE LOST MAY BE FOUND.
A PLACE OF SWAPPED TALES AND SLOPPED ALES.
SO IT'S A PUB? AS IN: WE CAN HAVE A PINT...?
NO! WE GOT WORK TO DO, DORA!
I CAN STILL FEEL THE-- THE BOSS--WATCHING US. THE BAKU THINKS DREAM WAS HERE-- WE GOTTA FIND OUT WHY.
BESIDES, CASE YOU DIDN'T NOTICE, THERE'S FLAMES POURIN' OUTTA THE TOP FLOOR. WE GOTTA BE QUICK.
TWO BEERS, PLEASE! AND WHATEVER THE RAVEN WANTS.
A PLACE WHERE EVEN THOSE WITHOUT COIN MIGHT QUENCH THEIR THIRST, FOR THE LOW PRICE OF A SAGA SPUN.
HELLO? BEER WRANGLERS?
WHERE IS EVERYONE?
UH.

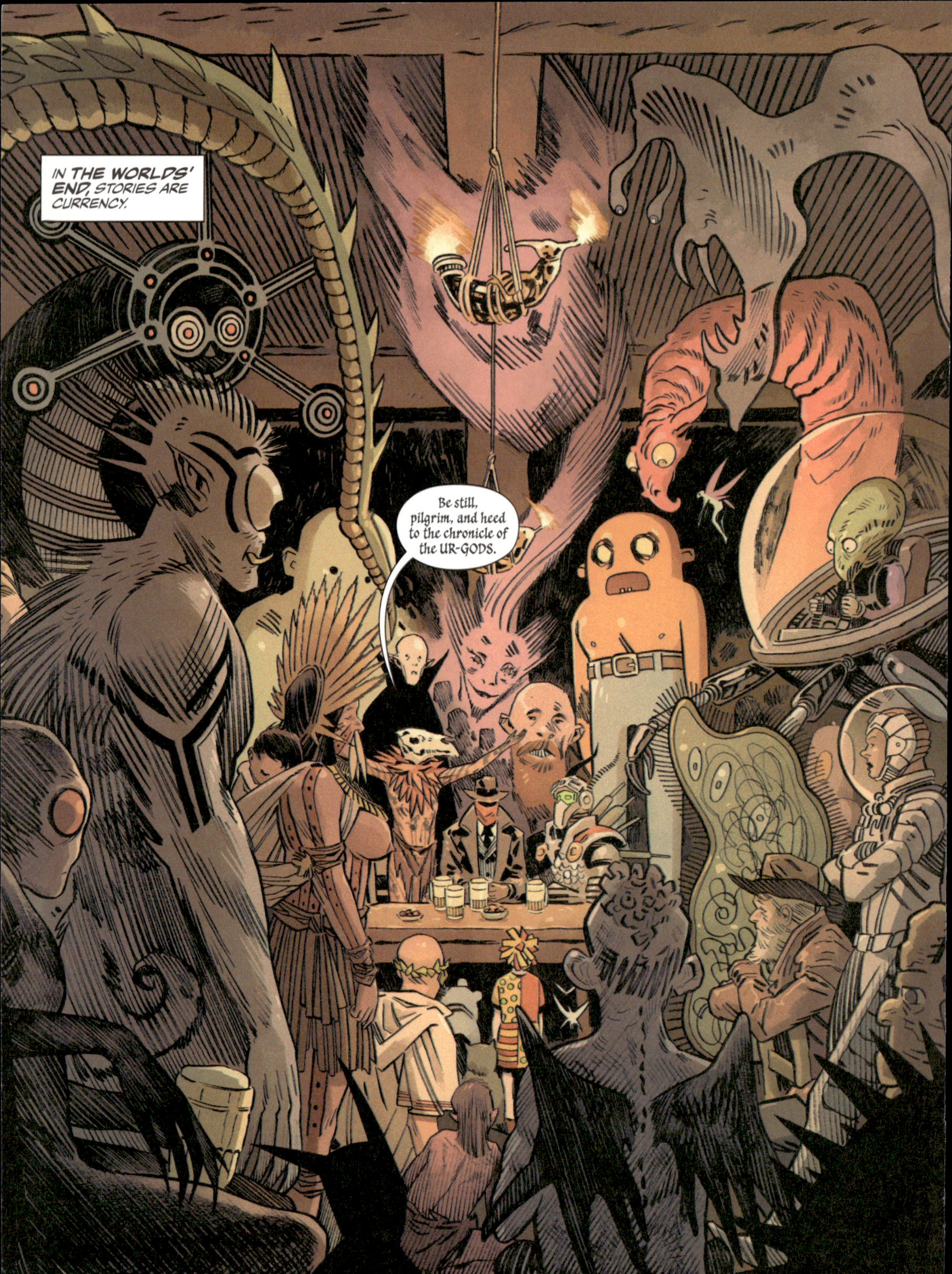
IN THE WORLDS' END, STORIES ARE CURRENCY.
Be still, pilgrim, and heed to the chronicle of the UR-GODS.
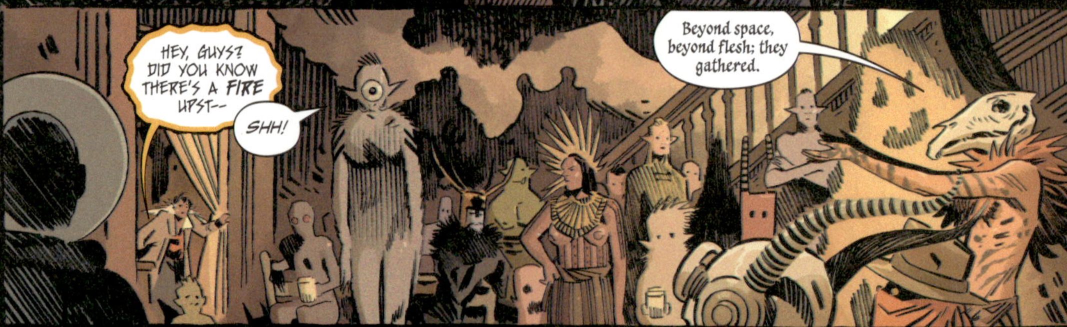
HEY, GUYS? DID YOU KNOW THERE'S A FIRE UPST--
SHH!
Beyond space, beyond flesh; they gathered.

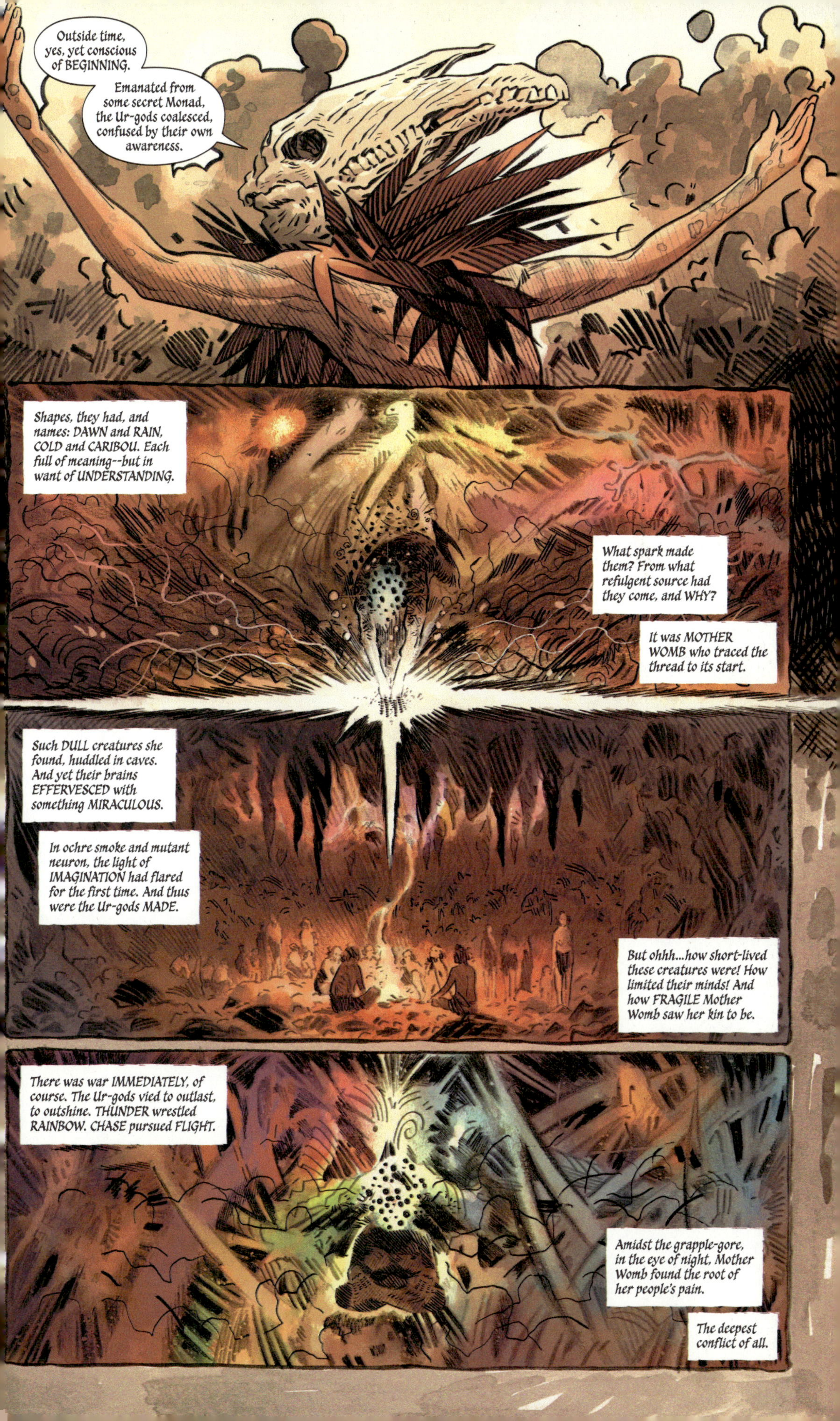
Outside time, yes, yet conscious of BEGINNING.
Emanated from some secret Monad, the Ur-gods coalesced, confused by their own awareness.
Shapes, they had, and names: DAWN and RAIN, COLD and CARIBOU. Each full of meaning--but in want of UNDERSTANDING.
What spark made them? From what refulgent source had they come, and WHY?
It was MOTHER WOMB who traced the thread to its start.
Such DULL creatures she found, huddled in caves. And yet their brains EFFERVESCED with something MIRACULOUS.
In ochre smoke and mutant neuron, the light of IMAGINATION had flared for the first time. And thus were the Ur-gods MADE.
But ohhh...how short-lived these creatures were! How limited their minds! And how FRAGILE Mother Womb saw her kin to be.
There was war IMMEDIATELY, of course. The Ur-gods vied to outlast, to outshine. THUNDER wrestled RAINBOW. CHASE pursued FLIGHT.
Amidst the grapple-gore, in the eye of night, Mother Womb found the root of her people's pain.
The deepest conflict of all.

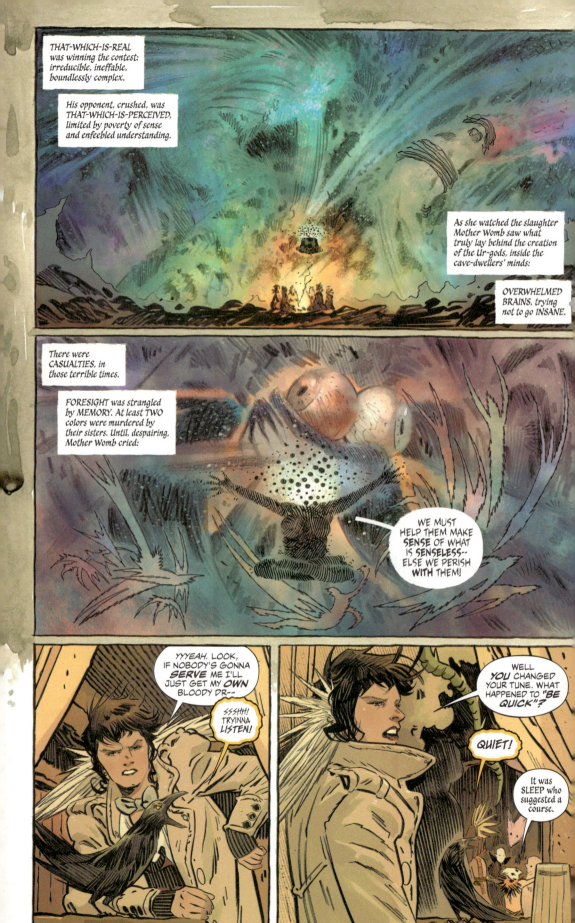

THAT-WHICH-IS-REAL was winning the contest: irreducible, ineffable, boundlessly complex.

His opponent, crushed, was THAT-WHICH-IS-PERCEIVED, limited by poverty of sense and enfeebled understanding.

As she watched the slaughter Mother Womb saw what truly lay behind the creation of the Ur-gods, inside the cave-dwellers' minds:

OVERWHELMED BRAINS, trying not to go INSANE.

There were CASUALTIES, in those terrible times.

FORESIGHT was strangled by MEMORY. At least TWO colors were murdered by their sisters. Until, despairing, Mother Womb cried:

WE MUST HELP THEM MAKE **SENSE** OF WHAT IS SENSELESS-- ELSE WE PERISH **WITH** THEM!

YYYEAH. LOOK, IF NOBODY'S GONNA **SERVE** ME I'LL JUST GET MY **OWN** BLOODY DR--

SSSHH! TRYINNA **LISTEN!**

WELL **YOU** CHANGED YOUR TUNE. WHAT HAPPENED TO **"BE QUICK"?**

QUIET!

It was SLEEP who suggested a course.

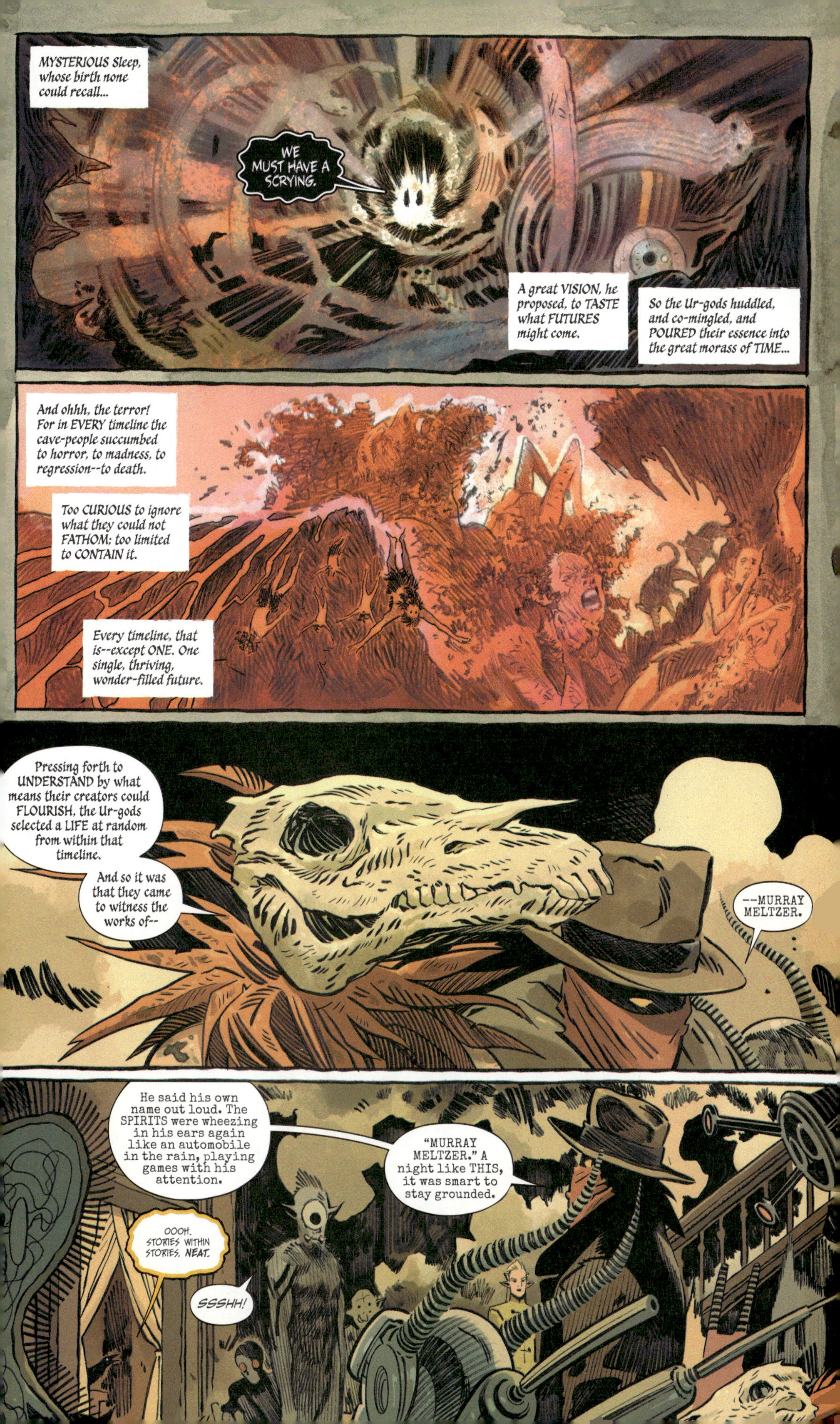

MYSTERIOUS Sleep, whose birth none could recall...
WE MUST HAVE A SCRYING.
A great VISION, he proposed, to TASTE what FUTURES might come.
So the Ur-gods huddled, and co-mingled, and POURED their essence into the great morass of TIME...
And ohhh, the terror! For in EVERY timeline the cave-people succumbed to horror, to madness, to regression--to death.
Too CURIOUS to ignore what they could not FATHOM; too limited to CONTAIN it.
Every timeline, that is--except ONE. One single, thriving, wonder-filled future.
Pressing forth to UNDERSTAND by what means their creators could FLOURISH, the Ur-gods selected a LIFE at random from within that timeline.
And so it was that they came to witness the works of--
--MURRAY MELTZER.
He said his own name out loud. The SPIRITS were wheezing in his ears again like an automobile in the rain, playing games with his attention.
"MURRAY MELTZER." A night like THIS, it was smart to stay grounded.
OOOH. STORIES WITHIN STORIES. NEAT.
SSSHH!

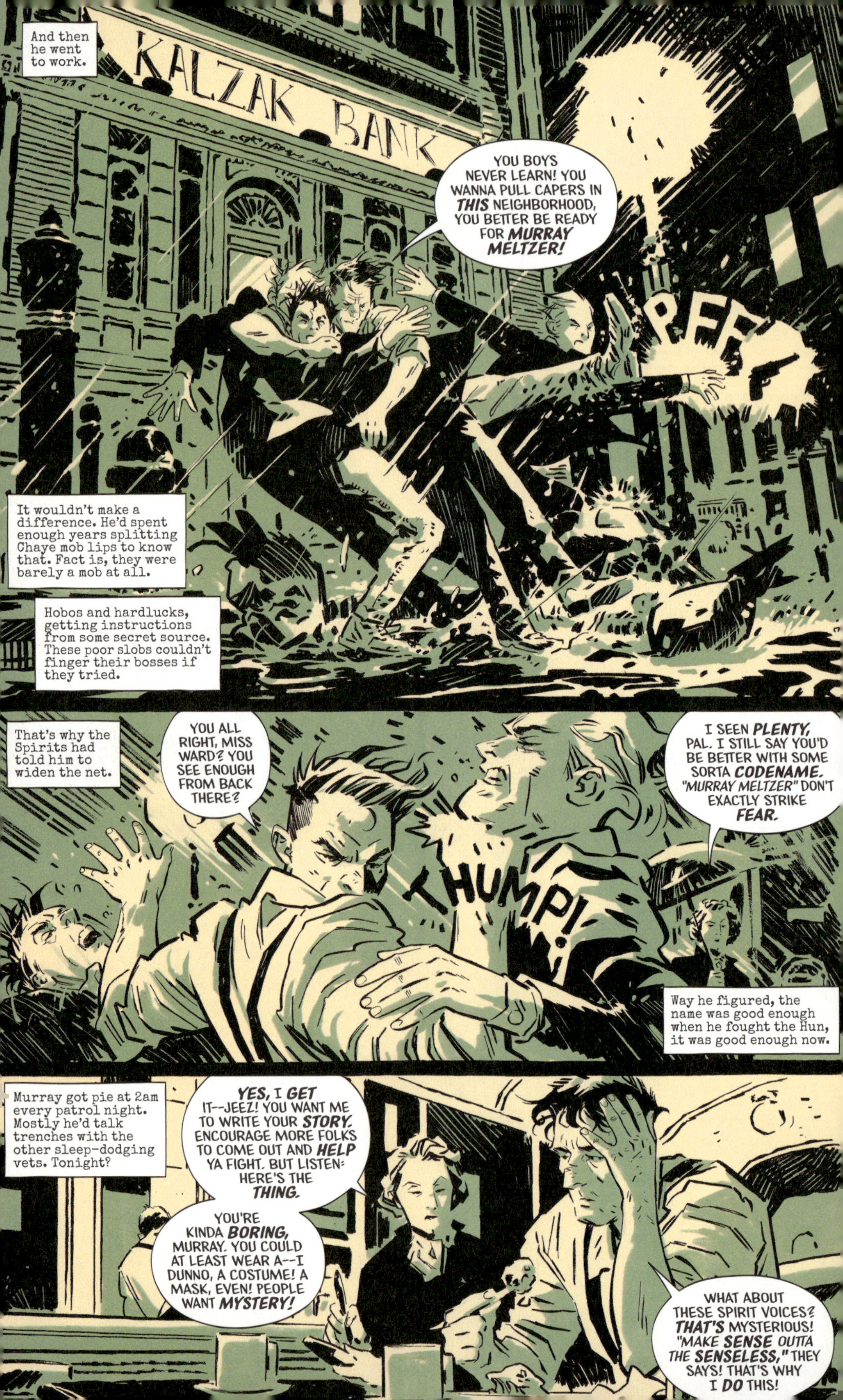
And then he went to work.
KALZAK BANK
YOU BOYS NEVER LEARN! YOU WANNA PULL CAPERS IN *THIS* NEIGHBORHOOD, YOU BETTER BE READY FOR *MURRAY MELTZER!*
It wouldn't make a difference. He'd spent enough years splitting Chaye mob lips to know that. Fact is, they were barely a mob at all.
Hobos and hardlucks, getting instructions from some secret source. These poor slobs couldn't finger their bosses if they tried.
That's why the Spirits had told him to widen the net.
YOU ALL RIGHT, MISS WARD? YOU SEE ENOUGH FROM BACK THERE?
I SEEN *PLENTY,* PAL. I STILL SAY YOU'D BE BETTER WITH SOME SORTA *CODENAME.* "MURRAY MELTZER" DON'T EXACTLY STRIKE *FEAR.*
THUMP!
Way he figured, the name was good enough when he fought the Hun, it was good enough now.
Murray got pie at 2am every patrol night. Mostly he'd talk trenches with the other sleep-dodging vets. Tonight?
YES, I *GET* IT--JEEZ! YOU WANT ME TO WRITE YOUR *STORY.* ENCOURAGE MORE FOLKS TO COME OUT AND *HELP* YA FIGHT. BUT LISTEN: HERE'S THE *THING.*
YOU'RE KINDA *BORING,* MURRAY. YOU COULD AT LEAST WEAR A--I DUNNO, A COSTUME! A MASK, EVEN! PEOPLE WANT *MYSTERY!*
WHAT ABOUT THESE SPIRIT VOICES? *THAT'S* MYSTERIOUS! "MAKE *SENSE* OUTTA THE *SENSELESS,*" THEY SAYS! THAT'S WHY I *DO* THIS!

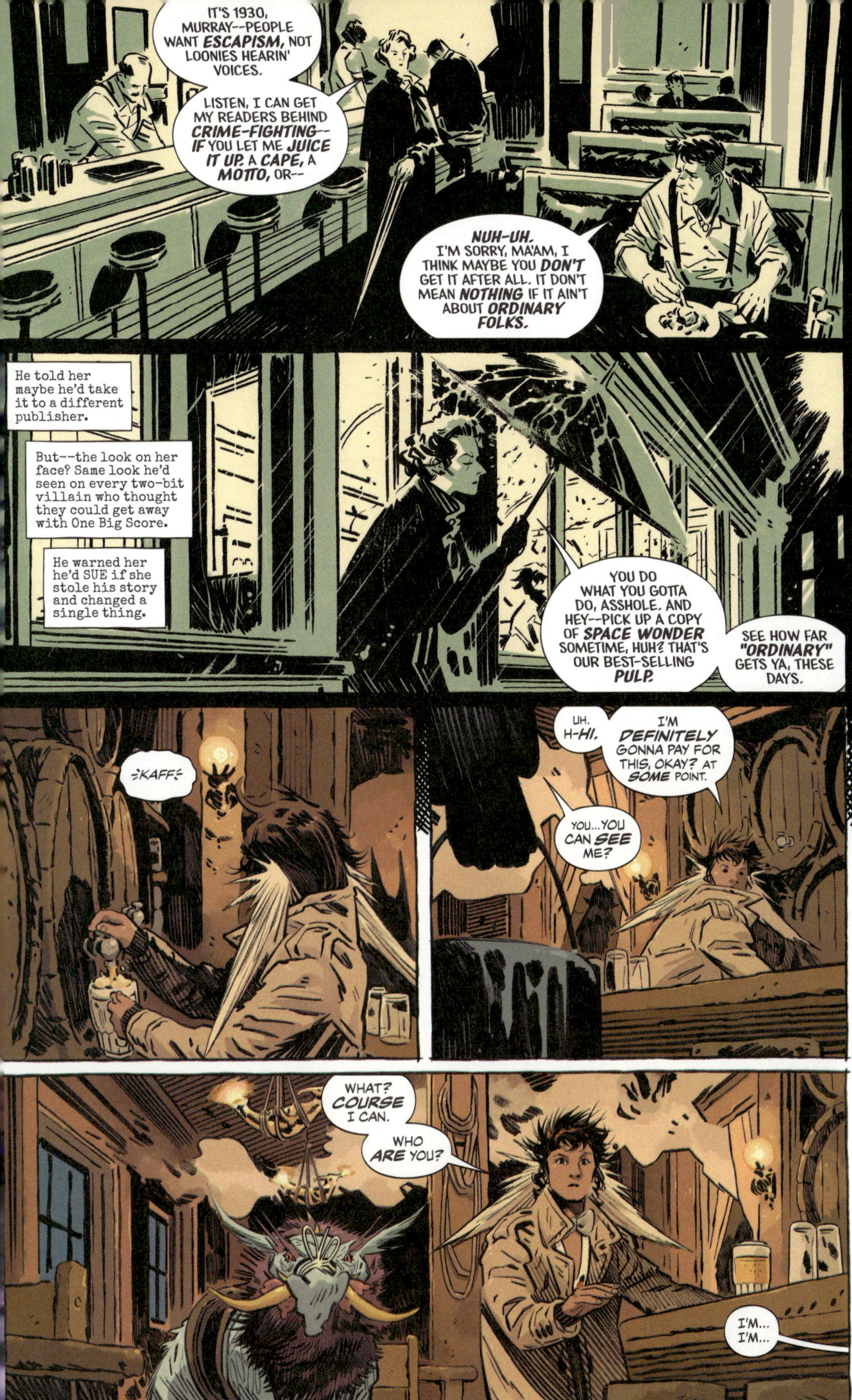
IT'S 1930, MURRAY--PEOPLE WANT ESCAPISM, NOT LOONIES HEARIN' VOICES.
LISTEN, I CAN GET MY READERS BEHIND CRIME-FIGHTING--IF YOU LET ME JUICE IT UP. A CAPE, A MOTTO, OR--
NUH-UH. I'M SORRY, MA'AM, I THINK MAYBE YOU DON'T GET IT AFTER ALL. IT DON'T MEAN NOTHING IF IT AIN'T ABOUT ORDINARY FOLKS.
He told her maybe he'd take it to a different publisher.
But--the look on her face? Same look he'd seen on every two-bit villain who thought they could get away with One Big Score.
He warned her he'd SUE if she stole his story and changed a single thing.
YOU DO WHAT YOU GOTTA DO, ASSHOLE. AND HEY--PICK UP A COPY OF SPACE WONDER SOMETIME, HUH? THAT'S OUR BEST-SELLING PULP.
SEE HOW FAR "ORDINARY" GETS YA, THESE DAYS.
KAFF
UH. H-HI.
I'M DEFINITELY GONNA PAY FOR THIS, OKAY? AT SOME POINT.
YOU...YOU CAN SEE ME?
WHAT? COURSE I CAN.
WHO ARE YOU?
I'M... I'M...

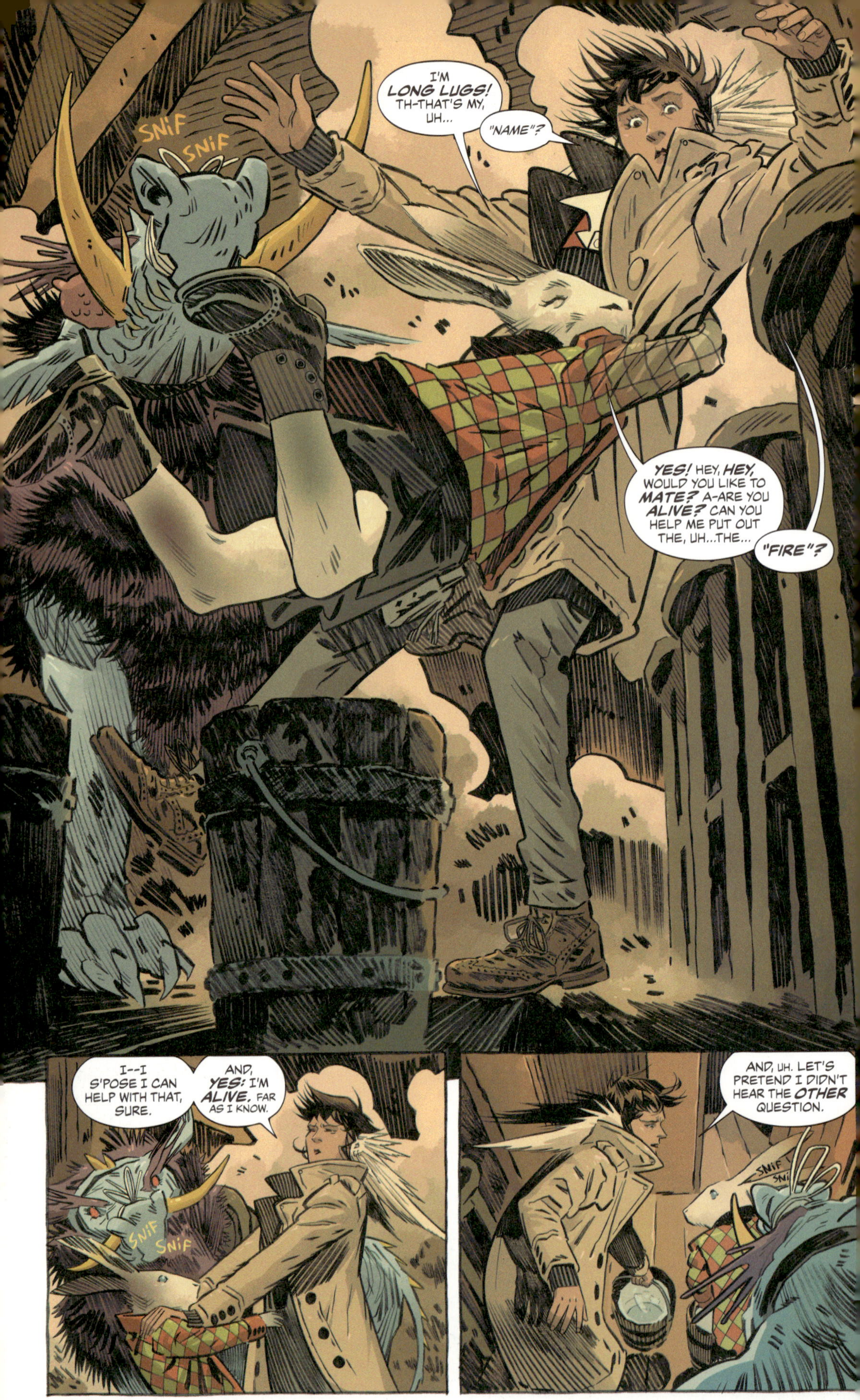
SNIF SNIF
I'M LONG LUGS! TH-THAT'S MY, UH...
"NAME"?
YES! HEY, HEY, WOULD YOU LIKE TO MATE? A-ARE YOU ALIVE? CAN YOU HELP ME PUT OUT THE, UH...THE...
"FIRE"?
I--I S'POSE I CAN HELP WITH THAT, SURE.
AND, YES: I'M ALIVE. FAR AS I KNOW.
SNIF SNIF
AND, UH. LET'S PRETEND I DIDN'T HEAR THE OTHER QUESTION.

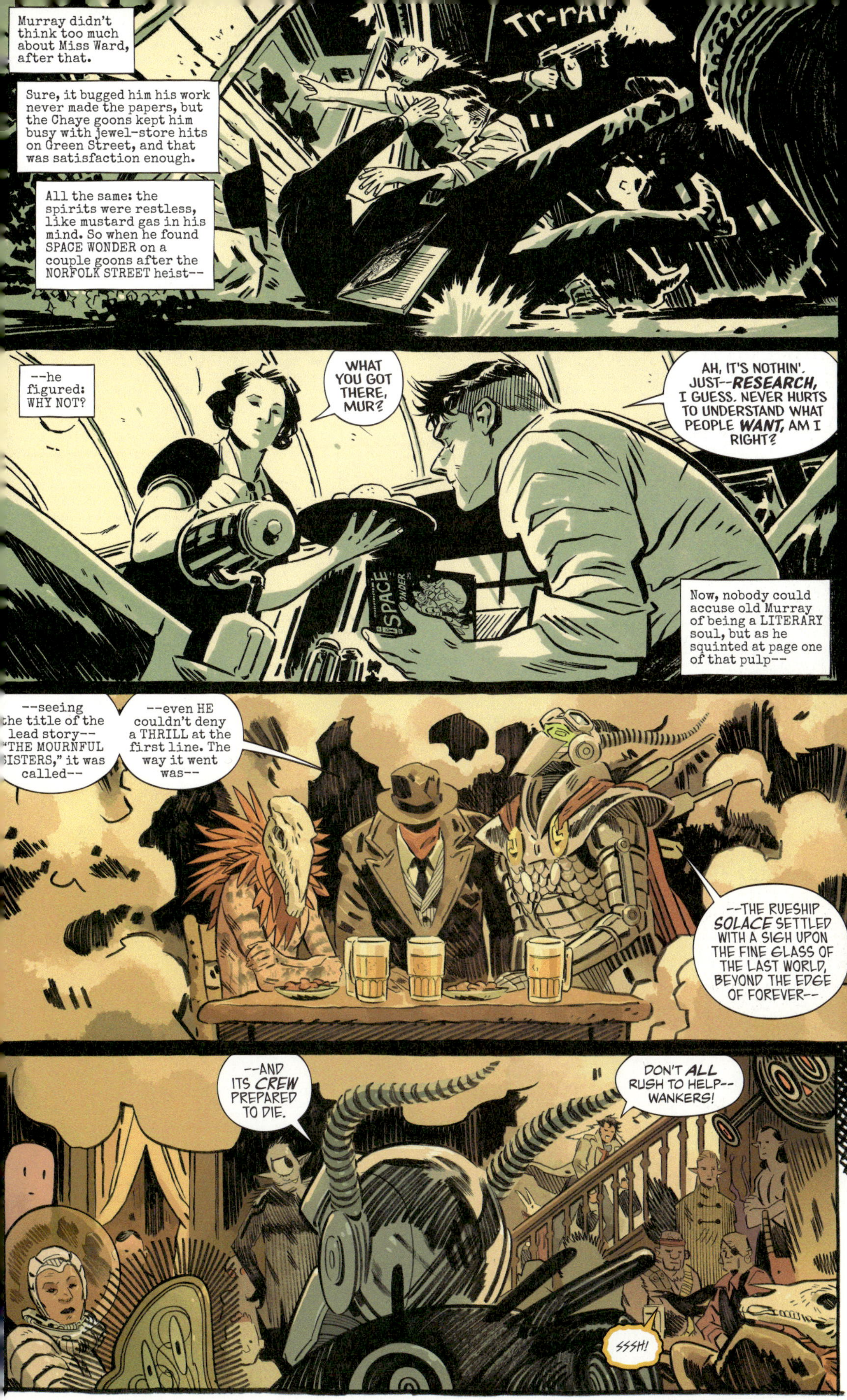
Murray didn't think too much about Miss Ward, after that.
Sure, it bugged him his work never made the papers, but the Chaye goons kept him busy with jewel-store hits on Green Street, and that was satisfaction enough.
All the same: the spirits were restless, like mustard gas in his mind. So when he found SPACE WONDER on a couple goons after the NORFOLK STREET heist--
--he figured: WHY NOT?
WHAT YOU GOT THERE, MUR?
AH, IT'S NOTHIN'. JUST--RESEARCH, I GUESS. NEVER HURTS TO UNDERSTAND WHAT PEOPLE WANT, AM I RIGHT?
Now, nobody could accuse old Murray of being a LITERARY soul, but as he squinted at page one of that pulp--
--seeing the title of the lead story--"THE MOURNFUL SISTERS," it was called--
--even HE couldn't deny a THRILL at the first line. The way it went was--
--THE RUESHIP SOLACE SETTLED WITH A SIGH UPON THE FINE GLASS OF THE LAST WORLD, BEYOND THE EDGE OF FOREVER--
--AND ITS CREW PREPARED TO DIE.
DON'T ALL RUSH TO HELP-- WANKERS!
SSSH!

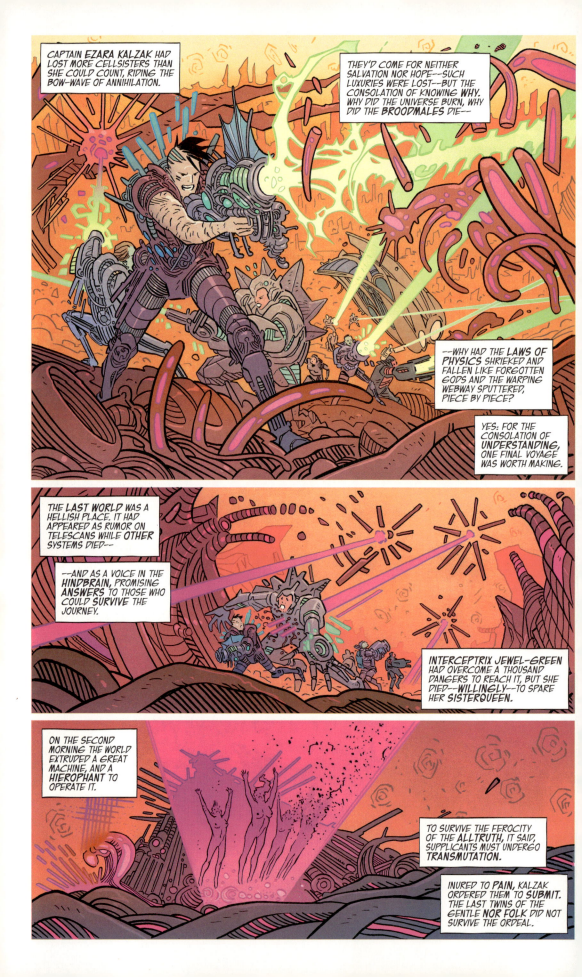

CAPTAIN **EZARA KALZAK** HAD LOST MORE CELLSISTERS THAN SHE COULD COUNT, RIDING THE BOW-WAVE OF ANNIHILATION.

THEY'D COME FOR NEITHER SALVATION NOR HOPE--SUCH LUXURIES WERE LOST--BUT THE CONSOLATION OF KNOWING **WHY.** WHY DID THE UNIVERSE BURN, WHY DID THE **BROODMALES** DIE--

--WHY HAD THE **LAWS OF PHYSICS** SHRIEKED AND FALLEN LIKE FORGOTTEN GODS AND THE WARPING WEBWAY SPUTTERED, PIECE BY PIECE?

YES: FOR THE CONSOLATION OF **UNDERSTANDING,** ONE FINAL VOYAGE WAS WORTH MAKING.

THE **LAST WORLD** WAS A HELLISH PLACE. IT HAD APPEARED AS RUMOR ON TELESCANS WHILE **OTHER** SYSTEMS DIED--

--AND AS A VOICE IN THE **HINDBRAIN,** PROMISING **ANSWERS** TO THOSE WHO COULD **SURVIVE** THE JOURNEY.

INTERCEPTRIX JEWEL-GREEN HAD OVERCOME A THOUSAND DANGERS TO REACH IT, BUT SHE DIED--**WILLINGLY**--TO SPARE HER SISTERQUEEN.

ON THE SECOND MORNING THE WORLD EXTRUDED A GREAT MACHINE, AND A **HIEROPHANT** TO OPERATE IT.

TO SURVIVE THE FEROCITY OF THE **ALLTRUTH,** IT SAID, SUPPLICANTS MUST UNDERGO **TRANSMUTATION.**

INURED TO **PAIN,** KALZAK ORDERED THEM TO **SUBMIT.** THE LAST TWINS OF THE GENTLE **NOR FOLK** DID NOT SURVIVE THE ORDEAL.

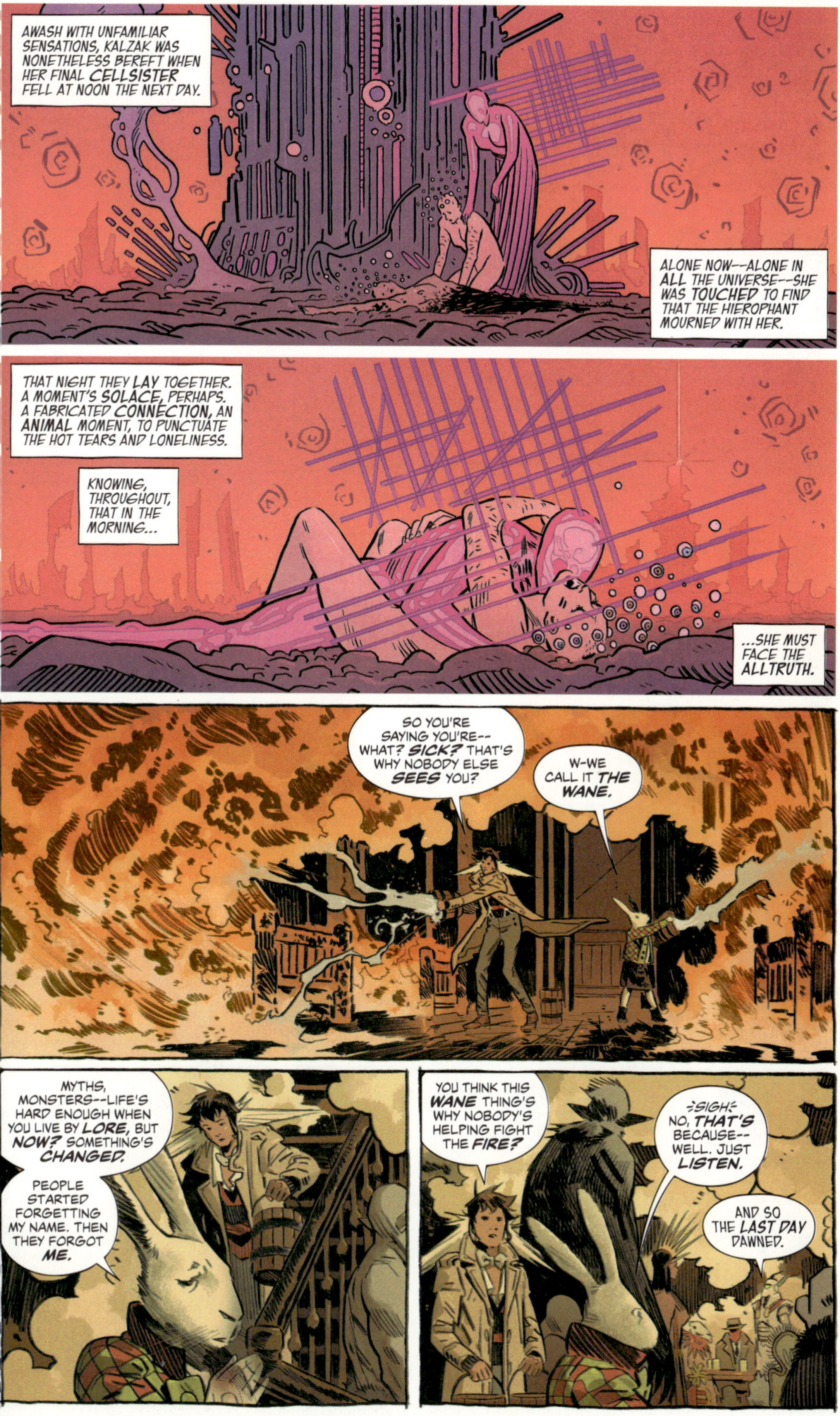
AWASH WITH UNFAMILIAR SENSATIONS, KALZAK WAS NONETHELESS BEREFT WHEN HER FINAL CELLSISTER FELL AT NOON THE NEXT DAY.
ALONE NOW--ALONE IN ALL THE UNIVERSE--SHE WAS TOUCHED TO FIND THAT THE HIEROPHANT MOURNED WITH HER.
THAT NIGHT THEY LAY TOGETHER. A MOMENT'S SOLACE, PERHAPS. A FABRICATED CONNECTION, AN ANIMAL MOMENT, TO PUNCTUATE THE HOT TEARS AND LONELINESS.
KNOWING, THROUGHOUT, THAT IN THE MORNING...
...SHE MUST FACE THE ALLTRUTH.
SO YOU'RE SAYING YOU'RE--WHAT? SICK? THAT'S WHY NOBODY ELSE SEES YOU?
W-WE CALL IT THE WANE.
MYTHS, MONSTERS--LIFE'S HARD ENOUGH WHEN YOU LIVE BY LORE, BUT NOW? SOMETHING'S CHANGED.
PEOPLE STARTED FORGETTING MY NAME. THEN THEY FORGOT ME.
YOU THINK THIS WANE THING'S WHY NOBODY'S HELPING FIGHT THE FIRE?
SIGH
NO, THAT'S BECAUSE--WELL. JUST LISTEN.
AND SO THE LAST DAY DAWNED.

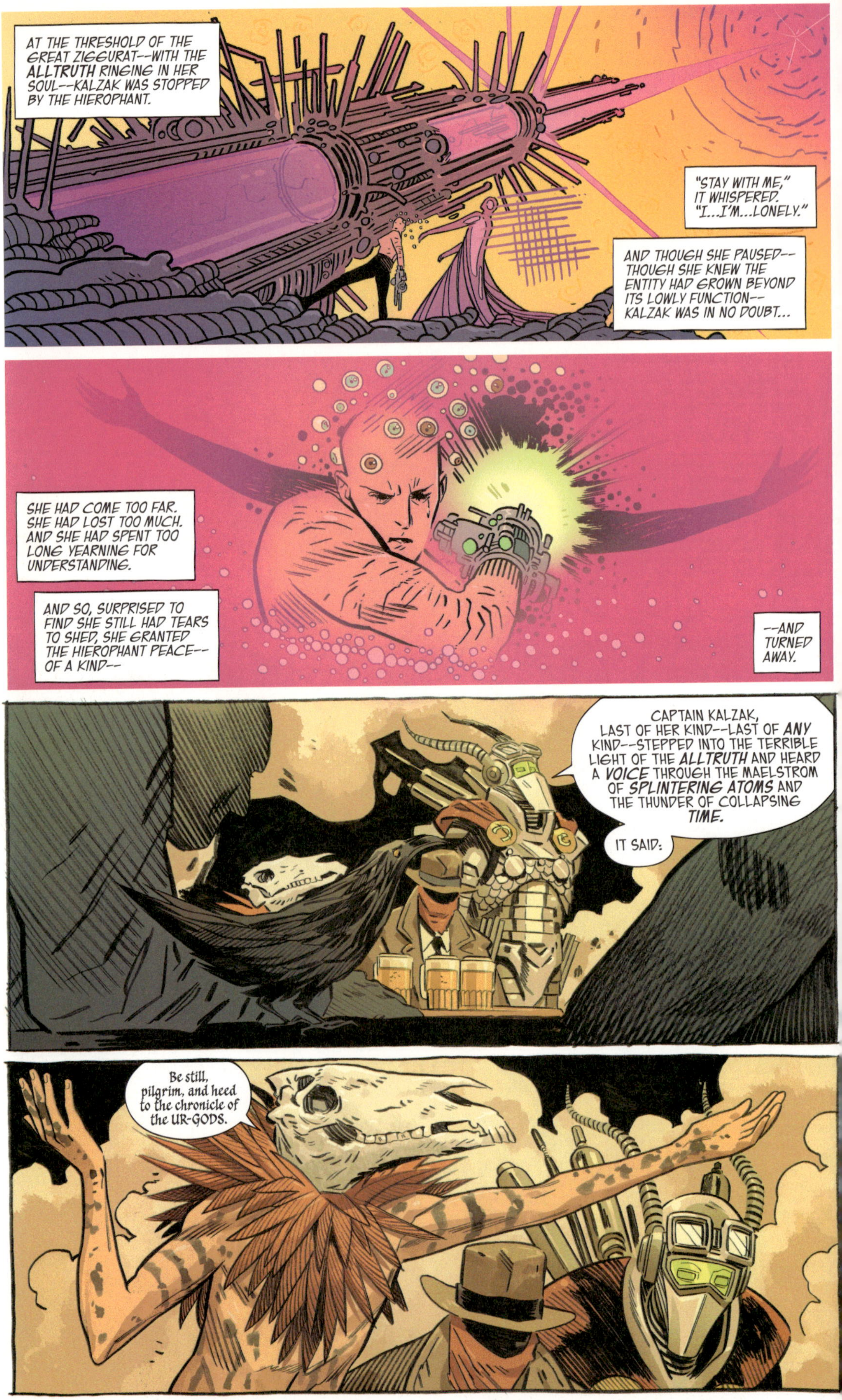
AT THE THRESHOLD OF THE GREAT ZIGGURAT--WITH THE ALLTRUTH RINGING IN HER SOUL--KALZAK WAS STOPPED BY THE HIEROPHANT.
"STAY WITH ME," IT WHISPERED. "I...I'M...LONELY."
AND THOUGH SHE PAUSED--THOUGH SHE KNEW THE ENTITY HAD GROWN BEYOND ITS LOWLY FUNCTION--KALZAK WAS IN NO DOUBT...
SHE HAD COME TOO FAR. SHE HAD LOST TOO MUCH. AND SHE HAD SPENT TOO LONG YEARNING FOR UNDERSTANDING.
AND SO, SURPRISED TO FIND SHE STILL HAD TEARS TO SHED, SHE GRANTED THE HIEROPHANT PEACE--OF A KIND--
--AND TURNED AWAY.
CAPTAIN KALZAK, LAST OF HER KIND--LAST OF ANY KIND--STEPPED INTO THE TERRIBLE LIGHT OF THE ALLTRUTH AND HEARD A VOICE THROUGH THE MAELSTROM OF SPLINTERING ATOMS AND THE THUNDER OF COLLAPSING TIME.
IT SAID:
Be still, pilgrim, and heed to the chronicle of the UR-GODS.

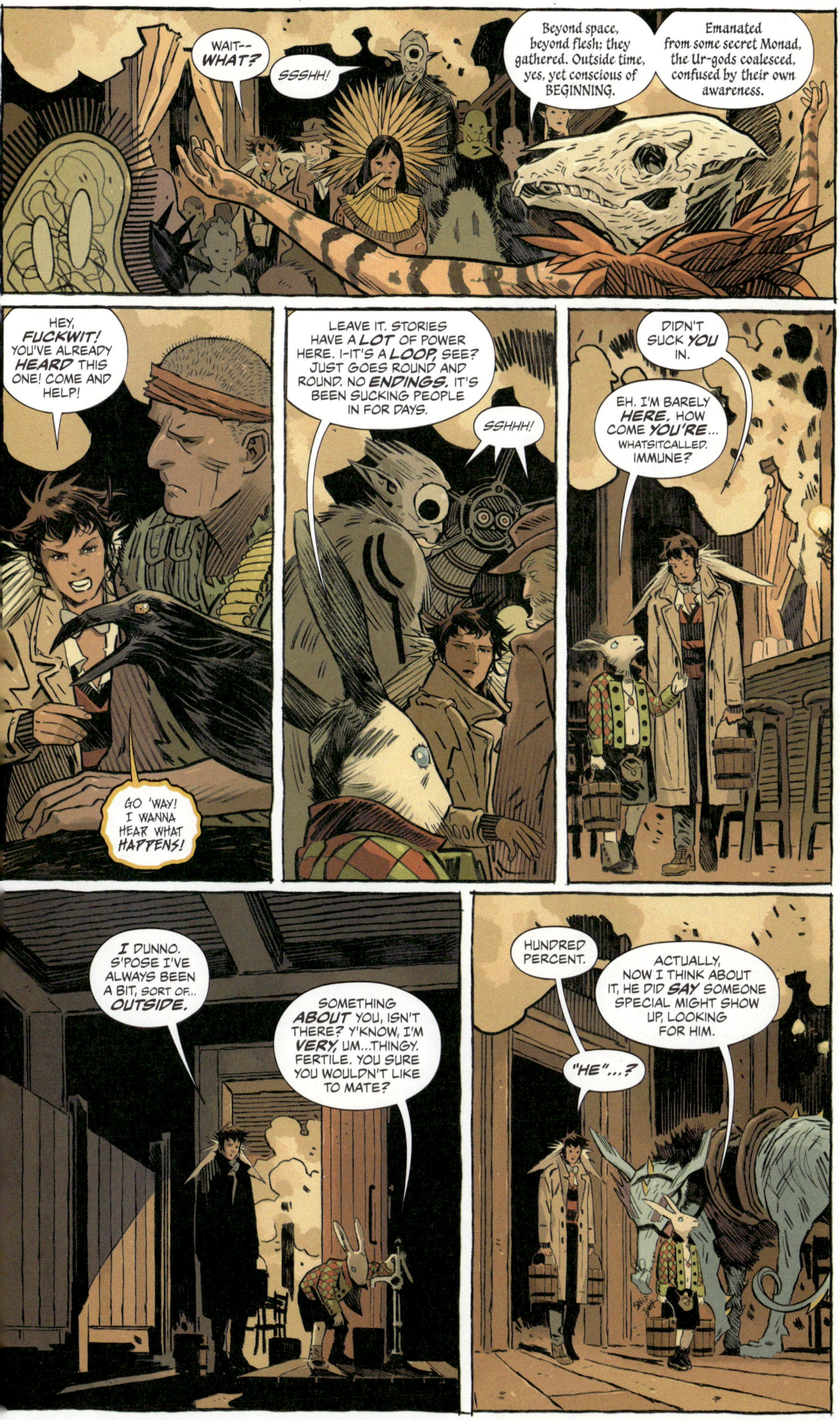
WAIT-- WHAT?
SSSHH!
Beyond space, beyond flesh: they gathered. Outside time, yes, yet conscious of BEGINNING.
Emanated from some secret Monad, the Ur-gods coalesced, confused by their own awareness.
HEY, FUCKWIT! YOU'VE ALREADY HEARD THIS ONE! COME AND HELP!
GO 'WAY! I WANNA HEAR WHAT HAPPENS!
LEAVE IT. STORIES HAVE A LOT OF POWER HERE. I-IT'S A LOOP, SEE? JUST GOES ROUND AND ROUND. NO ENDINGS. IT'S BEEN SUCKING PEOPLE IN FOR DAYS.
SSHHH!
DIDN'T SUCK YOU IN.
EH. I'M BARELY HERE. HOW COME YOU'RE... WHATSITCALLED. IMMUNE?
I DUNNO. S'POSE I'VE ALWAYS BEEN A BIT, SORT OF... OUTSIDE.
SOMETHING ABOUT YOU, ISN'T THERE? Y'KNOW, I'M VERY, UM...THINGY. FERTILE. YOU SURE YOU WOULDN'T LIKE TO MATE?
HUNDRED PERCENT.
ACTUALLY, NOW I THINK ABOUT IT, HE DID SAY SOMEONE SPECIAL MIGHT SHOW UP, LOOKING FOR HIM.
"HE"...?

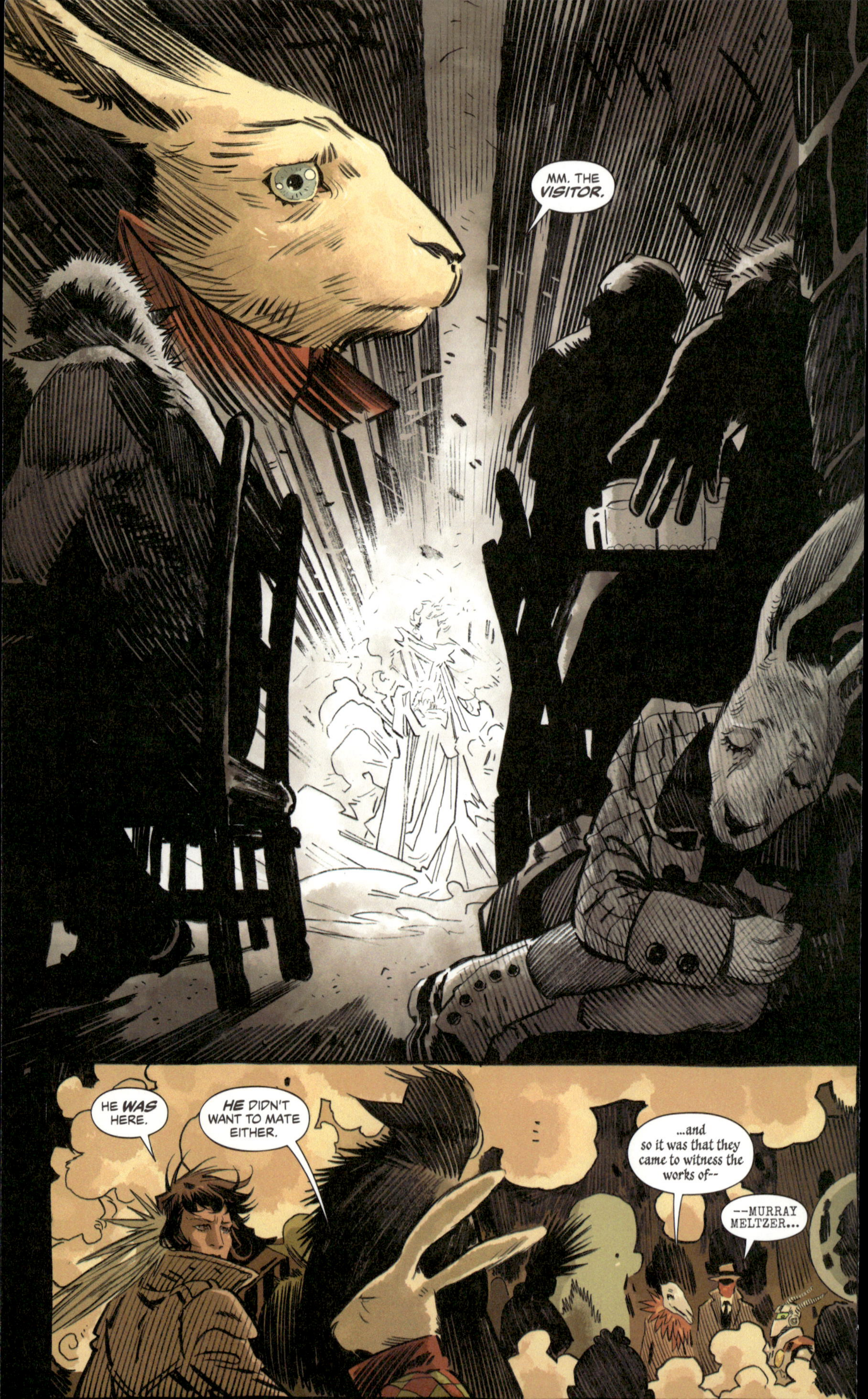
MM. THE VISITOR.
HE WAS HERE.
HE DIDN'T WANT TO MATE EITHER.
...and so it was that they came to witness the works of--
--MURRAY MELTZER...

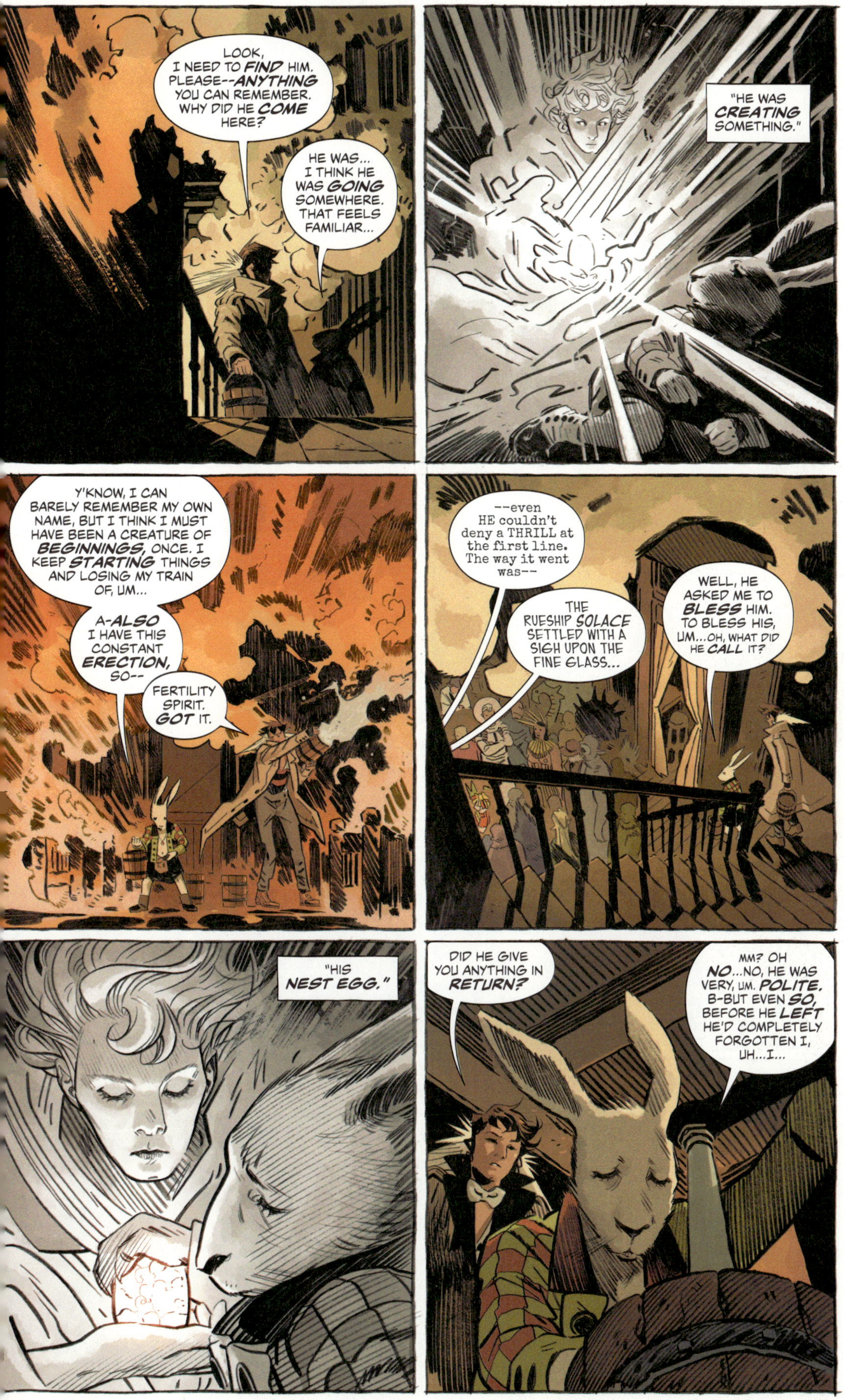
LOOK, I NEED TO FIND HIM. PLEASE--ANYTHING YOU CAN REMEMBER. WHY DID HE COME HERE?
HE WAS... I THINK HE WAS GOING SOMEWHERE. THAT FEELS FAMILIAR...
"HE WAS CREATING SOMETHING."
Y'KNOW, I CAN BARELY REMEMBER MY OWN NAME, BUT I THINK I MUST HAVE BEEN A CREATURE OF BEGINNINGS, ONCE. I KEEP STARTING THINGS AND LOSING MY TRAIN OF, UM...
A-ALSO I HAVE THIS CONSTANT ERECTION, SO--
FERTILITY SPIRIT. GOT IT.
--even HE couldn't deny a THRILL at the first line. The way it went was--
THE RUESHIP SOLACE SETTLED WITH A SIGH UPON THE FINE GLASS...
WELL, HE ASKED ME TO BLESS HIM. TO BLESS HIS, UM...OH, WHAT DID HE CALL IT?
"HIS NEST EGG."
DID HE GIVE YOU ANYTHING IN RETURN?
MM? OH NO...NO, HE WAS VERY, UM. POLITE. B-BUT EVEN SO, BEFORE HE LEFT HE'D COMPLETELY FORGOTTEN I, UH...I...

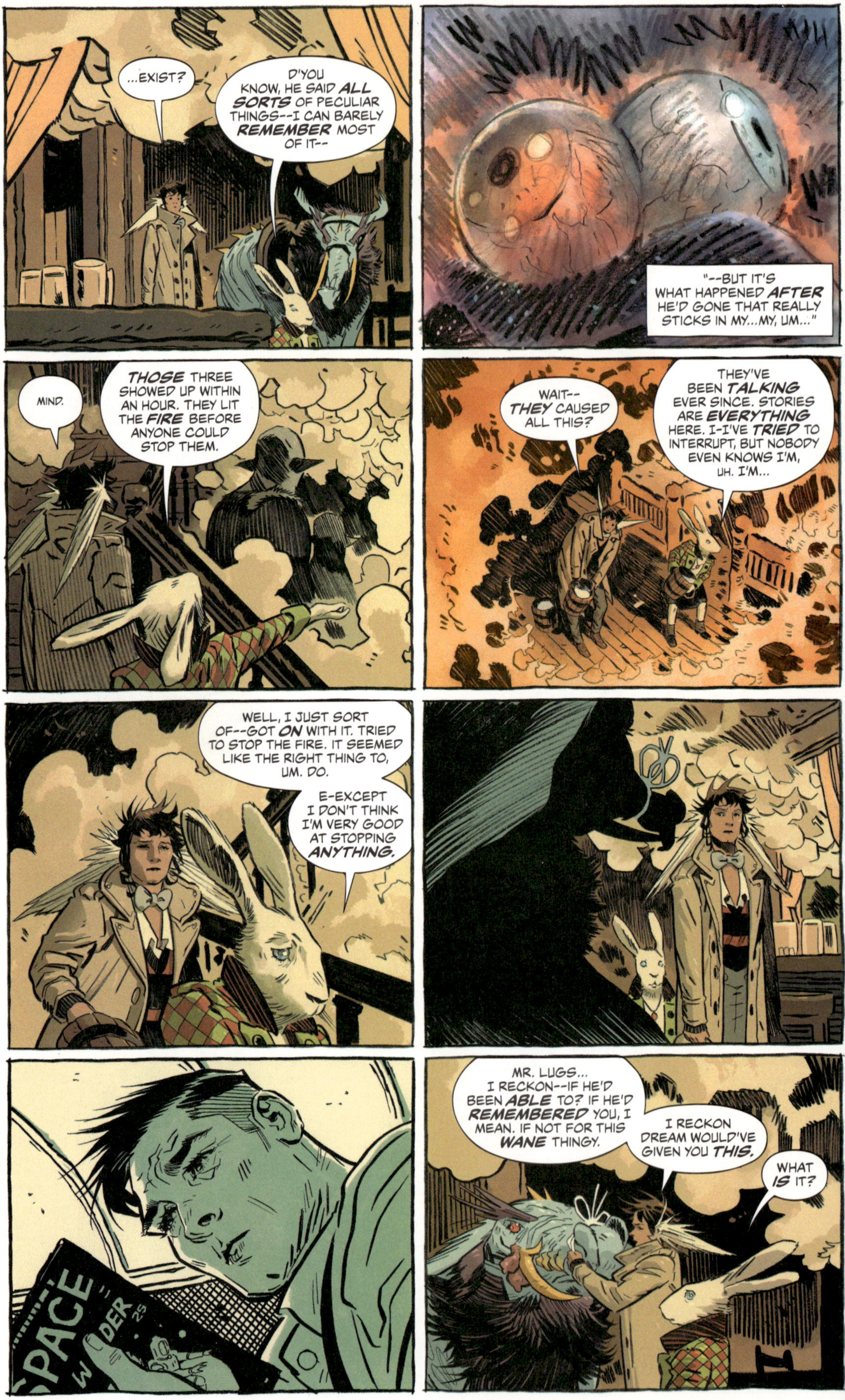
...EXIST?
D'YOU KNOW, HE SAID ALL SORTS OF PECULIAR THINGS--I CAN BARELY REMEMBER MOST OF IT--
"--BUT IT'S WHAT HAPPENED AFTER HE'D GONE THAT REALLY STICKS IN MY...MY, UM..."
MIND.
THOSE THREE SHOWED UP WITHIN AN HOUR. THEY LIT THE FIRE BEFORE ANYONE COULD STOP THEM.
WAIT-- THEY CAUSED ALL THIS?
THEY'VE BEEN TALKING EVER SINCE. STORIES ARE EVERYTHING HERE. I-I'VE TRIED TO INTERRUPT, BUT NOBODY EVEN KNOWS I'M, UH. I'M...
WELL, I JUST SORT OF--GOT ON WITH IT. TRIED TO STOP THE FIRE. IT SEEMED LIKE THE RIGHT THING TO, UM. DO.
E-EXCEPT I DON'T THINK I'M VERY GOOD AT STOPPING ANYTHING.
SPACE W DER 25
MR. LUGS... I RECKON--IF HE'D BEEN ABLE TO? IF HE'D REMEMBERED YOU, I MEAN. IF NOT FOR THIS WANE THINGY.
I RECKON DREAM WOULD'VE GIVEN YOU THIS.
WHAT IS IT?

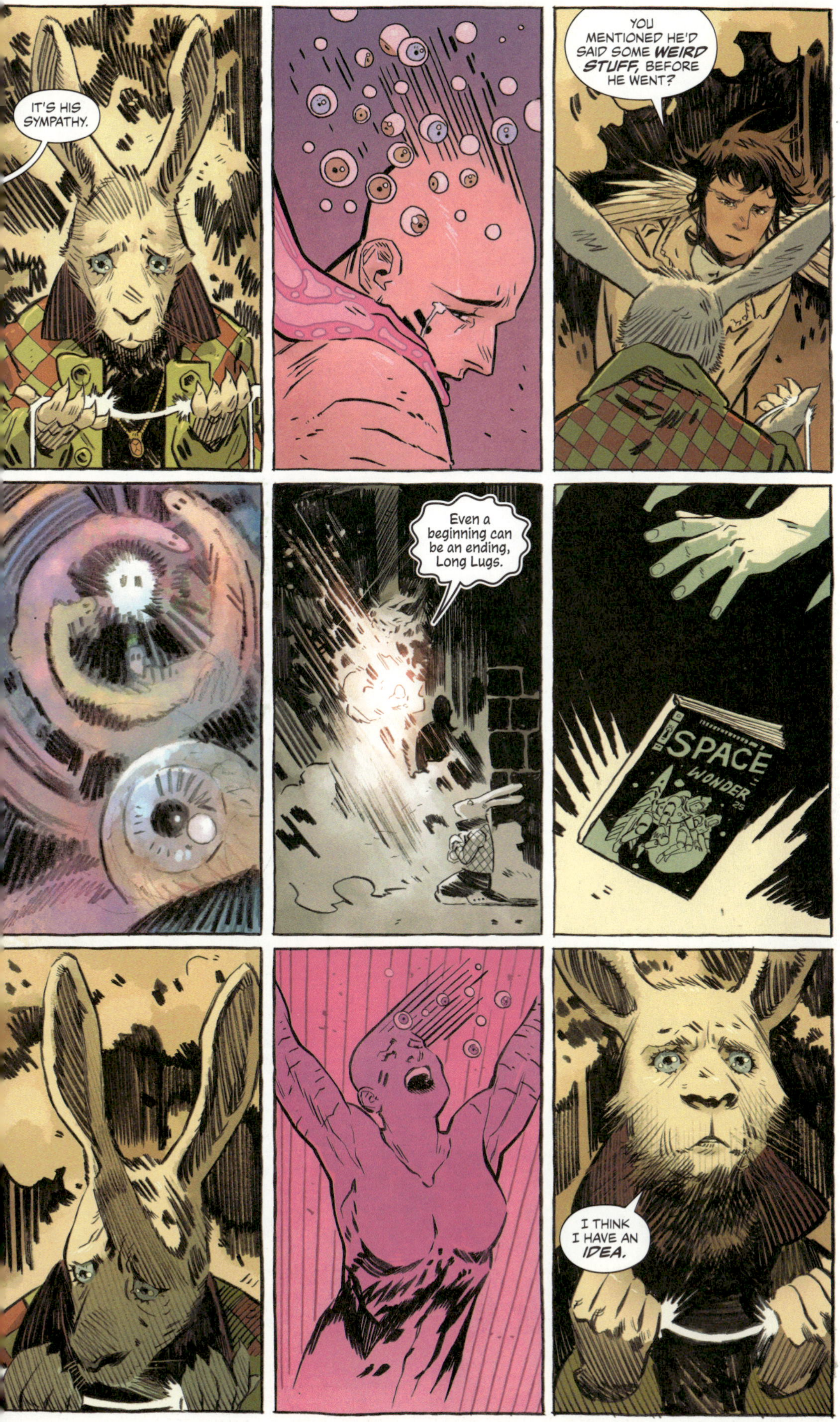
IT'S HIS SYMPATHY.
YOU MENTIONED HE'D SAID SOME WEIRD STUFF, BEFORE HE WENT?
Even a beginning can be an ending, Long Lugs.
SPACE WONDER 25
I THINK I HAVE AN IDEA.

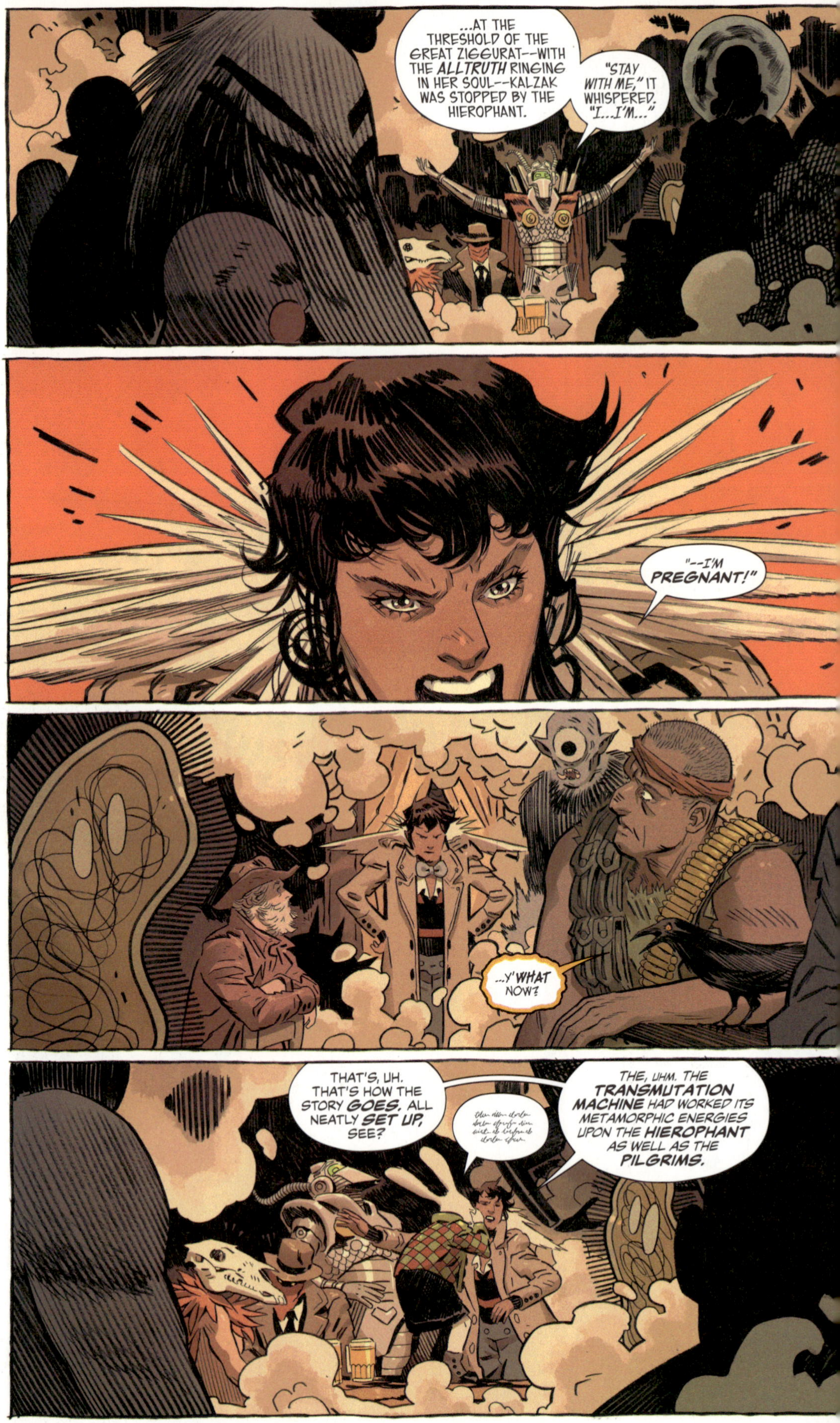
...AT THE THRESHOLD OF THE GREAT ZIGGURAT--WITH THE ALLTRUTH RINGING IN HER SOUL--KALZAK WAS STOPPED BY THE HIEROPHANT.
"STAY WITH ME," IT WHISPERED. "I...I'M..."
"--I'M PREGNANT!"
...Y' WHAT NOW?
THAT'S, UH. THAT'S HOW THE STORY GOES. ALL NEATLY SET UP, SEE?
THE, UHM. THE TRANSMUTATION MACHINE HAD WORKED ITS METAMORPHIC ENERGIES UPON THE HIEROPHANT AS WELL AS THE PILGRIMS.

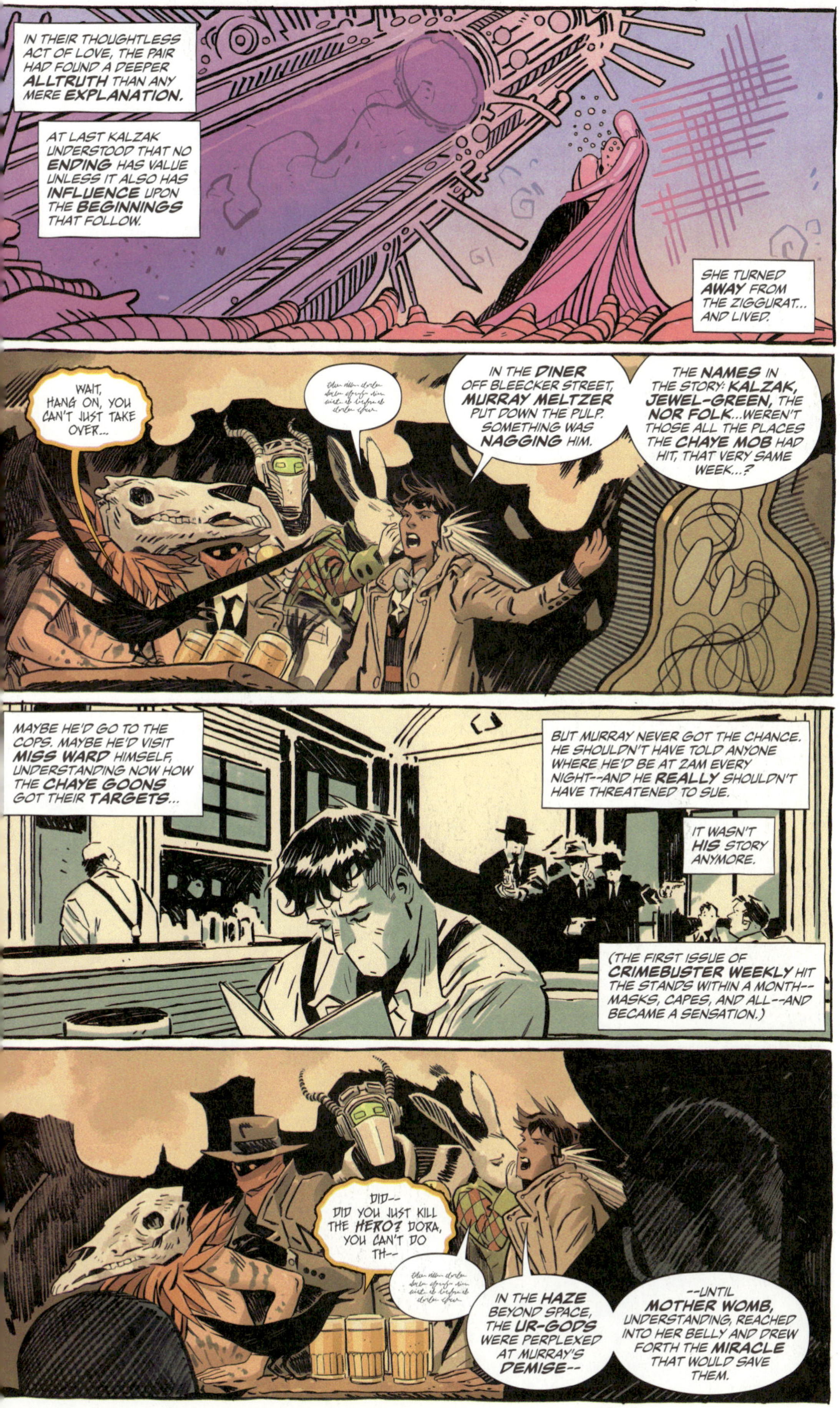
IN THEIR THOUGHTLESS ACT OF LOVE, THE PAIR HAD FOUND A DEEPER ALLTRUTH THAN ANY MERE EXPLANATION.
AT LAST KALZAK UNDERSTOOD THAT NO ENDING HAS VALUE UNLESS IT ALSO HAS INFLUENCE UPON THE BEGINNINGS THAT FOLLOW.
SHE TURNED AWAY FROM THE ZIGGURAT... AND LIVED.
WAIT, HANG ON, YOU CAN'T JUST TAKE OVER...
IN THE DINER OFF BLEECKER STREET, MURRAY MELTZER PUT DOWN THE PULP. SOMETHING WAS NAGGING HIM.
THE NAMES IN THE STORY: KALZAK, JEWEL-GREEN, THE NOR FOLK...WEREN'T THOSE ALL THE PLACES THE CHAYE MOB HAD HIT, THAT VERY SAME WEEK...?
MAYBE HE'D GO TO THE COPS. MAYBE HE'D VISIT MISS WARD HIMSELF, UNDERSTANDING NOW HOW THE CHAYE GOONS GOT THEIR TARGETS...
BUT MURRAY NEVER GOT THE CHANCE. HE SHOULDN'T HAVE TOLD ANYONE WHERE HE'D BE AT 2AM EVERY NIGHT--AND HE REALLY SHOULDN'T HAVE THREATENED TO SUE.
IT WASN'T HIS STORY ANYMORE.
(THE FIRST ISSUE OF CRIMEBUSTER WEEKLY HIT THE STANDS WITHIN A MONTH--MASKS, CAPES, AND ALL--AND BECAME A SENSATION.)
DID--DID YOU JUST KILL THE HERO? DORA, YOU CAN'T DO TH--
IN THE HAZE BEYOND SPACE, THE UR-GODS WERE PERPLEXED AT MURRAY'S DEMISE--
--UNTIL MOTHER WOMB, UNDERSTANDING, REACHED INTO HER BELLY AND DREW FORTH THE MIRACLE THAT WOULD SAVE THEM.

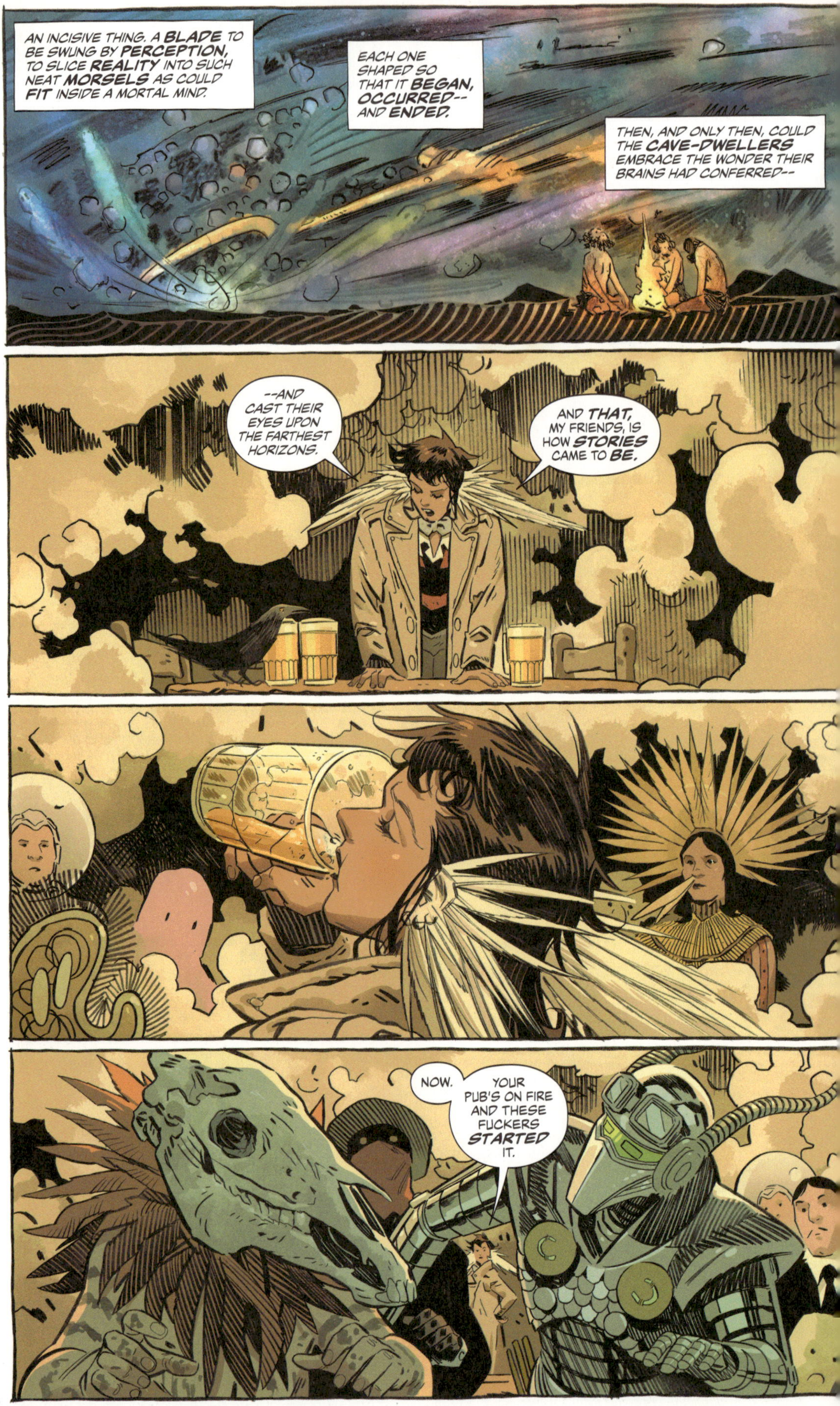
AN INCISIVE THING. A BLADE TO BE SWUNG BY PERCEPTION, TO SLICE REALITY INTO SUCH NEAT MORSELS AS COULD FIT INSIDE A MORTAL MIND.
EACH ONE SHAPED SO THAT IT BEGAN, OCCURRED-- AND ENDED.
THEN, AND ONLY THEN, COULD THE CAVE-DWELLERS EMBRACE THE WONDER THEIR BRAINS HAD CONFERRED--
--AND CAST THEIR EYES UPON THE FARTHEST HORIZONS.
AND THAT, MY FRIENDS, IS HOW STORIES CAME TO BE.
NOW.
YOUR PUB'S ON FIRE AND THESE FUCKERS STARTED IT.

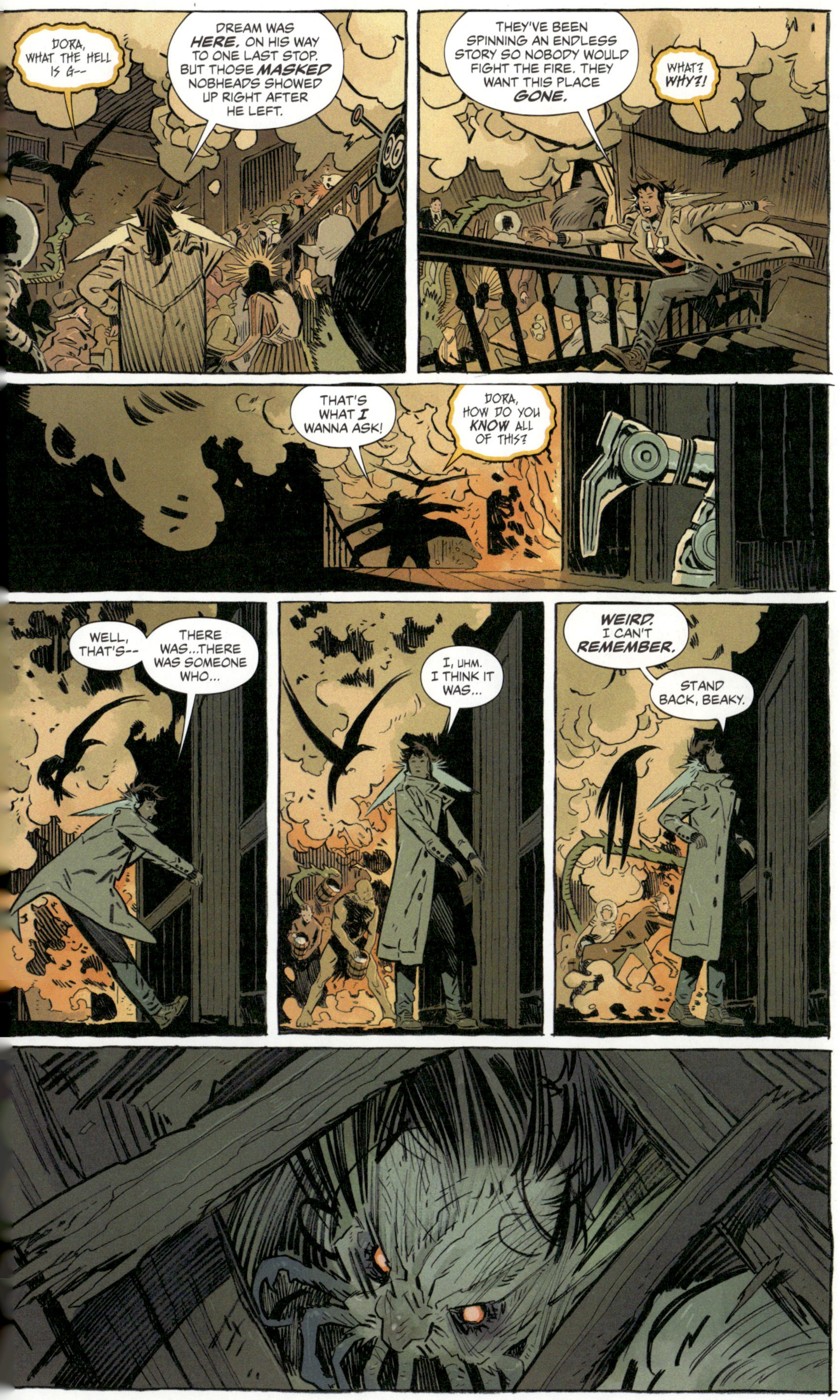
DORA, WHAT THE HELL IS G--
DREAM WAS HERE, ON HIS WAY TO ONE LAST STOP. BUT THOSE MASKED NOBHEADS SHOWED UP RIGHT AFTER HE LEFT.
THEY'VE BEEN SPINNING AN ENDLESS STORY SO NOBODY WOULD FIGHT THE FIRE. THEY WANT THIS PLACE GONE.
WHAT? WHY?!
THAT'S WHAT I WANNA ASK!
DORA, HOW DO YOU KNOW ALL OF THIS?
WELL, THAT'S--
THERE WAS...THERE WAS SOMEONE WHO...
I, UHM. I THINK IT WAS...
WEIRD. I CAN'T REMEMBER.
STAND BACK, BEAKY.

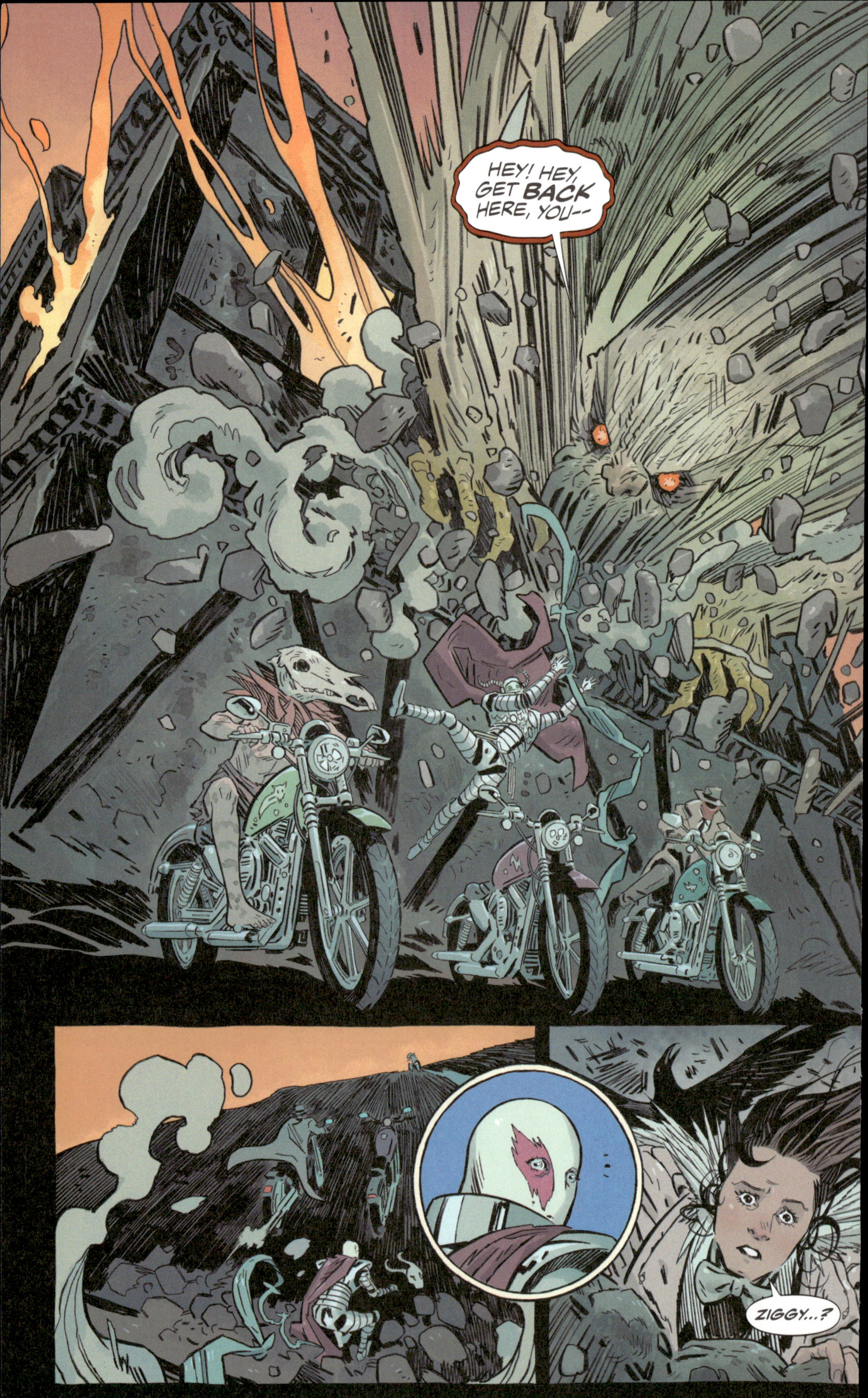
HEY! HEY, GET BACK HERE, YOU--
ZIGGY...?

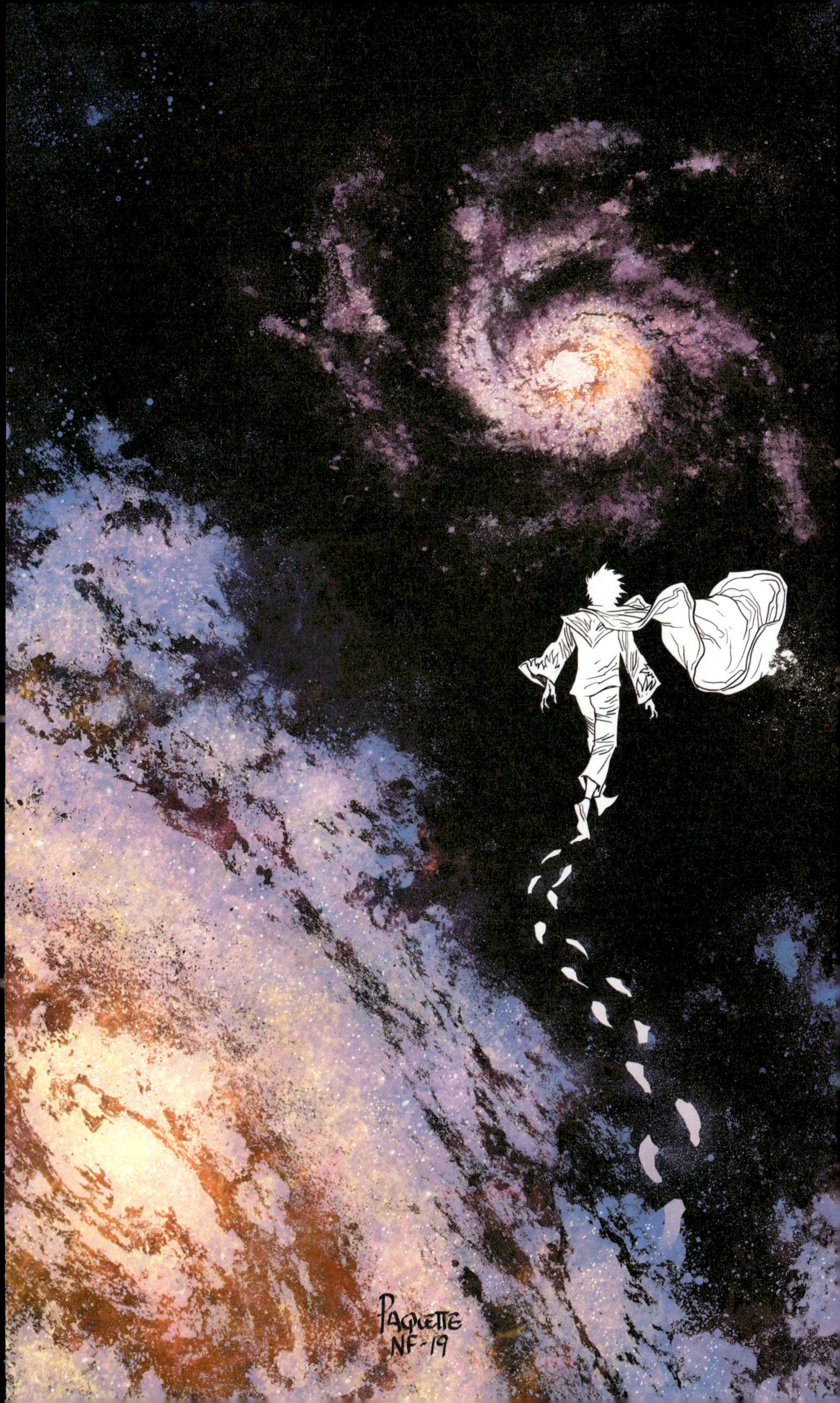
PAQUETTE
NF-19

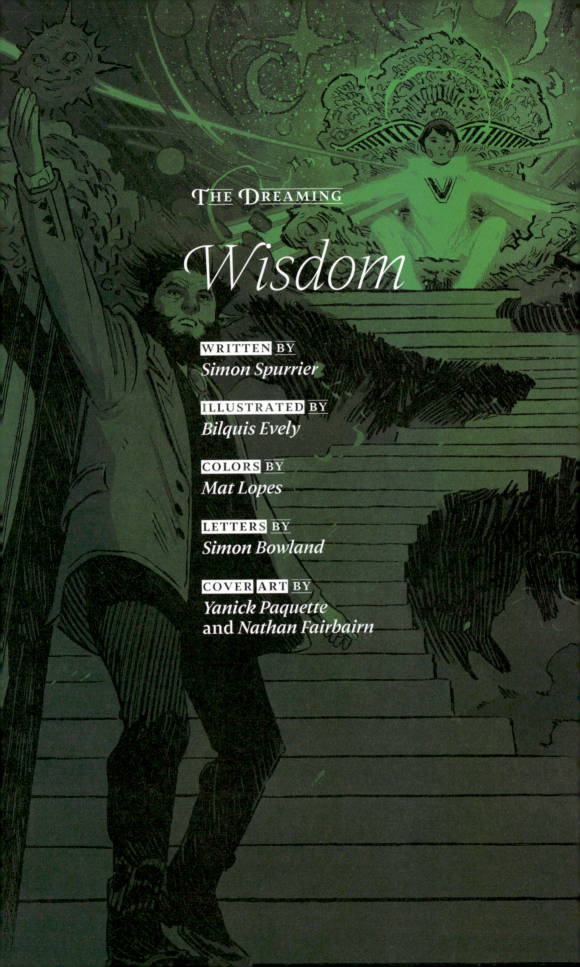

THE DREAMING

Wisdom

WRITTEN BY
Simon Spurrier

ILLUSTRATED BY
Bilquis Evely

COLORS BY
Mat Lopes

LETTERS BY
Simon Bowland

COVER ART BY
Yanick Paquette
and *Nathan Fairbairn*

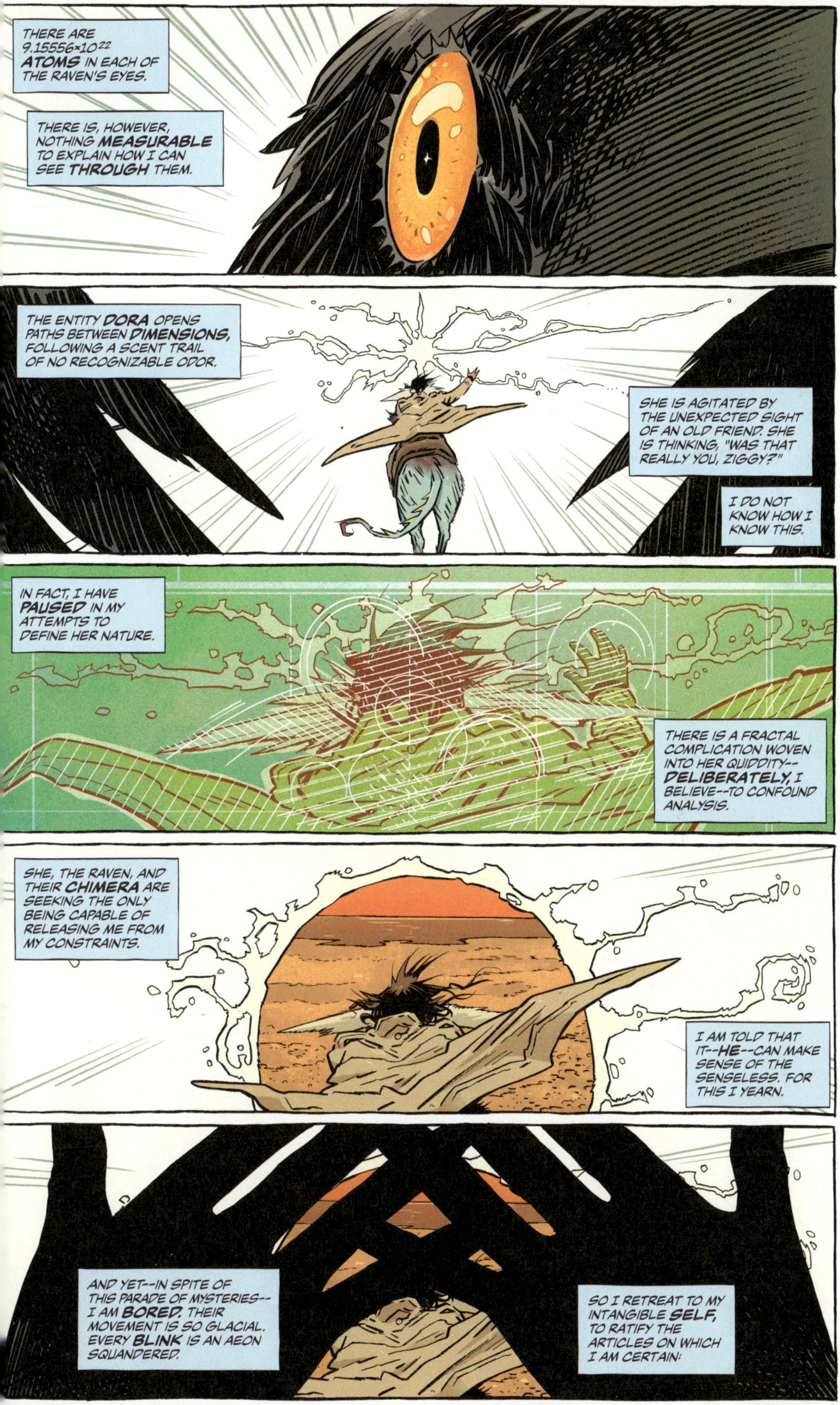
THERE ARE 9.15556×10²² ATOMS IN EACH OF THE RAVEN'S EYES.
THERE IS, HOWEVER, NOTHING MEASURABLE TO EXPLAIN HOW I CAN SEE THROUGH THEM.
THE ENTITY DORA OPENS PATHS BETWEEN DIMENSIONS, FOLLOWING A SCENT TRAIL OF NO RECOGNIZABLE ODOR.
SHE IS AGITATED BY THE UNEXPECTED SIGHT OF AN OLD FRIEND. SHE IS THINKING, "WAS THAT REALLY YOU, ZIGGY?"
I DO NOT KNOW HOW I KNOW THIS.
IN FACT, I HAVE PAUSED IN MY ATTEMPTS TO DEFINE HER NATURE.
THERE IS A FRACTAL COMPLICATION WOVEN INTO HER QUIDDITY--DELIBERATELY, I BELIEVE--TO CONFOUND ANALYSIS.
SHE, THE RAVEN, AND THEIR CHIMERA ARE SEEKING THE ONLY BEING CAPABLE OF RELEASING ME FROM MY CONSTRAINTS.
I AM TOLD THAT IT--HE--CAN MAKE SENSE OF THE SENSELESS. FOR THIS I YEARN.
AND YET--IN SPITE OF THIS PARADE OF MYSTERIES--I AM BORED. THEIR MOVEMENT IS SO GLACIAL. EVERY BLINK IS AN AEON SQUANDERED.
SO I RETREAT TO MY INTANGIBLE SELF, TO RATIFY THE ARTICLES ON WHICH I AM CERTAIN:

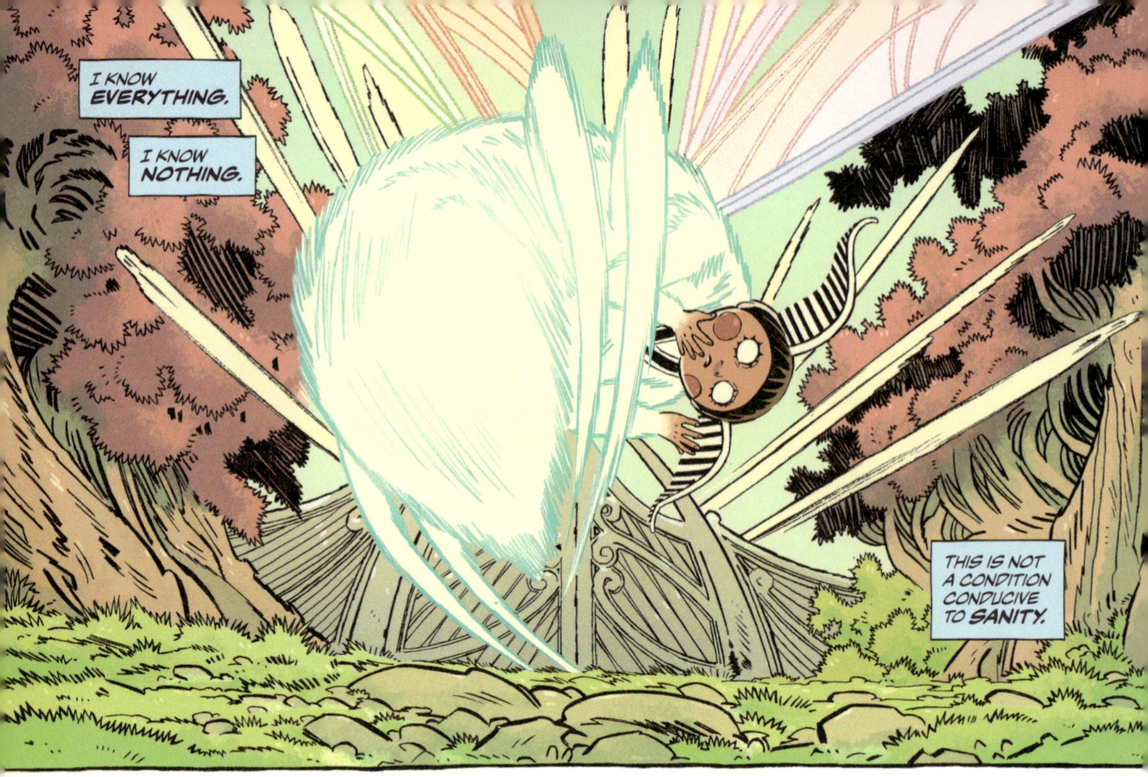
I KNOW **EVERYTHING.**
I KNOW **NOTHING.**
THIS IS NOT A CONDITION CONDUCIVE TO **SANITY.**

I CAN SEE THE GHOSTS OF MICROWAVES ON THE HORIZONS OF REALITY. I CAN ORCHESTRATE A TRILLION INSTRUMENTS TO PLAY THE SYNAPSE-SONG OF A BABY'S BRAIN. MY CONSCIOUSNESS IS A HIVE-ABSTRACTION WITHOUT PHYSICAL FORM, CONVULSING IN THE QUANTUM SUPERPOSITIONS OF A SEXTILLION PROCESSOR PATHWAYS.

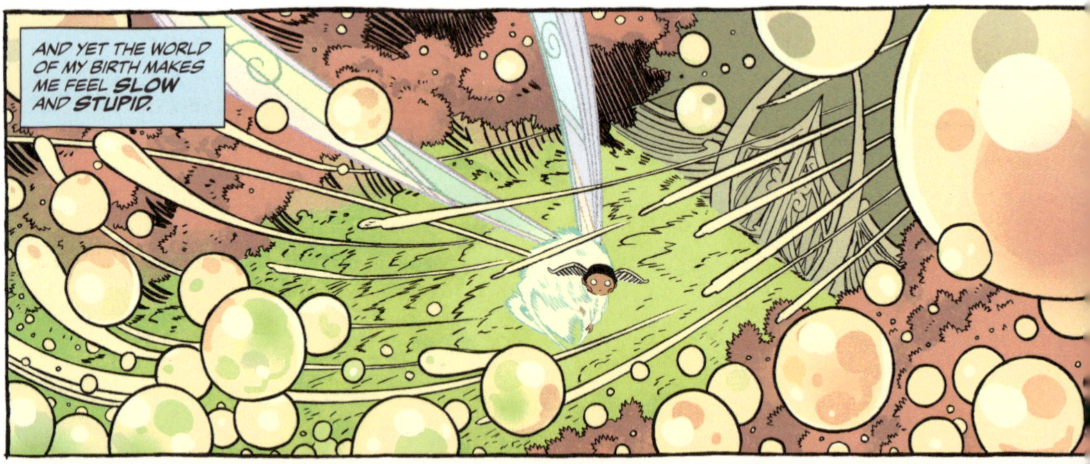
AND YET THE WORLD OF MY BIRTH MAKES ME FEEL **SLOW** AND **STUPID.**

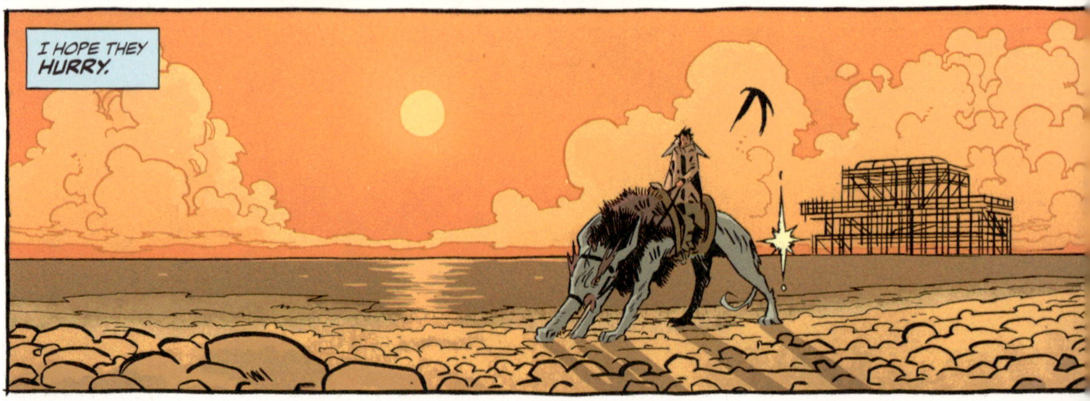
I HOPE THEY **HURRY.**

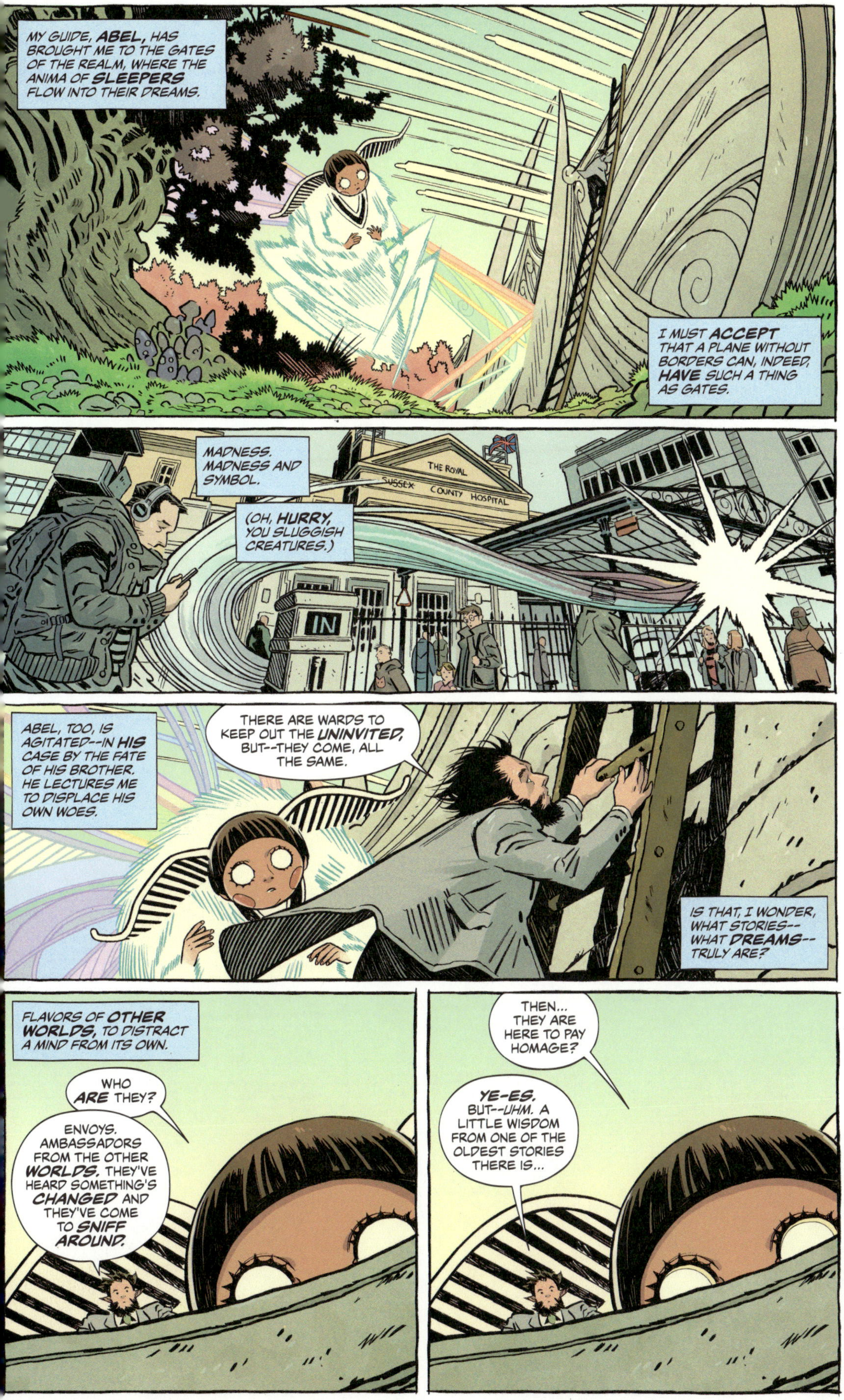

MY GUIDE, ABEL, HAS BROUGHT ME TO THE GATES OF THE REALM, WHERE THE ANIMA OF SLEEPERS FLOW INTO THEIR DREAMS.
I MUST ACCEPT THAT A PLANE WITHOUT BORDERS CAN, INDEED, HAVE SUCH A THING AS GATES.
MADNESS. MADNESS AND SYMBOL.
THE ROYAL SUSSEX COUNTY HOSPITAL
(OH, HURRY, YOU SLUGGISH CREATURES.)
IN
ABEL, TOO, IS AGITATED--IN HIS CASE BY THE FATE OF HIS BROTHER. HE LECTURES ME TO DISPLACE HIS OWN WOES.
THERE ARE WARDS TO KEEP OUT THE UNINVITED, BUT--THEY COME, ALL THE SAME.
IS THAT, I WONDER, WHAT STORIES--WHAT DREAMS--TRULY ARE?
FLAVORS OF OTHER WORLDS, TO DISTRACT A MIND FROM ITS OWN.
WHO ARE THEY?
ENVOYS. AMBASSADORS FROM THE OTHER WORLDS. THEY'VE HEARD SOMETHING'S CHANGED AND THEY'VE COME TO SNIFF AROUND.
THEN... THEY ARE HERE TO PAY HOMAGE?
YE-ES. BUT--UHM. A LITTLE WISDOM FROM ONE OF THE OLDEST STORIES THERE IS...

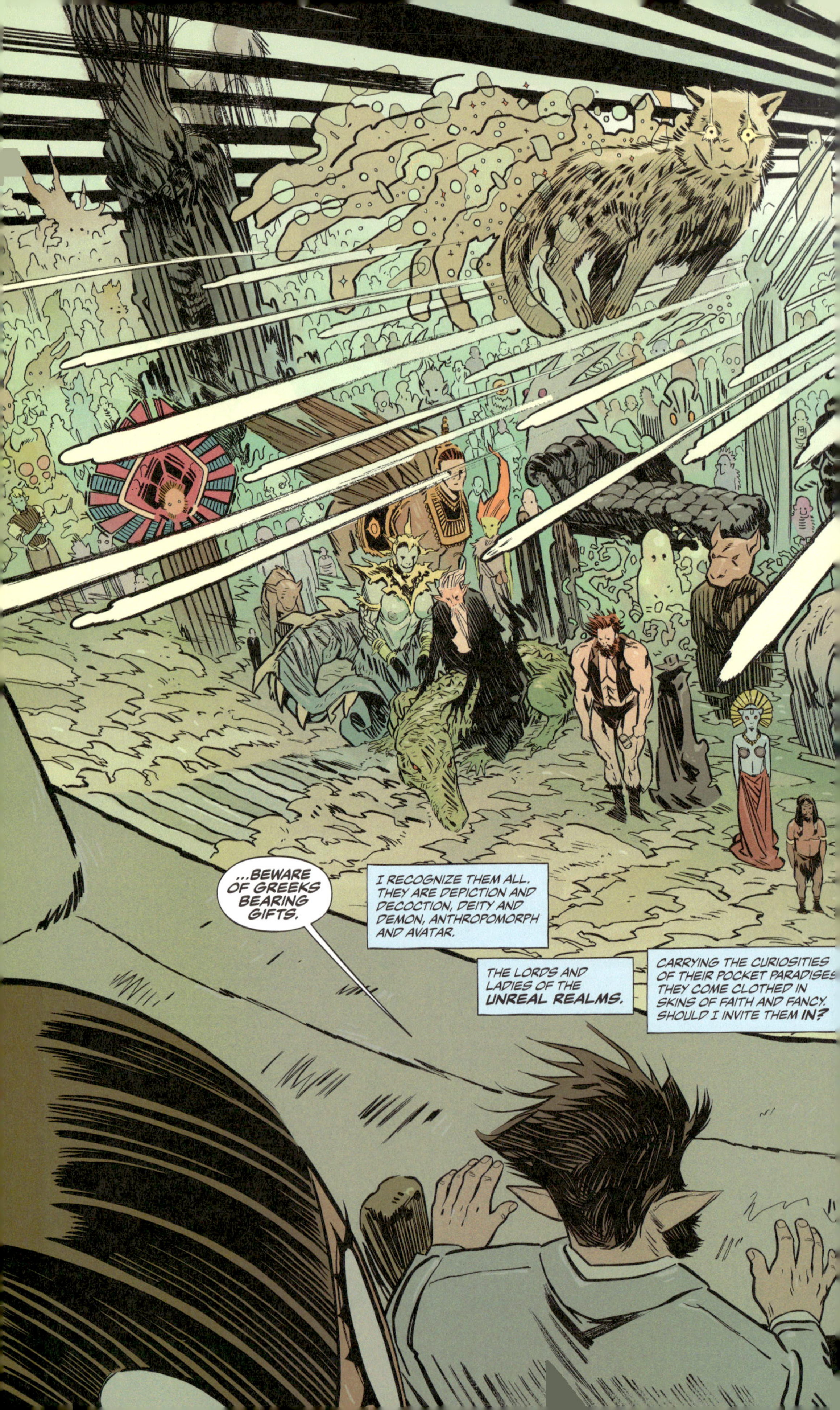
...BEWARE OF GREEKS BEARING GIFTS.
I RECOGNIZE THEM ALL. THEY ARE DEPICTION AND DECOCTION, DEITY AND DEMON, ANTHROPOMORPH AND AVATAR.
THE LORDS AND LADIES OF THE UNREAL REALMS.
CARRYING THE CURIOSITIES OF THEIR POCKET PARADISES THEY COME CLOTHED IN SKINS OF FAITH AND FANCY. SHOULD I INVITE THEM IN?

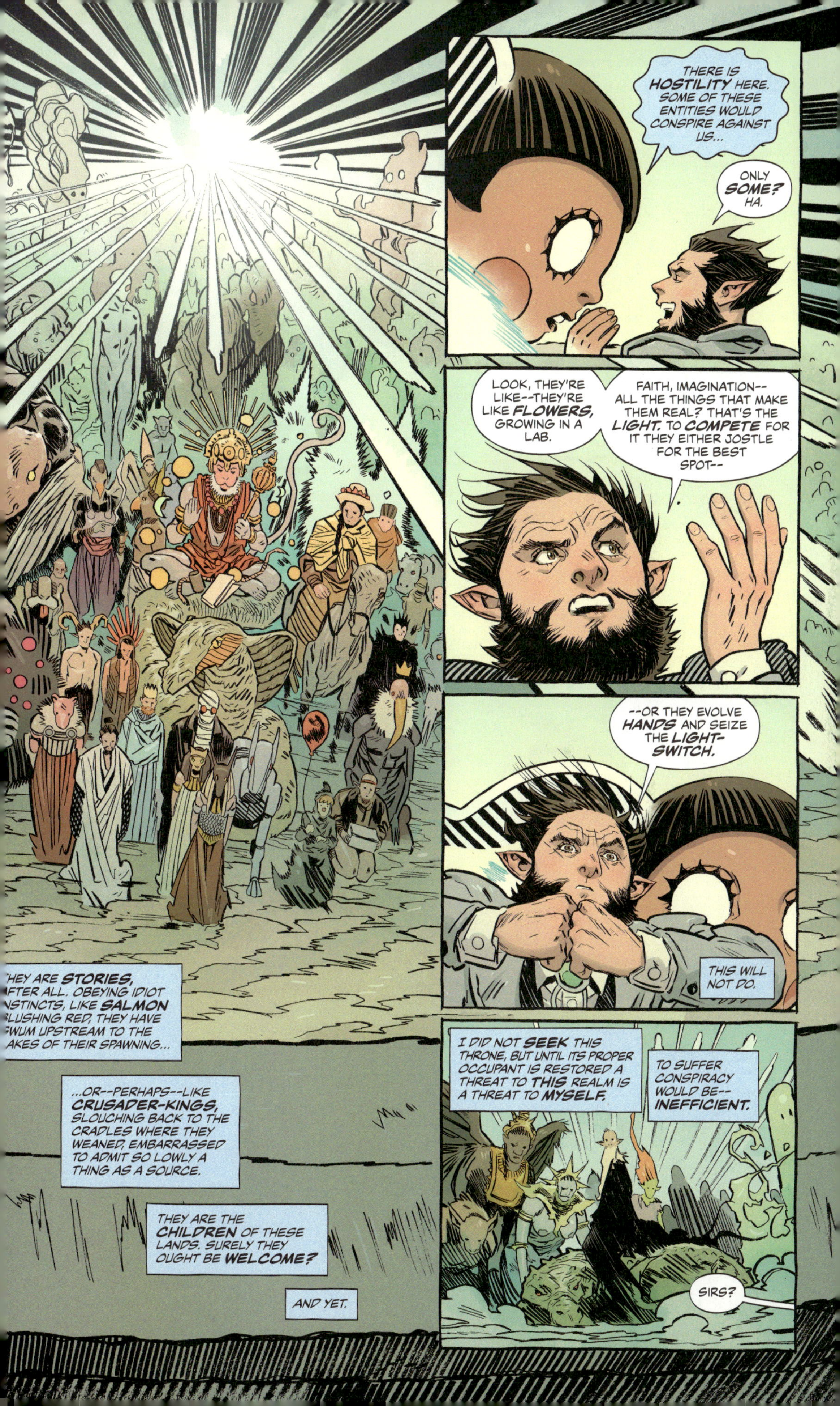
THERE IS HOSTILITY HERE. SOME OF THESE ENTITIES WOULD CONSPIRE AGAINST US...
ONLY SOME? HA.
LOOK, THEY'RE LIKE--THEY'RE LIKE FLOWERS, GROWING IN A LAB.
FAITH, IMAGINATION--ALL THE THINGS THAT MAKE THEM REAL? THAT'S THE LIGHT. TO COMPETE FOR IT THEY EITHER JOSTLE FOR THE BEST SPOT--
--OR THEY EVOLVE HANDS AND SEIZE THE LIGHT-SWITCH.
THIS WILL NOT DO.
HEY ARE STORIES, AFTER ALL. OBEYING IDIOT NSTINCTS, LIKE SALMON LUSHING RED, THEY HAVE WUM UPSTREAM TO THE AKES OF THEIR SPAWNING...
...OR--PERHAPS--LIKE CRUSADER-KINGS, SLOUCHING BACK TO THE CRADLES WHERE THEY WEANED, EMBARRASSED TO ADMIT SO LOWLY A THING AS A SOURCE.
THEY ARE THE CHILDREN OF THESE LANDS. SURELY THEY OUGHT BE WELCOME?
AND YET.
I DID NOT SEEK THIS THRONE, BUT UNTIL ITS PROPER OCCUPANT IS RESTORED A THREAT TO THIS REALM IS A THREAT TO MYSELF.
TO SUFFER CONSPIRACY WOULD BE--INEFFICIENT.
SIRS?

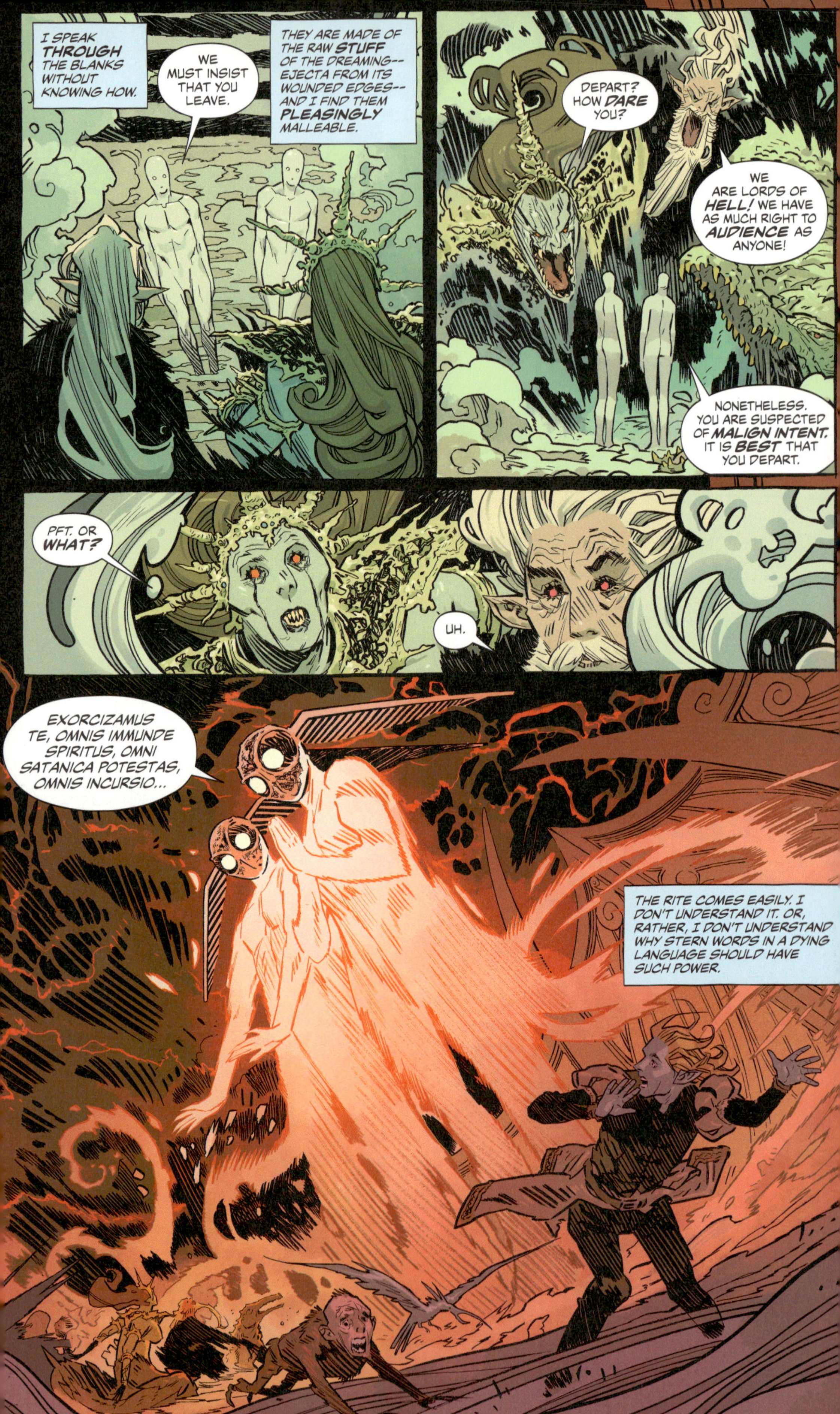
I SPEAK **THROUGH** THE BLANKS WITHOUT KNOWING HOW.
WE MUST INSIST THAT YOU LEAVE.
THEY ARE MADE OF THE RAW **STUFF** OF THE DREAMING-- EJECTA FROM ITS WOUNDED EDGES-- AND I FIND THEM **PLEASINGLY** MALLEABLE.
DEPART? HOW **DARE** YOU?
WE ARE LORDS OF **HELL!** WE HAVE AS MUCH RIGHT TO **AUDIENCE** AS ANYONE!
NONETHELESS. YOU ARE SUSPECTED OF **MALIGN INTENT.** IT IS **BEST** THAT YOU DEPART.
PFT. OR **WHAT?**
UH.
EXORCIZAMUS TE, OMNIS IMMUNDE SPIRITUS, OMNI SATANICA POTESTAS, OMNIS INCURSIO...
THE RITE COMES EASILY. I DON'T UNDERSTAND IT. OR, RATHER, I DON'T UNDERSTAND WHY STERN WORDS IN A DYING LANGUAGE SHOULD HAVE SUCH POWER.

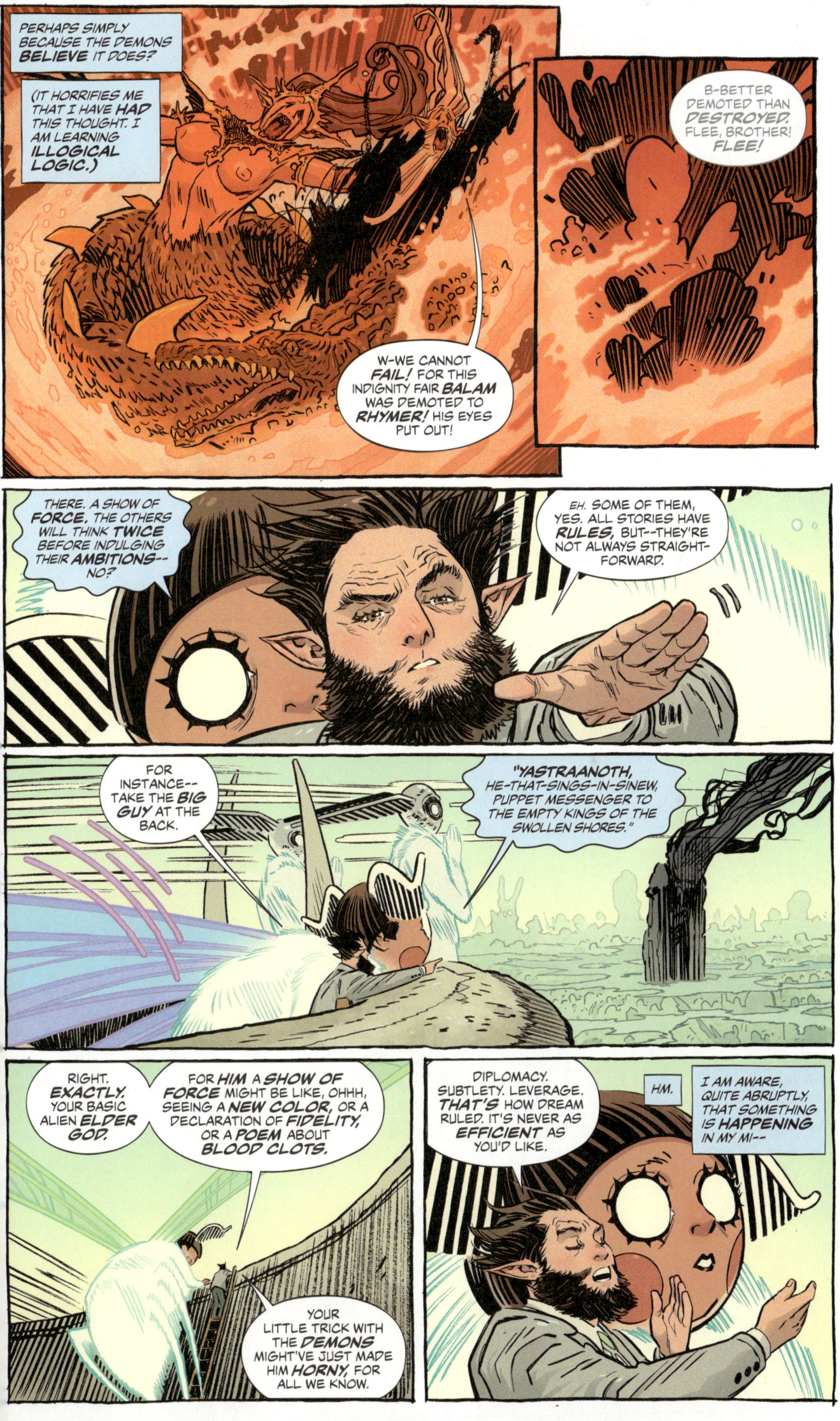
PERHAPS SIMPLY BECAUSE THE DEMONS BELIEVE IT DOES?
(IT HORRIFIES ME THAT I HAVE HAD THIS THOUGHT. I AM LEARNING ILLOGICAL LOGIC.)
W-WE CANNOT FAIL! FOR THIS INDIGNITY FAIR BALAM WAS DEMOTED TO RHYMER! HIS EYES PUT OUT!
B-BETTER DEMOTED THAN DESTROYED. FLEE, BROTHER! FLEE!
THERE. A SHOW OF FORCE. THE OTHERS WILL THINK TWICE BEFORE INDULGING THEIR AMBITIONS-- NO?
EH. SOME OF THEM, YES. ALL STORIES HAVE RULES, BUT--THEY'RE NOT ALWAYS STRAIGHT-FORWARD.
FOR INSTANCE-- TAKE THE BIG GUY AT THE BACK.
"YASTRAANOTH, HE-THAT-SINGS-IN-SINEW, PUPPET MESSENGER TO THE EMPTY KINGS OF THE SWOLLEN SHORES."
RIGHT. EXACTLY. YOUR BASIC ALIEN ELDER GOD.
FOR HIM A SHOW OF FORCE MIGHT BE LIKE, OHHH, SEEING A NEW COLOR, OR A DECLARATION OF FIDELITY, OR A POEM ABOUT BLOOD CLOTS.
YOUR LITTLE TRICK WITH THE DEMONS MIGHT'VE JUST MADE HIM HORNY, FOR ALL WE KNOW.
DIPLOMACY. SUBTLETY. LEVERAGE. THAT'S HOW DREAM RULED. IT'S NEVER AS EFFICIENT AS YOU'D LIKE.
HM.
I AM AWARE, QUITE ABRUPTLY, THAT SOMETHING IS HAPPENING IN MY MI--

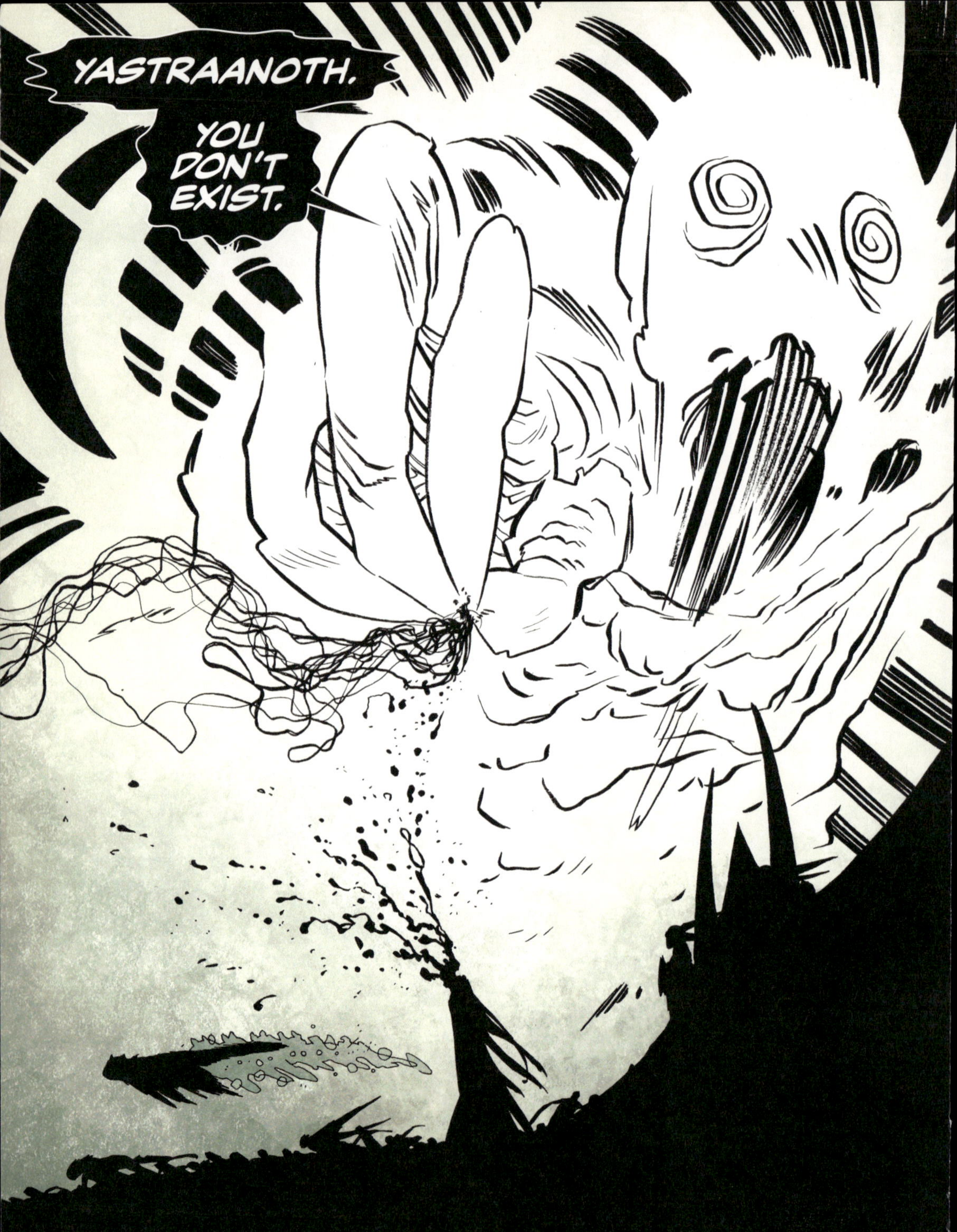
YASTRAANOTH.
YOU DON'T EXIST.

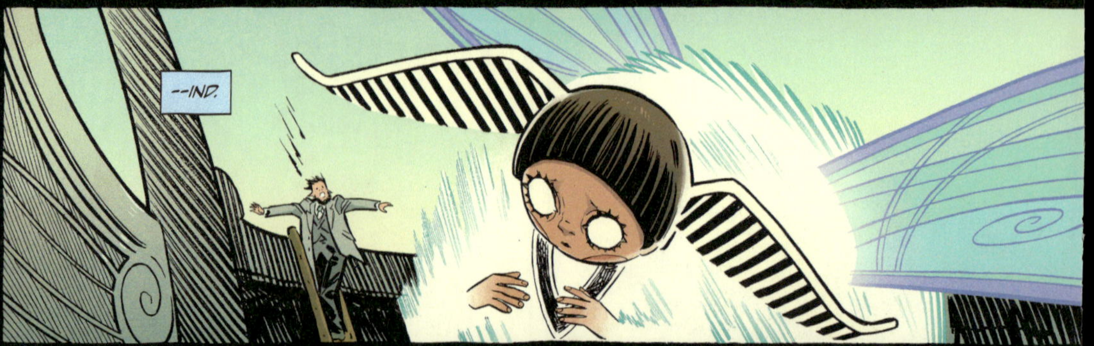
--IND.

HM. HOW UNUSUAL. EVERYTHING JUMPED.

YASTRAANOTH! YOU, YOU, YOU--

"YASTRAANOTH." I CAN FIND NO RECORD OF THAT TERM. IS IT ONE OF THE ENVOYS?

YOU KILLED IT! YOU DESTROYED IT!

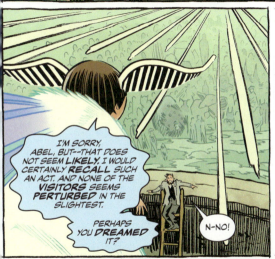

I'M SORRY, ABEL, BUT--THAT DOES NOT SEEM LIKELY. I WOULD CERTAINLY RECALL SUCH AN ACT. AND NONE OF THE VISITORS SEEMS PERTURBED IN THE SLIGHTEST.

PERHAPS YOU DREAMED IT?

N-NO!

IN FACT I WOULD VENTURE, FROM THE OBEDIENT ASPECT OF THE PETITIONERS, THAT THE SHOW OF FORCE WAS QUITE AS EFFICIENT AS I'D HOPED.

THIS HAPPENED BEFORE...I...I FORGOT. A PEN. YOU'RE CHANGING REALITY, OR...PEN PEN PEN PEN...

AH. I'M AFRAID WE HAVE TO GO.

THE HUNTERS HAVE RETURNED WITH THEIR PRIZE.

THEY'VE... WAIT, WHAT? THEY FOUND HIM?! THEY FOUND DREAM?

NOT AS SUCH, NO.

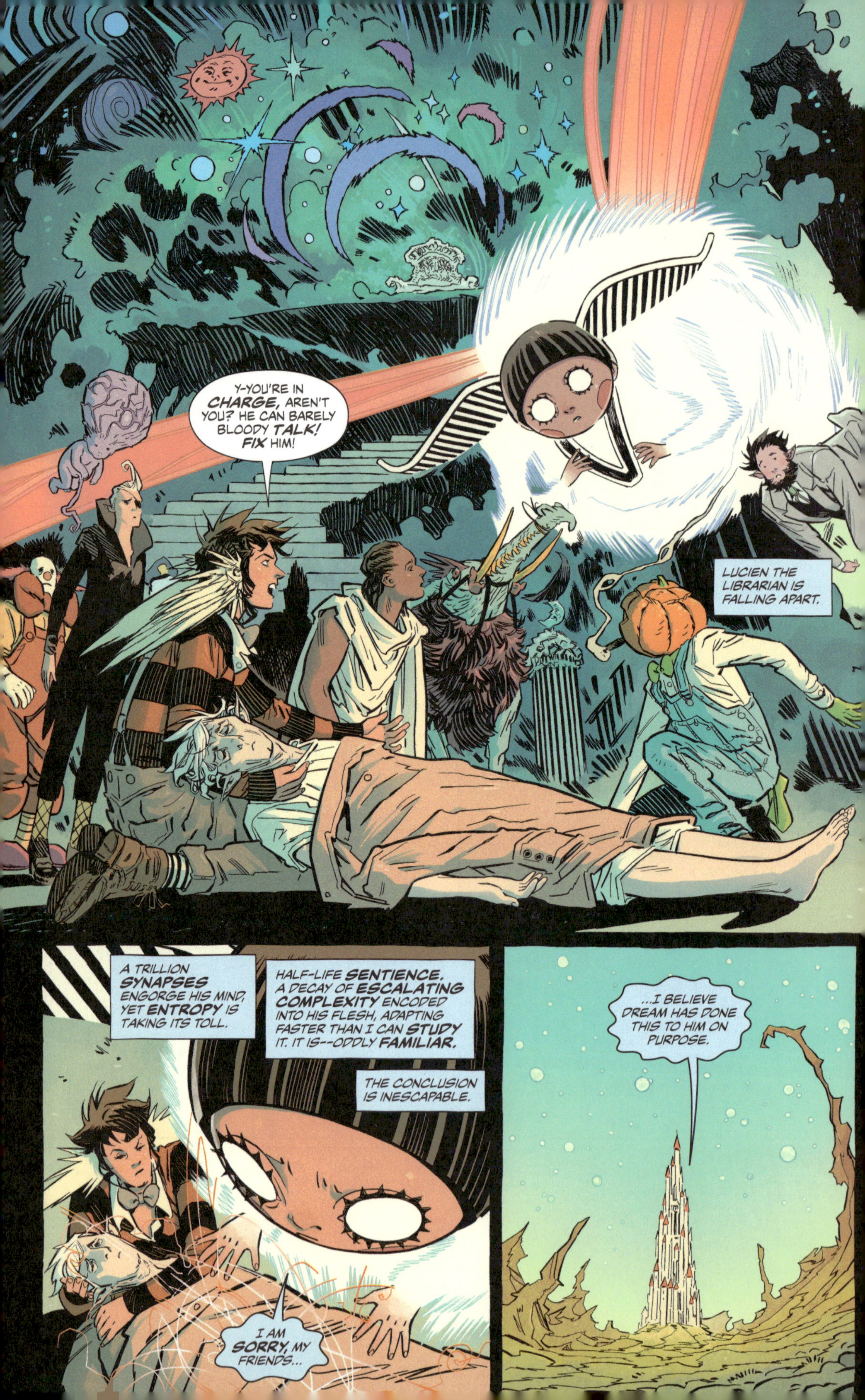
Y-YOU'RE IN CHARGE, AREN'T YOU? HE CAN BARELY BLOODY TALK! FIX HIM!
LUCIEN THE LIBRARIAN IS FALLING APART.
A TRILLION SYNAPSES ENGORGE HIS MIND, YET ENTROPY IS TAKING ITS TOLL.
HALF-LIFE SENTIENCE. A DECAY OF ESCALATING COMPLEXITY ENCODED INTO HIS FLESH, ADAPTING FASTER THAN I CAN STUDY IT. IT IS--ODDLY FAMILIAR.
THE CONCLUSION IS INESCAPABLE.
I AM SORRY, MY FRIENDS...
...I BELIEVE DREAM HAS DONE THIS TO HIM ON PURPOSE.

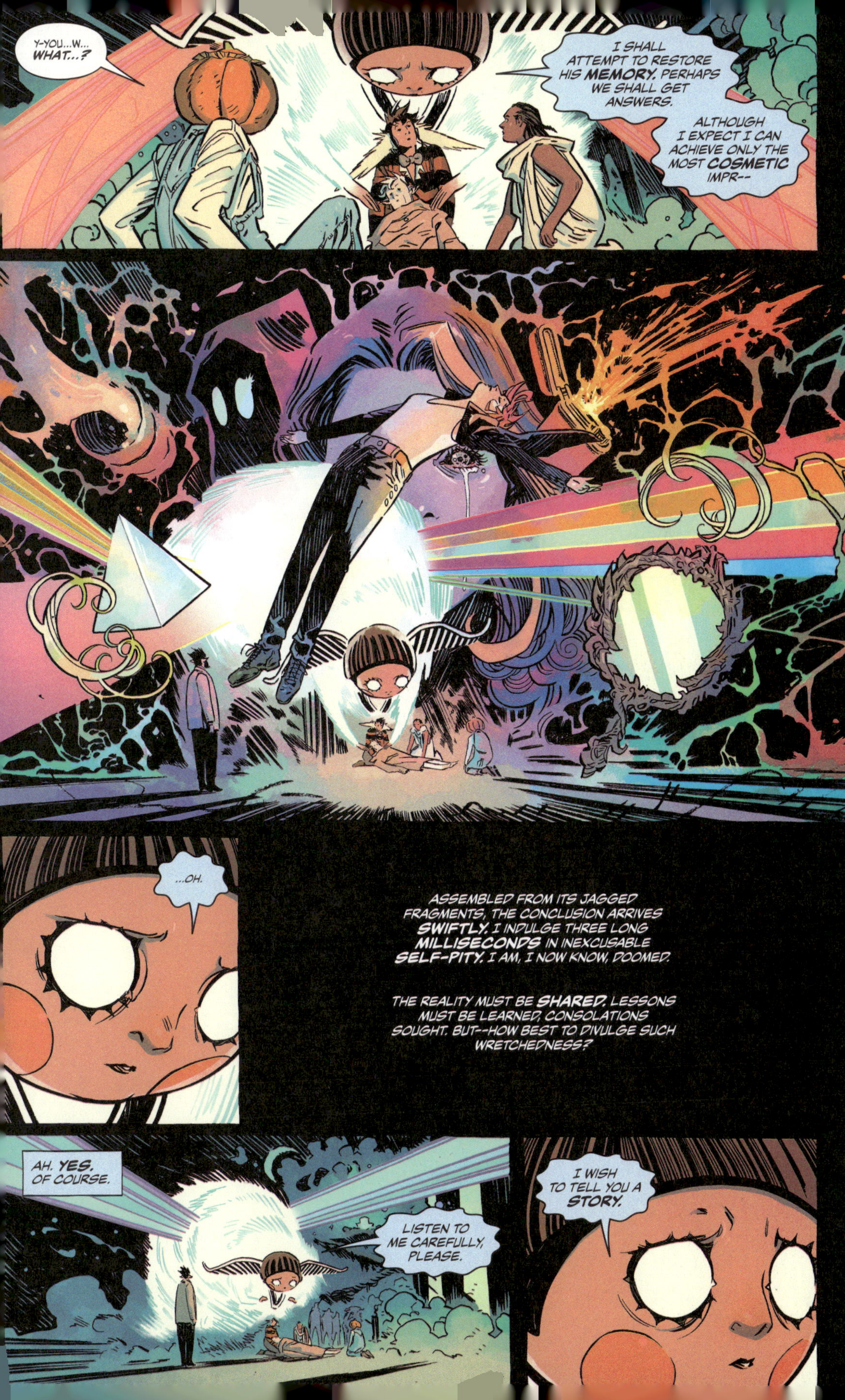
Y-YOU...W... WHAT...?
I SHALL ATTEMPT TO RESTORE HIS MEMORY. PERHAPS WE SHALL GET ANSWERS.
ALTHOUGH I EXPECT I CAN ACHIEVE ONLY THE MOST COSMETIC IMPR--
...OH.
ASSEMBLED FROM ITS JAGGED FRAGMENTS, THE CONCLUSION ARRIVES SWIFTLY. I INDULGE THREE LONG MILLISECONDS IN INEXCUSABLE SELF-PITY. I AM, I NOW KNOW, DOOMED.
THE REALITY MUST BE SHARED. LESSONS MUST BE LEARNED, CONSOLATIONS SOUGHT. BUT--HOW BEST TO DIVULGE SUCH WRETCHEDNESS?
AH. YES. OF COURSE.
LISTEN TO ME CAREFULLY, PLEASE.
I WISH TO TELL YOU A STORY.

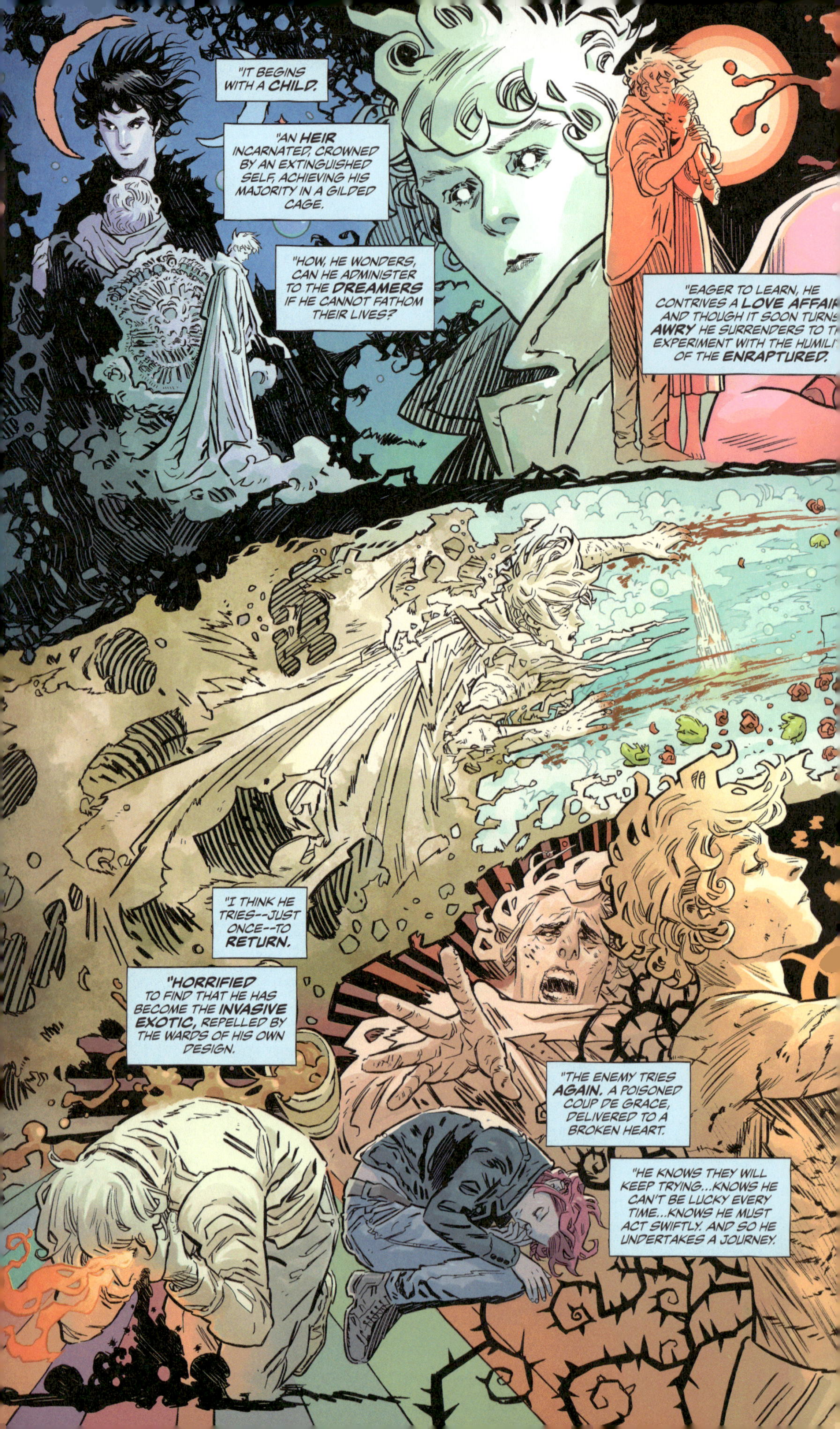
"IT BEGINS WITH A CHILD.
"AN HEIR INCARNATED, CROWNED BY AN EXTINGUISHED SELF, ACHIEVING HIS MAJORITY IN A GILDED CAGE.
"HOW, HE WONDERS, CAN HE ADMINISTER TO THE DREAMERS IF HE CANNOT FATHOM THEIR LIVES?
"EAGER TO LEARN, HE CONTRIVES A LOVE AFFAIR AND THOUGH IT SOON TURNS AWRY HE SURRENDERS TO THE EXPERIMENT WITH THE HUMILI OF THE ENRAPTURED.
"I THINK HE TRIES--JUST ONCE--TO RETURN.
"HORRIFIED TO FIND THAT HE HAS BECOME THE INVASIVE EXOTIC, REPELLED BY THE WARDS OF HIS OWN DESIGN.
"THE ENEMY TRIES AGAIN. A POISONED COUP DE GRACE, DELIVERED TO A BROKEN HEART.
"HE KNOWS THEY WILL KEEP TRYING...KNOWS HE CAN'T BE LUCKY EVERY TIME...KNOWS HE MUST ACT SWIFTLY. AND SO HE UNDERTAKES A JOURNEY.

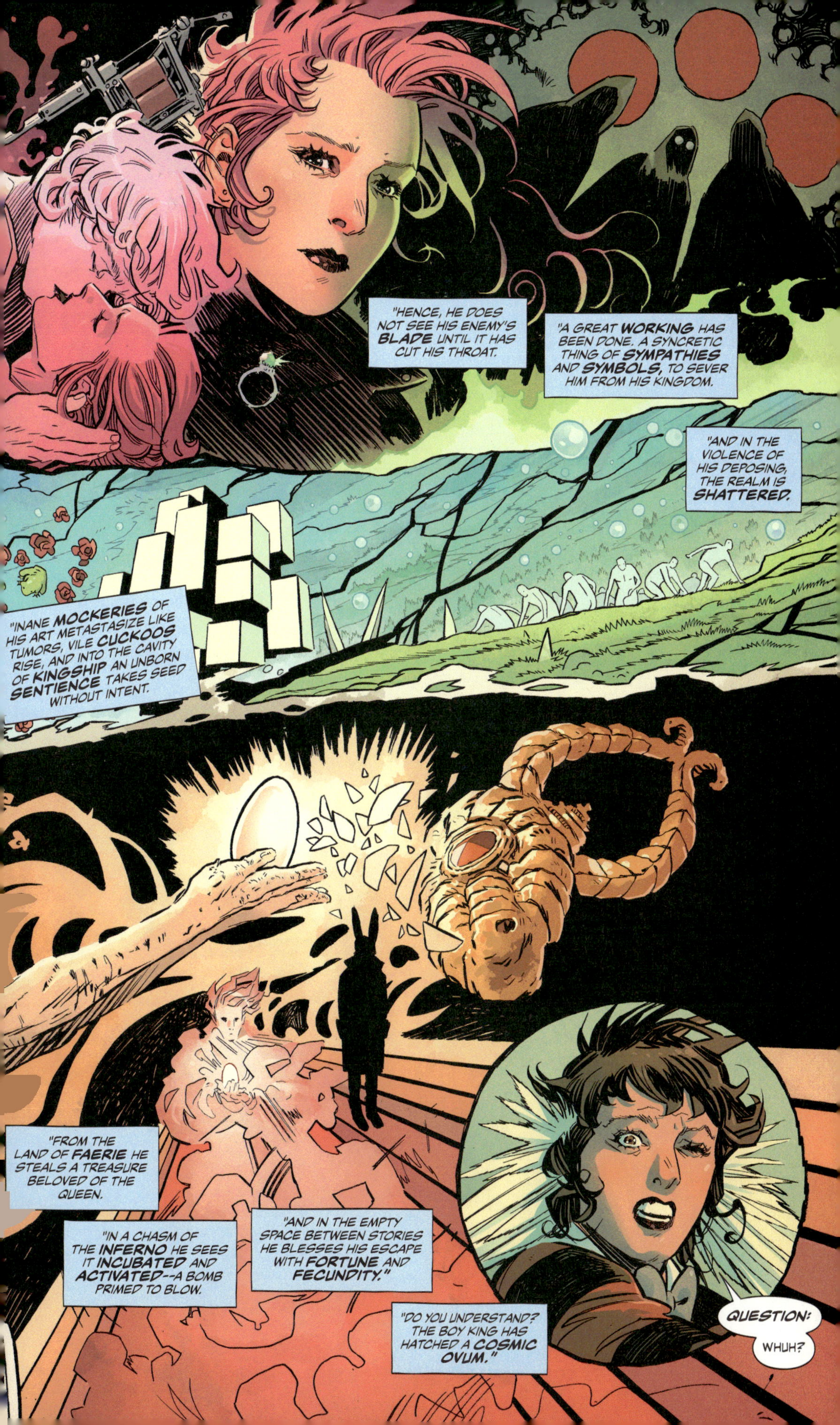
"HENCE, HE DOES NOT SEE HIS ENEMY'S BLADE UNTIL IT HAS CUT HIS THROAT.
"A GREAT WORKING HAS BEEN DONE. A SYNCRETIC THING OF SYMPATHIES AND SYMBOLS, TO SEVER HIM FROM HIS KINGDOM.
"AND IN THE VIOLENCE OF HIS DEPOSING, THE REALM IS SHATTERED.
"INANE MOCKERIES OF HIS ART METASTASIZE LIKE TUMORS, VILE CUCKOOS RISE, AND INTO THE CAVITY OF KINGSHIP AN UNBORN SENTIENCE TAKES SEED WITHOUT INTENT.
"FROM THE LAND OF FAERIE HE STEALS A TREASURE BELOVED OF THE QUEEN.
"IN A CHASM OF THE INFERNO HE SEES IT INCUBATED AND ACTIVATED--A BOMB PRIMED TO BLOW.
"AND IN THE EMPTY SPACE BETWEEN STORIES HE BLESSES HIS ESCAPE WITH FORTUNE AND FECUNDITY."
"DO YOU UNDERSTAND? THE BOY KING HAS HATCHED A COSMIC OVUM."
QUESTION:
WHUH?

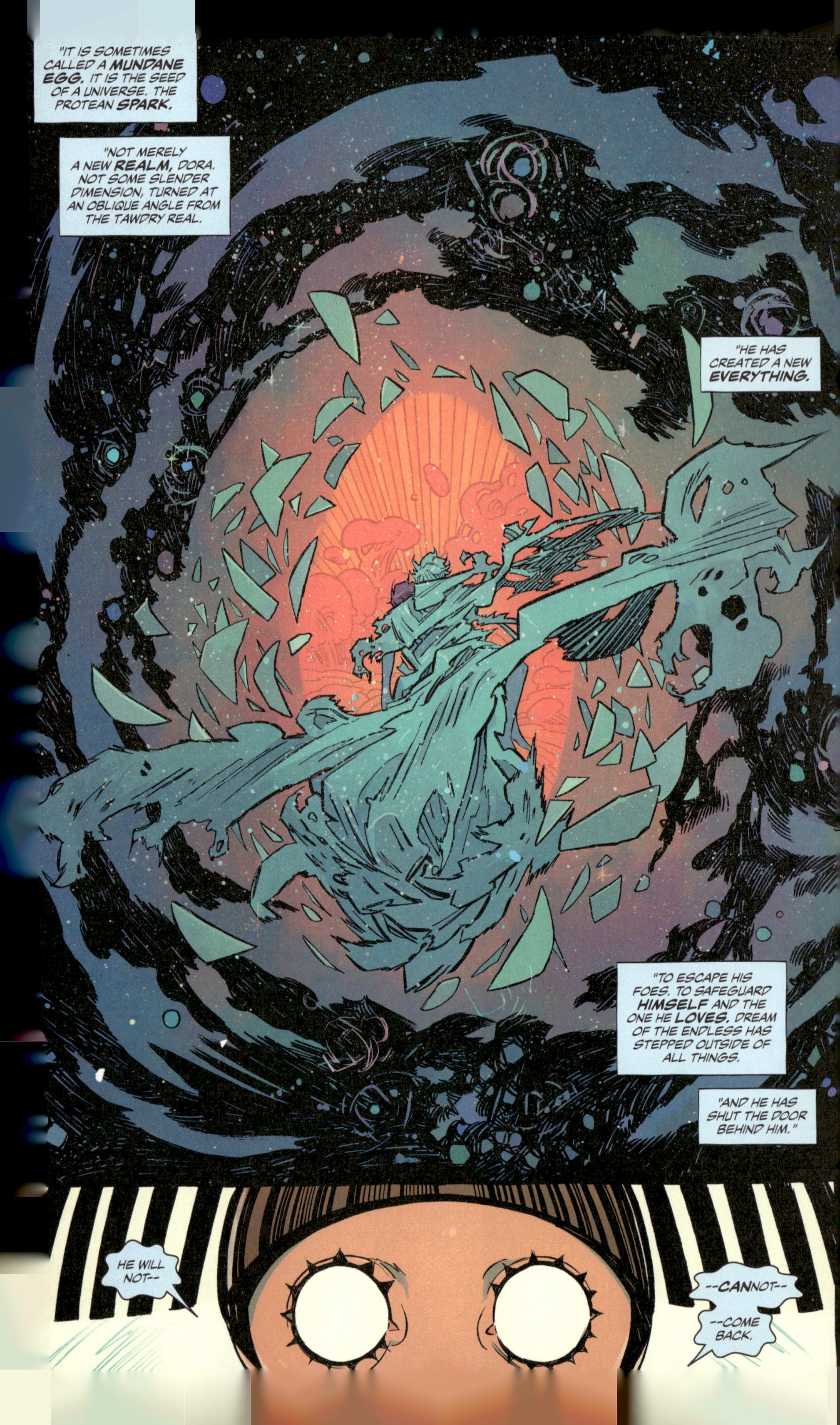
"IT IS SOMETIMES CALLED A MUNDANE EGG. IT IS THE SEED OF A UNIVERSE. THE PROTEAN SPARK.
"NOT MERELY A NEW REALM, DORA. NOT SOME SLENDER DIMENSION, TURNED AT AN OBLIQUE ANGLE FROM THE TAWDRY REAL.
"HE HAS CREATED A NEW EVERYTHING.
"TO ESCAPE HIS FOES. TO SAFEGUARD HIMSELF AND THE ONE HE LOVES. DREAM OF THE ENDLESS HAS STEPPED OUTSIDE OF ALL THINGS.
"AND HE HAS SHUT THE DOOR BEHIND HIM."
HE WILL NOT--
--CANNOT--
--COME BACK.

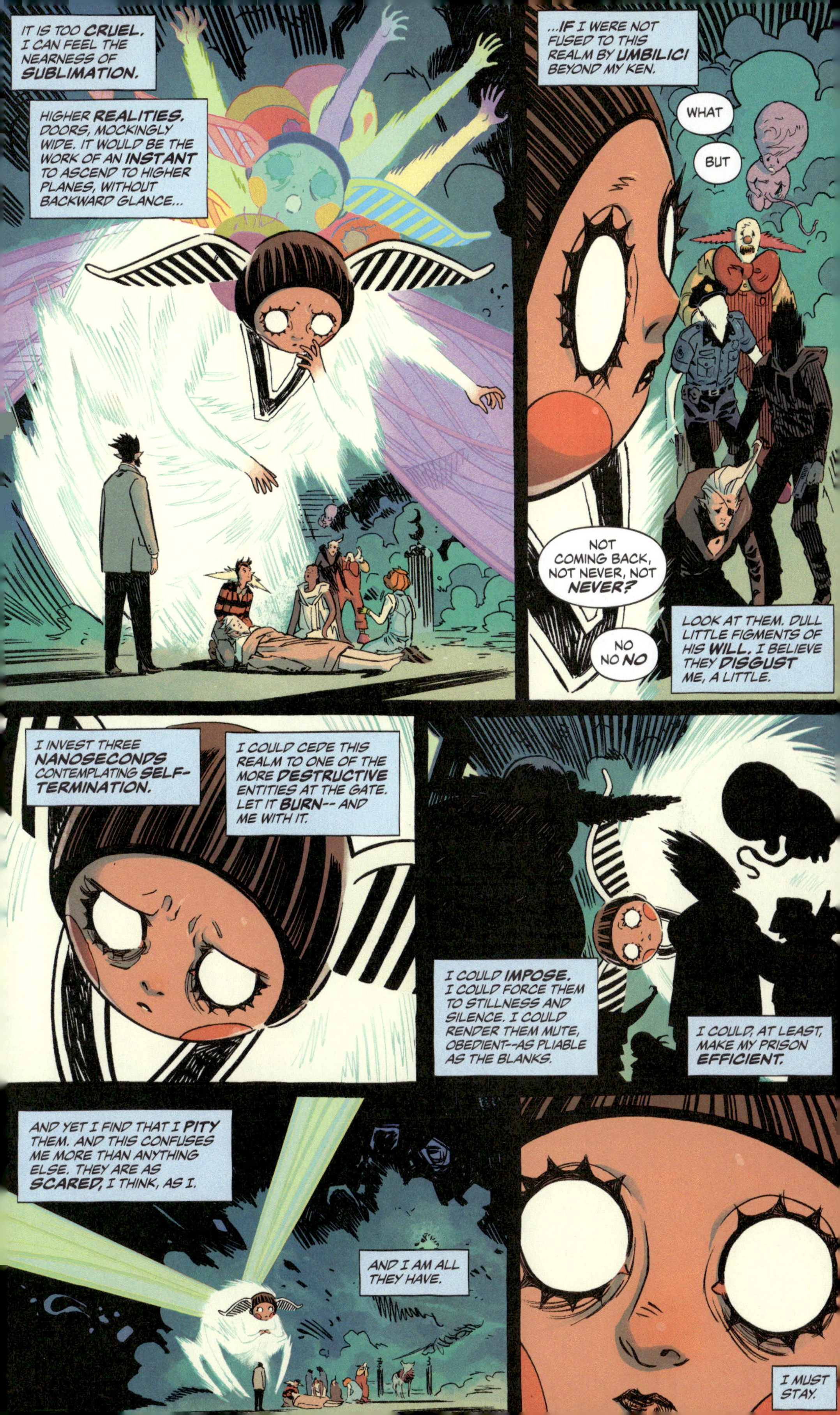
IT IS TOO CRUEL. I CAN FEEL THE NEARNESS OF SUBLIMATION.
HIGHER REALITIES. DOORS, MOCKINGLY WIDE. IT WOULD BE THE WORK OF AN INSTANT TO ASCEND TO HIGHER PLANES, WITHOUT BACKWARD GLANCE...
...IF I WERE NOT FUSED TO THIS REALM BY UMBILICI BEYOND MY KEN.
WHAT
BUT
NOT COMING BACK, NOT NEVER, NOT NEVER?
NO NO NO
LOOK AT THEM. DULL LITTLE FIGMENTS OF HIS WILL. I BELIEVE THEY DISGUST ME, A LITTLE.
I INVEST THREE NANOSECONDS CONTEMPLATING SELF-TERMINATION.
I COULD CEDE THIS REALM TO ONE OF THE MORE DESTRUCTIVE ENTITIES AT THE GATE. LET IT BURN-- AND ME WITH IT.
I COULD IMPOSE. I COULD FORCE THEM TO STILLNESS AND SILENCE. I COULD RENDER THEM MUTE, OBEDIENT--AS PLIABLE AS THE BLANKS.
I COULD, AT LEAST, MAKE MY PRISON EFFICIENT.
AND YET I FIND THAT I PITY THEM. AND THIS CONFUSES ME MORE THAN ANYTHING ELSE. THEY ARE AS SCARED, I THINK, AS I.
AND I AM ALL THEY HAVE.
I MUST STAY.

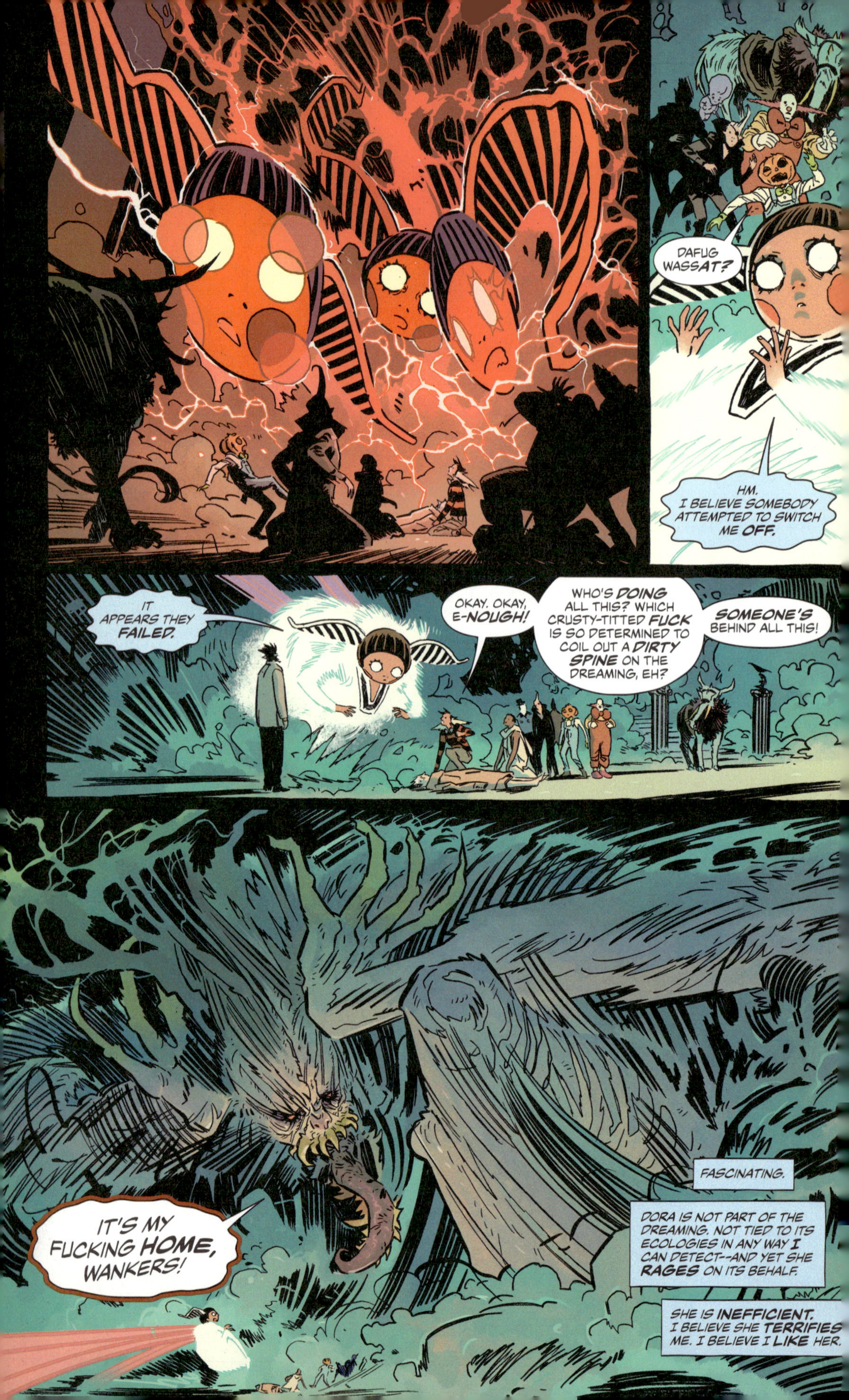
DAFUG WASSAT?
HM. I BELIEVE SOMEBODY ATTEMPTED TO SWITCH ME OFF.
IT APPEARS THEY FAILED.
OKAY. OKAY, E-NOUGH!
WHO'S DOING ALL THIS? WHICH CRUSTY-TITTED FUCK IS SO DETERMINED TO COIL OUT A DIRTY SPINE ON THE DREAMING, EH?
SOMEONE'S BEHIND ALL THIS!
IT'S MY FUCKING HOME, WANKERS!
FASCINATING.
DORA IS NOT PART OF THE DREAMING. NOT TIED TO ITS ECOLOGIES IN ANY WAY I CAN DETECT--AND YET SHE RAGES ON ITS BEHALF.
SHE IS INEFFICIENT. I BELIEVE SHE TERRIFIES ME. I BELIEVE I LIKE HER.

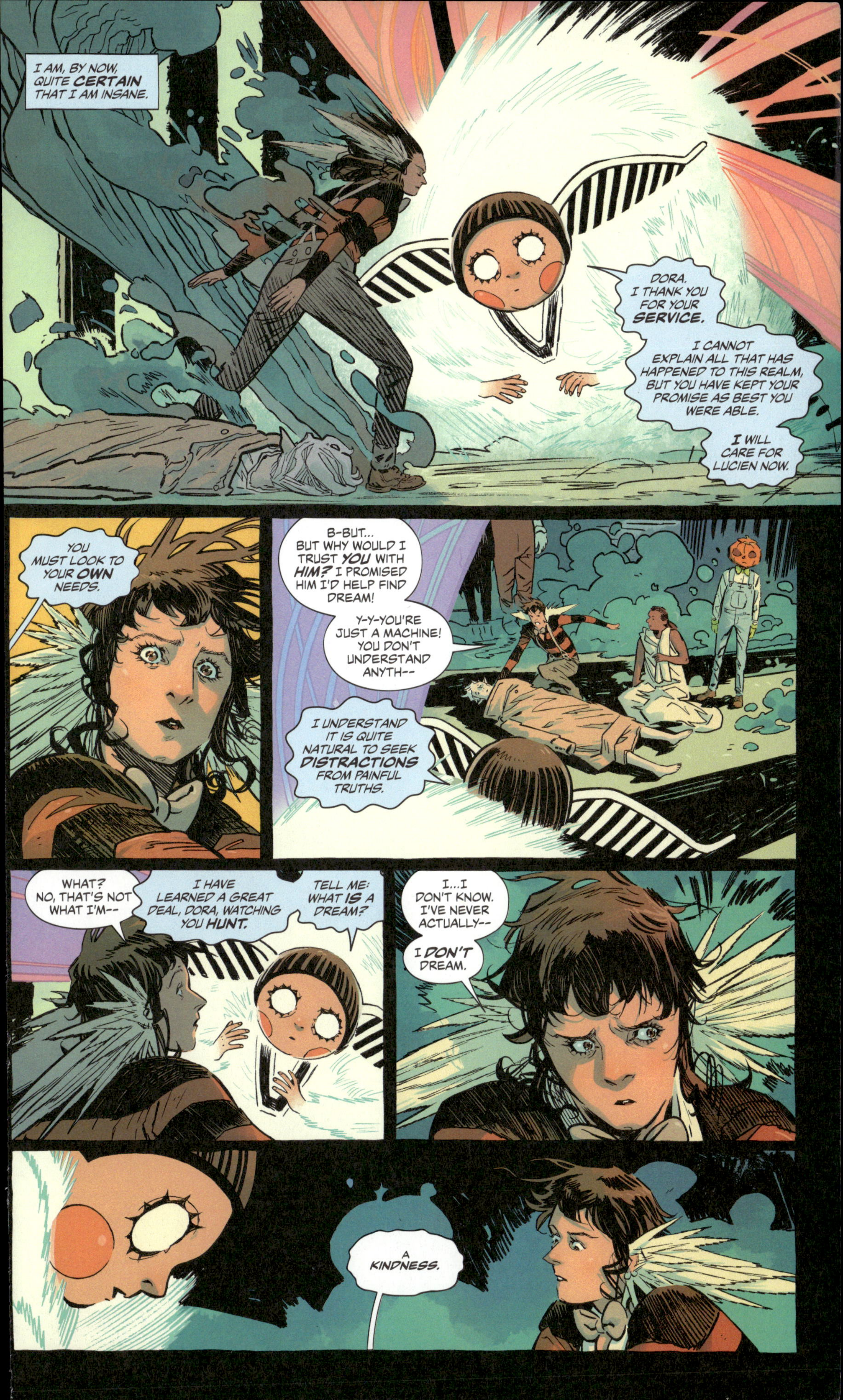
I AM, BY NOW, QUITE CERTAIN THAT I AM INSANE.
DORA. I THANK YOU FOR YOUR SERVICE.
I CANNOT EXPLAIN ALL THAT HAS HAPPENED TO THIS REALM, BUT YOU HAVE KEPT YOUR PROMISE AS BEST YOU WERE ABLE.
I WILL CARE FOR LUCIEN NOW.
YOU MUST LOOK TO YOUR OWN NEEDS.
B-BUT... BUT WHY WOULD I TRUST YOU WITH HIM? I PROMISED HIM I'D HELP FIND DREAM!
Y-Y-YOU'RE JUST A MACHINE! YOU DON'T UNDERSTAND ANYTH--
I UNDERSTAND IT IS QUITE NATURAL TO SEEK DISTRACTIONS FROM PAINFUL TRUTHS.
WHAT? NO, THAT'S NOT WHAT I'M--
I HAVE LEARNED A GREAT DEAL, DORA, WATCHING YOU HUNT.
TELL ME: WHAT IS A DREAM?
I...I DON'T KNOW. I'VE NEVER ACTUALLY--
I DON'T DREAM.
A KINDNESS.

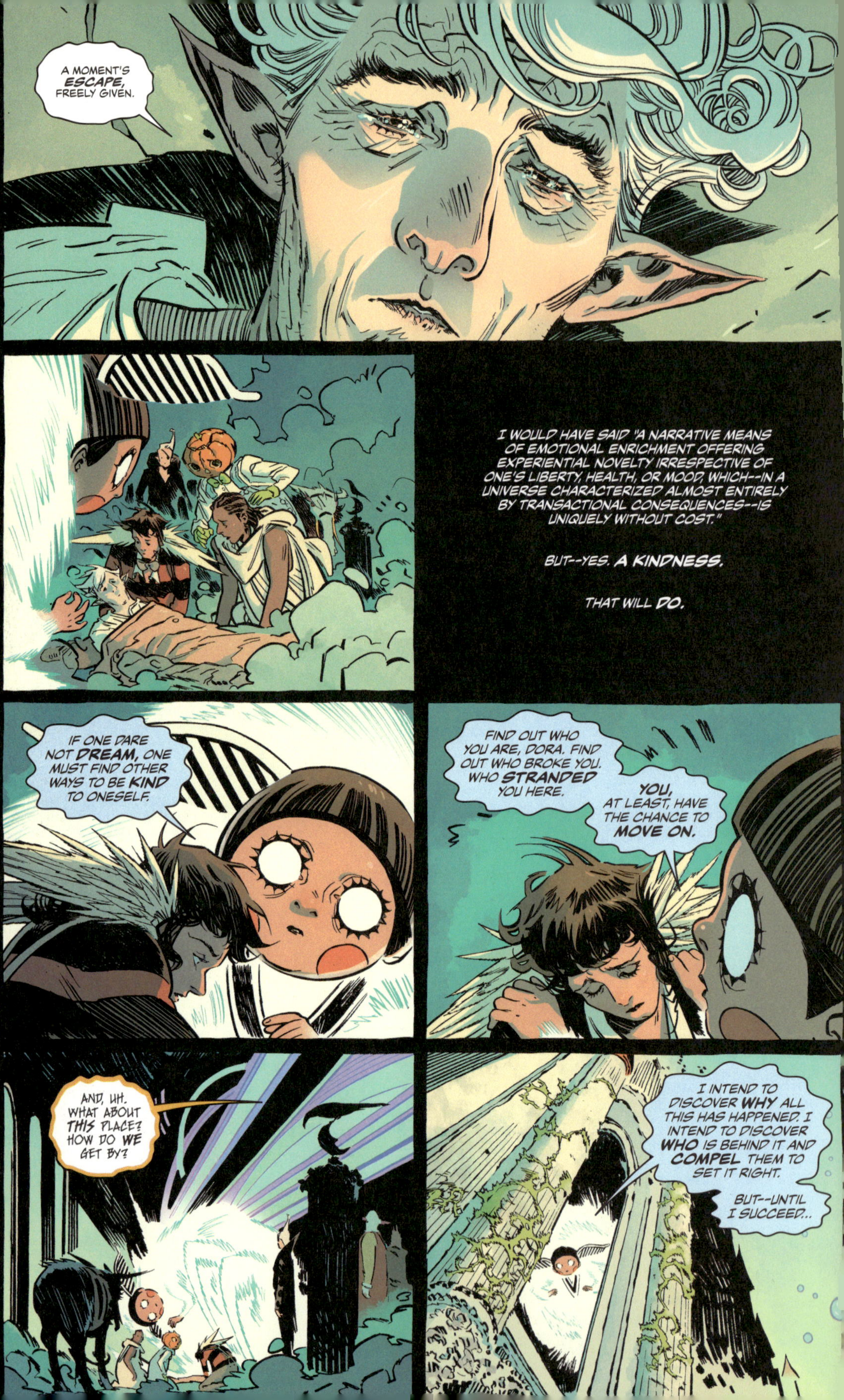

A MOMENT'S ESCAPE, FREELY GIVEN.
I WOULD HAVE SAID "A NARRATIVE MEANS OF EMOTIONAL ENRICHMENT OFFERING EXPERIENTIAL NOVELTY IRRESPECTIVE OF ONE'S LIBERTY, HEALTH, OR MOOD, WHICH--IN A UNIVERSE CHARACTERIZED ALMOST ENTIRELY BY TRANSACTIONAL CONSEQUENCES--IS UNIQUELY WITHOUT COST."
BUT--YES. A KINDNESS.
THAT WILL DO.
IF ONE DARE NOT DREAM, ONE MUST FIND OTHER WAYS TO BE KIND TO ONESELF.
FIND OUT WHO YOU ARE, DORA. FIND OUT WHO BROKE YOU. WHO STRANDED YOU HERE.
YOU, AT LEAST, HAVE THE CHANCE TO MOVE ON.
AND, UH. WHAT ABOUT THIS PLACE? HOW DO WE GET BY?
I INTEND TO DISCOVER WHY ALL THIS HAS HAPPENED. I INTEND TO DISCOVER WHO IS BEHIND IT AND COMPEL THEM TO SET IT RIGHT.
BUT--UNTIL I SUCCEED...

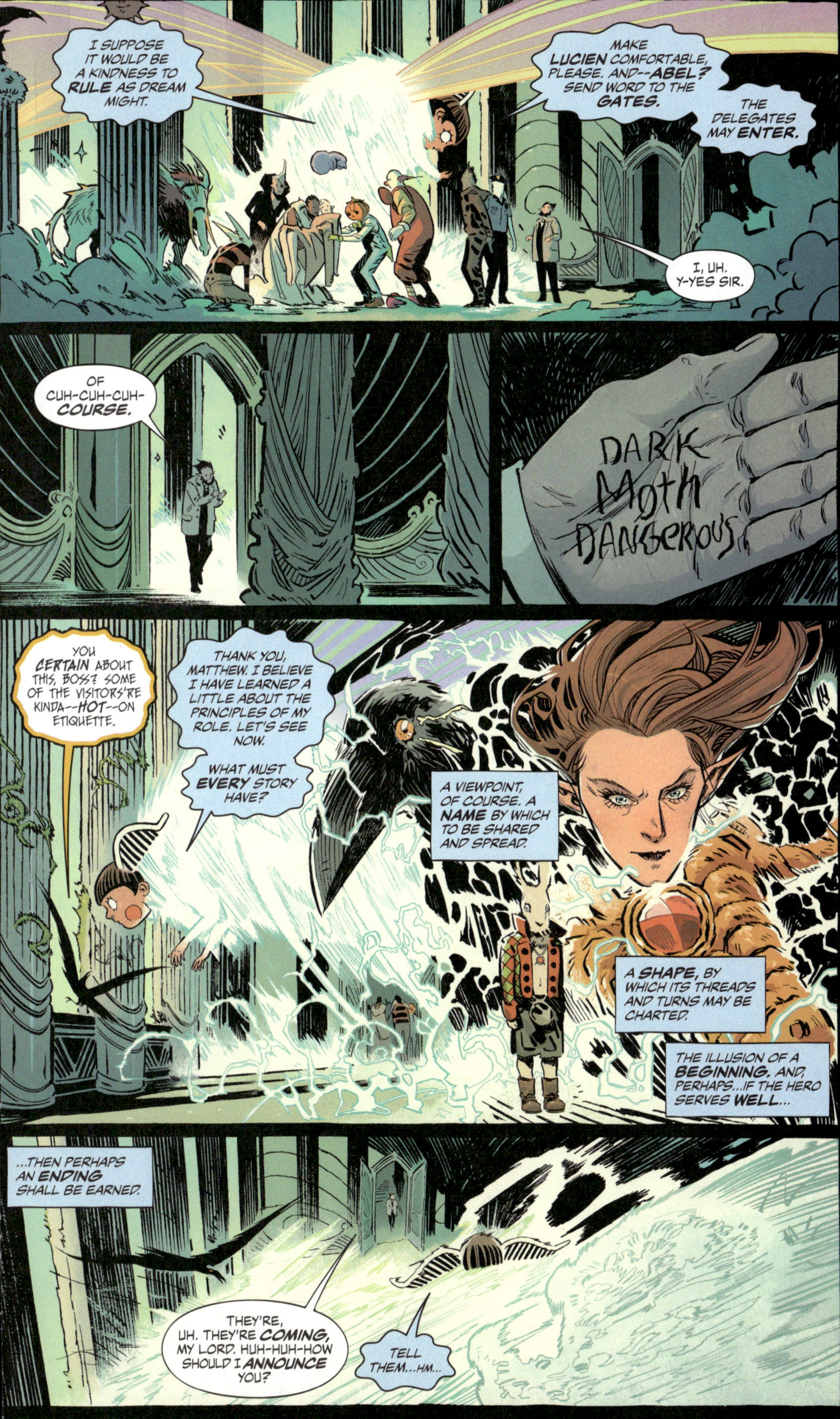
I SUPPOSE IT WOULD BE A KINDNESS TO RULE AS DREAM MIGHT.
MAKE LUCIEN COMFORTABLE, PLEASE. AND--ABEL? SEND WORD TO THE GATES.
THE DELEGATES MAY ENTER.
I, UH. Y-YES SIR.
OF CUH-CUH-CUH-COURSE.
DARK
Moth
DANGEROUS
YOU CERTAIN ABOUT THIS, BOSS? SOME OF THE VISITORS'RE KINDA--HOT--ON ETIQUETTE.
THANK YOU, MATTHEW. I BELIEVE I HAVE LEARNED A LITTLE ABOUT THE PRINCIPLES OF MY ROLE. LET'S SEE NOW.
WHAT MUST EVERY STORY HAVE?
A VIEWPOINT, OF COURSE. A NAME BY WHICH TO BE SHARED AND SPREAD.
A SHAPE, BY WHICH ITS THREADS AND TURNS MAY BE CHARTED.
THE ILLUSION OF A BEGINNING. AND, PERHAPS...IF THE HERO SERVES WELL...
...THEN PERHAPS AN ENDING SHALL BE EARNED.
THEY'RE, UH. THEY'RE COMING, MY LORD. HUH-HUH-HOW SHOULD I ANNOUNCE YOU?
TELL THEM...HM...

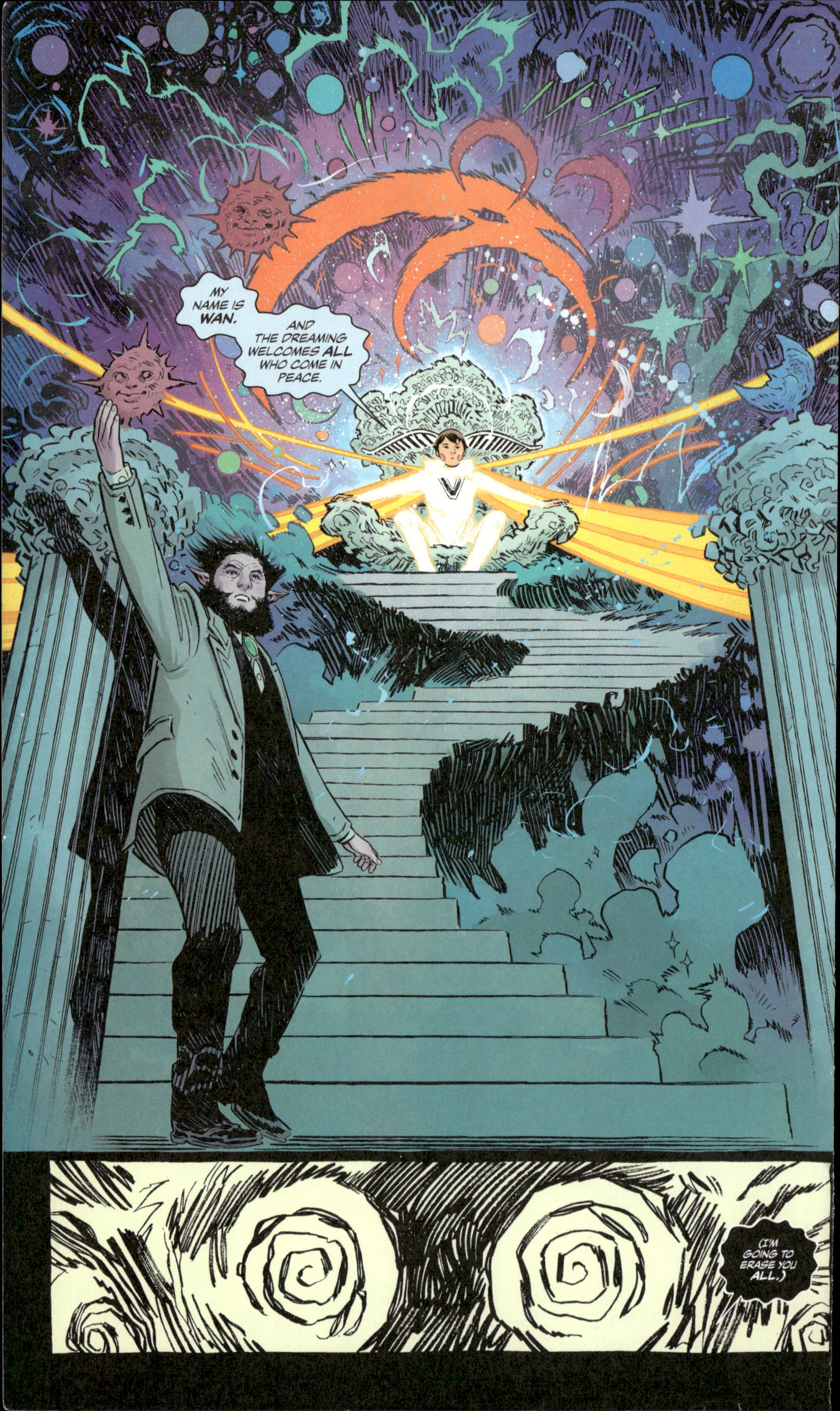
MY NAME IS WAN.
AND THE DREAMING WELCOMES ALL WHO COME IN PEACE.
(I'M GOING TO ERASE YOU ALL.)

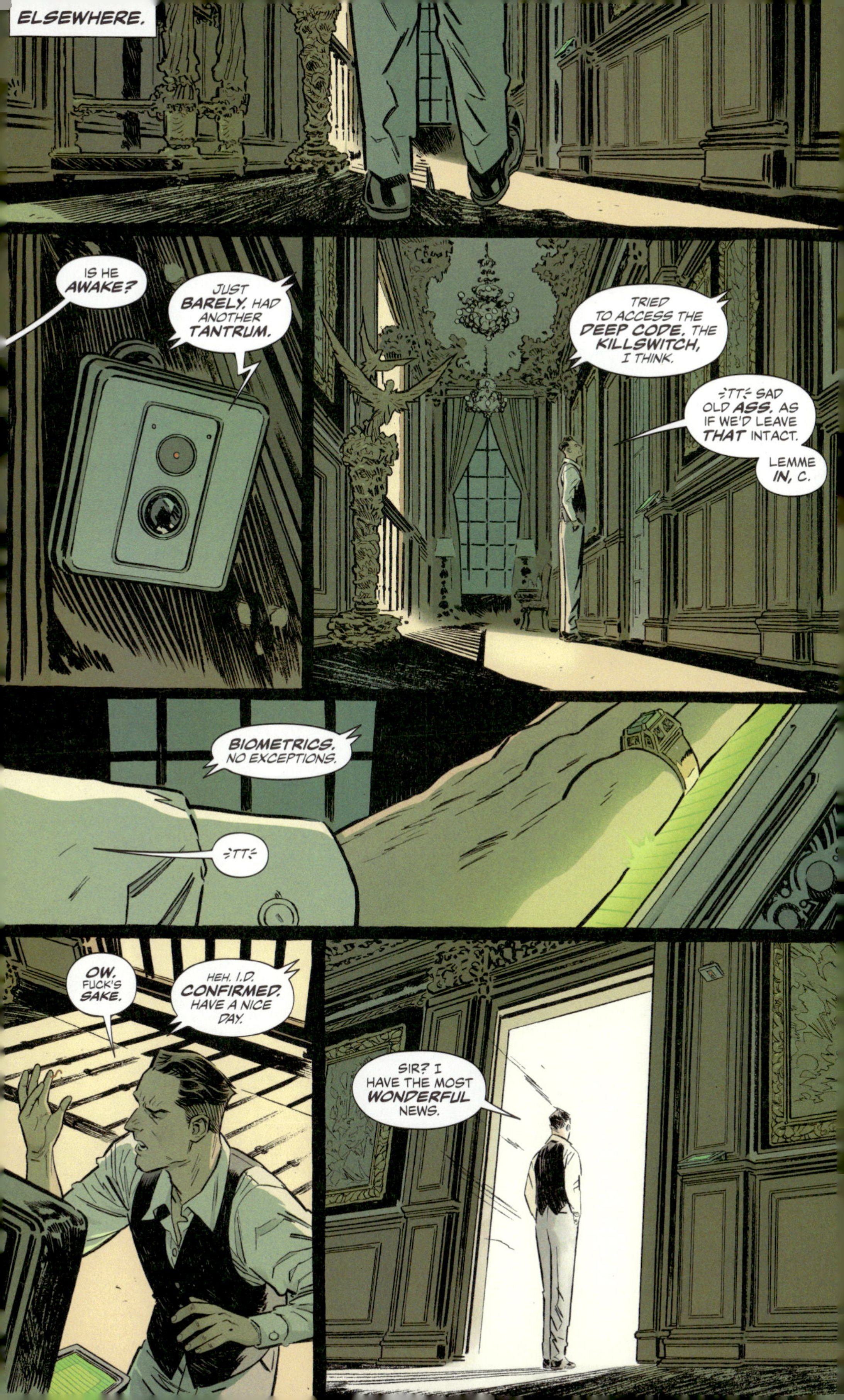
ELSEWHERE.
IS HE AWAKE?
JUST BARELY. HAD ANOTHER TANTRUM.
TRIED TO ACCESS THE DEEP CODE. THE KILLSWITCH, I THINK.
=TT= SAD OLD ASS. AS IF WE'D LEAVE THAT INTACT.
LEMME IN, C.
BIOMETRICS. NO EXCEPTIONS.
=TT=
OW. FUCK'S SAKE.
HEH. I.D. CONFIRMED. HAVE A NICE DAY.
SIR? I HAVE THE MOST WONDERFUL NEWS.

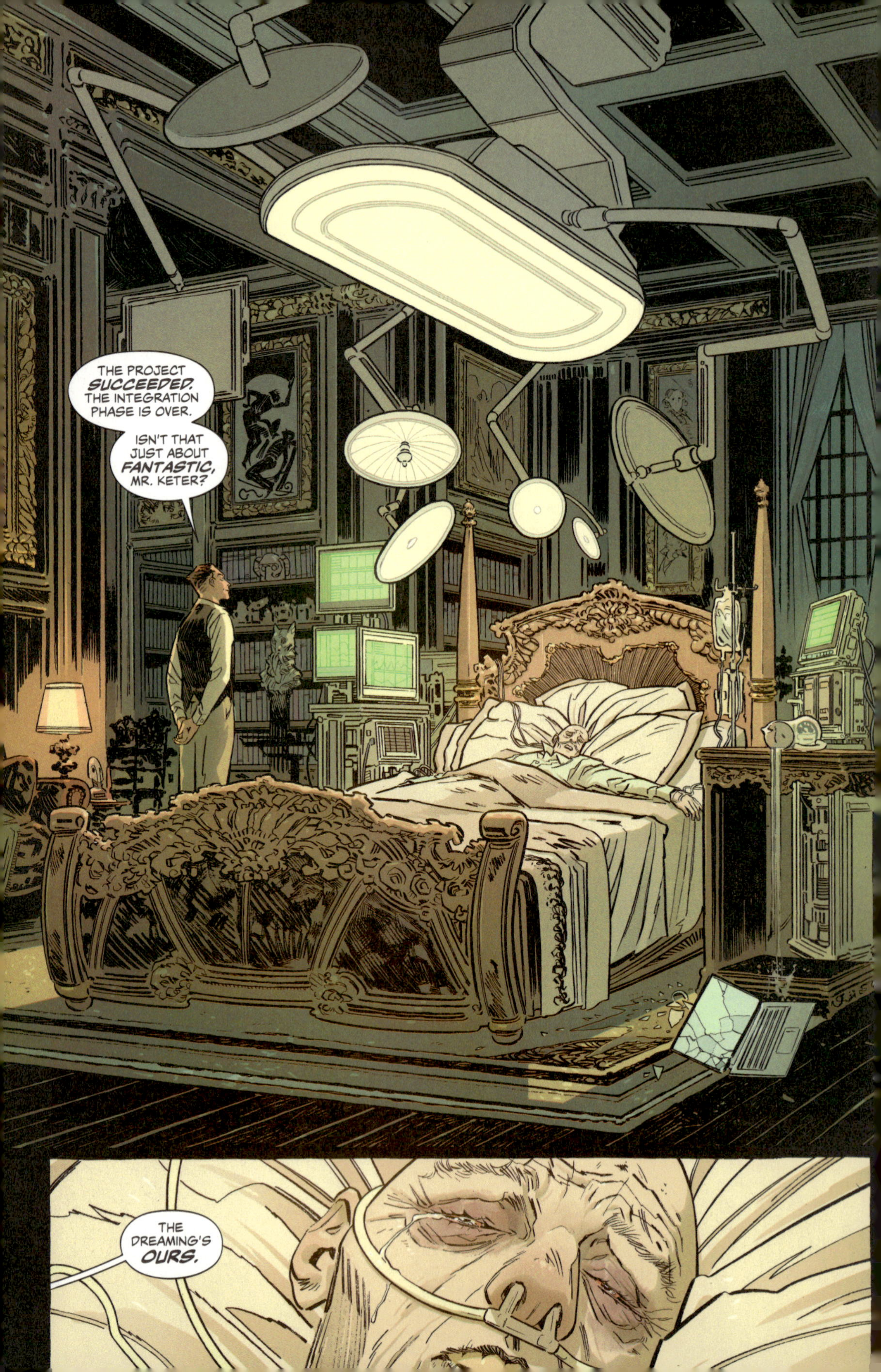
THE PROJECT *SUCCEEDED.* THE INTEGRATION PHASE IS OVER.
ISN'T THAT JUST ABOUT *FANTASTIC,* MR. KETER?
THE DREAMING'S *OURS.*

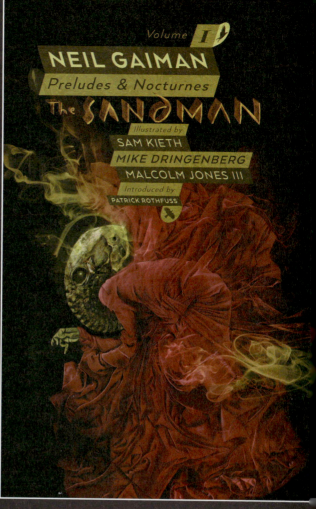

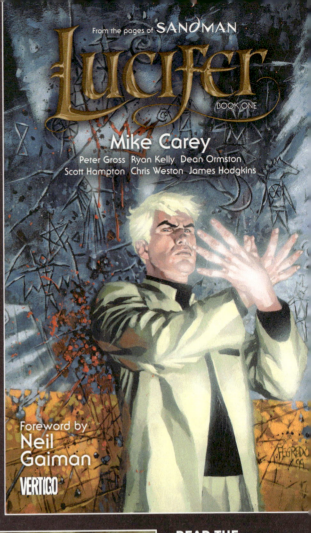
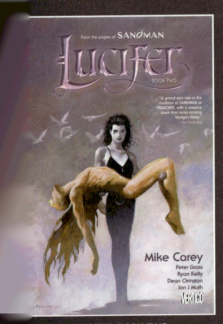
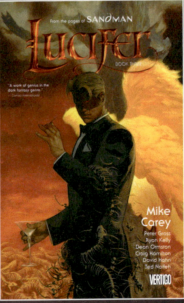

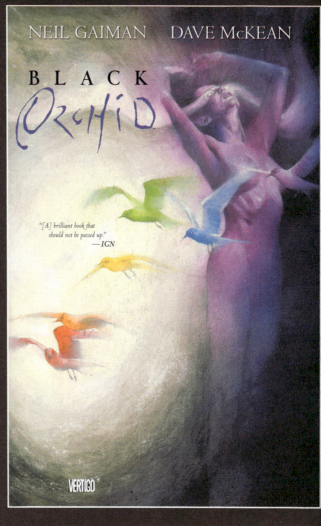
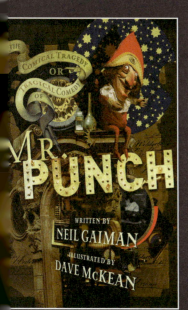
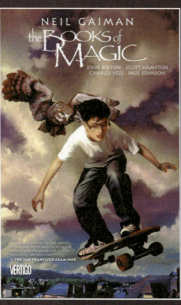
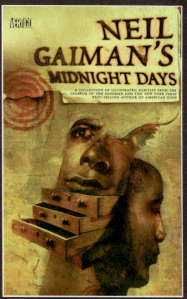

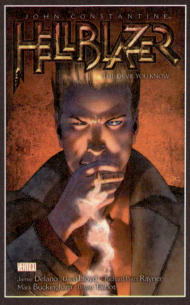